MARTINŮ AND HIS WORLD

THE BARD MUSIC FESTIVAL

LEON BOTSTEIN AND CHRISTOPHER H. GIBBS
SERIES EDITORS

MARTINŮ
AND HIS WORLD

EDITED BY
ALEŠ BŘEZINA AND MICHAEL BECKERMAN

THE UNIVERSITY OF CHICAGO PRESS
CHICAGO AND LONDON

The University of Chicago Press, Chicago 60637
The University of Chicago Press, Ltd., London
© 2025 by The Bard Music Festival
All rights reserved. No part of this book may be used or reproduced in any manner whatsoever without written permission, except in the case of brief quotations in critical articles and reviews. For more information, contact the University of Chicago Press, 1427 E. 60th St., Chicago, IL 60637.
Published 2025
Printed in the United States of America

34 33 32 31 30 29 28 27 26 25 1 2 3 4 5

ISBN-13: 978-0-226-84571-5 (cloth)
ISBN-13: 978-0-226-84573-9 (paper)
ISBN-13: 978-0-226-84572-2 (ebook)
DOI: https://doi.org/10.7208/chicago/9780226845722.001.0001

This publication has been produced by the Bard College Publications Office:
Irene Zedlacher, project director
Karen Spencer, design
Text edited by Paul De Angelis and Erin Clermont
Music typeset by Christopher Deschene
Indexed by Scott Smiley

This publication has been underwritten in part by a grant from
Roger and Helen Alcaly.

Library of Congress Control Number: 2025931558

♾ This paper meets the requirements of ANSI/NISO Z39.48-1992
(Permanence of Paper).

Authorized Representative for EU General Product Safety Regulation (GPSR) queries:
Easy Access System Europe—Mustamäe tee 50, 10621 Tallinn, Estonia,
gpsr.requests@easproject.com
Any other queries: https://press.uchicago.edu/press/contact.html

To our wonderful families
Our wives
Ivana Březinová and Karen Palmore Beckerman
and our children
Štěpán
the two Annas
Bernie
Hadallia
Artur
Charlie

Contents

Permissions and Credits

The following copyright holders, institutions, and individuals have graciously granted permission to reprint or reproduce the following materials:

Universal Edition, Vienna, © 1961 for Examples 1, 2, 4, 5, 6, in Christou, "Byzantine Music in Martinů's Opera *The Greek Passion.*"

Marios Christou, for Figures 1–4 in Christou, "Byzantine Music in Martinů's Opera *The Greek Passion.*" Collection of the author.

DILIA, Prague, © 1965 for Figure 1 in Meadow, "Meditation on the First *Ave Maria* of Bohuslav Martinů's *Sister Paskalina*"; and © 1947 for Examples 4a and 5a in Rentsch, "The Long Shadow of *Juliette*: Martinů's Late Musical Aesthetic and the *Fantasies symphoniques* (Symphony No. 6)."

Boosey & Hawkes © 1953 for Examples 1–14 in Nedbal, "Ambiguous Historicism in Martinů's *The Marriage*"; and © 1957 for Examples 1, 2, 3, and 4b in Rentsch, "The Long Shadow of *Juliette*: Martinů's Late Musical Aesthetic and the *Fantasies symphoniques* (Symphony No. 6)"; and © copyright 1969 for Example 5b in Rentsch, "The Long Shadow of *Juliette*." Reprinted by permission of Boosey & Hawkes, Inc.

Bohuslav Martinů Center, Polička, ©, for Figures 1 and 2 in Rentsch, "The Long Shadow of *Juliette*: Martinů's Late Musical Aesthetic and the *Fantasies symphoniques* (Symphony No. 6)"; for unassigned Figure 1 on page 85, photograph of Bohuslav Martinů in Darien, Connecticut; for Figures 1–3 in Březina, "'I changed practically nothing'": Bohuslav Martinů's Collaboration on *The Kitchen Revue*"; for Figures 1 and 2 in Körner, "Martinů, Benjamin, and the Changing Experience of Historical Time"; for Figure 1 in Ottomano, "Challenging Modernism: Bohuslav Martinů's Works at the Venice International Festival of Contemporary Music"; for Figures 1 and 2 in Zouhar, "On the Complete Edition of Bohuslav Martinů's Correspondence"; and for Figure 1 in Beckerman and Březina, eds., "Martinů in the U.S.A.: Interviews with the Composer's American Friends and Students."

Editio Bärenreiter, Prague, ©, for Examples 1b, 2a, and 2b in Locke, "Negotiating the 'Concerto Grosso type' in Paris and Princeton: Martinů's Multi-Soloist Concertante Works from a Generational Perspective."

The Cleveland Orchestra, for Figures 1–3 in Kratochvilová and Pechač, "'To My Countrymen-Workers of Cleveland': The World Premiere of Bohuslav Martinů's Symphony No. 2." Used with permission from The Cleveland Orchestra Archives.

Archivio Storico della Biennale di Venezia, ASAC, ©, for Figures 2 and 3 (photographs by Giacomelli) in Ottomano, "Challenging Modernism: Bohuslav Martinů's Works at the Venice International Festival of Contemporary Music."

Michael Beckerman, for Figure 1 in Beckerman, ed., "Martinů's Notebook of Dreams." Collection of Michael Beckerman.

The Juilliard School Library for the Appendix and for Figure 1 in Botstein, "Music and Politics in the Twentieth Century: The Parallel Lives of Bohuslav Martinů and Rudolf Firkušný."

Acknowledgments

The editors would like to specially thank Tereza and Pavel Žůrek for their careful proofreading (as well as source and literature research), and the line editor Paul De Angelis for his meticulous work and dedication. We could not have completed this project without the solid and ongoing support of Irene Zedlacher and Christopher Gibbs of Bard College who have to put into play all the things we merely imagine. And of course, our deepest gratitude to Leon Botstein who is an inspiration to us all.

Aleš Březina's biggest personal thanks go to Michael Beckerman, his co-editor, who, more than twenty years ago, came up with the idea of extending the Czech footprint at the Bard Festival, already established with events around Dvořák and Janáček, into the second half of the twentieth century through the legacy of Bohuslav Martinů. Michael Beckerman in turn gives a huge shout out to his fellow-editor Aleš Březina who gives new meaning to the Czech word, *šikovný* (look it up…). It seems completely inadequate to say, "I couldn't have done it without you!" What a pleasure it has been!

Introduction: Martinů and His Worlds

MICHAEL BECKERMAN

Much has changed since the Bard Music Festival began in 1990 with the idea of presenting the music of the past to contemporary audiences in innovative ways. At that time, almost all music departments in the United States still had Western music at the center of their curricula. Graduate musicology programs featured courses on paleography, repertoire, sketch studies, and archival research; most had Early Music ensembles. While concert audiences have retained their passion for standard repertory, enlivened by exciting new works and historical discoveries, there are elite graduate programs in the United States where Western classical music is now not much taught, not considered particularly important, or even treated with deep suspicion for a range of political reasons having to do with race, gender, colonialism, social justice, and other factors.

Since the Bard Festival is unique in featuring the interface between an educated audience primarily of non-specialists, superb performers, and the academic world, we may ask what might be at stake for each of these groups with *Martinů and His World* in 2025.

For audiences, we believe the answer is simple: Martinů is one of the most exciting composers for a listener to encounter. Among the most prolific composers of the twentieth century—if not the most prolific—his catalogue offers a feast of beautiful and profound works: fifteen operas and fourteen ballets; more than twenty concertos; six symphonies; well over 200 songs, choral works, and cantatas; and a similar number of chamber works, including seven string quartets; altogether totaling almost 400 opus numbers and over a thousand separate pieces. From the voluptuous interiority of the Andante moderato from the Violin Concerto No. 2 to the folklike exuberance of *Špalíček*, and from the haunted surrealism of *Juliette* to the starkness of *The Epic of Gilgamesh*, Martinů provides us with an almost inexhaustible collection of works, approaches, and ideas. His fascinations, with such things as madrigals, Stravinsky, the Virgin Mary, jazz, Baroque music, Bartók, surrealism, neoclassicism, Byzantine chant, medieval miracle plays, and the folk cultures of Czechoslovakia, give his works shadings both subtle and powerful.

Further, Martinů's life and career in and of themselves unfold in a series of extraordinary stories. Born in a church tower high above a small town in the

Bohemian Moravian highlands in 1890, like many young Czech composers (Smetana, Dvořák, Suk) he eventually moved to Prague, but unlike others, he made Paris a second home in the 1920s and '30s. Forced out by the Nazis, he arrived in the United States in 1940 and quickly became one of the most successful composers of the decade, his symphonies premiered by major orchestras. Set to go back to Prague after the war, he was derailed by a tragic fall from a balcony in Great Barrington, Massachusetts in 1946, and by the time he recovered, the Communist coup of 1948 had taken place. Until the end of his life, he was a kind of exile, traversing back and forth between the United States, France, Italy, and Switzerland. He never returned to Czechoslovakia. Each of these places left an indelible mark on his creative life, from the church tower on the Bohemian-Moravian border with its view of the static landscape which, according to the composer, he always saw in his mind's eye, to the vibrant world of Paris where he encountered jazz, surrealism, and Stravinsky. But starting in Paris in the 1930s and continuing for the rest of his life, Martinů also reimagined a Czech world he had left behind in a series of operas, cantatas, and nostalgic miniatures. In the United States, he became a symphonist and returned to opera. His years of wandering resulted in stark works of great philosophical and political power, such as *The Greek Passion*, *Gilgamesh*, and the *Prophecy of Isaiah*. While Martinů himself might have despaired that tales told around his life color our response to certain works, that is simply one of the realities of art reception.

For performers the field is equally rich. Not only are there compositions for practically every instrument and combination of instruments, but Martinů's music offers both ease and intense challenges. There is far more to Martinů than his trademark lyrical syncopation, but there is a core aspect of his style based on subtle rhythmic displacements—this is one of the reasons it is difficult to imagine a more "dancerly" composer than he. When these kinds of moments are coupled with radically different ones, performers, whether chamber players, soloists, or conductors, have to forge a certain through-line that requires both skill and intuition. Since Martinů often combines moments of seeming exquisite musical clarity with ideas that seem to undercut them, performers cannot rely on intuition alone to execute the works, but have to think through how they might be most effective in performance. The figures who have managed to work with his music over the years—such as Rudolf Firkušný, Garrick Ohlsson, Julia Fischer, Jiří Bělohlávek, Stephen Isserlis, Magdalena Kožená, and Jakub Hrůša—consider Martinů among the most rewarding composers to perform.

We arrive then at the question of what the study of Martinů, or the encounter with Martinů's music, can offer the academic world, particularly one that is often steeped in critical and cultural theory and harboring deep suspicions of "nesses," whether "greatness," "Whiteness," or "Czechness." We ask this not as apologists for Martinů or for the world of "classical music," nor as a critique of the academic status quo, but in genuine curiosity. Some of the answers to this question are found in the essays collected in this volume, which will be addressed in the second part of this introduction, and I offer some additional thoughts below.

One of the most profound questions raised by Martinů's music has to do with what we might call the presence (or absence) of composers at the "philosophers' table." In other words, there is a tacit assumption, for example, that works of prose, such as the writings of Michel Foucault or Judith Butler, can explicate and be applied to artworks in various ways. Do we accord artworks, such as a Martinů symphony, a philosophical vantage point, which could be used, say, to explicate those same works of theorizing prose, or other things in the world? Is art simply in need of theory, or can and should art function *as* theory? And if it can, does it force our hands to admit that rather than focusing on any purported "inability" of music to address real-world issues, is it actually prose that exceeds the authority of what we know and can say?

This can be extended to ask how much of the nature of an artwork is ultimately related to external reality, and how much finds its value only in the rigorously abstract relationship between parts, a question that has been hanging in the air for centuries. Martinů certainly believed in abstraction, or at least he was suspicious of overdetermined notions of expression and meaning. This is borne out in what we learn about Martinů's creative process from the letters of his student, Jan Novák. According to him, far from being a kind of intuitive machine, Martinů was an absolute micromanager of his structures and other material. And yet, much of Martinů's music—operas, ballets, songs, and choral works—is attached through its subject matter to specific aspects of the world outside music. Are we then to imagine that there is some kind of impenetrable barrier between texted and untexted works, such that none of the meanings associated with the former can ever be productively considered in connection with the latter? And if the answer is that there is no such barrier, how then should we proceed?

This kind of inquiry is typical of the way in which almost all of Martinů's works can open up into a world of thoughts, questions, and revelations. For example, a seemingly "minor" work such as the *Five Madrigal Stanzas for Violin and Piano* (1943), with its combination of restlessness and lyricism, is perfectly balletic in its implications for physical movement. It also invokes the composer's fascination with madrigals, for their antiquity, their independence of voices, and their lyricism. These "stanzas" are simultaneously completely of the world, and completely apart from it all at once. But there is also the question of the dedicatee of this composition: Albert Einstein. The two were acquainted and became colleagues at Princeton. In his recollections Martinů reveled in his encounter with Einstein's ideas and enjoyed reading his work. Whether he would have considered Einstein's theories as parallel to his own work in their combination of abstraction and concrete implications is unknown.

Martinů's music also encourages us to interrogate the knotty relationship between wholes and parts. In a play like *Hamlet*, where one character has not only the title role, but more than a third of the lines, and is on stage far more than anyone else, it is not particularly difficult to think about who the main character is. But we understand that over four movements, a symphony, whether by Beethoven or Martinů, may have as many as twenty or thirty different "characters." Is there any way to know which of these is central, and which peripheral? Martinů plays with this question by combining elements in mysterious and inexplicable ways. In one of the interviews we reproduce, Charles Rosen describes how Martinů gave students an opening theme and asked them how the piece should continue. He was indignant when they all *developed* the original idea, saying that with a theme like that, what follows has to be different. I refer to this notion of composition as reflecting Martinů's *Špalíček* aesthetic. Not only does the word refer to a wonderful ballet/cantata the composer wrote in 1932 based on various folk legends, but the actual object, "Špalíček," recalls something like a bulky, wooden chapbook, in which one might have found such things as a song, a pressed flower, a poem, or a picture. In other words, a collection of unlike things. Martinů once said that as a composer, he simply presents such things, and that it is the role of the audience to "cooperate" in putting them together. This seems to echo, in a way, Faust's lament in the first scene of Goethe's poem: "These ten years long, with many woes / I've led my scholars by the nose," or the famous line of Eugene V. Debs, "I would not lead you into the promised land if I could, because if I led you in, someone else would lead you out." Thus, Martinů insists that the audience, in some sense, act as the composer of the piece and not be led around by the ear, as it were. We can feel this aesthetic at work in compositions as different as the finale of the ballet *The Kitchen Revue*, which ricochets from French neoclassicism to the Charleston to Czech folk music, or the 1959 Nonet which, even before the first main cadence, has at least ten different "looks." The listener must cooperate.

Further intriguing issues emerge around the question of how we should understand Martinů's extraordinary productivity and his personality. There are, of course, many kinds of composers, but for the sake of (over)simplicity we might speak of Type Beethoven and Type Schubert. With Type Beethoven we have some clear concurrence, at least in the minds of his contemporaries and today's audiences, between the personality of the composer and the music they compose. While, of course, this cannot apply to every note or every composition, there is a general sense that the personal force of Beethoven is part of the reception of his works.

Then we have Type Schubert, a composer who seemed to show few external traces of the drama we find in his music, although recent biographies have teased out a more nuanced picture. In this sense, Martinů is very much Type Schubert, but even more so. He did not comport himself like a superstar à la Beethoven,

Wagner, Stravinsky, or Schoenberg—nor was he really ever taken as one. His self-styling was minimal, if it existed at all, and so it has perhaps taken longer for performers, audiences, and scholars to realize what power lies within his oeuvre.

And like Schubert, music seemed to pour out of him. Impressive as this is, there has also been a critical downside. Since Martinů was so extraordinarily prolific, he sometimes is treated as if he suffered from the "Vivaldi syndrome," referring to a figure who was put down as someone who wrote one concerto 600 times (a genuine misapprehension of that composer). So too, there has been a tendency to consider Martinů a composer whose works are "too similar," or at least that they tend to draw upon a repeating set of materials. It is somewhat puzzling, and even amusing, that audiences do not seem to be bothered by the fact that Mark Rothko, for example, created over 800 paintings on canvas (in addition to more than a thousand on paper), considering the wild demand for them. And of course, any good art critic would point out that within the seeming similarity of Rothko's late, huge canvases lie enormous differences. So it is with Martinů's music: the more you engage it, the more you notice how different, original, and precise each composition is.

There is another problem to be confronted in thinking about Martinů's work: in his notebook, presented in the last part of this volume, Martinů asks the trenchant question, "Are we sincere at all?" Martinů is one of the world's great pastoral artists. So much of his work seems to move in and out of idyllic spaces, such as the opening of Symphony No. 6 or the Cello Sonata No. 3. And of course, there are works that are almost entirely anchored in the idyllic, such as the cantata *Opening of the Springs*, or the *Songs on One Page*. In fact, works without the vestige of an idyll, such as the Double Concerto and *Gilgamesh,* may be considered exceptions. But what are we to make of the composer's idyll? Is it sincere? Is it an affirmation, or an escape? Is it real or an illusion? Is it the nostalgic longing of the exile, a smokescreen to set off a world of affective complexity, or just an abstract means of controlling the pace of a composition?

As we try to answer such questions, we are aided by our access to an almost endless amount of data. For example, even if in recent decades there certainly were many recordings of Martinů's music available in the form of LPs, cassettes, and CDs, it cannot possibly compare with the thousands of tracks available today on YouTube, Spotify, and other streaming platforms at the touch of a laptop key or a voice command. When writing about a composition one can now assume most readers can have access to it if they want to listen. So, for example, if I were to say that the opening of Jiří Bělohlávek's recording of Martinů's Symphony No. 6 with the BBC opens with a kind of restless insect-like buzzing, references the Dvořák Requiem in the cello at 1:18, and after some exploratory moments, moves to a gorgeous cadence at 1:39, it is possible for many of those reading this passage to instantly access the music and find those places, testing the ideas of any writer making arguments about a composition. And this is true for any of the works that have so far been mentioned, and those that are forthcoming. Thus, when we write about music in this volume, our views can be tested and verified by readers with startling immediacy. If there is a danger that too much accessibility somehow diminishes value, this is offset by the opportunities for detailed exploration, the kind of exploration that Martinů's music needs and deserves.

Finally, Martinů is a person of continual surprises. He had a *practice*, but never a system. According to those who knew him, and to his diaries and notebooks, he was a fantastic reader. In fact, he never stopped reading, studying, and trying to understand things. That through all this, he still refused to show himself as any kind of "authority" is a remarkable testimony to the humility and modesty so often presented as essential virtues, but so rarely encountered.

While Martinů's symphonic and chamber music is performed regularly outside of the Czech Republic, his fifteen operas, except perhaps *Juliette* and *The Greek Passion*, have the status of rarities. And yet taken together they are breathtaking in their scope, dramaturgy, and difference.

Six of the essays in this volume directly confront the operas. We begin with a poetic, ironic, witty, and profound essay by the Czech novelist and poet Jiří Gruša, based on a speech he gave at the Bregenz Opera House in Austria. A leading dissident and later ambassador to Austria, author of brilliant novels such as *The Questionnaire*, Gruša places the composer in the context of his time, our time, as well as the surreal time in which he spent most of his life, powerfully referencing the pull of Martinů's opera *Juliette*.

Aleš Březina both introduces Martinů's *Juliette* and raises thoughtful questions about the relationship between the opera and the events that followed shortly after its creation in 1937. Březina is particularly attuned to the question of memory, seeing the unnamed town of the opera and its inhabitants who have lost their memories as a "parable about a century that had enormous trouble with historical memory."

It was startling to learn, from the work of Marios Christou, that the opera, *The Greek Passion*, draws on specific pieces of Byzantine music, and that Martinů undertook a serious study of some of the theoretical aspects of this music. This essay raises engaging questions about the relationship between knowledge and apprehension. For example, I had always found the opening of the opera's second version somewhat banal with its oversimple harmonies. Discovering that Martinů has actually used a melody associated with the beginning of Passion Week for the opening of his "passion" opera casts quite a different light on how we hear and process the material. There are always those who believe that we should never need such bits of knowledge in order to approach a work, but that idea seems misplaced, and Christou's essay opens up an entirely new way of hearing Martinů's work.

If *The Greek Passion* has been performed several times outside the Czech Republic and is probably the best known of the composer's operas other than *Juliette*, the *Plays of Mary* has left no traces in the larger operatic world. And yet, as Jon Meadow makes clear in his essay, it is an astonishing and completely original creation. A work made up of two one-act operas introduced by Prologue and Pastorale, it links together four episodes around the Virgin Mary. Meadow gives us a fresh perspective on the whole cycle through his exploration of the opening scene of the last part, *Sister Paskalina*. Drawing on Gregorian chant in ways similar to his use of Byzantine material in *The Greek Passion*, Martinů creates dissonances and paradoxes that are explored by Meadow.

Martinů's operatic reach is staggering: few composers have written stage operas, television operas, radio operas, and even operas with embedded film. With precision, Martin Nedbal explores aspects of his television opera, *The Marriage*, from its adaptation of the Gogol original, to its historical contexts, motivic developments, operatic allusions, and even questions around its "Czechness." Nedbal also argues convincingly that the somewhat uneven reception of the opera was related to cuts made specially for the television production, and concludes by demonstrating that what Martinů aimed for, rather than offering something Czech, was the creation of "a comic opera for the twentieth century."

If one were to overdetermine a metaphor for Martinů himself, it might be through that elusive and haunting opera, *Juliette.* To some extent this is accomplished in a powerful way in Ivana Rentsch's essay on links between the opera and the composer's *Fantaisies symphoniques*, which also allows us to bridge our sections on opera and instrumental works. Her detailed evaluation, involving analysis, archival sources, and an extensive meditation on Martinů's ideas around form, raises subtle and knotty problems about just what a composer does and what kinds of meanings we can tease out (or not) from self-quotation. That Martinů himself was ambivalent in various ways, comes out in both quotations from his published and unpublished writings, but also in the careful way Rentsch threads the needle and sews the two works together in both the spirit of modern scholarship and surrealism itself.

In Part II of this volume, both Giselher Schubert and Brian Locke wrestle with and show the importance of Martinů's involvement with concerto-type works. Schubert places the issue tellingly in the context of Martinů's search for simplification in Paris, with reference to similar changes in the compositions of Strauss, Reger, Schoenberg, and others. He charts the rise of the chamber orchestra at the time, involving a move away from symphonic and concerto sound in favor of a more fluid concertante approach with solo instruments. Schubert designates these moves as "minimally instrumentalized neoclassicism" and stresses an "ambivalence between Impressionism and neoclassicism." He offers an artful comparison of Roussel and Martinů serenades, and concludes with an extensive comparison of the three versions of the first Cello Concerto (1930, 1939, and 1955), each of which represents a different creative period of Martinů and the changes in his musical style.

Locke delivers a breathtaking tour of Martinů's concertante type works for multiple soloists, noting and trying to explicate the composer's own words, "I am a concerto grosso type composer." Exploring these works from a broad historical and theoretical vantage point, he shows Martinů to be both thoughtful and intuitive, aware of the past, but flirting with different ways of transforming it. Like Giselher Schubert, Locke places the composer's activity alongside similar efforts by composers such as Hindemith, Strauss, Vaughan Williams, Krenek, and Bloch.

Aleš Březina reminds us in his writing on *The Kitchen Revue* of how significant was ballet in Martinů's development. Part analysis and part historical reconstruction, we concur with the assertion that "There is no musical trend of the 1920s to 1940s in which Bohuslav Martinů did not participate in some significant manner." This delightful work, a ballet of kitchen implements, is breathtaking in its combination of unlike elements. As the composer suggests, it is a Czech dance with the piano playing the rhythm of a Charleston.

In Part III of our book, Axel Körner writes movingly about the parallels between Martinů and Walter Benjamin, exploring, "how artistic and philosophical production is closely intertwined with its own materiality, how the emergence of texts and music is determined by external factors, by physical and environmental conditions, but also by societal and political circumstances." In this probing essay, haunted by Benjamin's suicide, Körner explores, "how flight, exile, and existential fear caused both men to experience a profound change in the relationship between past, present, and future," and the way this impacted the thinking of both figures. Writing of Martinů's "polystylistic response to historical time," Körner persuasively argues for the broadest possible understanding of the sources of Martinů's creativity.

Markéta Kratochvílová and Marek Pechač give an intricate and detailed view of the processes that led up to the Cleveland premiere of Martinů's Symphony No. 2, teasing out how the main actors in the drama made the performance possible, and offering a vivid view of the nuts and bolts of getting a work performed at that time. Most compelling are an extensive collection of letters from the archives of the Cleveland Symphony Orchestra which allow the writers to precisely document the activities around the symphony, and show that the work had both local and international significance at the time.

In her provocatively essay titled "Challenging Modernism," Vincenzina C. Ottomano not only gives a detailed history of the Venice Biennale, from its inception during the fascist period through the Second World War and beyond, but also offers an intricate overview of Martinů's relationship to the Biennale, and through that, his relationship to modernist currents of the time. The essay offers a detailed evaluation of responses to Martinů's music at the festival, shedding light on both the scope and limitations of the notion of modernism.

The "Documents and Editions" section of this volume is devoted to presenting the results of editorial research as well as previously unavailable materials. We include two articles by Aleš Březina and Vít Zouhar on, respectively, the complete edition of Martinů's works and the collected letters of the composer. It is critical to note that the study of Martinů and his music has been beautifully nourished by the activities of the Bohuslav Martinů Institute in Prague, supported by the Bohuslav Martinů Foundation. Brilliantly led by my co-editor, Aleš Březina, the institute continues to subsidize and produce a range of Martinů-related publications.

Aleš Březina provides a justification and overview of the process of the compiling a complete edition of Martinů's compositions. An ambitious project, eventually it will consist of over one hundred volumes, and will gather together all the sources and other materials related to the compositions. Several volumes have already been published, and a certain amount of information is already available on the website www.martinu.cz. Here Březina provides information about the contents, and in writing about compositions such as the *Field Mass* makes clear the challenges that have faced the editors.

Vít Zouhar provides not only an overview of the publication of the complete letters of Martinů, more than 700 letters in twelve volumes, but gives valuable samples of the material in his writing. He shows how critical are the letters for understanding not only the composer's creative process, but everything from his general state of mind to the tiniest details of composition and performance.

Michael Beckerman presents a recently discovered notebook from around 1953— written mostly in English, but also in French and Czech—that gives us a kind of snapshot into Martinů's, thinking, and also takes us through some of the literary sources he was engaging. We encounter in this notebook a persistent searcher, preoccupied with human dignity, and with a deep empathy for his fellow human beings. We also see his rejection of totalizing theories, and his insistence in finding answers for himself. He rarely provides categorical statements, and his most characteristic move is to ask questions.

We also present for the first time a collection of interviews about Martinů conducted by Aleš Březina with some of the most important figures in American musical life. Taken together, these interviews create a portrait of an anti-celebrity. While it would be misleading to label the composer simply as "modest," because, after all, his confidence in his abilities was absolute, he comported himself as if he was superior to no one. In these interviews we encounter his teaching style, his views on composers of the past as well as on his contemporaries, his privileged position on the American music scene in the mid-twentieth century, his fondness for food and wine, his distaste for the bustle of New York (or at least that around

58th Street), his recovery from a serious fall and its repercussions, his sadness and sometimes desperate circumstances, and ultimately, his great humanity.

In a concluding essay, Leon Botstein speaks about the friendship between Martinů and Rudolf Firkušný, framing the two within the context of war, exile, and Czechoslovak democratic ideals. He casts them as closely connected parts of what almost amounts to a single organism: the introverted composer providing material for the virtuoso performer, and the performer delivering that composer's compelling music to a broad and appreciative public. The essay is also a powerful meditation on what the author calls, "the specific potential of music to promote the neighborly love that Masaryk believed was the essential basis of democracy's commitment to freedom."

Part I. Operatic Perspectives

Office for Dreaming—or the Simple Future

Commemorative speech on the occasion of the performance of Juliette *at the opening of the fifty-seventh Bregenz Festspiele, 17 July 2002*

JIŘÍ GRUŠA
TRANSLATED BY SUSAN H. GILLESPIE

I have come from Prague to Bregenz—from "Braga" to "Brigentia"—to speak with you about a music that one could actually call "*Musica Bohemica.*" You see, our ties are long-standing. They bring life to what is ours, since what we have in common is revealed in them. Your decision to perform Bohuslav Martinů is in fact a contextual action. For Martinů is Czech and European, is *heimat* and world. Born in a small town in "Kakania,"[1] in the tower room of the local church, he was poor enough to fit into a biblical crèche. And Polička, the town, was a little bit reminiscent of Bethlehem. It also made crèches as Christmas products. The city, itself no redoubt of the wealthy, was cozy and modest in size. Bohemian idyll. Eerily safe and sound. As Spitzweg would have it: "And in the evenings poems I write."[2] Poetically sleepy. Hypnos could have a field day here. The tower room—with foyer and coal-burning stove—was lit by an oil lamp. Its light didn't yet mingle dark and light, like the electric lightbulbs of our big cities. The windows suggested a dirigible. Thus Bohuslav sailed over Bohemia and harkened to the landscape. His father, a shoemaker and tower-keeper, kept watch over the clock. Made the measure of the region. Every night on the rounds with the lantern. In the daytime with a megaphone. Both, today, still stand in the entryway. A magical stage—the watershed of Europe. United the North Sea with the Black Sea. The winters are long and the late summers magnificent. Daily ascent and descent of the stairways. "He who lives in the height of a tower feels the trembling of the world sooner and in farther-reaching oscillations"—this is how it will soon sound in Heideggerian language.[3] A tricky praise of homely things. But even those who are born in the air must ultimately land. They turn the symbol of the tower on its head: here, towering becomes earthen. The way the birds let themselves down on the water out beyond the Gothic city walls. Martinů landed among the earthly, took his leave of the tower. But never of the clarity of its things. He won't be a fog sculptor, no harbinger of darkness. Nor a trumpeter of theses. Born in the air does not mean having taken off. Only being a seer. "I see the music," he will say later. Since the hearing of it was already inside him. But first he built himself a fiddle and played it like Orpheus. Enthralled the world around him. The city was fascinated, inwardly larger. It helped him and let him go. But his departure was Orphean, too. The ascent was drawn out. And every turnabout cost something beloved. The conventional vanished with every step. Origin and arrival became separated. Just as the fledgling twentieth century began to separate everything that previously seemed bound together. Young Martinů was astonished. And took it in. For the person who had to land, separation meant flight. Landing, freedom. He felt it literally: What is left behind does not determine what is coming. Leaving does that. So he went. Wanted his Now. For the future was by no means traditional, either. It simply "unfolded"[4]—and wanted to be wanted. Asked not for models, only for mettle. The name of the future was—Praha. Prague. The world there was more colorful. Czech and Jewish and German. Harmonious and astir. It was not yet producing manic fears and exclusivity. Hybris and Phobos did not yet reign as gods—hubris and fear, the deadliest princes. And towers were here, a hundredfold. No guard with a megaphone could outshout the racket, it is true. Although Polička was here, too! And a tower-dweller.[5] In the Klementinum, on the gallery of the observatory. He had a flag and waved it in time with the pendulum of the astronomical clock. And a fire worker on the Hradschin saw this signal, put his match to the gunpowder, and a shot thundered over the heads of Prague's inhabitants. They stopped and corrected their pocket watches. The stars still stood, as they should. The chronometer measured no Chronos. Meant no powerful god of time who devours his own children. It tested the cyclical. Peace and rules. Only the doves flew up briefly, but they soon settled down. On Kampa Island.[6] Where they picked around, so numerously. And where Martinů could feed them from his window. He lived near the Charles Bridge. And was supposed to become a Paganini. Only—he was no careerist, submitted to no drill in order to rise. As the son of a tower-keeper he understood "above" very factually. In a tower room, time becomes material. There, one sees that even silence already trembles. And vibrations soon become rifts. One can touch them. Notate and play them. A mere interpreter, a person who repeats, can do nothing here. A setter of musical notes, though, almost everything! And Martinů perceived life's trembling. He composed, worked away stubbornly, and earned much ridicule and a reprimand. Considering that he actually smelled of success. For this we forgive no one. "Irredeemable negligence" is what we accused him of. But he was no longer to be caught with our line. New interpretation of established things was not his objective. Flowing things are what suits him. Now-time, the present, its reasoning. We call the present "*přítomnost.*" Literally, a "present," with an ending for abstraction. In other words, it is not about a "*Gegenwart*"[7]—no "*Wart*" (attendant), and no "*gegen*" (against). The way Czechs understand presence sees, in humans, a kind of sluicegate in the river.

In that *panta rhei*, the all-flowing of being. Even Martinů's tower room reinforced this position. It taught him to relativize every vanishing point. For even towers become tiny if you view them from afar. As a result, the signs showing the only correct direction become eternally suspect. He liked neither philosophizing music nor music-making philosophy. Contents that can be told are urns full of ashes. Something that may be full, but is simultaneously empty. He sensed that the old saying "The clearer the signs, the lighter the steps" is not entirely correct. Since it takes the ground of the future for guaranteed. Nice and perfectionist, European in its thinking. We Europeans do love salvation in the future. But our will to arrive there is tricky. It devalues the present, turns it into a valueless nowhere. We sacrifice our "there" to an "out there" and turn it into a "back there." The future, facing backward, is what we call "history." No other culture ever hallowed so many martyrs, painted them in such large numbers. As long as we only used them to decorate temples, it seemed healthy. But we have become secular. Our perfectionism gave birth to folkish chosenness and wanted to raise it. That was not simple, for no one comes by that much pedigree without falsifying documents. So we gave a magisterial spin to what, before that, was only magnificent. Turned output into input. And loaded our canons with the stuff. The ones at Hradčany Castle, too. They fired, and the doves on Kampa were really terrified. They took off and roamed around in the heights. Wanted to get to Radetzky Square, but came to earth on Republic Square. And the soldiers who departed the city from Franz-Josef Station returned to the one called Wilson. Czech Prague felt fine and enjoyed the days. The other part[8] became bewildered and fearful. This wasn't something to go to war for! A musician's ear could hear the undertone, the strange rustle of the region. And it all seemed more like a folk festival in Polička than an opera by Wagner in the Deutsches Theater. But it didn't sound bad. If one no longer saw it deterministically, not theatrically. As if another message were becoming perceptible there. Not prefabricated, just something that could be built upon, in us and through us. It no longer wanted to beautify. As if the beautiful were merely a manner of being of our ethos. Martinů wrote this music, but his Prague fellow residents didn't understand him, as opposed to the Mozart of once upon a time. Prague was living euphorically, in its politics, but it opened up cautiously. And, in fact, the first years of Czechoslovakia were characterized by the will to take care, domestically, of what only yesterday people had been seeking in Paris, London, or Berlin. And many were still rhyming *czeský* with *hezký*: "Czech" with "beautiful." We don't actually claim that our *czeský* essence can save anyone else. *Czeský* plus *hezký* just seems more modest. Martinů's Prague neighbors saw him not as a cosmopolitan, but as an alien. At first, they accused him of not being one of us. Not one of the Czeskies and Heskies. The accusation was not aimed at the usual Germanophilia, as with Smetana, for example. But at the other great man,[9] born not far from Polička. For us, Martinů was too francophile and Russophile: Too much Debussy and Stravinsky. But he did not suffer. He became resistant. He, who was "irremediably irresponsible,"[10] was irreversible and full of fun. And gave back. Wrote a sentence never heard here before: "I have time!" In other words: My "*přitomnost*" is cooler than your "being there." It makes the music. Unboundedness is my boundary! My visual and aural space. So he smiled, and became—biographically—once again a *Musicus Bohemicus*. A "worldski" like so many before him. When music was still the homeland of musicians, and not the nation. Ergo, he also won't have to sell any brides—as Smetana did with his ingenious *buffa*. But become a bridegroom—of Juliette. She was already awaiting him . . . by the Seine. Dear Bregenzers, you have also selected Puccini's *La bohème* for the program of your festival. Accident or no, I see a nexus here. Naturally, during Martinů's time in Paris there was no more Mimi and her friends. Their pleasure in life, though, for sure. And also their belief, which values the day today more than yesterday's or tomorrow's. *Bohème* and Bohemia are connected. A bit incorrectly, but splendidly. And in Austria I don't have to explain that someone who goes "*auf lepschi*"[11] is not running to the cemetery or the office. *Bohème*, itself, is simply powerful praise of now-time. Have no fear, the Czech ambassador, here, is not claiming patent rights or seeking the repatriation of elderly relatives.[12] At best, he is merely imagining an amusing "homepage"[13] for himself. It recalls the '20s, which later seemed golden to people. In Paris, Berlin, and Prague. And golden is always a little bit "Bohemian." Martinů made his way through Paris and liked unprepossessing addresses. Courtyards and gardens in which one could converse Socratically until dawn. And when night came, dreams came too. Naturally, humanly private and thus not embarrassing. Waking people had a common world, sleepers a private one. But they were allowed to wake up. Sometimes refreshed, even cleansed. Before the war, a Viennese professor, it is true, had claimed that we also had a sleep world in common. And dreams in it that don't seem so isolated at all. This claim, though, was considered Viennese. A cellar of the soul? Where we put things that disturb us? Unheard of. Perhaps at the Prater.[14] But on the Champs Élysées and Picadilly? No. But now this belief could no longer be stopped. As if the losers as well as the victors in the war now wanted to know where the murdering came from that made them so happy. As if they also wanted to dig up the things that disturbed them as well. Make the unconscious conscious. In France, people even saw the beautiful in this and wanted to put it to use to make the world better. They saw what was underneath as on the very top. And called it superreality. Surreality. Many artists baptized themselves Surrealists. They thought relativistically, multi-causally, and anti-poetically. But they were great poets. One of them wrote *Juliette ou La clé des songes*. Juliette or the book of dreams. An *ad causam* play on behalf of the depths one can wade in. Like at ebb tide. Or even, specifically after this cruel war. Everything lay fallow. Not just cathedrals, charterhouses, too. Chaotically strewn about. Reconstructable, though, any way one wanted.

Earlier, people would have spoken of the transient nature of humanity. Now only of the transience of the past. Making the unconscious conscious? Why not? All you need to do is realize the unreal. Georges Neveux portrayed this process. But still as a kind of wading in the shallow water of the coasts. In his *Juliette* there is a small town, almost Bohemian-like, in a Bohemia by the sea.[15] The people here have no memory. A loss of the scope of time, normally a sign of madness, now becomes the norm. And people have arrived here bureaucratically. Not, in other words, that they just fall asleep and land in Hypnos. Here, they walk into an office. And a bureaucrat takes down their name. They get a ticket and receive the dream they wished for. No differently than nowadays in a video shop. What a concrete vision, and dated so early, in 1930! Peepshow[16] of the soul. A newbie like Michel, a bookseller and main character in the play, appears here. He still remembers, but he is infatuated with a fatal reminiscence. A girl in the window, a song. Something one of a kind. Michel can't let go of it. "Yesterday, barely fallen asleep, you came here," the official says to him. "You should wake up and get out of here!" Apparently he already feels sorry for him. Knows, in other words, what is on offer here. In this "dream book play," not a single dream is interpreted. No omen for the future deciphered. People here are in bondage to the past. As if, in them, the stream of time were drying up. And their now time turning into a black hole. Michel could offer up his memory. He, however, prattles on, completely unconcentrated; searches for his Juliette. But since all the girls here have this name, it looks as if he wants a mass-produced article. In France, death is feminine. *La mort*—as it is in Czechia. So, is Juliette a Moira, more of a Norn? And mild-mannered Hypnos—a Thanatos, the god of death? Transformed into this official, a factotum of eternal consummation? The person who looks for the Hotel Sailor, like Michel, boards not a dreamboat, but a galley. When Neveux's *Juliette* had its premiere, Paris was still *bohémien*, and yet it was not up to the drama. The text seemed provocative. As if the author were not a dreamer, but a fortune teller who prophesies the demise of the current authority. A whiff of Sophocles was in the air. How, otherwise, would all the good bourgeois citizens have gotten so up in arms? They felt misled. Did not want to know, in a waking state, what they already knew when sleeping. They were afraid. But fulfilling the wishes of fearful people is easy. You just need to convince them of them. Then the dream fulfills what reality denied. It is enough to offer the values of insanity as sensible values. To open an office, Commission for What Is Coming. When Martinů discovered the play by Neveux, Surrealism had already reached its zenith. The "sur-" of reality was incapable of further intensification. Even Prague now wanted Martinů back. The opportunity eventually arrived; the usual enviers were silent. And Martinů's success, too, could no longer be gainsaid. Yes, Prague had its own group of excellent Surrealists. It was, indeed, in the eye of the hurricane, but only wanted its *přítomnost* all the more. The danger without helped speed the setting of the scene.

Martinů could count on the country's best. And it even seemed as if, with his opera, he had once more conjured up cyclical time. But it was the last swing of its pendulum. As prescribed by the composer, something unnatural should adhere to the decoration. The wish was fulfilled. As the office was being erected on the Prague stage, with its desk where everyone can come to pick up his dream, as the insignia were being polished yet again, to decorate the hero who has a "story" at the ready that is preparing to become historic, and then, to the wild applause of the people, deliver the governorship of the city to the storyteller, something occurred in Vienna that made the Prague premiere into a reprise. The day before, namely, along the Danube, a black Mercedes began to move. It carried a man who pretended to be able to tell a story for a thousand years and more. He drove, in step, to his masses. The hotel was not named Le Navigateur—but Imperial. And the rejoicing was for an announcement that declared the fulfillment of the most daring dreams. I don't know whether the man knew anything about his Polička connection. This too, namely, was surrealistic. For among the people in front of the new Hofburg[17] there might have been Marie Zákrejsová. His landlady from the Stumpergasse.[18] He paid her 20 crowns a month for a room in the basement. He was still forced to pay for his super-reality—psychically and physically. But he was full of hope of realizing the irreal. The landlady liked him. And he liked her too, although her Bohemian accent was conspicuous. Beyond that, the man surely did not know that in Polička the name Zákrejs means something. One of the Zákrejs left behind a street and a scary drama: "Last public execution on Mount Gallows." Ominous? I don't know, but bizarre enough. Almost in character for Neveux. The performance was splendid. Also as an upbeat to the creepiness. After a year and a bit, Prague will see the black Mercedes too. And the professor in Vienna, the discoverer of the collective nightmare, will pack his things. And have to flee—into the individual. And soon the whole continent begins to be in motion. Soldiers, refugees, tanks, and baby carriages. Martinů leaves Paris, finds a hiding place in the South. Like Michel in his play, he barely escapes a death sentence. Flees to Spain, Portugal, and the States. He will describe his life after *Juliette* as "*Juliette in actu*." But the hallucinatory continues. His Czechs also get an office for dreaming. A politburo for "a morning that means a yesterday." So excellently one of them will formulate the purpose of our utopia. And a commissar for the folkish in music will write, about Martinů: "Take a look. Where is the content? Not a single melody resounds within it that would fit in the mouths of our soldiers . . . !" Once more, he becomes a stranger, this time for life. And he will be homesick. Until he, too, sees and gets his Juliette—for he will die soon. But listen to his music. It is the Ionian Muses who make their appearance here. The beautiful as practice. It is the praise of the present tense. The pre-sent has become a now-sent.[19] Reality is not an object, up against something. But rather a conjecture. Life in it creates courage to want the future. It is the reason why Martinů becomes more and more timely.

He almost reminds us of the *actus purus*. Of the divine. The phrase "In the beginning" here becomes a thought. It turns into an endless point in time, vibrating and trembling. And finding resonance within us.

NOTES

All notes are by the translator.

1. Kakania is a slang term based on the abbreviation "k. u. k," for the phrase "*Kaiserlich und Königlich,*" which refers to the empire and the kingdom of Austria. It was made famous by Robert Musil's 1930 novel *The Man Without Qualities*.

2. Carl Spitzweg (1808–1885), was a German genre painter who also wrote poetry. Both his paintings and his poems betray a rather conventional, sometimes humorous bourgeois sensibility. An English translation of the poem in question: "But please, on earth your sole refrain / Should be to stay away from pain / As for me, all day I paint / And in the evening poems I write."

3. "Wer in der Höhe einer Turmstube wohnt, spürt das Erzittern der Welt eher and in weiter auslandenden Schwingungen." The English version of this Heidegger quote, cited in the text, is taken from the Translator's Foreword to Heidegger's *Country Path Conversations*, trans. Bret W. Davis (Bloomington: Indiana University Press, 2016), xv.

4. The German verb used here, "*west*," is Heideggerian language.

5. This is a pun. German "*Türmer*" can mean someone who escapes, or, theoretically and grammatically (although the word is not in the dictionary), can mean a "tower person."

6. Kampa Island is located on the left bank of the Vltava River and is reached by the Charles River Bridge. During Martinů's time there, it would have been home to poorer segments of the population.

7. German for "present time."

8. The German population of Prague, which until then had been economically and culturally dominant.

9. I.e. Bedřich Smetana.

10. In German, "*der unverbesserliche Vernachlässiger*." This is a double pun.

11. Viennese slang for going out to have a good time.

12. At the time Jiří Gruša delivered this speech, he was the Czech ambassador to Austria.

13. English in original.

14. Vienna's amusement park.

15. An allusion to Act 3, scene 3 from Shakespeare's *Winter's Tale*.

16. English in original.

17. The Hofburg is the former Imperial Palace of the Habsburg dynasty, in Vienna.

18. Adolf Hitler once lived at Stumpergasse 31 in Vienna.

19. The German "*Die Gegenwart ist hier ein 'Mit-Wart,'*" another untranslatable pun, is replaced here with a different one.

“We Have No Railway Station”: *Juliette* or the Renunciation of Memory

ALEŠ BŘEZINA

The opera *Juliette* by Bohuslav Martinů, after a play of the same name by the French surrealist Georges Neveux, is frequently defined as a dream opera, by which I mean the positive aspects of the ability to dream. But this is only one aspect of this immensely complex and ultimately not fully explicable piece.

Shadow Figures Without Properties

The only somewhat real person in the opera is Michel. He, a Parisian bookseller, once came to a small harbor town and heard a woman’s voice sing out of a mansard window. Out of fear that he might have fallen in love with the girl, he hastily left the city. Three years later he returns to find the window, the girl, and the song again. In the meantime, however, the inhabitants of the city have strangely changed: it gradually becomes clear that for some inexplicable reason they became shadow figures, with no context. Only Michel is equipped with a little information about his origin, clothing, occupation, parents, place of residence, and appearance. We know nothing at all about Juliette, all others are only partially characterized by race affiliation (small and old Arabs), occupation (various saleswomen), or clothes (Man with a Fur Hat). They are characterized mainly by obsessions: a “Man with Helmet” imagines himself to be the owner of a steamer, a “Bird Seller” is obsessed with the idea that a canary has been stolen from her, etc.

Juliette is an opera about dreams. But gradually it becomes clear that what these “men without qualities” (Robert Musil) are experiencing is not so much an imaginative, continuing dream that enriches the world perceived with the senses and giving it new dimensions, but are, rather, escaping into a dream world. They continuously invent little stories, or lure passing visitors into recounting their experiences, then give the invented or stolen “memories” an unrestricted predominance over their real life, which in its banality and everydayness cannot match the dream life.

Actually, in this strange world, only objects are real; the people vegetating between them appear vague and have no coherence. In their changeability, they produce an unstable impression, like the melting clock in a famous painting by

Salvador Dalí. They are unable to love, because they are in love not with a counterpart, but with their own wishful thinking. Since their respective stories are not compatible, they also cannot communicate with each other.

The play *Juliette* was written in 1927. Martinů set it to music ten years later. In "the age of mechanical reproduction" (Walter Benjamin), with the increasing popularity of mass culture, it is not surprising that the prefabricated dreams of all protagonists by no means look unique, but resemble each other. Dreams have degenerated into commodities and are treated as such. Neveux and Martinů illustrate this first in the character of a "Seller of Memories" and much more directly in the third act with the depiction of a "Central Dream Office," a marvellous monstrosity, a vacuum inhabited by grey figures that is responsible for the mass duplication of a limited number of dreams. Among the clients of this office is a blind beggar, who sells fortune-telling cards in the daytime but who, in the evening, longs to experience some elements of the promises described in his cards, at least in the form of a dream.

But Martinů and Neveux do not treat these cheap dreams in a derogatory manner; they do not emphasize their obvious ridiculousness. Through the poetry of language and beauty of music, they somehow make them understandable, almost credible. They show sympathy for the tragedy of their protagonists, but without giving them an excuse for their constantly changing, incoherent identities: one must not forgive, only understand, the reasons that led to this incoherence. However, the opera ends tragically: Michel shoots Juliette (or maybe just thinks he shot her), killing the positive side of his dream, i.e. his desire for her. Faced with the possibility of returning to real life with the certainty he would lose her, he recoils. Instead of returning to reality, he plunges through the door of the Central Dream Office.

Loss of Memory

What has turned all these people into incoherent shadow figures? The inhabitants of the small harbor city have all lost their memory. As a result, they cannot develop their own thoughts but can only repeat or parrot other people's ideas. Significantly, after his appointment as "Captain of the Town" Michel receives as one of the three visible symbols of his authority a parrot in a cage who "repeats a refrain every fifteen minutes" to remind everybody of his rank.

But is this really a loss, a kind of amnesia? Did not Martinů and Neveux want to build a parable in which the protagonists voluntarily renounce memory and thus become an easily manipulated mass? When the strange events in the opera reach a temporary climax, Michel wants to go to the station and leave the city. "We have no railway station here!" says the Man at the Window. But Michel knows for certain he arrived on the Northwest Railroad Line. "There is no railway station here!" replies the Little Arab and everyone agrees. And with the words "No, no!

You cannot leave here!" the Commissioner concludes the whole discussion.

And so Michel's position in the city fundamentally changes within just a few hours. He is first regarded as a stranger and interrogated; the inhabitants of the town even want to arrest him. Several people want to carry out the interrogation ordered by the Commissioner: "Please, please, that's what I'd like to do," offers The Man with a Helmet, the prototype of a follower. Michel owes it only to his (still) good memory that he is not—yet—arrested. The Commissioner announces that he will not arrest Michel on the spot because Michel kept in mind the Commissioner's rank. But the possibility of a completely arbitrary arrest remains an option. Suddenly Michel is admired by the same people who had wanted to interrogate him for his "more than ten seconds" of back memory, who appointed him Captain of the City. Only a short time later, the residents forget this fact and want to execute him because they believe he shot Juliette.

Isn't this a parable about a century that had enormous trouble with historical memory? In a world without historical memory, in a world of generally accepted lies, people can easily be manipulated. Think of the Munich Agreement, the two World Wars and the Cold War, the belated compensation of forced laborers and the few Jews who survived the Holocaust, the expulsion of Czech Germans from Czechoslovakia after World War II, and much more. The renunciation of memory allows the city dwellers what Václav Havel has described in his essay "The Power of the Powerless" as a comfortable and undisturbed "life in lies."

Neither Neveux nor Martinů offer an explanation of why the city dwellers renounced their memory. They do not say what fundamentally changed their mentality in the three years between Michel's first and second stay. The power they have bowed to remains invisible, as in the novels of Franz Kafka. But the development of the figure of Michel shows that everyone has a free choice to face or negate reality: after he "shoots" his Juliette, he gradually begins to lose his memory. At the end of the opera, he voluntarily leaves reality and takes refuge in a dream world.

It is hard to prove whether the authors of this piece asked similar questions. In the 1920s and mid-1930s, they had not yet been exposed to totalitarian power. However, only a few years later Martinů noticed that this "surrealist" piece had something in common with the events of the day: in a short autobiographical sketch written in September 1945, he noted: "How many times did it occur to me during the whole time [i.e. during Martinů's several months' flight from Hitler's occupied France], that I was living through scenes from this opera: what was truth and reality only five minutes ago, after that it was not anymore."

Like all good parables, this parable of the renunciation of memory is timeless. The opera *Juliette* is by no means merely a review of the past; it is also valid for the present, the time after the collapse of Communist systems in Eastern and Central Europe. On 13 August 2001, the *New York Times* published the following quote from Jürgen Liftin, whose brother was the first to be shot while trying to get across the Berlin Wall to West Berlin: "Fewer and fewer Berliners ever go to see the wall or care about it. People want to forget about it. They want to be rid of it and think that life is beautiful. It's a tragedy." The fall of the Berlin Wall at the end of the last millennium may now seem like a distant memory. However, one need not go that far to confirm the timelessness of Juliette's main theme, since we are now experiencing a situation in which the clear victim of the current war is being labelled by its main ally as the aggressor and, what is more, even as the perpetrator of this war.

Juliette is more than just a dream opera about unfulfilled love. It is also a bittersweet parable about human yearnings in general, as well as about the lack of communication, and above all, about the renunciation of memory and the resulting easy manipulability of the people who have embarked on this comfortable but dangerous game. The humorous presentation of a serious and at times dark theme with distinct, beautiful, and captivating music makes this highly original work a unique contribution to twentieth-century opera.

This text was written within the project GA21-21228S Bohuslav Martinů's Music Theatre 1913- 1937. Processing and publication of a monograph with critical edition by the Grant Agency of the Czech Republic (GACR).

Byzantine Music in Martinů's Opera *The Greek Passion*

MARIOS CHRISTOU

The Greek Passion, the last opera and one of the most significant works of Bohuslav Martinů, has been considered a bridge between Greek and Czech culture in the twentieth century. This, for the obvious reason that the libretto is based on the celebrated novel by the Greek writer Nikos Kazantzakis, *Christ Recrucified*, and that the two artists had a genuine friendship.[1] Eleni Kazantzaki stated boldly, "The names Martinů and Kazantzakis will be connected forever."[2] It is surprising, considering Martinů's correspondence with Šafránek and Kazantzakis, that so little has been written about how this cultural bridge is present in the musical fabric of the score. Apart from the Greek origin of the work's libretto, there are several different kinds of evidence that Martinů drew on Greek sources to create the musical character of the opera.[3] The main intention of this essay is to demonstrate that Byzantine music played an essential role in the musical construction of *The Greek Passion*.

The study of Byzantine music in *The Greek Passion* was triggered in 2016 by the discovery of a manuscript in Martinů's hand, consisting mostly of Byzantine chants.[4] This manuscript was, obviously, a part of the composer's research into Greek music for the opera.[5] Using this manuscript as a starting point, and after further research in secondary sources, I have analyzed the opera and discovered that Byzantine music serves as a foundational element of the work. In this study, nonetheless, I aim not only to demonstrate the significance of Greek music in it but also illustrate how Martinů utilized and adapted what might be considered a remote musical culture into his work.

The opera exists today in two different versions. The first version, known as the London version, H 372 I, was composed between 1954 and 1957 for the Covent Garden Royal Opera House.[6] The work was rejected by the Royal Opera and therefore remained unknown to the public until 1999.[7] Soon after the1957 rejection, Martinů began work on a new version of the opera, which is known today as the Zurich version, H 372 II. This study concerns only the first version of the opera.

Leitmotifs

"Alleluia of the Bridegroom"

The hymn notated in Figure 1 is the "opening melody" of the Palm Sunday service of the Greek Orthodox Church, known as the "Alleluia of the Bridegroom" (Το Αλληλούια του Νυμφίου / To Alliloulia tou Nymphiou) and is chanted in the fourth plagal mode (not to be confused with the third mode!).[8] Thus, its extra-musical association conveys the meaning of the beginning of the Great and Holy Week, the beginning of the *Passion*. And for Martinů, this is the beginning of *The Greek Passion*.[9]

Figure 1. Excerpt from Martinů's manuscript on Byzantine music.

The "Alleluia of the Bridegroom" appears in the first scene of Act 1 when the priest Grigoris sings "How can I become worthy to bear the terrible weight of the Cross!"

Martinů uses the original chant melody without any modifications, but still, his harmonization fundamentally changes its character (see Example 1).[10] The "Alleluia of the Bridegroom" is the most frequently used Byzantine melody in the opera and has a substantial function in the macrostructure of the work. It appears in every act, always when the question of the Passion comes up. In fact, this chant melody is a leitmotif of an idea (not a character), the leitmotif of the Passion itself. According to Aleš Březina, this is also called the "Cross theme" (*téma kříže*).[11] Although this study deals only with the first version of the opera, it is noteworthy to mention that the second version of the opera actually begins with this theme.

"O Lord, Save Thy People"

"O Lord, Save Thy People,"[12] another Byzantine chant melody that appears several times in the opera, is the Apolytikion of the Feast of the Holy Cross. This theme is not included in Martinů's manuscript but is referred to in his letters to Kazantzakis.[13] Again, Martinů chooses a chant that expresses the given situation in the plot of the opera. The English translation of the original Greek text is:

> Save, O Lord, Your people and bless Your inheritance; grant victory to the faithful over their adversaries. And protect Your commonwealth, by the power of Your Cross.[14]

Example 1. Martinů, *The Greek Passion*, Act 1, scene 1.

Example 2. Martinů, *The Greek Passion*, Act 1, scene 3.

Example 2. Continued

The Apolytikion is actually an invocation for God's help and it is introduced at the point when a group of refugees arrives at the village of Lykovrisi, starving, exhausted, begging for help, and asking for shelter.

Example 2 shows that Martinů used only the first words of the original text. It seems that he had to modify it in order to fit the music. In a letter to Miloš Šafránek he wrote, "Of course, I have used Byzantine chant, but there is a problem with that, because the English translation of the text does not fit the music."[15] Nevertheless, considering that there are several English translations of this text and that we do not know which one of them got into the possession of the composer, we cannot be certain about the changes he made on the text.

This Apolytikion is very popular among the Greek people and it is customarily sung by heart from generation to generation. Consequently, there is a plethora of variations, which makes it difficult to pin down what might be the original melody. Example 3 displays one of the most common versions, that is also quite close to the version we find in the opera.[16]

An analysis of Examples 2 (Martinů's elaborated version) and 3 (the original chant melody) reveals that this is not simply a harmonization of the original chant melody, but a free variation. Before proceeding to an analysis of the chant's elaboration in the opera, it is important to remind ourselves that we do not know which version of the chant Martinů had in mind.[17] Hence, we cannot be sure if minor differences from the melody displayed in Example 2 are variations by the composer or a part of the version of the melody he received from Greece. In any case, what occurs here is a transposition and variation of approximately the first eight measures of the original melody.

Example 3. Common version of the Apolytikion chant melody.

Another aspect of Martinů's elaboration lies in the sixteenth notes sung on the syllable "my." To any chanter of Byzantine music it would be immediately clear that this is nothing other than an effort to write down the ornaments that always appear in that music when a syllable is sung on more than one tone (see second measure of Example 2).

The Apolytikon of the Holy Cross also functions as a leitmotif, though it does not appear as frequently as the "Alleluia of the Bridegroom."

Direct Quotations: Wedding, Gladsome Light, Funeral

In addition to the variations (including simple harmonizations) of chant melodies used as leitmotifs, several melodies are introduced directly, in their original one-voice form, at crucial points of the opera. The examples that follow display three of them. All of them "preserve" their original extramusical association (wedding, funeral, etc.) in the new musical environment of the opera.

Wedding

The first of the direct quotations is another popular Greek chant known as the "Dance of Isaiah" ("Ο χορός του Ησαΐα" / O choros tou Isaia), from the wedding service. As can be seen in the excerpts that follow, Martinů copies this melody from his manuscript to the score of the opera without any changes (Figure 2). The only modification of the original chant concerns the text, where he easily solves the problem fitting the music to the text by replacing the words with meaningless syllables "la, la, la . . ." (Example 4).

Gladsome Light (Phos Hilaron)

"God called up the day": with these words the commentator closes the first scene of the last act of the opera. And again the Czech composer uses a very suitable and enchanting early hymn for this last part of the scene, *Phos Hilaron* (Φως Ιλαρόν). This hymn is known in English as "O Gladsome Light." One of its English translations is the following:

> Gladsome Light of the Holy Glory of the Immortal Father, Heavenly, Holy, Blessed: O Jesus Christ. Now that we have come to the setting of the sun, and behold the light of evening, we praise God: Father, Son, and Holy Spirit, for meet it is at all times to worship Thee with voices of praise, O Son of God and Giver of life: therefore, all the world doth glorify Thee.[18]

After an examination of Figure 3 and Example 5 we can see that Martinů made only minor changes. At points he altered the metric structure by prolonging some of the tones, he ignored the micro-intervals of the second mode (see Figure 3, at the beginning) and he did not use the entire hymn.

Figure 2. "Dance of Isaiah," excerpt from Martinů's manuscript on Byzantine music.

Example 4. Martinů, *The Greek Passion*, Act 4, scene 1.

Figure 3. "Gladsome Light," excerpt from Martinů's manuscript on Byzantine music.

Example 5. Martinů, "Gladsome Light," *The Greek Passion*, Act 6, end of scene 1.

Funeral

The last direct quotation of Byzantine chant in the opera is taken from the service for the dead (Νεκρώσιμος ακολουθία / Nekrosimos akolouthia) and it serves as a prayer for the soul of Manolios following priest Fotis's inducement "Manolios is dead, let's pray for him" (see Figure 4 and Example 6.)

Figure 4. Martinů, Funeral chant, excerpts from Martinů's manuscript on Byzantine music.

Allusions

Another way that Byzantine chant penetrates the opera is by the principle of allusion, which, according to Alfred Schnittke, "manifests itself in the use of subtle hints and unfulfilled promises that hover on the brink of quotation but do not actually cross it."[19] One of the many examples of this principle in *The Greek Passion* is "Kyrie eleison" sung by the choir in the third scene of the first act of the opera. The melody here is reminiscent of the Greek "Kyrie eleison" sung at the beginning of the Divine Liturgy known as Great Litany or Litany of Peace. What is reminiscent of the Great Litany here is the rhythmic organization and the melodic contour (see Example 7).

Example 6. Martinů, funeral chant in *The Greek Passion*, Act 4, scene 3.

Example 6. Continued

Conclusion

The intention here is not to demonstrate thoroughly all the Greek chants and songs used in the opera nor all the techniques of their elaboration. But the analysis leaves no doubt that Byzantine music played a fundamental role in the creation of Martinů's *Greek Passion*. It is not only important that Martinů used Byzantine chant, but to note the way he adapted an essentially remote musical culture into his work and succeeded in making it an integral part of a twentieth-century opera. In the end, the work is a result of the elaboration of Greek music in the mind of a Czech composer.

A reading of the correspondence between Martinů and Kazantzakis along with a careful study of the opera suggests that there is even more Greek music, both sacred and secular, in *The Greek Passion*. This analysis is the first step in exploring this critical connection, which should be an assignment for a large project consisting of a team of experts from Greece—Byzantine music scholars—and the Czech Republic, and elsewhere.

NOTES

1. See Aleš Březina and Růžena Dostálová, *Řecké pašije, Osud jedné opery Korespondence Nikose Kazantakise s Bohuslavem Martinů* (Prague: Set Out, 2003).

2. In Greek: "Τα ονόματα Μαρτινού και Καζαντζάκη θα συνδέονται αιώνια." Quotation can be found in Giorgos Anemogiannis, Το Χρονικό μιας δημιουργίας / To Chroniko mias demiourgias), Ανέκδοτη αλληλογραφία Καζαντζάκη-Μαρτινού (Athens: Nikos Kazantzakis Museum,1986), 39.

Example 7. Martinů, "Kyrie eleison" melody, *The Greek Passion*, Act 1, scene 3.

3. For example, see Martinů's letters to Miloš Šafránek in Miloš Šafránek, ed., *Divadlo Bohuslava Martinů* (Prague: Editio Supraphon, 1979), 284 and 287; and Březina and Dostálová, *Řecké pašije*.

4. See Marios Christou, "A newly discovered manuscript by Bohuslav Martinů on the Byzantine Octoechos," *Journal of the International Society for Orthodox Church Music* 3/2018 (1. 1. 2020): 112–20.

5. Ibid.

6. For further reading about the discovery of the first version of the opera see Aleš Březina, "Řecké pašije – dvě opery Bohuslava Martinů," notes in the program brochure *Bohuslav Martinů – Řecké pašije* (Prague: National Theatre, 2006), 26.

7. Ibid.

8. For a comprehensive theory of Byzantine music modality see, for example, *Theory and Practice of Church Music* (Θεωρία Και Πράξη Της Εκκλησιαστικής Μουσικής / Theoria kai Praxi tis Ekklisiastikis Mousikis) by Giorgos Konstantinou (Athens: Holy Great Monastery of Vatopedi, 2013).

9. A fine recording of this chant is to be found in the CD Αλληλούια (Hallelujah) performed by the Greek choir Ιλισιώτες Ψάλτες (Ilisiotes Psaltes) published by the association Η Αγία Μαρίνα Άνω Ιλισίων (Saint Marina of Ano Ilisia). The liner notes include a noteworthy study on this hymn by the conductor of this choir, Grigorios Anastasiou, including further bibliography.

10. Byzantine music is monophonic, thus all the chants discussed here consist of only one voice originally.

11. Březina and Dostálová, *Řecké pašije*, 38.

12. In Greek: Σώσον, Κύριε, τον λαόν Σου / Soson Kyrie ton laon Sou.

13. Březina and Dostálová, *Řecké pašije*, 70.

14. The translation is taken from the website of the Greek Orthodox Archdiocese of America, https://www.goarch.org/el/-/hymns-of-the-feast-of-the-exaltation-of-the-cross.

15. Šafránek, *Divadlo Bohuslava Martinů*, 284. Translated by the author.

16. This version of the chant melody is taken from Georgios Loizou (Γεώργιος Λοΐζου) Αινείτε παίδες Κύριον (Praise the Lord, o Children), (Nicosia: Holy Monastery of Kykkos, 2000), 44.

17. This chant melody is not included in Martinů's notebook on Byzantine music, but it is mentioned on his correspondence with Kazantzakis.

18. This translation is taken from the official website of the Orthodox Church in America (OCA), https://www.oca.org/files/PDF/Music/Rubrics/Horologion/office-vespers.pdf.

19. Alfred Schnittke, "Polystylistic Tendencies of Modern Music," in *A Schnittke Reader*, ed. Alexander Ivashkin (Bloomington: Indiana University Press, 2002), 88.

Meditation on the First *Ave Maria* of Bohuslav Martinů's *Sister Paskalina*

JON KANTOR MEADOW

> Even when I'm here in his arms,
> I know you're somewhere in his heart.
>
> —Dua Lipa, "Maria"

Hry o Marii (*The Plays of Mary*), H 236, is Bohuslav Martinů's Czech-language cycle of four one-act opera-ballets. *The Plays of Mary* premiered in Brno's National Theatre on 23 February 1935, and the cycle takes a little over two hours to perform. The balletic sections of the cycle tend toward the abstract, the essential, the oneiric, the impersonal, and the visionary. Martinů's approach to musical style throughout is eclectic. All *The Plays of Mary*[1] include a legal trial of some kind, and each one-act opera's libretto conveys an impression of being farced in the ecclesiastical sense of being augmented with additional materials.[2] The cycle also contains many vocal choruses, which is a likely indicator of the work's interwar contemporaneity, its anti-Wagnerian bona fides, since Richard Wagner famously sought to reduce the presence of vocal choruses in his stage works, so much so that "while conceiving of the *Ring* in 1850" he "even toyed with banning a singing chorus outright, so extreme was his antipathy to the conventions of modern opera."[3] *The Plays of Mary* channels something of the spirit of medieval Christendom's liturgical dramas and its mystery and miracle plays, and like other operas of the times, reflects the everyday experiences and lived realities of the interwar moment, especially its social, spiritual, and economic conditions.[4] Staying with the matter of reflective surfaces a little longer, *The Plays of Mary*, with its plays within plays and performances within performances, exhibits the kinds of self-referentiality and structural recursion characteristic of the visual, literary, and dramaturgical device known in French as *mise en abyme* (placed in the void or abyss), which is suitably captured in the baroque imagery of mirrors within mirrors containing figures in infinite regress.

The Plays of Mary commence with *Panny moudré a panny pošetilé* (*The Wise and Foolish Virgins*), Martinů's setting of Vítězslav Nezval's retelling of the liturgical drama *Sponsus* (The Bridegroom). *Sponsus* is an Old Provençal and Latin enactment of Christ's parable of Mary and Martha from the Gospel According to St. Matthew, written down in the twelfth-century in the Benedictine abbey of Saint Martial Limoges.[5] Although *Mariken z Nimègue* (*Mariken of Nimègue*) follows *The Wise and Foolish Virgins* in *The Plays of Mary*'s original performance sequence, it was the one-act opera of the cycle that Martinů composed first. *Mariken of Nimègue* is Martinů's setting of Vilém Závada's astonishing take on the tale of a pact made around the waning of the Middle Ages between the Devil and a young Dutch girl named Mariken.[6] *The Plays of Mary*'s third one-act opera is a Christmas pastorale called *Narození Páně* (*The Nativity*) and its libretto is based on Moravian folk poetry. Remarkably, *The Nativity*, offers different accounts of the events surrounding Christ's birth.

Sestra Paskalina (*Sister Paskalina*) is *The Plays of Mary*'s fourth and final one-act opera. Martinů wrote the libretto by reducing Julius Zeyer's ornately written Czech-language novella, *Sestra Paskalina*, and Maurice Maeterlinck's French-language Symbolist play, *Sœur Béatrice*, to their essentials then adding in various passages of Moravian folk poetry, prosaic dialogue in the Czech vernacular, and Latin-texted psalms, hymns, and portions of the liturgy. In a self-penned Czech-language *Plays of Mary* publicity article titled "Remarks on the Cycle *The Plays of Mary*" Martinů alludes to the cycle's broader intra- and inter-play reflections when he notes that of all *Mary*'s plays, *Sister Paskalina* is the one within which his "principles and rules are reflected best."[7] Granted, as Martinů notes in another *Plays of Mary* publicity essay called "On the Brno Premiere," some of these principles and rules "only pertain directly" to *The Plays of Mary*.[8] The nature of some of the principles and rules he is referring to can be gleaned from another statement he writes in "On the Brno Premiere." There he makes note of his ideal of textual integrity and purity of transmission. He writes, "I want the text to be understood, and ask the singer for clarity."[9] At the same time he takes some responsibility, acknowledging that in order for the singers to deliver the words with minimal degradation, he must compose in a way that simultaneously keeps the text's integrity in mind and empowers the singers "to concentrate on both clear enunciation and the vocal and acoustic interpretation—the singing—without straining the voice and competing with the orchestra."[10]

The brief essay that follows shows how an easily neglected sonic prop—Martinů's setting of the *Ave Maria*'s Latin text, nine rehearsal numbers into *Sister Paskalina*, scene 1,[11] can reveal how some attributes and roles most habitually assigned to the Virgin Mary inform select principles and rules suggested by Martinů in his *Plays of Mary* publicity.

Objects and Things

Among *The Plays of Mary*'s most charming features are its numerous vocal choruses, and included in this multitude is Martinů's a cappella setting of the *Ave Maria*'s Latin text for a chorus of sopranos and altos that Martinů locates offstage. It is customary to set all three of the famous Marian hymn's sections. However, Martinů's initial treatment of the text is irregular in that he sets the hymn's angelic salutation (Ave Maria, gratia plena, Dominus tecum)[12] and Elizabeth's salutation (Benedicta tu in mulieribus, Et benedictus fructus ventris tui, Iesus)[13] sections in full, while only including the words "Sancta Maria" when setting the hymn's petition for intercession section (Sancta Maria, Mater Dei, Ora pro nobis peccatoribus, Nunc et in hora mortis nostrae. Amen).[14] One possible effect of cutting the hymn's petition section ("pray for us sinners, now and in the hour of our death") is that a prayer verging on instrumentality shifts towards being one of acknowledgment and reverence. Another is that the hymn becomes more impersonal.

In a portion of "On the Brno Premiere" Martinů makes it clear that for its first appearance the *Ave Maria* is sounding from a ritualistic site located offstage. He makes note of this while providing his reader with a more general sense of *Sister Paskalina*. First, he offers a sober plot summary, noting that *Sister Paskalina* "is the story of a girl who leaves the convent in order to follow her lover. After a great deal of suffering, she returns to the convent, where the Virgin Mary has taken her place without anyone noticing."[15] He then zooms in on aspects of *Sister Paskalina*'s first scene: "The beginning of the play, the exposition, takes place in a dream, a hallucination interrupted by an early morning prayer—*Ave Maria,* sung by the nuns from offstage. This scene has two layers: one with a precise and specific sense of reality, set to concisely developed music—the beginning of a new day, the awakening of life offstage, and the end of night. The other, on the threshold between her dream and awakening, is accompanied by unfinished, unreal music.[16] It is the ritualistic site located offstage that is tied to "a precise and specific sense of reality"[17] and "set to concisely developed music."[18]

When the audience first experiences the nuns singing the hymn, *Sister Paskalina*'s eponymous medieval antihero (mezzo-soprano) is, at least from the perspective of those sitting in the auditorium, on the main stage. She is isolated, asleep and having a nightmare. Although she sings in earlier parts of *Sister Paskalina*, scene 1, during the episode that contains the *Ave Maria*'s first appearance, the singer interpreting the role of Paskalina remains in bed and never sings any words. Instead, she vocalizes on different vowels. The dreams and nightmares that she has throughout the section are plagued by grotesque knights and invasive demons, and this legion of forces is balletically translated from the dreamscape of Paskalina's mind onto the main stage around her. Because Paskalina does not get out of bed until the second half of *Sister Paskalina*'s first scene, balletic episodes like this provide an appearance of movement, given that, without such episodes here, one could say that not much happens on the physical stage in the first half of *Sister Paskalina*, scene 1. In the second half, Paskalina gets out of bed to turn toward a statue of the Virgin Mary. She then offers a dramatic and virtuosic extemporaneous prayer to the Virgin. Her solo prayer at this moment is, in a word, operatic. The gist of the prayer consists of her asking the Virgin for advice about whether she should stay in the convent and become a nun or if she should leave the convent to follow her lover, an unnamed knight. At one point she even bargains with the Virgin. After receiving no answer (at least from the statue of the Virgin Mary), Paskalina puts her habit off to the side and exits the cloister. After this, the statue of the Virgin Mary comes to life, takes off her gold crown and puts on the habit that Paskalina leaves behind.

Throughout its first appearance the *Ave Maria* is plainly sung (see Figure 1).[19] Martinů's setting of the hymn's first two sections of text spans just a single measure. Granted, that measure has no written time signature and contains sixty-five eighth notes. Throughout the setting Martinů indicates subtle and gradual changes in dynamics, but there is none of the surrounding orchestral music's tumult and extremity of volume, dotted rhythms, agitated style, rhythmic complexity, and textural density. His setting also appears to avoid examples of what musicologist Derek B. Scott refers to as demonic signifiers, such as tritones (*diabolus in musica*) and quartal and quintal harmonies.[20] The contrast is jarring between the hymn's a cappella setting and the pit orchestra's infernal march music, which begins as a parody of heroic and romantic music strongly associated with the key of C minor.[21] Unlike the blustery infernal march, the more moderated *Ave Maria*'s predominant emotion is one of calm, so much so that one would be hard-pressed to argue that the setting's first two sections exhibit extremes rather than any sort of emotional arc. The chorus of nuns starts off singing a cappella in a two-voice texture, and because they are singing a cappella, these sopranos and altos, almost by definition, are liberated from having to negotiate (compete) with the orchestra. By mirroring the Virgin's compassion and care at this moment, Martinů thereby spares the singers and audience from having to experience a kind of fateful clash, a situation that he describes in "Has Opera Had Its Day?" which is another *Plays of Mary* publicity essay, as a "losing battle between singer and orchestra,"[22] onc in which "the orchestra is barely boastful of the victory of which it was assured from the beginning."[23] The two-voice texture soon expands into a three-voice texture. By the terminus of the setting's "Sancta Maria" portion, the three-voice texture reduces to a two-voice texture, ending on a "pure" C octave. The hymn's harmonic language is accessible in its tonality and there is very little chromaticism throughout. The musical style is the stuff of Christmas pastorales (for example, *Mary*'s third one-act opera, *The Nativity*), especially the succession of sweet parallel intervals over a sustained note sung by the lowest voices that Martinů uses to set the words "Sancta Maria." The rhythmic values employed are simple: eighth

Figure 1. Martinů, Latin-texted *Ave Maria* for soprano-alto chorus from *Sister Paskalina.*

notes, quarter notes, or half notes. The lengths of phrases are not very long, which takes each chorister's vocal health into account. As a rule, Martinů sets the text syllabically, with one note per syllable, and when this is not the case, he employs smaller divisions of notes for the purposes of subtle expressive inflection. Up until the setting of the words "Sancta Maria," when the violas, cellos, and contrabasses from the pit orchestra agitate the tranquil surface of things, the hymn's sense of time, given that it contains fermatas and has no written time signature, is freer, more leisurely. It is worth noting that after the strings from the pit orchestra infringe upon the calm setting with their crushed notes, the composer does deploy dotted quarter notes in the altos on the first syllable of "Sancta" and for all three voices on the last syllable of "Maria." Each voice type is assigned a melody that is relatively comfortable to sing. The three-voice texture's strands generally stay contained and make space for the other voices. The melodic lyricism of each voice can be sensed in how at different points throughout the setting each has a leap followed by a stepwise descent. The sopranos go first. After that the second sopranos leap followed by a stepwise descent. A few phrases later, the altos leap upward followed by a stepwise descent. When the voices are not set in a lyrical style, they are rocking back and forth, sustained on a single pitch or flowing in undulating curves.

The *Ave Maria*, due to its history and cultural associations, is perfectly equipped to evoke the character of the site of the daily ritual of morning prayer. This is because both the hymn and the site of ritual are tied to the commonplace (topical), the ubiquitous, the habitual, the routine, the repetitive, the regular, the stable, the ordinary—the stuff of the business as usual that binds an intentional community defined by Ora et Labora like a convent, and to a lesser degree, the world outside the convent.[24] For example, due to its repetition in the rosary "the *Ave Maria* remains the most widely uttered prayer in Christian devotional life."[25] The *Ave Maria* also "emerged as a natural component of the medieval day" and in some ways, with its connection to the ringing of the Angelus, the hymn "established a rhythm of life in [Medieval] urban culture."[26] Moreover, various "forms of the *Ave* found their way into the daily ritual of the Office as recitations and in musical settings."[27] The *Ave Maria* is also associated with a kind of practicality and utility. For his *Ave Maria*'s top line Martinů alludes to the hymn's plainchant[28] melody as it is placed in the *Liber usualis,* or Book of Common Use,[29] "which represent[s] the culmination of a tendency, particularly noticeable in the Western Church, to combine in one volume for practical use selections from liturgical books hitherto kept separate."[30] If one looks at the melody as it appears in the *Liber usualis,* it is clear that there is a concrete affiliation between the highest voice of Martinů's *Ave Maria* and the plainchant melody as it is rendered in the *Liber usualis* (see Figure 2).

It seems, then, that there is an intimate relationship between the plainchant melody Martinů references and the hymn's broader connections to a collection of terms clustered around the customary or ordinary. This speaks to how the Virgin Mary has often acted as a medial figure who both embodies and facilitates a kind of participation that encounters the sacred in the rather unextraordinary activities of everyday life. Here the Virgin—through her verbal and sonic icon—is acting in her role as bridge between the divine and the mundane, as well as between Paskalina and the nuns offstage who are calling to Paskalina to get out of bed and come participate in morning prayer. A Martinů choral composition predating *The Plays of Mary* does justice to this bridge concept better than any long-winded explanation

Figure 2. The melody is from the tenth century.

could: "Snídaní Panny Marie" (Our Lady's Breakfast), the third of Martinů's *Čtyři písně o Marii* (*Four Songs About Mary*), H 235, for SATB chorus (1934),[31] a collection of a cappella settings of Moravian folk poetry. These are some of Martinů's earliest substantial choral works. Their sound corroborates a more confessional statement that Martinů makes in some of his unpublished writing about *The Plays of Mary* from 1934: "I realized that I could write choral pieces, but in a different way than it had usually been done—my own way."[32] For the purposes of this essay, I am only interested in the verbal contents of the Moravian folk poem he sets, not the music to which he sets it. The words focus on the quotidian dealings of the Virgin Mary and her newborn child. The song starts with Mary washing in the cold water of a brooklet. She then steps out onto the shore to give birth to Baby Jesus. She soon informs her newborn child that they need to cross the hill to procure some breakfast. Baby Jesus then tells his mother not to worry because he will go catch some fish in the cold water. Then two gentlemen riding by stop to meet the Baby Jesus, who holds a red rose in his hand. Mary is surprised that Baby Jesus knows where roses grow, given that he was born only an hour ago. Baby Jesus then tells the two gentlemen to follow him to a place where they can tether their horses below a lime tree and wait for the sun to come out from behind the clouds. Even though the poem's Baby Jesus is rather extraordinary, the Mary in this folk text, who, admittedly, does not literally sit down to eat breakfast, still comes off more like an ordinary "bundle of accident and incoherence that sits down to breakfast" than Regina Caeli.[33] Through his combination of this folk text and some rhythmically complex and harmonically sophisticated music the composer adds magic to some very real, practical concerns as well as everyday activities such as looking for breakfast and waiting for the sun to come out.

This practicality and bridging carry over into how the composer writes for the chorus while setting the *Ave Maria*'s Latin text. *Sister Paskalina*'s Latin-texted choral *Ave Maria* is emblematic of the kinds of choral writing that were stock-in-trade of *Gebrauchsmusik*, or "music used by amateur performers in ordinary social situations."[34] *Gebrauchsmusik*, or in English, utility music, became commonplace throughout the interwar period, emerging in Weimar-era Germany and circulating throughout the world. According to musicologist Stephen Hinton, a leading authority on *Gebrauchsmusik*, composers such as Kurt Weill and Paul Hindemith were professionals who "remained modern professional composers, with all the aims and aspirations implied by the ultimately irreversible division of labour."[35] However, due to an outgrowth of two critical factors, one of which was financial, the other spiritual, these modern composers, facing a crisis of vocation, sometimes chose to adopt compositional attitudes and modes of conduct distinct from those associated with the composition of highly virtuosic pieces for opera houses and chamber and concert music settings. A primary motivation involved questions of financial precarity. As the title of Lesley L. Hughes's excellent dissertation, "Survival Strategies: The Professional, Political, and Artistic Negotiations of Paul Hindemith, 1918–1934" suggests, survival for a professional composer (and virtuosic performer) like Paul Hindemith was not guaranteed in the interwar period, especially in the wake of the economic, spiritual, and geopolitical crises that plagued the world. So, economic expediency encouraged professional composers to craft pieces for amateur music-making, which "was a relatively inexpensive form of entertainment, in contrast to attending a traditional concert or opera,"[36] and these amateur music makers demanded access to compositions that they themselves could sing and/or play.[37] However, the financial crisis was not the only thing driving this change in attitude. By crafting *Gebrauchsmusik* for amateur singers and players professional composers were responding to a more spiritual impetus, and this spiritual impetus was the desire to bridge a distance, "to reconnect with, and compose works for the Volk, breaking down the barriers between professional and amateur."[38] Such demand for composing works reflecting a more practical musicianship associated with more mundane tasks and situations spoke to vehement interwar critiques of both the composer and the virtuoso, as well as being a call to explore modes of musical activity not associated with the modern institutions of the concert hall or the opera house. What I am ultimately suggesting here is that "impersonating" the Virgin Mary, humbly mirroring some of her roles and attributes while composing a piece of choral music like *Sister Paskalina*'s *Ave Maria* holds much in common with composing music based upon a commitment to the interwar philosophy and practice of *Gebrauchsmusik*.

This brief essay has attended to how Martinů assigns his setting of the *Ave Maria*'s Latin text to a chorus of medieval nuns (sopranos and altos) that is initially located offstage. Martinů's setting of the hymn shows him obeying his own Mary-inspired compositional principles and rules. His treatment of the *Ave Maria*'s words and how he considers the singers singing those words are informed by Mary's reported purity, her care and compassion, her calming presence, and how she acts as a channel between the divine and the human, the extraordinary and the mundane, even the amateur and the professional. With this moment of collective song Martinů not only reaffirms the enduring relevance of Marian values in the arts but also demonstrates how music can serve as a bridge that unites distant realms.

NOTES

The title of this essay alludes to the Bach/Gounod *Ave Maria* or "Méditation sur le Premier Prélude de S. Bach" (1853), for solo violin and piano accompaniment. This essay is an abridged version of "Chapter 3: Utility, Vanishing Acts, and *Ave Marias*" from my dissertation. See Jon Kantor Meadow, "Traveling with Mary: Explorations of Bohuslav Martinů's Opera Cycle *Hry o Marii*" (PhD diss., New York University, 2023).

1. For the remainder of the essay, I will refer to the name of the cycle in its English translation.

2. Jessica Milner Davis, *Farce* (New Brunswick, NJ.: Transaction, 2003), nonpaginated. "Farced" here refers to the interleaving of different kinds of texts.

3. Laurence Dreyfus, "Sunk in the 'Mystic Abyss': The 'Choral' Orchestra in Wagner's Music Dramas," in *Choruses, Ancient and Modern,* ed. Joshua Billings, Felix Budelmann, and Fiona Macintosh (Oxford: Oxford University Press, 2013), 229.

4. For more on the relationship between the economic hardships at the start of the 1930s and Martinů's stylistic and dramaturgical shifts, see Aleš Březina, "'So we have a new musical and social form—opera crisis': The Transformation of Bohuslav Martinů's Music Theatre after 'Black Tuesday' 1929," *Hudební věda (Musicology)* 60/1 (2023): 42.

5. Jon Kantor Meadow, "Traveling with Mary," 126.

6. Before composing the music for Závada's *Mariken* libretto Martinů composed music for *Mariken de Nimègue*, H 236/2 (1933), which is Henri Ghéon's French-language retelling of the tale of Mariken. The two Mariken operas share the same source text, but they are both textually and musically distinct. Závada did not use Ghéon's libretto.

7. Translation by Katarina Važanová. In Czech: "Moje řešení a zásady se nejlépe odrážejí v této hře." Bohuslav Martinů, "Poznámky k cyklu *Hry o Marii*" (Remarks on the Cycle *The Plays of Mary*), in Miloš Šafránek, ed., *Divadlo Bohuslava Martinů* (Prague: Editio Supraphon, 1979), 208. The article was originally published in the Czech-language periodical *Divadelní list* 10/14 (2 February 1935), 289–94. The contents of *Divadlo Bohuslava Martinů* are only in Czech. Katarina Važanová's English translation of the article can be found in *Martinů's Mysterious Accident: Essays in Honor of Michael Henderson,* ed. Michael Beckerman (Hillsdale, NY: Pendragon Press, 2007), 141–43.

8. Translation by Katarina Važanová. In Czech: "Vztahují se ve svém celku přímo." Bohuslav Martinů, "*Hry o Marii.* K brněnské premiéře" (On the Brno Premiere), in Šafránek, *Divadlo Bohuslava Martinů*, 222. Važanová's translation of the composer's illuminating caveat reads: "I also want to point out that these issues are not fundamental, because they only pertain directly to my setting of *The Plays of Mary*" ("Také upozorňuji, že všechny podrobnosti nejsou zásadní, nýbrž vztahují se ve svém celku přímo

jen k mé skladbě Hry o Marii"). The article was originally published in the Czech-language periodical *Tempo: listy hudební matice* 14/5–6 (1934–35), 141–51. Also included in *Martinů's Mysterious Accident*, 144–54.

9. "Chci, aby bylo textu rozuměti, vyžaduji od zpěváka zřetelnost." Šafránek, *Divadlo Bohuslava Martinů*, 222.

10. "Aby se mohl věnovati bez přepínání hlasu v boji s orchestrem jak péči o zřetelnou výslovnost, tak i o hlasový, zvukový projev, tedy o zpěv." Ibid. While Martinů is writing about soloists in this excerpt, his thinking is transferable to composing for choruses. Važanová's translation of the whole quote reads: "Even though I am speaking mainly about the musical side of the work, I have not forgotten the text, the words. I want the text to be understood, and ask the singer for clarity. To achieve clarity, I use entire phrases found in natural speech, in the language of common people (and not the very popular systems of "correct" declamation). I also choose verses and text that 'have a sound of their own,' and I do not cover them up with layers of orchestral writing and emotional description. In short, I allow the singer to concentrate on both clear enunciation and the vocal and acoustic interpretation—the singing—without straining the voice and competing with the orchestra. The singer must not forget that he is on stage, not in a concert hall; but apart from this requirement, he is completely free in the interpretation of the character. One cannot ask the singer to sing beautifully, but one can ask him to make himself clearly understood" ("Ačkoli mluvím nejvíce o hudební stránce díla, nezapomínám na text, na slovo. Chci, aby bylo textu rozuměti, vyžaduji od zpěváka zřetelnost. Abych toho mohl dosáhnout, deklamuji celé fráze melodií přirozené mluvy (tedy ne systémem 'správné' deklamace, u nás oblíbeným), mluvy lidové, volím rovněž verše a text, který, abych se vyjádřil, 'zní sám o sobě', nepřikrývám jej nánosem orchestru, ani líčením stavů. Zkrátka dovoluji zpěvákovi, aby se mohl věnovati bez přepínání hlasu v boji s orchestrem jak péči o zřetelnou výslovnost, tak i o hlasový, zvukový projev, tedy o zpěv. A ovšem nesmí zase zapomenouti, že není v koncertě, nýbrž na scéně, ale kromě těchto požadavků má ve vytvoření své role úplnou volnost. Žádati na zpěvákovi, aby krásně zpíval, není vlastně požadavek, ale aby mu bylo rozuměti, to je požadavek velmi vážný).

11. He repeats the hymn's music several other times throughout *Sister Paskalina*. Sometimes he repeats the Latin text. In scene 1 he references the music again at rehearsal number 11 (mm.1–18); at rehearsal numbers 17 through 20; and at rehearsal number 22. In scene 2 it appears he references the music again at rehearsal number 55, which is the *dolce* and *tranquillo* section that concludes Paskalina's "Last Appeal." In scene 3 we find it at rehearsal number 75 (mm. 1–4) and rehearsal number 78 (mm. 6–8). The *Ave Maria* returns in the singing of a vocal choir, or when Paskalina rehearses the hymn as a soloist. Toward the end, portions of the music are taken up by the orchestra.

12. The text in this section of the *Ave Maria* is based upon Luke 1:28.

13. This text of this section of the *Ave Maria* is based upon Elizabeth's exaltation in scripture (Luke 1:42).

14. This is the *Ave Maria*'s petition section. From approximately the seventh century A.D., the *Ave Maria* consisted of a combination of texts from Luke 1:28 and Luke 1:42, and so it remained into the late Middle Ages. Use of the petition part in prayer did not become official until 1568, when the Dominican Pope Pius V finalized the reformed Breviary. See Nicolas Ayo, *The Hail Mary: A Verbal Icon of Mary* (Notre Dame, IN: University of Notre Dame Press, 1994).

15. Translation by Katarina Važanová. In Czech: "Je příběh dívky, která opustila klášter, aby šla za svým milencem. Po mnohých utrpeních se vrací do kláštera, kde její místo bylo převzato a opatrováno celý ten čas Matkou Boží, aniž kdo co pozoroval." Martinů, "*Hry o Marii.* K brněnské premiéře," 219.

16. "Začátek hry, expozice, je prostředí snu, halucinace, do něhož zasahuje ranní Ave Maria sester. Zpívajících za scénou. Dostává tím dvojitý rámec scény, precizní a konkrétní motiv reality, probouzející se den, začínající život za scénou, s hudbou koncízně rozvedenou – a dohasínající noc, na samé hranici snu a probuzení, s hudbou kusou, nedopověděnou, nereální." Ibid.

17. "Precizní a konkrétní motiv reality." Ibid.

18. "S hudbou koncízně rozvedenou." Ibid.

19. Bohuslav Martinů, *Hry o Marii*, ed. Karel Šolc, rev. Jan Hanuš, German trans. Kurt Honolka, vocal score (Prague: Panton, 1979), 229–30.

20. Derek B. Scott, "*Diabolus in Musica*: Liszt and the Demonic," in *From the Erotic to the Demonic: On Critical Musicology* (New York: Oxford University Press, 2003), 132. Liszt's First and Third *Mephisto Waltzes* are good illustrations of quartal and quintal harmonies functioning as demonic signifiers. Instead of stacking thirds, quartal and quintal harmonies are built by stacking intervals of fourths and fifths, respectively.

21. An example of the Romantic association of the key of C minor with heroism is Beethoven's *Coriolan Overture*, Op. 62 (1807).

22. "Předem prohraném mezi zpěvákem a orchestrem." Bohuslav Martinů, "Přežila se opera?", in Šafránek, *Divadlo Bohuslava Martinů*, 228.

23. Translation by Adam Prentis. In Czech: "Orchestr není ani dost málo pyšný na toto vítězství, o němž byl od začátku přesvědčen." Martinů, "Přežila se opera?", 228. The original version was published in the Czech-language periodical *Přítomnost* 12/7 (1935): 105–7. Adam Prentis's translation was published in *Martinů Revue* 20/2 (2020): 12–15.

24. During the interwar period, this *Ave Maria* might have felt too sentimental and too religious—what in object relations theory is referred to as a "bad object." For more on opera and bad objects, see David Levin, *Richard Wagner, Fritz Lang, and the Nibelungen: The Dramaturgy of Disavowal* (Princeton: Princeton University Press, 1998).

25. Michael Alan Anderson, "Enhancing the *Ave Maria* in the Ars Antiqua," *Plainsong and Medieval Music* 19/1 (2010): 35.

26. Ibid., 36.

27. Ibid., 38.

28. Plainchant is unadorned in style, monophonic, and rhythmically free, following the flow of the text and without instrumental accompaniment or harmonic support. Martinů's three-voice *Ave Maria* has harmonic support, but by the end of "Sancta Maria" it has gone from two voices to three voices to two voices, ending on an octave.

29. The compendium was first issued by the monks of Solesmes in 1896. The full title is *Liber usualis missae et officii pro dominicis et festis duplicibus cum cantu gregoriano* (Book of common practice for Mass and Office for Sundays and double feasts, with Gregorian chant).

30. N.A., "Liber usualis (Lat.: Book of common practice)," *Grove Music Online*, ed. Dean Roote, http://www.oxfordmusiconline.com.

31. Martinů completed the composition on 17 January 1934. It was premiered in Prague by the ensemble Vinohradský Hlahol under the leadership of Karel Šejna. The work includes three other a cappella settings for mixed chorus: "The Annunciation," "Dream," and "The Virgin Mary's Picture." See Bohuslav Martinů, *Čtyři písně o Marii* (*Four Songs About Mary*), H 235 (1934), ed. Zdeněk Zouhar (Prague: Tempo, 1993).

32. Translation by Katarina Važanová. In Czech: "Současně jsem komponoval sbory na lidové texty a shledal jsem, že umím psát i pro sbor, jenomže jinak, než se sbory obyčejně píší, jaksi po svém." Martinů, "Bohuslav Martinů k *Hrám o Marii*," in Šafránek, *Divadlo Bohuslava Martinů*, 205. See "Unpublished 1934 Article About *The Plays of Mary*," in *Martinů's Mysterious Accident*, 139–40.

33. Yeats quoted in Hermione Lee, "Against Biography," in *Biography: A Very Short Introduction* (New York: Oxford University Press, 2009), 93.

34. Caleb T. Boyd, "Gebrauchsmusik as Wartime Exile Response: Hanns Eisler's *Woodbury Liederbüchlein*," *Danish Yearbook of Musicology* 43 (2019): 49.

35. Stephen Hinton, "Gebrauchsmusik," *Grove Music Online*, ed. Dean Roote, http://www.oxford musiconline.com.

36. Lesley L. Hughes, "Survival Strategies: The Professional, Political, and Artistic Negotiations of Paul Hindemith, 1918–1934" (PhD diss., University of Wisconsin, Madison, 2020), 212–213.

37. Such situations were not restricted to Weimar-era Germany, or even Nazi Germany, although interwar Czechoslovakia's economic conditions were more favorable than those of Weimar Germany.

38. Hughes, "Survival Strategies," 230.

Ambiguous Historicism in Martinů's *The Marriage*

MARTIN NEDBAL

In discussing Bohuslav Martinů's 1953 opera *The Marriage*, based on Nikolai Gogol's play *Zhenit'ba*, critics use two somewhat opposing sets of characteristics. In his 1979 book on Martinů's theatrical works, biographer Miloš Šafránek claims that the work "lacks any kind of sentimentality."[1] By contrast, musicologist Jaroslav Mihule, in his comprehensive 2002 biography of Martinů, writes that the opera "dampened the satirical edge and reduced the sparkling social critique, typical of the keen observer Nikolai Gogol,"[2] and that "the defining tone of the work then became more lyrical."[3]

A similar contrast marks the reactions of American and Czech critics to the opera's premieres in the United States and in Czechoslovakia. After *The Marriage* was first performed on American television in February 1953 (as part of the *NBC Opera Theater*), Olin Downes wrote a generally positive review for the *New York Times*. He noted—prefiguring Šafránek's views—that in certain parts of the score "a little plain operatization might help—when a quintet or a duet of more than a conversational and fleeting nature would contribute gaiety and melodic substance to the effect—as Mr. Martinů accomplished so charmingly with his little operatic comedy of a former season, 'The Bridge.'"[4] By contrast, in response to the work's first production in Brno, Czechoslovakia, in 1960, Czech musicologist Jiří Vysloužil argued that in *The Marriage* "the music of B. Martinů depicts the plot and . . . characters in overly embellished colors, so much so that it blunts the edge of the satire, its biting mockery, with which Gogol endowed all the little people of his comedy without exception."[5]

As one of the first television operas, Martinů's *The Marriage* encapsulates the long-standing ambiguities and contradictions associated with opera as a genre, particularly the tension between lyrical and non-lyrical elements—or, to use Richard Wagner's terms, between opera and drama. The following exploration shows that Martinů's opera resolves this contradiction by subtly referencing the operatic traditions of the past. Although it is often viewed as a neoclassical work, *The Marriage* is more accurately a piece of operatic historicism, drawing on the styles of composers such as Mozart, Smetana, Wagner, and, indirectly, Musorgsky.

Furthermore, a closer look at critical responses to *The Marriage* illustrates that whether operatic works are perceived as too lyrical or too dramatic/satirical often depends more on external circumstances and ideological biases than on purely musical and aesthetic criteria.

The Libretto

In preparing the opera's libretto, Martinů engaged with a significant set of operatic conventions and traditions. There is no indication that he was aware of Modest Musorgsky's 1868 operatic fragment based on the first scene of Gogol's play. Nevertheless, both composers took a similar approach to Gogol's text by setting it directly to music without having a librettist arrange it for a musical adaptation. In Musorgsky's time, this approach was highly innovative—the only other composers attempting to set prose directly to music was Musorgsky's Russian colleague Alexander Dargomyzhsky, in *The Stone Guest*, based on an 1830 play by Alexander Pushkin. By the time Martinů began work on *The Marriage*, the practice of using prose plays as librettos had become common, with significant precedents, such as Claude Debussy's *Pelléas et Mélisande* (based on a play by Maurice Maeterlinck), Leoš Janáček's *Jenůfa* (based on a play by Gabriela Preissová), and Alban Berg's *Wozzeck* (based on fragments of a play by Georg Büchner). Martinů had previous experience adapting spoken plays into opera librettos, notably with his 1935 radio opera *Veselohra na mostě* (*Comedy on the Bridge*), H 247, based on a comedy by the nineteenth-century Czech dramatist Václav Kliment Klicpera, and his 1937 *Julietta aneb Snář*, H 253, which was based on *Juliette ou La clé des songes* (*Juliette, Key of Dreams*), a play by Georges Neveux.

Martinů's approach to Gogol's text brings a cosmopolitan element to the practice of adapting preexisting prose texts. Whereas Dargomyzhsky, Musorgsky, Debussy, Janáček, Berg, and Martinů himself (in *Veselohra na mostě*) used texts in the original language, which was also their native tongue, *The Marriage* involved a series of multilingual adjustments. The multilingual aspect of *The Marriage*'s libretto was partially foreshadowed in Martinů's *Juliette*, where he created his own Czech libretto from Neveux's French play.[6] In constructing the libretto for *The Marriage*, Martinů first read Gogol's Russian play in a Czech translation, as evidenced by his correspondence and the extant Czech text of the play containing Martinů's autograph comments.[7] Martinů mentioned Gogol's play as early as September 1934 in a letter to Oldřich Vrbovec. Vrbovec had sent him texts of several plays as potential sources for musical works, including what was likely a Czech translation of Gogol's *The Marriage*. Martinů disliked the translation because it "distorted both Gogol and the play itself," yet he still hoped to find "an ideal subject for a new comic opera in Gogol."[8] The idea of a comedic work based on Gogol remained with Martinů over the years. This is evident in a 1937 letter to the Melantrich publishing house, in which he wrote that he needed someone for "a certain comedy, satire, someone who would have a good relationship with Russian literature and particularly with Gogol for arranging a libretto."[9] This letter suggests that at this point, Martinů envisioned the potential Gogol opera as a Czech work and one that would follow the traditional collaboration between a composer and a librettist.

Martinů returned to the idea of an opera based on Gogol's *The Marriage* in June 1951 when he asked music publisher Karel Šebánek as well as his family in Polička for a Czech edition of Gogol's play.[10] By then the main concept of the opera had changed. It was no longer going to be an "ideal" comic opera in Czech but rather a television opera in English.[11] During his preparation for *The Marriage*, Martinů no longer mentioned working with a librettist and instead began arranging the text himself. The process started with the Czech edition of the play that Martinů had received from his family. Comments in Martinů's autograph copy show that he was already thinking about cuts, other changes, and the musical setting at this point. But the preparation of the opera's script later relied on an English translation of Gogol's play by Alexander Bakshy, several copies of which (some with Martinů's comments) survive in the Martinů estate.[12] Thus, Martinů's approach to the libretto of *The Marriage* transformed a Russian play into an English libretto by way of a Czech translation.

Transforming the Story

In his approach to the text adaptation, Martinů resembles his operatic predecessors in that he does not use the Gogol text verbatim. His transformation of the original play is more substantial, especially compared to Musorgsky. In the fragment that he set to music, Musorgsky retained most of Gogol's original text, making only minimal cuts and occasional changes in phrasing.[13] In contrast, Martinů executed radical cuts, likely because the television opera was limited to roughly 60 minutes.

A comparison of the opera's libretto with the text of the play shows that Martinů left out most of the passages in which Gogol engages in social criticism and psychological characterization of his protagonists, focusing instead on the basic comedic storyline. This approach transformed the nineteenth-century realist play into a twentieth-century version of a generic comedy that pokes fun at human foibles, akin to eighteenth-century commedia dell'arte.

This transformation is clearly illustrated in Martinů's approach to the opening scene, which introduces Podkolyosin, a bachelor, and his servant, Stepan. Podkolyosin has been contemplating marriage and has even taken steps in that direction, but his conversation with Stepan suggests that he is more concerned about how the marriage will be perceived by his social milieu than about the match itself. In the opening scene, Podkolyosin tries to find out from Stepan whether the tailor and cobbler who supply him with a coat and shoes deduce from the nature of his order that he is planning to get married. Whereas Gogol's play provides extensive details that highlight Podkolyosin's self-complacency and arrogance, including his sense of self-importance as a civil servant and nobleman, Martinů's shortened libretto straightforwardly emphasizes humorous elements rather than psychological and social satire. Despite the overall cuts, Martinů expands on some aspects of basic clowning present in Gogol's play, such as Stepan's and Podkolyosin's exchange about buttonholes:

Original English Text	**Martinů's Libretto** (the composer's inserts in bold)
Podkolyosin: How far [ha]s [the tailor] gone?	Podkolyosin: How far [ha]s [the tailor] gone?
Stepan: Pretty far. Right now he's doing the buttonholes.	Stepan: Pretty far. Right now he's doing the buttonholes.
Podkolyosin: What did you say he's doing?	Podkolyosin: What did you say he's doing?
Stepan: I said the buttonholes.	**Stepan:** **The buttonholes!**
	Podkolyosin: **The buttonholes?**
	Stepan: **The buttonholes!!!**

Similar transformations, focusing on basic comedic elements rather than psychological motivation and social criticism, continue throughout the entire libretto. A prominent example of this approach is Martinů's introduction of Podkolyosin's friend Kochkaryov, who visits Podkolyosin as he is discussing a potential bride with the matchmaker Fyokla. Seemingly without any motivation, Kochkaryov decides to take over from Fyokla—he throws her out of Podkolyosin's apartment—and arrange the marriage himself. Gogol's play provides a reason for Kochkaryov's interest in seeing Podkolyosin get married: Fyokla has recently arranged Kochkaryov's own marriage, which is not going well, and Kochkaryov wants Podkolyosin to be as miserable as he is.[14] By removing this motivation, Martinů's libretto focuses on the slapstick moment of Kochkaryov pushing Fyokla out of the apartment.

Martinů also completely cuts one character from the plot, the middle-class merchant Starikov, who visits the home of Agafya Tichonovna, the potential bride. Agafya's aunt, Arina Panteleymovna, favors Starikov as a suitor, but Agafya, a merchant's daughter herself, is only interested in marrying a noble bridegroom. At Agafya's home, Starikov encounters three other suitors invited by Fyokla—Yayishnitsa, Anuchkin, and Zhevakin—as well as Kochkaryov and Podkolyosin.[15] When the suitors criticize Agafya's presumed lack of knowledge of the French language and one of them, Yayishnitsa, reveals his main interest is Agafya's dowry, Starikov leaves, saying, "They put on airs in this house. Well, Agafya Tichonovna, you'll think of me one day yet."[16] The words prove prophetic, as, at the end of the play, Agafya finds herself left alone. After rejecting Fyokla's three suitors and accepting Podkolyosin's proposal, she is abandoned when he gets cold feet and escapes through her window. The presence of Starikov highlights the class structure of nineteenth-century Russian society, ridicules members of the middle class obsessed with marrying into the nobility, and perhaps even suggests the moral superiority of the middle class.

Emphasizing his disregard for Gogol's criticism of Russian nobility, Martinů also cuts dialogue in the final scene, when Agafya, Arina, Fyokla, and Kochkaryov discover Podkolyosin's escape through the window. Among the lines cut are Arina's tirade, which ends by connecting Kochkaryov's failure as a matchmaker to his noble origin: "To disgrace a girl before the whole world! I'm a peasant's daughter, but I wouldn't stoop so low. And you call yourself a nobleman. It looks to me all your nobility is good for is scurvy things and swindling people."[17] Martinů replaces the dialogue with stage directions that highlight the comical confusion Podkolyosin's unexpected departure causes in Agafya's apartment:

> Agafya, wearing her wedding dress, walks in timidly with lowered head, looks around diffidently: "Where is he?"—opens the door to the entrance hall. Enter Fyokla—same [reaction]. Enter Arina. All are running all over the room, opening doors, looking everywhere for Podkolyosin. Enter maid and Kochkaryov. Maid shows that Podkolyosin jumped out of the window. Kochkaryov stands thunderstruck . . . Fyokla is laughing at him . . . Agafya is fainting.—Consternation.—Kochkaryov, furious, takes a hat and rushes out.[18]

Neoclassical Setting

Just as the libretto illustrates Martinů's awareness of comedic traditions from the eighteenth through the twentieth centuries, his musical setting is full of allusions to operatic styles of the past. Most prominently, Martinů references the tradition of number opera, particularly eighteenth- and early nineteenth-century opera buffa. These allusions, however, are always mixed with references to later operatic styles with less predictable formal structures. Thus, Martinů incorporates static and formulaic moments, but the overall structure of the work is fluid, blending spoken dialogues, recitatives, and ariosos. Several scenes are interrupted, and most conclude with short ensemble *tutti*, yet these are always fleeting, hinting at earlier operatic styles rather than truly emulating them. The first such moment occurs in Act 1, scene 3, in which Podkolyosin tries to assure Kochkaryov he is not thinking of marriage, even though Fyokla the matchmaker is present in the room. Martinů has Podkolyosin repeat the phrase "Ridiculous! The thought never entered my head!" multiple times, juxtaposing it to newly created phrases for Fyokla—"What? The thought never entered his head! Ha, ha, ha, ha! Is that so?"—and Kochkaryov—"It hasn't? Ha, ha, ha, ha! The thought never entered his head!" The vocal line is filled with fast patter, linking it to the rapid exchanges found in *buffo* finales and ensembles. At the same time, the trio is brief, and the plot soon continues.

A different kind of tutti appears in the introspective quintet in the middle of Act 1, scene 7, in which the four suitors and Kochkaryov reflect on the situation and express their feelings about Agafya, who has just fled the room, feeling overwhelmed and embarrassed. Here, Martinů juxtaposes phrases from the play's cut dialogue that convey the characters' general attitudes: Ivan thinks the other suitors are too weak, Anuchkin is concerned about Agafya's lack of knowledge of French, Podkolyosin worries that something may be wrong with her, the suitor Zhevakin appreciates her beauty (although, unlike in the play, he repeats Anuchkin's and Podkolyosin's concerns), and Kochkaryov fears that Zhevakin's infatuation with Agafya could spoil his plan to arrange a marriage between her and Podkolyosin. Ultimately, these inner monologues are mostly unintelligible, hinting at traditionally operatic lyricism, though with only fleeting musical, psychological, or dramatic effect.

Martinů also incorporates aria-like sections that combine musical lyricism with psychological introspection. Although lyrical and sometimes tuneful, these sections cannot be considered fully fledged arias typical of opera buffa. One such section occurs at the beginning of Act 2, when Agafya reflects on her conflicted and troubled feelings about her suitors. Her entrance is introduced by flowing melodies in the violins, which she then imitates in two flights of coloratura, similar to the opening of Baroque arias with instrumental ritornellos. But after the opening coloratura, Agafya shifts to a speech-like arioso that relies on repeated notes rather than lyrical melodies. At the end of the monologue, Martinů brings back the flowing melodies in the strings as if a varied repetition of the opening were commencing, but this return is cut short by the entrance of Ivan.

Similar ambiguity marks the most clearly aria-like section of the entire opera: Agafya's soliloquy at the beginning of Act 2, scene 11. Martinů created his own text for this moment. In the play, Agafya speaks about her fondness for Podkolyosin and worries that she talked too much when she was with him. In the opera, she is more introspective, expressing uncertainty and apprehension about her upcoming marriage, her inability to stop thinking about Podkolyosin, the prospect of being alone with him, and regrets not being a girl anymore. The soliloquy's musical setting hints at the possibility of a traditional aria, especially in the orchestral introduction and the first vocal section, both of which present tuneful melodic phrases in B-flat major. However, there is no clear structure or phrasing in Agafya's opening melodic line, which relies on irregular melodic segments that avoid repetitions. Martinů then shifts to other tonal centers with new melodic ideas, and the traditional-sounding lyricism from the opening never returns. As in most other references to traditional operatic lyricism in *The Marriage*, Agafya's soliloquy mixes classical means of expressing emotional earnestness with modernist detachment and satire. Although Martinů's aria-like lyricism radically departs from the structure and ethos of Gogol's play, the modernist ambiguity in his approach to musical classicism actually strengthens the satirical aspects of the original characters.

Motivic Development

Despite the work's neoclassical leanings, *The Marriage* resonates with nineteenth-century Wagnerian traditions of operas characterized by organic structures and the symphonic development of themes and motives. The most prominent example of musical organicism in *The Marriage* is the opera's cyclic conclusion, which was added by Martinů. Whereas Gogol's play ends in Agafya's apartment, Martinů includes an additional scene that takes place back in Podkolyosin's apartment. In this scene, Podkolyosin is lying on the couch when Stepan enters, bringing him his black tailcoat and announcing that the tailor has just finished the buttonholes.

Martinů's use of dramaturgical and musical cyclicity is irreverent, however, and subverts the Wagnerian tradition. At the end of the penultimate scene (in Agafya's apartment), Martinů appended a note on the score: "Opera could finish here." This shortened, alternate ending may have been designed with stage presentations in mind—the switch back to Podkolyosin's apartment is cinematic, reflecting the work's initial presentation on television, and might be challenging to execute on stage. By allowing the cyclic ending to be cut, Martinů also signals his detachment from traditional symphonic procedures in the opera. This detachment is further suggested by the final scene's music, which is nearly identical to that of the opening scene. Thus, Martinů creates a cyclic antithesis of the nineteenth-century tradition of symphonic and leitmotivic development in opera, where themes and motives are typically developed and reintroduced in new forms, leading to a final moment of catharsis or resolution. In *The Marriage*, this sense of transcendence, associated with nineteenth-century musical traditions, is hinted at but ultimately cut brutally short.

Martinů does add new music that develops previous motives in the opera's last few measures, but this "development" is so simplistic as to suggest parodistic intent. After the spoken exchange between Podkolyosin and Stepan about the new tailcoat and buttonholes, Martinů introduces broken C-minor chords in the bassoon, tuba, and timpani (see Example 1). These chords are clearly derived from the E-flat major tuba fanfare that concludes the repeated opening segment a few measures earlier. Thus, Martinů recycles and develops previous material, but in a strikingly banal and simplistic manner, reflecting the banality and futility of the opera's entire plot: despite all the action and drama, the main protagonist ends up in the same place, position, and state of mind as at the opera's beginning.

Martinů's motivic development is more predictable in other parts of the opera, associated with certain characters and recurring ideas. A clear example is the musical theme connected to Fyokla's presentation of potential brides and suitors. This theme first appears at the beginning of Scene 2, introducing Fyokla as she enters Podkolyosin's apartment (Example 2). The theme, in triple meter with flowing eighth notes, is related to an earlier waltz that was presented three times in Act 1, scene 1, linked to the idea of marriage (Example 3). In Act 1, scene 2, melodic variants of the waltz-like idea are developed in both the vocal line and the orchestra as Fyokla praises the bride she has found for Podkolyosin. This development is highlighted by expressive harmonic shifts, such as when Foykla becomes annoyed by Podkolyosin's indecisiveness after he asks her to return the next day, and the flowing idea shifts from E-flat major to a brief focus on E major. The

Example 1. Martinů, *The Marriage*, rehearsal number 73, mm. 18–22.

Example 2. Martinů, *The Marriage*, rehearsal number 9, mm. 5–9.

motive returns in Act 1, scene 5, when Fyokla comes to visit Agafya (Example 4). Upon Fyokla's entrance, the flowing theme reappears, this time in a compound 6/8 meter, possibly because this meter is associated with Agafya at the beginning of the scene. Martinů again provides numerous rhythmic and melodic variants of the basic theme, including one beginning with sixteenth-note rests and dotted rhythms, reflecting Fyokla's breathlessness upon arriving at Agafya's (Example 5). As Fyokla tells Agafya further details about the suitors, the motive is reduced to an ostinato. The motive also reappears in Scene 6, when Kochkaryov and Podkolyosin enter Agafya's apartment and encounter Fyokla along with the other three suitors. Here, Martinů combines the Fyokla motive with an earlier version of the waltz, previously linked to Podkolyosin and the idea of marriage (Example 6).

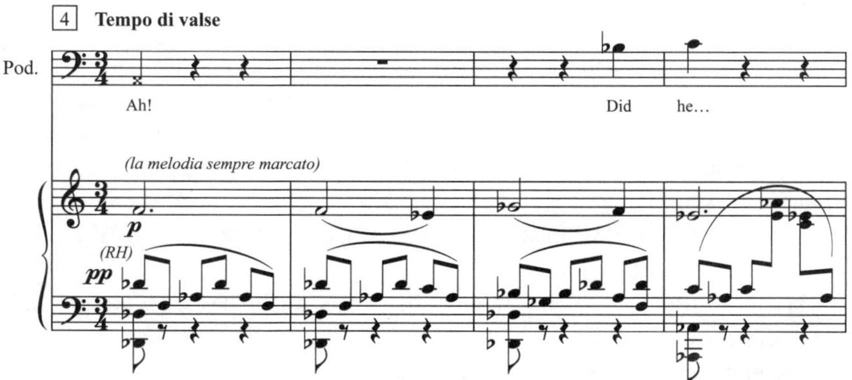

Example 3. Martinů, *The Marriage*, rehearsal number 4, mm. 1–4.

Example 4. Martinů, *The Marriage*, rehearsal number 27, mm. 1–4.

Another variant of the Fyokla motive closes Act 1, with Kochkaryov taking over from Fyokla and persuading Podkolyosin that Agafya "is a beauty," which leads to a rousing stretta in C major. In Act 2, motives related to Fyokla's waltz continue to appear occasionally. For example, in Scene 8, Kochkaryov convinces the other three suitors that Fyokla lied about Agafya's wealth and her ability to speak French. As Anuchkin and Ivan berate Fyokla for her presumed dishonesty, the orchestra juxtaposes ideas related to Fyokla's theme with sharp, angular motives associated with Kochkaryov (Example 7).

Martinů's use of recurring motives in connection to Fyokla contrasts with the deployment of motives linked to the other characters. Although motives or themes may be associated with these characters across several scenes, they eventually disappear, as if Martinů were creating expectations based on traditional

Example 5. Martinů, *The Marriage*, rehearsal number 27, mm. 5–7.

opera but then cutting them short, possibly to avoid becoming too conventional. This is evident in the treatment of thematic ideas associated with Podkolyosin. When Podkolyosin appears on stage, both at the beginning of the opera and in the concluding Scene 14 (if performed), his entrance is marked by a rhythmically awkward chromatic bassoon duet (Example 8), followed by a section in the strings and winds that is diatonic but retains the bassoons' awkward syncopations (Example 9). Metric ambiguity and syncopations become musical traits of Podkolyosin, reappearing in the next scene during various unpleasant experiences of the main protagonist. For instance, when Podkolyosin feels disappointed that the tailor did not ask Stepan if his master was getting married, the sentiment is conveyed by syncopations in the orchestra (Example 10). Similarly, when Podkolyosin hesitates about marriage in his discussion with Kochkaryov toward the end of Act 1, scene 3, the waltz-like melody in the orchestra, associated with marriage throughout the first act, is disrupted by syncopation and transforms into a variant of the rhythmically ambiguous section from the prelude (Example 11). However, the syncopations are not consistent throughout the opera, and Martinů

Example 6. Martinů, *The Marriage*, rehearsal number 35, mm. 1–10.

employs various other musical markers to express Podkolyosin's hesitation and social awkwardness. Thus, although motivic unity is one of the techniques Martinů uses in setting Gogol's text, he is not rigid about it. This inconsistency is particularly noticeable compared to Musorgsky's setting of *The Marriage*, where a limited number of motives are used more consistently, perhaps to compensate for the vocal lines' unmelodiousness, as Musorgsky aims to imitate the inflections of the Russian language.

49 **Allegro**

FYOLKA

What's that?

Anuch.

You fooled

Ivan

Come here, you old sin - ner! Come

mf

etc.

Anuch.

me, you fooled me!

Ivan

here!

Example 7. Martinů, *The Marriage*, rehearsal number 49, mm. 1–3.

CURTAIN. Podkolyosin is alone, lying on the couch, smoking a long Turkish pipe.

Example 8. Martinů, *The Marriage*, bassoon duet, measure 5 to first two beats of measure 8.

Example 9. Martinů, *The Marriage*, last two beats of measure 8 to downbeat of measure 11, violins, violas, and cellos.

Example 10. Martinů, *The Marriage*, rehearsal number 5, mm. 9–13.

Music-Historical Referentiality

The Marriage weaves in a web of musical allusions to specific works of the Western operatic and musical canons. However, these allusions are ambiguous and often irreverent. The most prominent reference occurs in the first act, where Martinů includes the theme from Mendelssohn's "Wedding March"—albeit with distortions to reflect its cheeky use at a moment when Kochkaryov is discussing not the marriage itself but the alcohol that would be consumed at the subsequent dinner. Similarly subversive is the quotation of the Russian folk tune "Song of the Volga Boatmen" in Act 2, scene 10 (Example 12). Podkolyosin and Agafya are trying to hold a conversation despite having nothing to say to each other. Podkolyosin tries to make a patriotic statement about the Russian people, but it falls flat. The first part of his sentence—"What brave people the Russians are!"—elicits the folk tune quotation from the orchestra. However, both the statement and the folk tune are immediately ridiculed when Podkolyosin cites his example of Russian bravery: "Well, take the workers. I saw a painter at the top of the house, whitewashing the wall, he wasn't the least bit afraid." The fact that there is nothing specifically Russian about whitewashing walls at a height, and that this is a mundane activity unrelated to common ideas of bravery or heroism, renders the patriotic opening and its musical accompaniment banal.

Example 11. Martinů, *The Marriage*, rehearsal number 22, mm. 8–19.

The opera also contains references that are ambiguous and possibly also unintentional. However, the numerous musical elements in Martinů's libretto and score that resemble operatic works of the past suggest that the composer aimed at emphasizing the idea of referentiality, without necessarily being concerned about whether the composers, styles, and works referenced were obvious. One such reference is indicated by Martinů's autograph note in the Czech edition of Gogol's play, which the composer's family sent to America. At the point of Kochkaryov's arrival in Act 1, Martinů wrote "Figaro." It is unclear whether he meant Beaumarchais's, Mozart's, or Rossini's *Figaro*, but it is not surprising that Martinů would associate the deceitful, matchmaking friend of Podkolyosin

Example 12. Martinů, *The Marriage*, rehearsal number 58, mm. 8–11.

with one of the most famous comedic characters. Moreover, the musical idea that Martinů links to Kochkaryov has a distinctly *buffo* character, featuring a fast-paced, fanfare-like style with a lot of patter-like staccato notes (Example 13).

The style of opera buffa, particularly as exemplified in Mozart's operatic comedies, resonates with many elements of *The Marriage*. For example, the opening of Scene 4, which introduces Agafya as she lays out cards and daydreams about her future husband, is somewhat analogous to the duet "Ah guarda, sorella" from Mozart's *Così fan tutte*, where Dorabella and Fiordiligi gaze at the portraits of their lovers. Both scenes use similar slow meters (6/8 and 3/8) and a pastoral style, with prominent use of horns and woodwinds. Additionally, the frantic musical accompaniment during Podkolyosin's leap from the window of Agafya's apartment resembles Mozart's accompaniment to Cherubino's leap from the Countess's chamber window in the second-act finale of *Le nozze di Figaro*.

Martinů's work also references nineteenth-century operatic comedies. When Kochkaryov announces to Podkolyosin that he is going to get him married ("Don't worry. I'll marry you, you won't even notice it"), his initially *buffo* theme becomes more melodious, with a strong rhythmic emphasis on every second beat (Example

Example 13. Martinů, *The Marriage*, rehearsal number 14, measure 1 to first two beats of measure 4.

14). This melodious polka connects Kochkaryov to the most famous Czech operatic matchmaker, Kecal from Smetana's *Prodaná nevěsta* (*The Bartered Bride*). In this way, Martinů subtly combines the tradition of opera buffa with allusions to nineteenth-century comic operas. This referentiality in *The Marriage* may also be connected to the work's status as one of the first television operas; by referencing the past in prominent yet not completely concrete ways, Martinů invites comparisons of his work and its genre to the hallowed specimens of the operatic canon.

American Film Version and the Complaints About Lacking Lyricism

Considering the ambiguity of Martinů's musical language in *The Marriage*, it is not surprising that critics have arrived at widely differing evaluations. Yet, some of these differences may also be due to the distinctions between two specific versions of the opera: the American television version and the theatrical version that appears in the published score. One of the main points in the American critics' responses to *The Marriage* was the lack of what Olin Downes called "operatization." Similarly, James Lyons noted that "there are no set pieces, no arias, no ensemble numbers, and some will find this multiple defection egregious. . . . I missed them myself, not out of fealty to custom but because they might have given *The Marriage* more shape and substance."[19] Jack O'Brian described the opera as "one of those discursive, gabby affairs with everyone yack-yacking away in recitative and no one taking time out for a simple aria, or simple anything except characterization."[20] He also felt that the work mostly consisted of "orchestral music" and seemed

Example 14. Martinů, *The Marriage*, rehearsal number 18, mm. 10–13.

"basically symphonic, rambling aimlessly instead of slowing occasionally to the melodic." H. W. L. complained, "There is missing the real bloodstream of musical ideas abounding in [Martinů's] earlier one-act opera, *Comedy on the Bridge*," adding that "most of the action takes place to rather insignificant recitative, and only rarely is there a short musical number of coherence."[21]

A comparison of the published score to the 1953 television version shows several cuts that omitted the lyrical moments that the critics felt were scarce. It seems as if the director wanted to emphasize the action and avoid even the short lyrical segments Martinů included in the score. For example, the film cuts the reflective quintet of the four suitors and Kochkaryov in Scene 7. Also cut is a short monologue for Zhevakin in Scene 9. In Martinů's musical setting, the scene presents the retired navy general as a potential sentimental match for Agafya. Unlike the other suitors, Zhevakin is fond of Agafya without any objections, calling her an "adorable cream puff," yet he allows Kochkaryov to speak to her on his behalf. As Zhevakin eagerly listens to what Kochkaryov will say to Agafya, his vocal line becomes lyrical, matching the pastoral idiom associated with Agafya throughout much of the opera. However, Kochkaryov tells Agafya that Zhevakin is a worthless fool, drunkard, and scoundrel, causing the disappointed Agafya to run into her bedroom. Zhevakin then begins an introspective soliloquy, which is cut in the film. Instead, the film shows Zhevakin accidentally tearing his uniform and becoming upset about it. Although Zhevakin's monologue is not particularly lyrical, it does enhance the sentimental, introspective aspect that American critics found lacking. Also significant is the film's removal of several sections of Agafya's aria in Scene 11, including the instrumental introduction and the entire second half of the aria, beginning with the words "They will lead me to the church." Furthermore, during much of the remaining part of the aria shown in the film, the camera cuts away from Agafya, focusing on Kochkaryov dragging Podkolyosin back to her apartment, thus de-emphasizing the element of sentimental reflection in favor of comedic action.

The Marriage and Czechness

The first Czech production of *The Marriage* (which was eventually also made into a film) made use of the published score, in which the cuts undertaken in the 1953 NBC television version were restored.[22] This may have prompted several Czech critics to view the work as quite appealing: the critic for *Tvorba* thought that the score was "full of fresh rhythmic excitement and musical wit" and "drew on Mozartian comic opera."[23] Jiří Vysloužil, in *Rovnost*, writes about "nobly tuneful, rhythmically vibrant, and cheerful music."[24] But this appeal may have also resulted from Czechcentric attitudes. For Jiří Vysloužil, the sensually appealing quality of Martinů's music, which was somehow lost on the American critics, was clearly connected to the work's Czechness. In his review for *Hudební rozhledy*, Vysloužil claims that the opera exudes "folk-likeness" (*lidovost*), and this quality makes *The Marriage* "particularly near and dear to us although we know that it is based on an English text and was commissioned by an American television company."[25] Vysloužil understands the opera as Czech, despite its American origin and English libretto and also despite its Russian subject. Similar ideas appear in the review by Bohumír Štědroň for *Svobodné slovo*: "The audience received the melodic music of our modern composer, who follows the style of Czech classics, the traditional Czech folksong, and realistic symbolism, with growing interest and pleasure."[26]

Vysloužil provides further insights into the Czech influences on Martinů's musical style. He argues that Martinů's nationality both makes him cosmopolitan and shields him from the pitfalls of cosmopolitanism. According to Vysloužil, Martinů's deep connection to Czech folksongs enriches his neoclassical musical style, as these songs are "closely related to the musical thought of the classical era; Czech folksongs drew from classicism and enriched it with their own elements."[27] Vysloužil also links the nationalistic idea of Martinů's inherent Czechness to the principles of socialist realism. He believes that the "wonderful imagery and liveliness" of Czech folksongs protected Martinů's genius from "self-serving artistry of many 'neoclassicists,' including Igor Stravinsky."[28]

Both Vysloužil and Štědroň reduce the rich, varied, and ambiguous web of historicist references in *The Marriage* to an expression of the composer's presumed national sentiments. These views have influenced later commentators, such as Miloš Šafránek whose 1979 book features one clear example of elements in Martinů's score supposedly drawing on Czech folksongs. According to Šafránek, the opera concludes with "a Czech polka, intensified with syncopation in [Martinů's] favorite key of B-flat major."[29] Šafránek likely refers to the dance-like music in B-flat major that first appears in Act 2, scene 12, accompanying Podkolyosin's excited arioso in which he extols his decision to marry Agafya. After Podkolyosin changes his mind and escapes through the window, the dance-like music comes back, underscoring the frantic confusion of the remaining characters. It therefore also serves as a conclusion to the version of the opera without the final scene. Although the music sounds folk-like and dance-like, Martinů does not provide any indication that it is meant to represent a polka, whereas his score clearly marks certain passages as waltz-like. Moreover, the dance-like conclusion's fast tempo, its 4/4 meter (as opposed to the typical polka-like 2/4), frequent syncopations, and repeating figurations also make it sound somewhat like a fiddle tune, similar to that used in "Hoedown" from Aaron Copland's 1942 ballet *Rodeo*. Rather than serving as a marker of Czechness, this dance-like music reflects Martinů's preference for ambiguity—a tune that sounds like a Czech polka to some but also contains elements of Anglo-American folk music is associated with a parody of several Russian characters. Thus, Martinů's *The Marriage* eludes simplistic national interpretations. Rather than being a straightforward example of the composer's Czech genius, *The Marriage* represents a diverse and sophisticated attempt at creating a comic opera for the twentieth century.

NOTES

1. In Czech: "je v ní zcela nepřítomná jakákoliv sentimentalita." Miloš Šafránek, ed., *Divadlo Bohuslava Martinů* (Prague: Editio Supraphon, 1979), 95.

2. In Czech: "ztlumila satirické ostří a ubrala na jiskřivé společenské kritice, typické pro bystrého pozorovatele Nikolaje Gogola." Jaroslav Mihule, *Martinů: Osud skladatele* (Prague: Karolinum, 2002), 446.

3. In Czech: "Určujícím laděním díla se pak stala spíše lyrika." Ibid., 446.

4. Olin Downes, "Martinu's Opera Scores in TV Bow," *New York Times*, 8 February 1953, 78.

5. In Czech: "Hudba B. Martinů líčí děj i . . . postavy v příliš přikrášlených barvách, že láme hrot satiry, její pichlavý výsměch, kterým Gogol obdařil bez rozdílu všechny lidičky své komedie." Jiří Vysloužil, "Československá premiéra opery B. Martinů," *Hudební rozhledy* 13/12 (2 June 1960): 527.

6. See Mihule, *Martinů: Osud skladatele*, 240.

7. Bohuslav Martinů Institute, Prague, shelfmark 341/TSA1.

8. In Czech: "jak Gogola tak i hru samu;" "v Gogolovi doufám nalézti ideální sujet pro novou komickou operu." A digitized copy of the letter can be found in Bohuslav Martinů Institute, Prague, shelfmark Vrb 1934-09-21. https://database.martinu.cz/mails/public_view/3492

9. In Czech: "na určitou komedii, satiru, někoho, kdo by měl dobrý poměr k ruské literatuře a zvlášť ke Gogolovi na úpravu libreta." A digitized copy of the letter from 2 May 1937 is in Martinů Institute, Prague, shelfmark Mel 1937-05-02. https://database.martinu.cz/mails/public_view/4132

10. Both letters are in Bohuslav Martinů Institute, Prague, shelfmark Šeb 1951-06-03, https://database.martinu.cz/mails/public_view/2481, and shelfmark Mar 1951-06-22. https://database.martinu.cz/mails/public_view/397

11. Martinů mentions *The Marriage* in connection to television in a letter to his family, 29 March 1952. Bohuslav Martinů Institute, Prague, shelfmark Mar 1952-3-29.

12. Bohuslav Martinů Institute, Prague, shelfmark 341/TSA2, LA.

13. These changes are outlined in the 1933 edition of the operatic fragment. Modest Musorgsky, *Die Heirat*, ed. Pavel Lamm (Vienna: Universal Edition, 1933).

14. Martinů's autograph score shows that he initially set to music Kochkaryov's exchange with Fyokla about his own marriage: Kochkaryov: "Ah, Fyokla, tell me now—why in the devil did you get me a wife?" Fyokla: "Nothing wrong in that. It's the law of life." Martinů eventually cut the line, and it does not appear in the published score, but it is unclear if the excision was part of his attempt to make the opera less psychological or whether it was cut to make the work shorter. Bohuslav Martinů Institute, Prague, shelfmark 341/A.

15. *Yayishnitsa* means omelet in Russian, and Gogol ridicules this in the play when Agafya says one of the reasons she does not want to marry him is her concern about being called Mrs. Omelet. Martinů cut this passage from the libretto, and changed Yayishnitsa's name to Ivan, possibly trying to reduce the conversation in favor of situational humor.

16. This according to the typescript English translation with Martinů's autograph comments, Bohuslav Martinů Institute Prague, 341/ TSA2, LA, 51.

17. Ibid., 100.

18. Text cited after the vocal score, Bohuslav Martinů, *The Marriage* (New York: Boosey and Hawkes, 1953), 130–31.

19. James Lyons, "Martinu Opera Composed for Television Given First Performance by NBC-TV," *Musical America* 73/2 (February 1953): 8.

20. Jack O'Brian, "TV News Notes," *The Call-Leader*, 11 February 1953, 4.

21. H. W. L., "NBC-TV Opera Premieres The Marriage, by Martinu," *The Musical Courier* 147/4 (15 February 1953): 8.

22. The Czech translation of Martinů's English libretto was by Eva Bezděková, and the composer did not like it, pointing out its "epic" style in a letter to Karel Šebánek, 10 January 1959. Bohuslav Martinů Institute, Prague, shelfmark Šeb 1959-01-10.

23. In Czech: "plná svěžího rytmického vzruchu a hudebního vtipu"; "těží z komické opery mozartovské." M. Č., "Brněnská premiéra," *Tvorba*, 25/21 (26 May 1960): 500.

24. In Czech: "ušlechtile zpěvná, rytmicky živá a radostná hudba." Jiří Vysloužil, "Dvě komické opery Bohuslava Martinů," *Rovnost* 75/129 (28 May 1960): 4.

25. In Czech: "zvláště pro tuto . . . vlastnost je nám i Ženitba milá a blízká, i když víme, že vznikla na anglický text a pro americkou televizní společnost." Vysloužil, "Československá premiéra opery B. Martinů."

26. In Czech: "Hlediště přijímalo zpěvnou hudbu našeho moderního skladatele, navazující na styl českých klasiků, na lidovou českou píseň a realistickou symboliku, s roustoucím zájmem a libostí." Bohumír Štědroň, "Skvělý Martinů v brněnské opeře," *Svobodné slovo*, 24 May 1960.

27. In Czech: "je blízký hudebnímu myšlení klasické epochy; česká lidová píseň z klasicismu čerpala a obohatila ho i o vlastní podněty." Vysloužil, "Československá premiéra opery B. Martinů."

28. In Czech: "úžasná obraznost a živost . . . samoúčelného artismu mnohých 'neoklasiků,' nevyjímaje z toho ani Igora Stravinského." Ibid.

29. In Czech: "českou polkou, vystupňovanou synkopami v jeho oblíbené tónině B dur." Šafránek, ed., *Divadlo Bohuslava Martinů*, 96.

The Long Shadow of *Juliette*: Martinů's Late Musical Aesthetic and the *Fantaisies symphoniques* (Symphony No. 6)

IVANA RENTSCH
TRANSLATED BY SUSAN H. GILLESPIE

His last symphony was "without form . . . but something holds it together, I don't know what, but it has a single line and I have expressed something in it."[1] Two core elements of Bohuslav Martinů's *Fantaisies symphoniques,* Symphony No. 6, first performed in 1955, nestle within his lapidary description as if in a nutshell: first, a formlessness within an obscure context and, second, a "something" in the way of content. An explanation of how, exactly, this should be conceived is lacking. In view of Martinů's fundamental reticence on aesthetic questions, this is hardly surprising.

For decades he repeatedly refused to express any opinion about his music, remarking that the works must speak for themselves. And if it was unavoidable, for instance, to deliver himself of a couple of comments for the program of a premiere, those comments generally remained on an abstract level that renders any direct reference to the music speculative. Even if one looks to the copious private correspondence and notebooks he kept in the 1940s, in Darien, Ridgefield, Cape Cod, and New York, the aesthetic statements remain strikingly diffuse.[2] Thus, it comes as no surprise that, as with many other composers, the consciously created theoretical void in the musical reception of Martinů's music is filled with biographical speculation.

In Martinů's case, an overly hasty linkage between biography and art is all the more dangerous because his life, after his escape from France to the United States in 1940, was dominated by a series of tragic circumstances. This began with the existential change in status from emigrant to exile, continued with the agonizing uncertainties of the war years, led to a postwar period overshadowed by a life-threatening accident and then, in 1948, the catastrophe of the Communist takeover of Czechoslovakia. As an American citizen, nothing remained for the Czech composer but lifelong involuntary exile. The political circumstances of that life already offer a cornucopia of suggestions for non-musical interpretations.

Beyond this, the breadth of potential explanations is further expanded by the private circumstance that Martinů sought his happiness in love in a variety of—shorter or longer—relationships.

The reception of Martinů's *Fantaisies symphoniques* provides a veritable lesson book on the ways in which biographical prejudices can channel one's perspective, even when the composer himself rejects every non-musical interpretation. In this case, a brief remark by Martinů that he had integrated a few measures from his opera *Juliette* into the symphony sufficed to make them resonate once again in his life.[3] Since *Juliette—Snář* (*Juliette—The Dream Book*) was first performed in 1938, it tends to be linked, in a biographical-aesthetic confabulation, with the extremely talented composer and conductor Vítězslava Kaprálová, with whom the married Martinů fell head over heels in love. A banal conclusion presents itself: The *Juliette* quotation appears as an homage to the young woman, who suffered an early death in 1940.[4] A direct connection with Kaprálová (or, perhaps, with Roe Barstow, who cared for the composer after his accident in 1946)[5] and the *Juliette* reminiscence in *Fantasies symphoniques* can neither be verified based on the sources, nor does it seem relevant from an artistic perspective. Moreover, the over-hasty biographical explanation obstructs the view of its aesthetic significance. A sober consideration of the matter makes it seem quite beside the point that the more than sixty-year-old famous composer should have used the occasion of a prize-winning work, commissioned to celebrate the seventy-fifth anniversary of the Boston Symphony Orchestra, to burst open the formal conception of the piece based on a private caprice. But, once we let go of the short-circuited link to the sentimental explanation, the evident musical reference of the *Fantaisies symphoniques* to *Juliette* seems all the more remarkable. As soon as the reminiscence is not dismissed as a private set piece, the aesthetic question of the "Why?" is posed in all of its fundamental potential. Precisely this broader aesthetic significance will be the subject of the following reflections. The search for a musical explanation focuses attention on the composer's artistic positioning after the end of the Second World War. Consequently, we will attend to fantasy as the principle of compositional form-creation that exceeds objectifiable principles of order and—necessarily inseparable from this—as the instrumental-musical adaptation of an aesthetic idea that goes back to *Juliette* and to the 1930s.

The "Musical Problem of Form" after 1945

In Martinů's considerable production, which on first glance may appear uneven and was created amid markedly changing background circumstances, closer inspection reveals two constants that are closely interwoven and would retain their determining role throughout his life.[6] The first was rejection of any non-musical or specifically psychological charge to be imposed on music; the second was the search for genuinely musical determinants. The fundamental nature of the ideal is demonstrated, not least, by the fact that it affected equally both Martinů's works for the stage and his instrumental compositions from the 1930s on. In regard to instrumental music, this meant a clear commitment to the concerto grosso form, whose productive adaptation goes back precisely to this period. As late as the 1941 "Autobiografie," written while in the United States, Martinů confessed, in third person: "Of the musical forms, the one that corresponds to him most strongly is the concerto grosso."[7] Or, four years later, "To tell the truth, I am a concerto grosso type."[8] The Baroque genre served him as the starting point for solutions to large instrumental forms whose objective inner coherence had no necessary need for extra-musical plot, dramatic narration, or psychological realization.[9] The gateway that symphonic music opened up, via borrowings, for *Weltanschauung*-like content, should be avoided in concerts.[10] The priority of musical principles should not be endangered by emotional excess. The attractiveness of the concerto grosso for the 1930s consisted, in principle, in the fact that the genre had not entered music history in the nineteenth century. Further stimulated by a temporal distance of over two hundred years, the concerts of Arcangelo Corelli—their historical context largely unknown—seemed especially unsullied by any external influence. The appearance of a purely musical logic in its fabrication, a "strict order," ultimately provided Martinů, too, with the impulse to give his own tonal language a new orientation in light of the concerto grosso.[11]

Martinů's focused search for a strict order that would adhere to solely musical laws was of a thoroughly moral nature. In 1933, he had spoken vehemently against the superficiality of Parisian concert culture, when he observed that music had become a social triviality that caused "no great damage."[12] The "quite ordinary banality" of the "new young school" seemed to him to be no more than an impoverished poor copy of the "great French tradition."[13] In contrast, he argued for a compositional self-understanding that was aimed at freeing music from the grip of mere entertainment and standing it up on its own foundations: a re-aestheticization that, paradoxically, should be committed to "life" precisely because it aimed at elementary laws that were ultimately more essential for human beings than social entertainment ever could be. From this perspective, the "longing for a definitive organization of the whole," as formulated by Martinů in 1933, proved to be the equivalent of a musical first draft for an ideal form of human existence.[14] The internally consistent compositional form became the model for a perfect system:

> There is always some program in the musical piece. It reflects, even if it is not especially or verbally indicated, the inner life of an artist, his conviction and his conception of the world, his struggle to express himself; it could mean even a refuge for a protest. He is

> always searching for a meaning of life, the life of mankind and his own, searching for truth.[15]

In this statement from 1956, Martinů's compositional claim still seems unchanged, and the ambitious search for the "meaning of life," as well as its transposition into a musical form—launched more than two decades earlier—seems to continue with unbroken validity. The description actually fits the image precisely—and yet the composer immediately revoked this ambitious claim: "As for the meaning of life and the program of the most recent works, I have already written to you that I had started to moralize (with a look at what we see around us in the world today—I didn't write this, but I thought it)"—this from Martinů to Miloš Šafránek. And further: "I have had enough of moralizing . . . I don't want to make the world better."[16]

The crisis situation of the 1930s had ultimately been the decisive factor in the composer's awareness of his moral responsibility; thereafter, the experiences of the Second World War and the Cold War that followed irrevocably put paid to that moral impetus. For even an artist who had replaced the ideologically suspect "subjectivity" with an "objective" expression—in keeping with the aesthetic paradigm of the interwar period—now appeared suspect. The programmatically expressed "longing for a definitive organization of the whole" revealed itself, against the contemporary background, as a dangerous chimera, as the equally totalitarian statements about order coming from National Socialism and, later, from Communism, were now impossible to ignore. For, just as the structure of society affected people in general yet in an extreme case could be determined by a single individual—in the same way, did the rules of the most objective art also depend necessarily on the individuality of the artist. But since the authority of the composer was unavoidable—without the voluntary establishment of ground rules not even aleatoric creations are possible—there remained only the possibility of capping the connection to social reality. And this is precisely what Martinů did in 1944 when he noted: "This idea of a 'message,' which places the [artistic] creator in the role of a benefactor of humanity (*bienfaiteur*), currently complicates his inner process, if it [the idea] is applied as a principle."[17] Even the most elevated purposes now appeared in the most negative sense of an egoistic, even egotistical nature, whereby "this entire question of egotism" could lead "all the way to Hitler, who in fact feels himself to be a benefactor of humanity."[18]

From Symphony to Fantasy

Given the issues raised above concerning the problematic nature of egotism in art and politics, the point of departure for Martinů's composing after 1945 had arrived at a complicated juncture. The still valid principle of a genuine musical form without extra-musical connotations was now joined by the challenge of reducing, as far as possible, the role of the composer as responsible for the work's structure, without thereby damaging the integrity of the work as a whole. Looking at the two key works from this period—the Symphony No. 6, *Fantaisies symphoniques*, and the Piano Concerto No. 4, *Incantation*—Martinů's procedure is clear. It is the emphatic move toward fantasy, a step that occurred as an immediate consequence of the thoroughgoing skepticism toward the composer acting as creator. Martinů himself was aware of the fundamental nature of the new starting point. Fantasy allowed him to concentrate at the level of small parts, without being responsible for the superstructure above it. This brought with it a large-scale vacuum that had to be filled somehow. Thus his comments from the 1950s speak not only of fantasy as a personal compositional ideal but always mention the challenge, inseparable from it, of achieving a manifestly musical unfolding in time. In the conviction that "music has . . . different laws," he saw the author as not in a position to comprehend the musical logic in its full extent.[19] For, as Martinů stated in the most diverse contexts, he by no means conceived music as the pure emanation of compositional will:

> To work through in detail: what the author "knows" during composition and what he "doesn't know" about the sense, subject, and about the unexpected chance. The aesthetic experts tend to believe what the author, in overconfidence, has revealed from within his laboratory.[20]

The characteristic starting point—"To work through in detail"—suggests that in the case of the above-cited entry in the Ridgefield notebook we are dealing with a lecture note for one of Martinů's American composition courses. Quite apart from his obvious choice not to use his pedagogical activities at Tanglewood, at the Mannes School of Music, or at Princeton to found his own school, but instead to respect to the fullest the personal style of the course participants,[21] an extensive relativizing of authorial intention seems to have been a central concern of his. Against this background, it is not surprising that Martinů turned with ever-increasing vehemence against analyses and publications offering technical compositional rules.[22] In the program booklet that accompanied the premiere of the *Fantaisies symphoniques*, he is then quoted as follows: "The textbooks have all the correct answers . . . and they can't produce a single measure of living music. With me, the students must think for themselves from the beginning."[23]

Musical laws eluded human penetration, thus naturally affecting not only musical production, but also, and equally, reception. So it seems thoroughly logical that Martinů drew a direct connection between the making of the *Fantaisies symphoniques* and the interpretive aesthetic of the dedicatee, Charles Munch, conductor of the Boston Symphony Orchestra:

> To come to my *Fantaisies*, there is one reason for this work which is clear and certain for me: I wished to write something for Charles Munch. I am impressed and I like his spontaneous approach to the music where music takes shape in a free way, flowing and freely following his movements. An almost perceptible slowing down or rushing up gives to the melody a sudden life.[24]

The analogy between Martinů's description of Munch's performance practice, the spontaneous approach of which aimed at a free unfolding of the musical movement, and his own turn toward the free form of the fantasy is striking: in both cases it is a matter of awakening music to "life." Composer and conductor relinquish any claim to mastery of the whole and instead focus on the musical moment—from which, as if on its own, an overarching movement grows. With this, however, the decisive compositional challenge consists in the formulation of a musical core—a "cellule"[25]—that first makes possible a free unfolding in time.[26]

The consequences of Martinů's musical ideal of the 1950s for his compositional practice are clearly evident in the *Fantaisies symphoniques.* The work begins with a chromatically oscillating sound field that emerges out of the void and without pressure for development. An actual movement appears only in the trumpets, which step forward out of the weave of sounds of the first nine measures with a stepwise musical arc: F–G♭–F–F♯–A–B♭ (see Example 1). The elementary minimal idea of a semitone step forms the starting point—the "cellule," as it were—not only for the first movement, but for the entire symphony. And so, just as the chromatically stamped trumpet motive emerges from the weave of sounds, that motive prepares a thematic phrase of the solo cello that will be relevant in what follows (Example 2, rehearsal number 3). The cello theme, with its chromatic character, underlines its derivation from the static beginning and, with the immediately following continuation in the flutes, develops a dynamic pull (measure 5 after rehearsal number 2 to measure 8 after rehearsal number 3; see beginning in Example 2).

Right at the beginning, the connection-creating elements are emphasized: The melodic idea of a semitone unfolds on the horizontal level and leads to a virtual kaleidoscope of motivic possibilities. The movement, as it unfolds, is supported by a long harmonic pulse, which makes a static impression. The harmonic central tones F, B♭, and E♭, which already crystallize themselves early in the symphony (mm. 1–14, double bass), stand unmistakably in a functional tonic-dominant relationship to one another, although this is not fully expressed, due to the avoidance of leading tone resolutions. The static verticals are confronted by a dynamic horizontal. It is the melodic structure, not the harmony, that is responsible for the temporal unfolding—the "life" of the fantasy. The cello theme (and its derivatives), which shines through repeatedly over the course of the symphony and which occasionally dominates, unfolds a force that creates coherence on the

Example 1. Martinů, *Fantaisies symphoniques* (Symphony No. 6), first movement, mm. 1–4.

Example 1. Continued

horizontal plane without its various harmonic possibilities ever coming into force in a way that would exceed sound color qualities.

In terms of larger forms, the associative melodic extension, which recalls Martinů's concerto grosso compositions of the 1930s and 1940s, remains determinative. Now completely lacking, compared to the earlier works, is a structure allied with concerto tutti principles. The free unfolding of the motives on the horizontal plane is complemented by a single formal support structure in the form of a latent harmonics, devoid of tension, and, in the first two movements, a simple reprise form. This applies in the first movement toward its end, in a repetition of mm. 1–15 in measure 2 starting after rehearsal number 25 to measure 5 after rehearsal number 27 until, immediately before the cello entrance, the movement with the elementary sound field dies away. The second movement, toward the end, brings

Example 2. Martinů, *Fantaisies symphoniques* (Symphony No. 6), first movement, measure 5 after rehearsal number 2 to measure 8 after rehearsal number 3.

Example 2. Continued

a repetition of measure 6 after rehearsal number 2 to measure 7 after rehearsal number 4, starting with measure 2 after number 22 until measure 7 after number 24. Evidently, the use of reprises did not fundamentally contradict Martinů's intent to let the musical movement grow, as if by itself, out of a motive's "cellule." That the arc form could be seen as primarily tied to "geometrical limits" and might perhaps have been broadly accepted due simply to "time savings for the composers" led Martinů to the conviction that the form model must not be evaluated as the "sole and organic law of nature."[27] Although he allowed that something prevented him from understanding this form as "absolute," he confessed that he himself was sensible of its "justification and formal logic."[28] And precisely this non-rationalized sense ultimately developed into a compositional authority—an authority that came together out of historically changeable and not entirely humanly comprehensible moments. The compositional power of the composer over his decision-making, now suspect, was thus transferred to the unconscious: "In fact, all the elements are subordinated to and develop in the direction of the generation of a living whole, and this also without *conscious* intervention of the composer."[29]

The musical consequences of the turn away from concerto grosso principles are considerable, as in the stylistic repositioning in the *Fantaisies symphoniques*, on which Martinů labored for two years—atypically long—from 1952 to 1953. Even if the

SEVENTY-FOURTH SEASON · NINETEEN HUNDRED FIFTY-FOUR AND FIFTY-FIVE

Eleventh Program

FRIDAY AFTERNOON, JANUARY 7, *at* 2:15 *o'clock*

SATURDAY EVENING, JANUARY 8, *at* 8:30 *o'clock*

MOUSSORGSKY.........................Prelude to "Khovanstchina"

SCHUMANN..................Symphony No. 4, in D minor, *Op.* 120

I. Ziemlich langsam; Lebhaft
II. Romanze: Ziemlich langsam
III. Scherzo: Lebhaft
IV. Langsam; Lebhaft

(Played without pause)

MARTINU..............Fantaisies Symphoniques (Symphony No. 6)

I. Lento; Allegro; Lento
II. Allegro
III. Lento; Allegro

(*First performance*)

INTERMISSION

BEETHOVEN....Concerto for Pianoforte, No. 5, in E-flat major, *Op.* 73

I. Allegro
II. Adagio un poco mosso
III. Rondo: Allegro ma non tanto

SOLOIST

ROBERT CASADESUS

Mr. Casadesus uses the Steinway Piano

This program will end about 4:15 o'clock on Friday Afternoon, 10:30 o'clock on Saturday Evening.

BALDWIN PIANO | RCA VICTOR RECORDS

[487]

Figure 1. Program of the premiere performance, *Fantaisies symphoniques* (Symphony No. 6), 7 and 8 January 1955, Boston Symphony Orchestra conducted by Charles Munch.

melodic unfolding from a core motive had already been established as characteristic of his personal style, the unrestricted priority that is accorded to the process here was new. Evidently, Symphonies Nos. 1–5, created in one-year intervals from 1942 to 1946 for big American orchestras, did not adhere to sonata principles.[30] They do, however, display formal divisions that no longer play a comparable role a few years later, in *Fantaisies symphoniques*. The hierarchical priority between the work's actual title and the name in parentheses must be taken literally: "*Fantaisies symphoniques* (Symphony No. 6)." The free symphonic form has been volatilized as fantasy (Figure 1).

The Instrumental Fantasy in *Juliette*'s Realm

As mentioned earlier, Martinů emphasized the formlessness ("without form") of the *Fantaisies symphoniques* as being held together only by a "single line." That this should have meant an associative spinning out of the chromatic idea and thematic derivatives is obvious. But if we accept Martinů's remark that "I have expressed something in it,"[31] we cannot avoid extending our attention beyond the borders of the work itself. It is in the nature of the *fantaisie* that musical ideas are manifested in it in an unfiltered way, without any claim to formal logic. As much as Martinů's choice of title may appear to give free rein to associative melodic continuation, the question of an aesthetic basis for the personal stylistic emphases persists. At any rate, this means forgoing generally valid principles of formal construction, however established, for which Martinů had been searching for decades in instrumental music. Ultimately, this amounts to a retreat to the individual subjectivity.

To judge the aesthetic import of Martinů's emphatic turn to fantasy, a look at the opera *Juliette*, which premiered in 1938, is revealing. This much in advance: such a look is significant above all for establishing the aesthetic position of the *Fantaisies symphoniques* within Martinů's creative work. For the American public at the premiere, it was evidently not relevant. Indeed, the printed program booklet contains not a single statement by Martinů on the genesis of the *Fantaisies symphoniques*, not even the comment now much cited in the secondary literature and originally included in the typed copy of a letter to Boosey & Hawkes (Figure 2).[32] The purpose of this text is not clear, nor, apparently, did it ever find public form. It is quite conceivable that in the end Martinů withheld the commentary given its potential for being misunderstood.

Although Martinů's description of the creative process appears to be paradigmatic for his artistic self-understanding during the American years, the composer is not able to explain his process comprehensively. Everything begins with an initial idea that develops gradually and only in combination with additional elements results in the "integrated formation of the idea":[33]

> But still the creative problem is not finished: then comes the daily work and with it many different difficulties which must be solved before the end is reached. So when you ask the composer to talk about his work for a programme, he is often reluctant and even embarrassed, and he usually tries to avoid doing so. Often the first impulse is already

> far away, or there are too many of them to enumerate. They may be a part of the composer's private life which he does not like to speak of, or perhaps he does not know how far they are connected with the piece because the real musical problem takes the place of many other things, which means more than the changing feelings.[34]

Although an extra-musical idea provides the starting point for the creative process, it is secondary for the understanding of the final composition. In the end, not even the composer himself is in a position to recognize which private influences

Extract from a Letter from Bohuslav Martinu
21st December 1954

Fantaisies Symphoniques

The creation of a piece of music goes through many metamorphoses. Sometimes it is a long way from the first idea to the composer's realisation. The idea remains germinating for years, and suddenly one day it pushes itself to the mind of the composer, almost ready to be written. All the changes of the first impulse and all the other elements suddenly take their place in the integrated formation of the idea. But still the creative problem is not finished: then comes the daily work and with it many different difficulties which must be solved before the end is reached.

So when you ask the composer to talk about his work for a programme, he is often reluctant and even embarrassed, and he usually tries to avoid doing so. Often the first impulse is already far away, or there are too many of them to enumerate. They may be a part of the composer's private life which he does not like to speak of, or perhaps he does not know how far they are connected with the piece because the real musical problem takes the place of many other things, which means more than the changing feelings.

To come to my Fantaisies, there is one reason for this work which is clear and certain for me: I wished to write something for Charles Munch. I am impressed and I like his spontaneous approach to the music where music takes shape in a free way, flowing and freely following his movements. An almost imperceptible slowing down or rushing up gives to the melody a sudden life. So I had the intention to write for him a symphony which I would call 'Fantastic'; and I started my idea in a big way putting three pianos in a very big orchestra. This was already fantastic enough, and during work I came down to earth. I saw it was not a symphony but something which I mentioned before connected with Munch's conception and conducting. I abandoned the title and finally I abandoned also my three pianos, being suddenly frightened by those three big instruments on the stage.

I called the three movements Fantaisies, which they really are. One little fantasy of mine is that I use a few bars quotation from another piece, from my opera Juliet, which to my mind fitted in perfectly well. That is of the nature of fantasy. I did it somehow for myself because I like the special orchestral colour in it, and thinking that I will never hear my opera, I could listen once more to these few bars, which I rewrote from memory.

Figure 2. Typescript copy of a letter from Bohuslav Martinů to Boosey & Hawkes, 21 December 1954.

Example 3. Martinů, *Fantaisies symphoniques* (Symphony No. 6), third movement, measure 2 to measure 10 after rehearsal number 12, transition to and beginning of musical reference to *Juliette*.

Example 3. Continued

Example 3. Continued

and additional factors played a role or how they are connected to the "real musical problem." Martinů formulated this peculiarity of the compositional process even more clearly a short time later in a handwritten comment on the no less "fantastic" Piano Concerto No. 4, *Incantation*, where he relates in its regard that the very instant an idea assumes musical form, the originally emotional impulse of the composer is extinguished.[35] A shift occurs from personal ideas to purely musical solutions, whereby the levels in Martinů's fragmentary descriptions are always changing—for example in the last paragraph of his reflections on the *Fantaisies symphoniques*:

> I called the three movements *Fantaisies*, which they really are. One little fantasy of mine is that I use a few bars quotation from another piece, from my opera *Juliet*, which to my mind fitted in perfectly well. That is of the nature of fantasy. I did it somehow for myself because I like the special orchestral colour in it, and thinking that I will never hear my opera, I could listen once more to these few bars, which I rewrote from memory.[36]

Setting aside the moving final sentence and soberly regarding the previous statements, one can see the emergence of an aesthetic positioning. Thus, all three movements involve true "*Fantaisies*." Martinů's above-cited description of the compositional process plays out against this background, in which personal impulses may perform a role at the inception that is gradually abandoned in favor of purely musical solutions, fitting the centuries-old genre definition of a musical *fantasy* in a way that can be termed virtually "ideal-typical." This coheres, too, with the few measures from *Juliette* that Martinů integrated because they "fitted in perfectly well." That the perfection of the fit must be understood as purely artistic—not somehow biographically determined—is made explicit by the reference to the shared "nature of fantasy." Since the reference to the opera fits seamlessly into the new composition means, in a reverse conclusion, that in *Fantaisies symphoniques* we are ultimately dealing with fantasies in the spirit of *Juliette*.

The opera *Juliette—Snář*, which had its premiere in 1938 at Prague's National Theatre, is entirely in the spirit of Czech Surrealism, whose representatives were in close contact with Paris artists. The conception of *Juliette* on a libretto of the French surrealist Georges Neveux is shaped, consequently, by a Czech-French expression of Surrealism of the 1930s. The opera is about Michel, who is confronted with an unending series of remarkable events. The protagonists, without exception, are odd, and Juliette, with whom—or with whose song—Michel is in love from the start, is constantly, like all the other inhabitants, forgetting everything and inventing ever new stories. The point of the opera consists, ultimately, in the fact that without exception Michel's experiences in the nameless city take place in a dream—a dream, furthermore, that in Neveux's Surrealist logic leads to surreality. Nothing less is at stake than the overcoming of reality in favor of an alternative world liberated from earthly causalities. And although Michel is aware of the flip side—that those who refuse to awaken and return to reality are all only skulking through the world like crazy gray figures—he ultimately remains in the dream. However dark this may seem from a realistic perspective, in Neveux's sense and in that of the Martinů of the 1930s, Michel's decision in favor of surreality in the eternal dream is a happy ending.[37]

As for Martinů's aesthetic motivation for referring to an opera of the prewar period in his *Fantaisies symphoniques*, the excerpt selected appears decisive. It consists of a total of fourteen measures in the third movement (measure 5 after rehearsal number 12 to measure 8 after rehearsal number 13; see the transition and the beginning of the passage in Example 3) that refer back to moments in the second act of *Juliette* when the heroine comes running breathlessly to Michel and the two listen to the stillness of the forest (*Juliette*, Act 2, rehearsal number 23).[38] As Michel meets Juliette for the first time here, he has literally arrived at the end goal of his dreams. In *Juliette*'s spirit world, this means entry into a sphere of surreality located on the far side of the logical-causal language of words, which consequently can be evoked only by instrumental means.

As for the relationship between the opera and *Fantaisies symphoniques*, it appears decisive that whereas the passage is an unmistakable recursion, it is not a citation in the formal sense. Motive and basic harmonic structure are largely congruent; in *Fantasies symphoniques* piano and harpsichord are lacking, but the woodwinds' part is remarkably similar. If one considers that Martinů, in his headlong flight to the United States in 1940, was not able to take the *Juliette* score with him and during the composition of the *Fantaisies symphoniques* was forced to rely on memory, the disparities are not too surprising. But it would be shortsighted to ascribe the musical differences between the opera and symphony segment solely to this circumstance. The subtle incorporation of the *Juliette* reference toward the end of the third movement of the *Fantaisies symphoniques* is by no means hermetic, or even specifically designed to be recognized, but aims for a complete harmonic and motivic integration into the musical proceeding. This is especially evident in the immediate approach (beginning with measure 4 after rehearsal number 11), as motivic references to the *Juliette* sphere and derivations from the cello theme intertwine (see Example 2 above). What we find here are not two distinct levels of sound, but the fusion into a consistent theme. The evocation of Juliette's dream world is seamlessly integrated into the overlapping process based on the chromatic "cellule" (see Example 1 above). Clearly, in the *Fantaisies symphoniques* Martinů's concern was not to refer concretely to *Juliette*. For this, the more obvious move would have been a reference to Juliette's song, whose function in the opera is to serve as a clearly contoured aural symbol of the dream woman.[39] Had the composer even wanted to point to a female figure—whether the main protagonist of the opera or, in a biographical connotation, to Kaprálová or Barstow[40]—citing the song in this way would have been a more obvious choice. But this does not seem to be at all what is occurring here. Neither the opera's plot, nor one of its protagonists, nor a real person becomes audible in the *Fantaisies symphoniques*, but solely the surrealistic sound sphere per se.

The musical characteristics of this *Juliette* sphere also encompass a plagal harmonic turn that is unmistakably linked to Michel's evocation of Juliette: Juliette's very first appearance, toward the end of the first act, when she finally emerges from her house, is underlined with an exposed phrase moving from G-flat major with an additional sixth to D-flat major (Example 4a). In contrast to Juliette's song, the cadence appears as a symbol less of the heroine than of her overwhelming impact on Michel. Its repetition at various key locations elevates it to the musical essence of Michel's untrammeled longing. No comments from Martinů himself have been identified on the subject—and certainly not its characterization as the "Moravian cadence," the label by which it has become known in the subsequent literature.[41] Apart from the plagal progression in *Juliette* having no folkloristic connotations and its being surely intended to point not to Moravia but to surreality, the narrow focus on harmonic issues is misleading. It is not merely the harmonic movement, but the specific tone coloring made up of strings, winds, and horn, that makes the simple plagal progression into a recognizable musical symbol.

At the start of the first movement of the *Fantaisies symphoniques* is a reference to the *Juliette* cadence that renders it identifiable as a core musical element (Example 4b). The cadence sounds immediately following the trumpets' chromatic emergence from the surging string and woodwind movement (see Example 1), and the solo cello and flutes' presentation of their thematic material (see Example 2). Here, too, as in the previously described *Juliette* reference in the third movement (see Example 3), we are dealing not with a note-for-note quotation, but with a subtle shift: The plagal cadence from E-flat minor with an added sixth to B-flat major (Example 4b, see the two measures before rehearsal number 4). That even here there is no citation from *Juliette* in the sense of an exact sequence of notes seems symptomatic. It is certainly possible to assume that Martinů would definitely have been able to retrieve the G-flat major with an added sixth to D-flat major sequence from memory if he had wanted to. This evidently is not to the case. Rather, the hermetic chord sequence that was utilized in *Juliette* as a surrealist symbol is expanded in a way that allows it to be seamlessly integrated into the course of the movement. In this respect, the orchestral work differs fundamentally from the opera. Unlike *Juliette*, the *Fantaisies symphoniques* contain no musical *objets trouvés*, whether hermetically emphasized cadence, acoustic set piece like the quacking of a toy duck (Act 1, scene 7), or recourse to striking examples drawn from music history.[42] The technique of building hermetic symbols into the tonal sequence of *Juliette* is immediately analogous to the Surrealists' puns and incoherent collages. Eventually, the surrealistic

Example 4a. Martinů, *Juliette*, Act 1, scene 8, 1 measure before to 1 measure after rehearsal number 75.

Example 4b. Martinů, *Fantaisies symphoniques* (Symphony No. 6), first movement, measure 9 after rehearsal number 3 to measure 2 after rehearsal number 4.

Example 5a. Martinů, *Juliette*, Act 1, scene 1, first five measures after rehearsal number 2 (bassoon solo).

Example 5b. Igor Stravinsky, *Le sacre du printemps*, Introduction, first five measures (bassoon solo).

libretto and the procedure of building hermetic symbols into the musical movement and its symbol-laden musical transformation are meant to undermine the opera public's belief in causal logic. This step toward musical provocation, which is ultimately intended to open the way to surreality, is entirely lacking in the orchestral work. The aesthetic consequences are far-reaching: In the *Fantaisies symphoniques* we are dealing with the emanation of a Surrealist sound world, one that—solely through the use of musical means and without any absurd narrative—fails to cut a path to surreality. To the contrary, the latter is there from the start. In contrast to Michel, who wanders, disoriented, into the nameless city, the symphony completely lacks signs of distress.

The decision to do without musical *objets trouvés* becomes particularly evident in the vague adaptation of a bassoon theme that is prominently utilized in *Juliette* (Example 5a).

The above-mentioned theme, thanks to its position, flow, and orchestration, serves in the opera as a surrealist sound cipher: an unmistakable reference to the bassoon solo in the opening five measures of Stravinsky's *Le sacre du printemps* (Example 5b).[43] Against the background of the structural and aesthetic meaning of the surrealist sound world of *Juliette* for *Fantaisies symphoniques*, the motivic relationship between the heavily surrealist bassoon theme from *Juliette* and the chromatic "cellule" becomes evident, and extends further to the cello theme of the *Fantaisies.* In contrast to the opera, however, the orchestra piece no longer even hints at a potential relationship to Stravinsky's *Sacre.* At stake is only the associative spinning out of a chromatic idea, without music-inspired references. The free, linear unfolding in time would not be compatible with the breaks introduced by *objets trouvés.*[44]

The integration of *Juliette*'s surreality (and not the surreal figure Juliette) reveals the aesthetic solution that Martinů found in the 1950s. The virulent problem of instrumental-musical form is resolved to the extent that in place of a logically reproducible form there now appears a sequence that is no longer rationally explicable but nevertheless adheres to a peculiar plausibility. This is a logic that the composer himself can no longer fully penetrate, the "I don't know what"[45] of a reality situated on the far side of human reason. Since what is at stake is a musical logic, one that, as Martinů repeatedly emphasizes, has nothing to do with the real world, the recourse to the genuine musical surreality of *Juliette* is consistent. The extent to which the composer was concerned with this purely musical solution is documented, not last, by the choice of the title. Although he had long played with the idea of labeling Symphony No. 6 the "*New Symphony Fantastique*,"[46] he ultimately decided on *Fantaisies symphoniques*. It is obvious that the direct reference to Hector Berlioz would have led to a whole series of implications that he preferred to avoid. Thus, Berlioz's *Symphonie fantastique* famously plays with the reinterpretation and deconstruction of sonata principles, and, in the legendary final movement with its Witches' Sabbath above the *Dies irae*, literally plays with *objets trouvés* of music history. Both compositional elements definitely play no role in the *Fantaisies symphoniques*. Moreover, popular reception of the *Symphonie fantastique* has tended to accord significant meaning to Berlioz's admiration for Harriet Smithson. It is easy to see that Martinů wanted to prevent just this kind of biographical short circuit.

Analogously to the way in which, in the opera, the characteristic sound world embodies surreality, in the *Fantaisies symphoniques* it stands for a musical reality that exceeds human rationality. Whether dream or fantasy is of no account: the work's associative, non-narrative unfolding eludes causal logic. Access to this sound world is of an intuitive, genuinely musical nature, which is why, ultimately, all commentaries on understanding the work have been superfluous. As opposed to an "objective" aesthetic like the one Martinů had explicitly embraced in the three preceding decades, his *Fantaisie* aesthetic of the 1950s abstains from any position on society. Still, this very abstention, *ex negativo*, results in a notable contribution to the history of the era. Society is not salvageable, what remains is only the step into surreality.

NOTES

1. Miloš Šafránek, *Bohuslav Martinů: His Life and Works* (London: Wingate, 1962), 271–72.

2. A collection of sources has been gathered in an undefined order, edited without critical commentary, and translated into Czech by Miloš Šafránek, as *Domov, hudba a svět* (Prague: Státní hudební vydavatelství, 1966), 125–267.

3. Typewritten copy of a letter by Bohuslav Martinů to Boosey & Hawkes, 21 December 1954, Bohuslav Martinů Center in Polička, BH 1954-12-21. See Figure 2.

4. See, among others, Michael Crump, *Martinů and the Symphonies*, Symphonic Studies 3 (London: Toccata Press, 2010), 407–8.

5. Harry Halbreich, *Bohuslav Martinů: Werkverzeichnis und Biografie*, 2nd rev. ed. (Mainz: Schott, 2007), 168.

6. The section that begins here is a revised excerpt from Ivana Rentsch, "Weder geometrisch noch neurotisch: Martinůs Klavierkonzerte und das musikalische Problem der Form," in *Kontinuität des Wandels: Bohuslav Martinů in der Musikgeschichte des 20. Jahrhunderts*, ed. Aleš Březina and Ivana Rentsch, Martinů-Studien 3 (Bern: Lang, 2010), 229–51.

7. Bohuslav Martinů, "Autobiografie," in Šafránek, *Domov, hudba a svět*, 322 ("Z hudebních forem nejvíce mu odpovídá concerto grosso").

8. Bohuslav Martinů, "1938–1945," in ibid., 340 ("Abych řekl pravdu, jsem typ concerta grossa"). For further discussion of Martinů's predilection for the concerto grosso form, see the essay in this volume by Brian Locke.

9. On Martinů's concerto grosso reception, see Daniela Philippi, "Die neue Klassizität im Instrumentalschaffen von Bohuslav Martinů," *Archiv für Musikwissenschaft* 60/3 (2003): 221–35.

10. Citation from Arnold Schering, *Geschichte des Instrumentalkonzerts bis auf die Gegenwart*, 2nd rev. ed. (Leipzig: Breitkopf & Schering, 1927), 225.

11. For additional information on Martinů's Corelli reception, see Halbreich, *Martinů: Werkverzeichnis und Biografie*, 71.

12. Bohuslav Martinů, "Hudba v Paříži," in Šafránek, *Domov, hudba a svět*, 55 ("nedělá velkých škod").

13. Ibid., 54 ("Nová mladá škola"; "s docela obyčejnou všedností"; "velké francouzské tradice").

14. Cited in ibid., *Domov, hudba a svět*, 329 ("Je to touha po definitivní organizaci celku").

15. Bohuslav Martinů, handwritten commentary on the Piano Concerto No. 4, *Incantation*, [May] 1956. Bohuslav Martinů Center in Polička, D 69/2010.

16. Bohuslav Martinů to Miloš Šafránek, 11 July 1958, in Šafránek, *Domov, hudba a svět*, 299n29 ("Pri tom smyslu života a programu poslednich del jsem ti psal ze jsem zacal moralisovat, (Vzhledem k tomu co vidime okolo sebe dnes na svete, to jsem nepsal ale myslel). . . . mne to moralizovani preslo. . . . nechci zlepsiti svet."). https://database.martinu.cz/mails/public_view/2757.

17. Bohuslav Martinů, Ridgefield Notebook, Bohuslav Martinů Center in Polička, fol. 18v. ("Tato idea 'message', která staví tvůrce do role dobrodince lidstva, (bienfaiteur) komplikuje současně jeho vnitřní proces, je-li applikována a-priori, jako princip"). Cited in Šafránek, *Domov, hudba a svět*, 175.

18. Ibid., fol. 19r. ("Celá ta otázka egotismu může vesti až k Hitlerovi který se skutečně považuje za dobrodince lidstva").

19. Martinů, handwritten commentary on the Piano Concerto No. 4.

20. Bohuslav Martinů, "Zápisky z roku 1947," in Šafránek, *Domov, hudba a svět*, 231 ("Rozebrati v detailu co autor 'vi' pri tvorbě a co 'nevi' o umyslu a pojeti a o nepredvidane Chance. Aesthetikove odpiraji verit to co autor nekdy v prilisne duverivosti prozradil ze svoji laboratore.").

21. Program booklet accompanying the premiere of the *Fantaisies symphoniques* by the Boston Symphony Orchestra, conducted by Charles Munch, 7 and 8 January 1955.

22. See Bohuslav Martinů, program booklet for Symphony No. 2, performed by the Cleveland Orchestra on 28 October 1943, cited in Šafránek, *Domov, hudba a svět*, 288 ("Taková analýza je druh hádanky (puzzle). Nekomponoval jsem symfonii jako skrývačku; a nepřeji si také, aby ji tak lidé poslouchali.")

23. Program booklet for the premiere of the *Fantaisies symphoniques*.

24. Letter to Boosey & Hawkes, 21 December 1954.

25. Martinů to Šafránek, 11 July 1958, in Šafránek, *Domov, hudba a svět*, 299n29.

26. Martinů, handwritten commentary on the Piano Concerto No. 4. See also Martinů, Ridgefield Notebook, fol. 18v.

27. Martinů, Ridgefield Notebook, in Šafránek, *Domov, hudba a svět*, 154 ("geometrických zákonů"; "získání času skladatele"; "přírodní zákon, jediný a organický").

28. In Czech: "absolutní"; "sám chápu a cítím oprávněnost i formální logiku této formy." Ibid.

29. In Czech: "A skutečně všechny složky se podřizují a vyvíjejí směrem k vytvoření živého celku, a to i bez *vědomého* zásahu skladatele") (emphases in original). Ibid.

30. For an analytical description of Symphonies Nos. 1–5, see Crump, *Martinů and the Symphonies*, 179–351.

31. Šafránek, *Bohuslav Martinů: His Life and Works*, 271–72.

32. Typewritten copy of a letter by Bohuslav Martinů to Boosey & Hawkes, 21 December 1954. I am grateful to Aleš Březina for discussion of the text and access to the relevant sources.

33. Ibid.

34. Ibid.

35. Martinů, hand-written commentary on Piano Concerto No. 4.

36. Typewritten copy of a letter by Bohuslav Martinů to Boosey & Hawkes, 21 December 1954 (emphases in original).

37. See Ivana Rentsch, "Anklänge an die Avantgarde: Bohuslav Martinůs Opern der Zwischenkriegszeit," in *Beihefte zum Archiv für Musikwissenschaft* 61 (Stuttgart: Steiner, 2007), 194–266.

38. For a comparative analysis of the two passages, see Crump, *Martinů and the Symphonies*, 492–94.

39. Ibid., 407.

40. Ibid.; Halbreich, *Martinů: Werkverzeichnis und Biografie*, 168.

41. See Crump, *Martinů and the Symphonies*, 112–15, 141–51; Halbreich, *Martinů: Werkverzeichnis und Biografie*, 170; Klaus Meyer, "Sport, Technik, Jazz and Mährische Kadenzen. Bohuslav Martinů aus der Sicht der Zeitgenossen und der Gegenwart," *Neue Musikzeitung* 47/12 (1998/99), https://www.nmz.de/ausgaben/1998-12.

42. See Rentsch, *Anklänge an die Avantgarde*, 227–42.

43. Ibid., 234–36.

44. For precisely this reason, Harry Halbreich's thesis that the chromatic motive is meant to refer back to the beginning of Antonín Dvořák's *Requiem*, Op. 89, fails to convince. Apart from the open question of why, then, Martinů should refer to Dvořák's *Requiem*—an assertion that is not supported by any evidence and is based on the mere circumstance that one of the two was a composer from Bohemia and the other came from Moravia—there is no musical evidence for an intertextual connection between the two generic motives. See Halbreich, *Martinů: Werkverzeichnis und Biografie*, 245; Crump, *Martinů and the Symphonies*, 376–77.

45. Šafránek, *Bohuslav Martinů: His Life and Works*, 271–72.

46. Crump, *Martinů and the Symphonies*, 368.

Figure 1. Martinů at the Darien, Connecticut, commuter station, 1943.

Part II. Experiments in Instrumental Music from Baroque to Jazz

Martinů and the Reduction of Music in the 1920s

GISELHER SCHUBERT
TRANSLATED BY SUSAN H. GILLESPIE

When Bohuslav Martinů decided to live in Paris in 1923, he was also, as he later expressed it in an autobiographical reminiscence, seeking an affirmation of fundamental "idiosyncrasies of Western culture,"[1] as he conceived them. He missed "lightness, clarity, a sense of pure form, economy of certain means, asentimentality or rationality" in the German-dominated culture of Prague's cultural and musical life.[2] In music, as we should understand Martinů, the characteristic of "lightness" had been opposed since the turn of the twentieth century to the heavily meaning-freighted *Weltanschauungsmusik*. "Clarity" stood against the labyrinthine development of expression in the oversized formal dispositions of individual movements; the "feeling for pure form" against the exaggerations that could be found in program music; "economy of certain means" was opposed to massively overblown orchestrations; "asentimentality" to overly emotionally laden, exaggerated subjective feelings; and "rationality" to arbitrary, out-of-control technical means of composition. In Germany, the protagonists of the music Martinů wished to leave behind were generally to be found among the Wagner succession, including, among many others, Strauss, Mahler, Pfitzner, Schreker, or the early Schoenberg—a succession that, to be sure, also influenced many French composers working primarily in Paris, from Fauré, Chausson, d'Indy, and Magnard through Dukas, in the sense of the impactful French "Wagnérisme" introduced by literary figures. Even a composer like Debussy developed an epochal, influential, completely new musical style—Impressionism—that also had a significant impact on the young Martinů, and could potentially be deployed against the German Wagner-succession. After all, it had been developed against the backdrop of Wagnerian music—one need only think of the "Prelude" (*Vorspiel*) to *Das Rheingold*, the "Siegfried-Idyll," the "Forest Murmurs" (*Waldweben*) from *Siegfried*, or the "Good Friday Magic" (*Karfreitagszauber*) of *Parsifal*. Moreover, Debussy had found his way to the unique sound world of his piano music through extensive practice of piano excerpts from Wagnerian music dramas.

The "idiosyncrasies of Western culture" that Martinů mentions—emerging in part from the catastrophe of the First World War and its devastating socioeconomic consequences—led to a pronounced distancing from late-Romantic and then Impressionist music in Germany and France, which was ultimately in line with critical commentaries on current developments in music around 1920. The work of influential German music critic Paul Bekker anticipated the trend, offered at the time with a sure sense of music's development—which, in a sense, he also anticipated. Bekker criticized the music of the post-Wagnerians as an external though certainly virtuosic "heightening of the conventional," which could scarcely be surpassed but had now finally reached its endpoint. He recognized, in 1919, that "we know, progress can only be achieved through simplification."[3] This tendency to musical simplification included a reduction in the size of the orchestra; a focus on the working out of inner-musical events; to musical forms of more manageable, limited dimensions; a simplification and clarification of tonal relationships; a recourse to pre-classical music; and finally, a reduction in musical ambition, which was experienced as liberation from "metaphysical" eccentricities of a quasi-religious belief in the power of art.

It was this kind of musical simplification—in the sense of a comprehensive reduction in all the dimensions of composing, as predicated by Bekker and largely corresponding to the characteristics of Western culture identified by Martinů—that Martinů sought in Paris. Meanwhile, it was precisely the composers who under the influence of Wagner had originally been creating works of this kind of "late-Romantic" music who had already taken or anticipated this turn, often in paradoxical simultaneity. Thus in 1911 Schoenberg completed the *Gurre-Lieder*, a work designed for one of the largest orchestras in music history, but in 1906 had already completed a "chamber symphony" for sixteen solo instruments (Opus 9). Reger was still completing his powerful *Symphonic Prologue to a Tragedy* for orchestra—*Weltanschauungsmusik*, in the true sense—in 1908 and had then with his 1912 *Concerto in Olden Style*, Op. 123, reverted to the simpler concerto forms of the musical Baroque, which he literally ennobled as "olden style." Even Strauss turned away from the robust orchestrations of his symphonic poems or his one-act operas *Salome* and *Elektra* and declared apodictically in 1929, "The orchestra of the future is the chamber orchestra, which, with its crystal clear background for all the events onstage, is solely capable of reproducing the intentions of the composer toward the vocal parts in all clarity."[4]

In 1928, Austrian composer and musicologist Egon Wellesz, who counted Schoenberg among his composition teachers, confirmed the general turn toward the chamber orchestra in his widely read 1928 essay "The New Instrumentation." The new direction—the emphatic focus on composing for chamber orchestra—essentially took for granted the significance of a particular kind of musical creation, for two main reasons: "It is a peculiar phenomenon that the emergence of cultural phenomena can be explained by several causes without it being possible any longer, to give precedence to one or the other. Thus, it is scarcely possible to determine whether the appearance of the chamber orchestra should be attributed to the economic needs of the period"—a reference to the devastating economic problems of the period following the First World War—"or to a sudden inner rejection of the large orchestra. Both impulses appeared almost simultaneously, and it is certain that the growing difficulties of supporting large orchestras and using them in performances helped encourage the mental shift from the late-Romantic, coloristic orchestra to the chamber orchestra. In the first case, the composer added the mood or subjective interpretation based on subjective internal forces; in the latter, he attempts to represent musical substance with the greatest possible clarity and concision."[5]

Besides, composing for the chamber orchestra made it possible to make immediate use of other above-mentioned musical methods, whether symphonic, concerto, or chamber-orchestral in their construction, while simultaneously emphasizing differences. The chamber orchestra differed from the symphonic orchestra in its solo instrument-oriented personnel and in its particular combination of instruments, and differed from the concerto in its leanings toward a concertante-soloistic use of all the included instruments. At the same time, it also differentiated itself from chamber music by its less demonstratively demanding musical structure and its singular instrumentation—often in works of more than one movement, even changing from one movement to the next, without any need for pedantic consistency in the incorporation of such changes. Instead, what dominated were mixed forms, so that composers such as Webern instrumentalized symphonic music in a chamber-orchestral manner, or composed concertos with chamber orchestra accompaniment, as did Jacques Ibert and the composers of "Les Six." Or, the larger chamber music groups they elected to use, all the way up to the nonet, could hardly be distinguished from chamber orchestras, which they sometimes even reduced to three instruments (as Schulhoff did, for example).

Such mixed forms clearly demonstrate the general compositional tendency in the 1920s toward musical simplification and a reduction of musical means, forms, and ambitions. This kind of chamber-orchestral composing was also encouraged institutionally, via thematic foci at festivals such as those in Donaueschingen/Baden-Baden or Salzburg, which were devoted to new music; through associations or groupings that performed works even written for large orchestra in reduced chamber-orchestral versions in Vienna, Prague, or Frankfurt am Main; in composition contests, for example those of Mainz's Schott Publishing; in the new medium of silent film, screened with chamber orchestras in the larger film palaces of big cities; or on the radio, where orchestras at first were limited in size due to broadcast-related constraints.

Peculiarly French Circumstances

In France, the distancing from "Wagnérisme" after 1909, which coincided with the epochal impact of the Ballets Russes of Serge Diaghilev, reached a point where, in 1923, a composer like Milhaud wanted a history of French music to exclude works that he saw as having been corrupted by an excessively intensive Wagner reception. In Paris, moreover, the Ballets Russes with Stravinsky established a composer who, with his spectacular ballets *The Firebird*, *Petrushka*, and *Le sacre du printemps*, and works like *Les noces* and *Histoire du soldat*, had found his way to special, singular, and often daring (chamber-)orchestral formations that lent his works an unmistakable specific coloring. This made a lasting impression on Martinů. Stravinsky, along with Ravel, Satie, or the other composers of "Les Six" (Poulenc, Milhaud, Auric, Tailleferre, Durey, and Honegger, to whom Martinů paid particular attention, while the others tended to disappoint him), was among the composers to whom Martinů was especially attached and whose work he experienced in Parisian concerts. He reported on them in detail in Prague journals and newspapers, engaging with them as a critic as well. And all these composers—to mention only a small number of examples—produced works in significantly reduced dimensions that made an entirely new impression. Stravinsky did it with *Histoire du soldat*, which he wrote for clarinet, bassoon, cornet à pistons, trombone, percussion, violin, and double bass. The orchestra, reduced to its sounding elements, also included references to popular music (tango, waltz, ragtime) or to intonations suggestive of marches, concertos, or choral music, and emancipated the percussion as a solo instrument. Schoenberg did the same with his melodrama *Pierrot lunaire*, in which each of the twenty-one pieces required a different combination of the eight instruments employed to accompany the *Sprechstimme*. Ravel, with his *Trois poèmes de Stéphane Mallarmé*, showed the influence of Schoenberg's *Pierrot lunaire*; and his remarkable sonata for violin and cello, which, coming after his opulent, sophisticatedly luxuriating orchestra scores, documents his turn to a minimally instrumentalized neoclassicism. Honegger's Sonatine for Two Violins or the *Rhapsodie* for two flutes, clarinet, and piano, attracted widespread attention at the 1922 Musikfest in Salzburg; another example is his Concertino for piano and orchestra. Poulenc, with the *Rhapsodie nègre*, gave musical exoticism and its wealth of sounds a turn toward the surrealistic; and especially Milhaud with five small, differently orchestrated symphonies; a sonata for piano, flute, clarinet, and oboe; or the ballet *L'homme et son désir*, which he wrote for a vocal quartet with the accompaniment of four small, entirely different chamber orchestras that sometimes play simultaneously.

The closest contact Martinů sought and found with a French composer, however, was with Albert Roussel, who had anticipated the later neoclassicism as early as 1906 with his *Divertissement* for flute, oboe, clarinet, horn, bassoon, and piano, Op. 6. It was only after Impressionist-influenced works like his first symphony *Poème de la forêt*, which the young Martinů especially cherished, that the young Roussel developed the characteristics that Martinů prized—clarity, lightness, musical economy, rationality or asentimentality—with works like *Sérénade*, Op. 30, for flute, harp, violin, viola, and cello; the *Concert pour petit orchestre*, Op. 34; or his Duo for Bassoon and Bass, without Opus. In the *Sérénade*, for example, Roussel completely forgoes bold thematic or motivic work; instead, he produces a clearly laid-out series of mainly rhythmically characterized, regularly colored and contoured sections, with *ostinati* in almost all the voices, which he separates with tempo changes; grounds in broad, wide-ranging melodies; and repeats with variations. In this way, the music, which remains listenable and transparent in every moment and is played with a light touch, takes on an entirely fresh, unsentimental expression and dissolves into its unusually characteristic sound presence without reference to any extramusical phenomena. With the *ostinati* it even seems to spin forward as if on its own power, so that it seems less as if the composer is expressing himself in an emphatic sense than that the music, once set in motion, is running on by itself in a compelling continuity of movement. With its sophisticated instrumental coloration, the robustly tonal *Sérénade* remains related to Impressionism; at the same time, the rhythmically inflected continuity of its movement identifies it as a neoclassical work. This ambivalence between Impressionism and neoclassicism, which is a feature of Roussel's style in his works of the 1920s, seems to have had special appeal for Martinů, without his making it his own. The relationship did not assume a teacher-student form, however, as has repeatedly been claimed (Martinů was twenty-one years younger than Roussel). Rather, the two mutually influenced each other, and one could even claim that in the 1920s Roussel was influenced by Martinů's composing. Indeed, the varied series of works that Roussel created in 1925—*Deux poèmes de Ronsard*, Op. 26, for flute and soprano; *Joueurs de flute*, Op. 27, for flute and piano; the Second Violin Sonata, Op. 28; *Ségovia*, Op. 29, for guitar; *Sérénade*, Op. 30; Duo for Bassoon and Bass—are more reminiscent of Martinů's composing. And, just as Martinů valued the company of Roussel—in an obituary, he wrote: "Roussel led me, with his modesty, amiability and noblesse, as well as his well-meaning irony, in such a way that I hardly noticed it. He left me time to reflect on everything and to reach maturity in my way."[6] Roussel in turn valued the music of Martinů, about whom he confessed: "My fame—that will be Martinů."[7] Comparison of a work like *Sérénade* for chamber orchestra (H 199), which Martinů composed in 1930 and dedicated to Roussel, with Roussel's *Sérénade* reveals commonalities and differences. Martinů's *Sérénade* is composed for a larger chamber orchestra of thirty-three players, and the *tutti* consequently sounds more massive and opulent; it is also significantly more dissonant and articulated. Martinů's *Sérénade* made varied use of different players, with parts for solo instruments; it uses *ostinato* techniques only to mark off formal sections, and its thematic inventions are significantly more consistent in adhering to the intended characteristics of its movements. It is as if Roussel composed and developed certain chamber-musical procedures and then put them to work, whereas Martinů composed with them in a more sovereign fashion, at least without exaggerated or intentional simplicity—as he complained when it came to the compositions of the Satie-inspired Paris École d'Arcueil. In his *Sérénade*, consequently, his personal musical style makes a stronger impression and, without losing the playful sense it shares with the *Sérénade* of Roussel, also reveals something of the turbulent times in which it was created.

Martinů's Contributions

In the 1920s Martinů, according to the dates listed in Harry Halbreich's work catalogue, composed no less than eighty works. They include just about all musical genres of the period and bear impressive witness to an original, sometimes even originary engagement with the compositional developments described above. These were reflected in a wealth of novel-seeming techniques in all genres and are closely related to the works' composition, expression, and purpose. Thus, it is noteworthy that, as his first work in Paris, Martinů turned to a type of chamber music grouping that had attracted little or no attention in France, composing his First String Trio, H 136, completed in January 1924. (Roussel wrote his string trio, Opus 58, only in 1937.) The work was not published in Martinů's lifetime and was considered lost until Eva Velická discovered and published it in 2005.[8] Martinů, relatively unburdened by historical models (even if those models had been created mainly by Mozart and Beethoven, with sometimes divertimento-like works), could create completely independently.

Characteristic of Martinů's work was the intensification of an almost concerto-like musical ductus, in which, after a brisk opening, he expanded the virtuoso part-writing (*Tonsatz*) with double stops right up to five voices. And this *concertante* composing, even in the more serene, melodically contoured parts, immediately draws attention to the eminently sensual process of music making, and less, as is more typically expected in chamber music, to the "abstract" compositional structure. The String Quartet No. 2, H 150, of September 1925 also can be played, despite its chamber-musical breadth, for example in the third movement, in the *concertante* style; the cadenza for the first violin is highly unusual in this genre (without this quartet being counted among the virtuoso genre of "*quatuors brilliants*" of the early nineteenth century). The Third String Quartet, H 183, from December 1929, differentiates the quartet sound, in turn, by means of articulation instructions that are seldom found in this fullness in chamber music. The first movement, for example, stipulates in the first measures that the second violin should lead with a mute, while the viola plays *collegno* and the cello *pizzicato*—with only the first violin articulating its staccato voice conventionally. The *ostinato*-like playing of all the rhythmically differentiated voices gives it a tightly woven sound texture that invokes distinctly chamber orchestral music associations. And the second larger work that Martinů completed in Paris, in April 1924, a quartet for the extremely unusual musical grouping of clarinet, horn, cello, and snare drum, H 139, seems even less like genuine chamber music than a chamber orchestra following Stravinsky's example. And in the suite-like Sextet, H 174, for winds and piano, from January–February 1929, Martinů does without consistent players in the sequence of five movements, and provides, as the third movement, a divertimento for flute and piano. (A first nonet, which Martinů had composed in 1924–1925, remained unperformed and unfortunately only its final movement is preserved.) In all these works, in other words, the traditionally rigid, extremely demanding chamber-music form has been considerably loosened up in favor of a more open, free, lively, but also emotionally present music making. Martinů, as it were, sublimates the traditionally demanding compositional structure of chamber music with procedures that are more typical of concerto, orchestral, and chamber orchestral style; they "over-form," so to speak, the chamber music requirements, simplify listeners' experience of chamber music, and lend the works a more varied appearance (however much they may heighten the technical difficulties for players). To this are added, in the Sextet, borrowings of musical elements typical of popular music. The fourth movement, for example, is a blues, which Martinů places beside the intensive-expressive, chamber-musical adagio of the second movement. The mixing of such elements in a single work points to a compositional practice that tends to open itself to the unlimited riches of the "whole" of music. The reduction of the rigid demands of chamber music, in this way, turns into an emphatic expansion of music's expressive possibilities.

In the 1920s, Martinů characteristically also created works written primarily in the style of popular music that was characterized by his contemporaries simply as "jazz." These were written for instruments rarely utilized in concert or symphonic music, typically including saxophone, percussion, and piano. He even titled a short one-movement work *Le jazz*, H 168, January 1928: an enchanting "portrait" of popular music of the time which, as music about music, could rival the "portrait" of Viennese music in Ravel's *La valse*. Two movements (*Präludium*, *Zwischenakt*) from his *Jazz Suite*, H 172, for chamber orchestra were introduced at the Deutsche Kammermusik 1928 festival, offering some lightness in between a series of three chamber operas (by the entirely forgotten composers Gustav Kneip, Hermann Reutter, and Walter Gronostay). Martinů frequently injected popular music into more extensive scenic works, using a corresponding selection of musicians, mostly for dramaturgical reasons. Examples include *Aufruhr* (*The Revolt*), H 151, 1925, and *On tourne*,[9] H 163, of June/August 1927. The suite for clarinet, bassoon, trumpet, violin, cello, and piano from his ballet *La revue de cuisine* (*The Kitchen Revue*), H 161, Easter 1927, offers with apparent delight genuine popular music; it gained a broad following and is counted among his most successful works from the 1920s. The traditional stylistic unity is replaced in these works by an open but by no means arbitrary stylistic diversity, which facilitates the general accessibility of this kind of music to the extent that it often disturbs the equanimity of "serious," ostensibly music-historically educated "connoisseurs" who, contemplatively, accept only stylistically "pure," "absolute" music.

The process of musical simplification and reduction had an impact on Martinů's composing in the *concertato* genre as well. The three concertos he wrote in the 1920s—the Concertino for Cello, Winds, Piano, and Percussion of December 1924, H 143, the First Piano Concerto from the summer of 1925, H 149, and the Divertimento for Piano Left Hand and Orchestra, of March 1926, which he reworked in 1928 and renamed Concertino, H 173—reduce the orchestral accompaniment entirely to the chamber orchestra, in keeping with the times. In the Cello Concertino, Martinů inserted a piano within the chamber orchestra, for the first time, rendering the sound of the *tutti* sharper, more characteristic, and in a certain sense—in comparison to the harp, which assumed a corresponding tonal function in late-Romantic orchestras—more "objective." In addition, Martinů reduced the formal dissonances in the Cello Concertino and the Piano Concertino (Left Hand); the Cello Concertino is even limited to a single movement. This alters the expressive character of the music, which hardly plays with the big, lofty, sovereign gesture of the dominant soloist, but instead opens itself, divertimento-like, to a maximally playful shared music making that the soloist leads or initiates. These concertos share an unsentimental emotional content, which very much responds to the modern, "democratic" attitude toward life accompanied by a more "objective" de-subjectification of music, with the orchestral works Martinů completed in this period. A subject like that of *Half-Time*, H 142, summer 1924, for larger orchestra, Martinů's first orchestral composition in Paris, turns with spectacular flair to soccer as a "lower," possibly "crude," in any case "ignoble" sport that is played before a noisy mass public, and that now wholly connects music to the ordinary world of society. Martinů created something analogous with his orchestra piece *La bagarre* (*The Tumult*), H 155, May 1926, which engages in an even more commonplace way with everyday life in a big city[10]—a demonstratively banal, but extremely unusual, eminently modern subject for an orchestral work that draws on and more generally expresses the everyday *Lebensgefühl* of the 1920s. The distance from the subjects of late-Romantic symphonic poetry, from sketches that range, for example, from flower-strewn meadows to a musical portrait of mermaids, could hardly have turned out more drastically.

On the Ambiguity of Musical Simplification

In all of these works, of which only a few small facets could be discussed here, Martinů reduces and simplifies the musical effort as compared to the late-Romantic, Impressionist style that had characterized his work prior to his move to Paris. But to call the change in his composing simplification and reduction remains difficult. It appears as simplification, above all, against the background of the roundly criticized and, in the 1920s, largely dismissed tendency toward an "intensification of the conventional"—a reduction of compositional effort and of means, forms, and aspirations. The aesthetic/compositional questions that accompanied this sort of simplification remained complex, and were judged and evaluated in correspondingly controversial ways, such as a regrettable decline in compositional level or as a progressive alignment with social reality. To avoid dogmatic judgments or conclusions, one must consider these questions individually and historically, identifying them, whether critically or affirmatively, with the forms of musical expression of the time in mind. We can illustrate this need for historical differentiation by examining Martinů's repeated reworking of one of his works as an example that requires us to rethink some judgments. Specifically, the three versions of his Cello Concerto No. 1, H 196, completed in 1930, 1939, and 1955.

The first version, from 1930, is a concerto with chamber orchestra accompaniment that Martinů enlarged somewhat in comparison to the Concertino for Cello, Winds, Piano, and Percussion composed six years earlier, H 143, 1924, but which should still be viewed entirely in the context of the compositional developments of the 1920s. The Cello Concerto received its premiere performance in 1931 in a Berliner Rundfunk concert without live audience, likely broadcast in a possibly too large orchestral setting with instruments that, at the time, were considered problematic to record, and without Martinů having planned the concerto as music for the radio. (A premiere originally planned for Paris had not materialized.) When he was able to hear the concerto live in concert for the first time, in 1938, he decided to thoroughly revise the instrumentation, which he now experienced as all too "aggressive," without altering the thematic material or the form—an indication of the extent to which he identified music's identity and impact with its instrumentation. In the summer of 1939, he completed the score with new instrumentation, which considerably enlarged the orchestra and simultaneously aligned the music's auditory flow with traditional solo concertos, including a dominant solo cello that more clearly distinguishes itself from the accompanying orchestra. This change can undoubtedly be considered an accommodation to convention, although with the changed instrumentation Martinů continued, for example, to utilize the piano as a sometimes even prominent orchestral instrument, lending a thoroughly unusual color to the orchestral *tutti*. As some critiques of the concerto had it, the piano occasionally even comes across as a second solo instrument. With this change, Martinů opened more possibilities for performance, as it no longer had to be organized as a chamber concert with special institutional conditions (honoraria for orchestra members performing solo roles, increased effort required in rehearsals). The outbreak of the Second World War and Martinů's flight from the Nazi troops in France prevented the timely performance and publication of this second version. For years, the cellist Pierre Fournier was the sole person who had access to this version and could perform it. When Martinů saw the score of this second version for the first time in 1955, after a lapse of sixteen years, he was utterly horrified by his instrumentation and remarked that 1939 had not been a good year for creative work—although in 1939 some masterworks did appear, for example the Cello Sonata No. 1, H 277, or the *Field Mass*, H 279. He reorchestrated the concerto once again, and this time he did alter the solo cello part, which he made easier (the precise treatment of the solo voice was, however, left to Pierre Fournier). In the orchestra, he now dispensed with the piano, which led not only to considerable changes in the orchestral movement, but also to a strikingly different coloration of the orchestral sound, which, for all its originality, now seems significantly more traditional. With this revision Martinů conventionalized the concerto even further than he had in 1939, seeking to make the piece, whose thematic and formal substance he continued to value, easier to perform. It now assumed the character of a traditional virtuoso concerto, and, ultimately, as was Martinů's wish and expectation, claimed and assumed its place in the cello repertoire. By contrast, in the first version of 1930, which is rarely performed, he had sought to overcome precisely this virtuoso character.

As of this writing, the second version has not been performed since 1955 because no performance material has been publicly accessible. It follows that the process of revision has led, paradoxically, to a situation whereby the first version of the Cello Concerto No. 1, which in the 1920s corresponded to historical-stylistic change and ideally achieved such social connection, is currently neglected because the historical context has changed again.

NOTES

1. In Czech: "vlastnosti západní kultury." Miloš Šafránek, ed., *Domov, hudba a svět* (Prague: Státní hudební vydavatelství, 1966), 317.

2. In Czech: "lehkost, jasnost, smysl pro čistou formu, ekonomii určitých prostředků a určitou asentimentalitu, racionalitu." Ibid.

3. Paul Bekker, "Neue Musik (1919)," in Paul Bekker, *Neue Musik*, Gesammelte Schriften 3 (Stuttgart: Deutsche Verlags-Anstalt 1923), 97.

4. Richard Strauss, *Musik heute und morgen* (1929), cited in Egon Wellesz, *Die neue Instrumentation*, Part II: Orchester (Berlin: Hesse, 1929), 170.

5. Egon Wellesz, *Die neue Instrumentation* (Berlin: Hesse 1928), 30.

6. In French: "Avec sa modestie, sa bonté et sa noblesse et aussi avec son ironie fine et amicale, il m'a guidé de telle façon, que cela s'est toujours passé presque sans que je m'en aperçoive. Il m'a laissé le temps de réfléchir et d'évoluer par moi-même." Bohuslav Martinů, *Témoignage tchécoslovaque. La Revue musicale,* special edition: "À la mémoire d'Albert Roussel" XVIII/178 (18 November 1937): 366. Czech translation in Šafránek, *Domov, hudba a svět*, 94.

7. Miloš Šafránek, *Bohuslav Martinů. His Life and Works* (London: Allan Wingate, 1962), 96.

8. Eva Velická, "Der unbekannte Wendepunkt in Bohuslav Martinůs Werk der 1920er Jahre," in *Bohuslav Martinů*, ed. Ulrich Tadday, Musik-Konzepte 11 (Munich: Ed. Text + Kritik, 2009).

9. Literally "This is being filmed," or "they're filming" *On tourne* is French for the director's instruction at the beginning of the shoot, so in English it's best matched by "Action!" (Translator's note.)

10. The work is dedicated to the memory of Lindbergh's landing at Le Bourget, outside Paris, where he was greeted by an enthusiastic and loud crowd of spectators. (Editors' note.)

Negotiating the "Concerto Grosso type" in Paris and Princeton: Martinů's Multi-Soloist Concertante Works from a Generational Perspective

BRIAN S. LOCKE

The neoclassical era was one of stylistic juxtapositions and disjunctions, by turns whimsical, nostalgic, disorienting, or even alienating. As Scott Messing and Richard Taruskin have shown, invoking a distant, largely imaginary musical "past" could be a highly contentious mode of expression for interwar composers seeking a way "forward" out of late Romanticism.[1] The sudden return in the mid-1920s of the multi-soloist concertante genre offered neoclassical composers a tangible opportunity to break with the Romantic inheritance (since that era had virtually ignored such works) and thereby reinvestigate a genre associated with the late-seventeenth and eighteenth centuries.[2] Bohuslav Martinů first turned to concertante instrumentation in 1931—whereupon it dominated the remainder of his Parisian years—and continued exploring this format to the end of his American period in the mid-1950s. Plentiful in number, Martinů's contributions do not represent a unified group but rather a heterogeneous series of compositional methods and aesthetic outcomes. As this essay will discuss, Martinů's concertante works are polysemic, resisting any monolithic reading of his neoclassical aesthetics: they bear musical traces of his historical models, but also of his own creative milieux. Thus, they reflect his generation's multivalent attitudes toward what Martha Hyde calls "metamorphic anachronism" across a thirty-year period.[3]

Two works from this broadly conceived genre, the Divertimento (Serenade No. 4), H 215 (Paris, 1931), and the Sinfonia Concertante No. 2, H 322 (Princeton, 1949), demonstrate Martinů's ability to transform specific pre-Romantic compositional models—Mozart and Haydn, respectively. But not all of Martinů's concertante works have such a clear genealogy; rather, they encompass an amalgam of freely associated historical forebears, including his contemporaries' recently premiered pieces. Martinů's writings about his music are also fascinatingly heterogeneous on the matter. Despite his overarching self-definition—that "I am a Concerto Grosso type" of composer—differences in compositional style between Martinů's Parisian and American years reveal his changing attitudes toward genre and neoclassicism.

In exploring Martinů's negotiation of the concertante genre, his historical models, and modernist practices, I employ Hyde's typology of metamorphic anachronisms, which she defines as the "deliberate dramatization of historical passage [of diachronic time], bringing the present into relation with a specific past and making the distance between them meaningful."[4]

Martinů's Concertante Pieces in the Context of His Generation

"Any attempt to work out a theory of neoclassicism in music, or even to give coherent content to the term, confronts a long history of careless or tendentious usage."[5] The same could be said for the concertante genre, wherein multiple soloists (collectively, the concertino) are accompanied by a large ensemble, or *ripieno*. Even by 1750, the title of "concerto grosso" was poorly defined, as was that of its subsequent incarnation, the "symphonie concertante" after approximately 1770. Differences between the two were subtle in their own day, and questions of what they did or did *not* include were also quite porous. In the "concerto for strings," a genre without named soloists, individual solo lines often emerge as the piece progresses: for example, in Bach's *Brandenburg Concerto* No. 3, either no one or everyone is a soloist, and the distinction between concertino and ripieno dissolves utterly. Its corollary might be the "divertimento" or "serenade" for outsized chamber ensemble, where the concertino *is* the ripieno.

Perhaps the most crucial element in this uncertain historical framework is that very few examples of concertante pieces were written in the nineteenth century (half of them by Louis Spohr). Even fewer—only two—made it into canonic repertoire: Beethoven's Triple Concerto for piano, violin, cello, and orchestra, Op. 56 (1803), and Brahms's Double Concerto for violin, cello, and orchestra, Op. 102 (1887). The neoclassicists' preoccupation with the concertante genre as a non-Romantic phenomenon is therefore easy to understand. Of the pre-1914 works, perhaps only Elgar's *Introduction and Allegro* (1905), with its string quartet concertino, string orchestra ripieno, clear form, and crisp articulation, looks ahead to the tremendous rush of metamorphic anachronism after 1924.

Several of the inclusions in Table 1 might at first be considered contentious or even polemic. I have deliberately included all multi-soloist-plus-orchestra pieces, regardless of style; I have left out several pieces named *Symphonie Concertante* that have only one soloist (for example, works by Prokofiev and Szymanowski); but I have retained the eighteenth-century overlap of "concerto grosso/concerto for orchestra" —or in some cases, multiple orchestras. Such a broad base of comparison yields two basic observations: an astonishingly wide variety of composers wrote concertante pieces in the thirty years between 1924 and 1954; and although they collectively outnumber Martinů's list, no individual composer contributed more to the genre than he. Investigating further, it is evident that this trend was by no means a unilaterally Parisian phenomenon, but international in scope from the outset. Nor can it be generalized as an offshoot of the "retour à Bach" movement that carried such political freight in its day. Indeed, the titles imply a heritage that stretches from before Corelli to the doorstep of Beethoven.

Quite possibly, mid-twentieth-century composers had a partial grasp of pre-Romantic repertoire at best, gleaned as it was via a small number of heavily edited scores and performances by modern orchestras. Are we to presume that a modernist composer—even one indulging in anachronism—made a clear distinction between the historical concerto grosso, the symphonie concertante, etc., and preserved those distinctions in their own work, two centuries on? Does a work titled *Concertino* reference the concerto grosso, or is it merely a diminutive that resists Romanticist grandeur? And if the concerto for orchestra uses soloists freely amid a heterogeneous texture, where is the barrier between concertante and orchestral works? Nor does every piece in Table 1 display neoclassical characteristics at all times, including entire movements by Martinů. It would seem, then, that a prescriptive reading of neoclassicist concertante practice—that is, what they *should have done*—would ultimately dismiss a vital part of the early twentieth-century listening experience.

A brief episode from Martinů's career illustrates the problem of overreliance on strict nomenclature. In late 1937, in the midst of fulfilling a commission for a double violin concerto (what would become H 264), Martinů writes to the artists, brothers Victor and Georges Desarzens: "As regards the details, I will ask if we agree as to the duration, namely, three movements of around 12–15 minutes, two violins conceived very much in a concertante manner. . . . What sort of title do you prefer? 'Concerto,' 'Duo' with orchestra, 'Sinfonia concertante'?"[6] One month later, he sends them a copy of the work with the note: "Regarding the title, I haven't written one in, but I think that the best would be *Le duo concertant* for two violins and orchestra."[7] Where the first interaction might imply Martinů's neutral or arbitrary stance toward titles—even sharing the choice with the commissioning artists—his attitude seems to have changed upon writing the work, ruling out Concerto and Sinfonia concertante in favor of its eventual title, *Duo concertant*.

In short, we must examine Martinů in his various historical contexts, starting halfway through his years in Paris. From Šafránek's chapter on "The Concerto Grosso," we learn that Martinů's first concertante work, the Concerto for String Quartet and Orchestra, H 207, came from a casual prompt by members of the Pro Arte Quartet after a concert in spring 1931, and furthermore, that Martinů had studied Corelli's concerti grossi and Bach's *Brandenburg Concertos*, and "for a number of years he had been considering the idea of writing a group of 'Prague Concertos.'"[8] I suggest, given the presence of concertante works among his contemporaries—thirteen written in the seven years prior to Martinů's String Quartet Concerto—that his generation's preoccupation with the genre may have guided his sustained interest in it.

Table 1. Multi-soloist Concertante Works and Concerti for Orchestra, 1924–1954

Works by Martinů				
Year	**H**	**Title**	**Soli**	**Orchestra**
1924				
1925				
1926				
1927				
1928				
1929				
1930				
1931	207 212 215 219	Concerto Partita Divertimento (Serenade No. 4) Sinfonia Concertante No. 1	str qt soli vn/va --	orchestra string orchestra chamber orchestra 2 orchestras
1932				
1933	231 232	Concerto Concertino	pf trio pf trio	string orchestra orchestra
1934				
1935	246	Concerto	hpd (pf obbl)	chamber orchestra
1936	252	Concerto	fl/vn	chamber orchestra
1937	263 264	Concerto grosso Duo concertant	2 pf 2 vn	chamber orchestra orchestra
1938	267 271	*Tre ricercari* Double Concerto	soli --	orchestra 2 string orchestras, piano, timpani
1939				
1940				

Works by other composers				
Year	**Composer**	**Title**	**Soli**	**Orchestra**
1924	Krenek Krenek Tcherepnin	Concertino Concerto grosso No. 2 Concerto da camera	fl/vn/pf str trio fl/vn	string orchestra orchestra chamber orchestra
1925	Berg Bloch Hindemith	Kammerkonzert Concerto grosso No. 1 Concerto	vn/pf pf obbl --	13 woodwind string orchestra orchestra
1926	d'Indy	Concert	pf/fl/vc	string orchestra
1927	Ghedini Schulhoff	Concerto grosso Double concerto	ww qnt fl/pf	string orchestra 2 horn, string orchestra
1928	Tansman	Suite	2 pf	orchestra
1929	Beck	Concerto	str qt	orchestra
1930	Holst Schulhoff	Double concerto Concerto	2 vn str qt	orchestra wind ensemble
1931	Ghedini Tansman Tcherepnin	*Pezzo concertante* Symphony No. 3 (Symphonie concertante) Triple Concertino	2 vn/va pf qnt pf trio	orchestra orchestra orchestra
1932	Poulenc	Concerto	2 pf	orchestra
1933	Casella Respighi Schönberg (Handel)	Triple Concerto *Concerto a cinque* Concerto	pf trio ob/tpt/vn/db/pf str qt	orchestra string orchestra orchestra
1934	Tailleferre	Concerto	2 pf	choir, orchestra
1935	Beck Françaix Rosenberg	Serenade Quadruple concerto Symphonie concertante	fl/cl fl/ob/cl/bn vn/va/ob/bn	string orchestra orchestra orchestra
1936				
1937	Françaix	*Musique de cour*	fl/vn	orchestra
1938	Malipiero Stravinsky	*Concerto a tre* *Dumbarton Oaks* Concerto	pf trio --	orchestra chamber orchestra
1939	Milhaud	Concerto	fl/vn	orchestra
1940	Kodály	Concerto	--	orchestra

Works by Martinů				
Year	**H**	**Title**	**Soli**	**Orchestra**
1941	285	Concerto da camera	vn/pf	percussion, string orchestra
1943	292	Concerto	2 pf	orchestra
1945				
1946				
1947				
1948				
1949	322	Sinfonia Concertante No. 2	vn/ob/bn/vc	chamber orchestra
1950	329	Concerto No. 2	2 vn	orchestra
1951				
1952				
1953	342	Concerto	vn/pf	orchestra
1954				

Works by other composers				
Year	**Composer**	**Title**	**Soli**	**Orchestra**
1941	Bořkovec Harsányi Milhaud	Concerto grosso Divertimento No. 1 Concerto	2 vn/vc/pf 2 vn 2 pf	orchestra orchestra orchestra
1943	Alwyn Bartók Ghedini	Concerto grosso No. 1 Concerto *Concerto 'dell' Albatro'*	tpt/vn/e.hn -- pf trio	orchestra orchestra orchestra
1945	Alwyn Martin	Concerto *Petite symphonie concertante*	ob/hp pf/hpd/hp	string orchestra string orchestra
1946	Giannini	Concerto grosso	soli	string orchestra
1947	Ghedini Strauss	Concerto Duett-Concertino	2 pf cl/bn	orchestra string orchestra, harp
1948	Alwyn Honegger Malipiero Vaughan-Williams	Concerto grosso No. 2 Concerto da camera *Quinta sinfonia, concertante in eco* Partita	str qt fl/e.hn -- --	string orchestra string orchestra 2 orchestras 2 string orchestras
1949				
1950	Bloch Ghedini Vaughan-Williams	Concertino *Concerto 'l'Alderina'* Concerto grosso	fl/va fl/vn --	string orchestra timpani, celesta, string orchestra 3 string orchestras
1951	Ghedini Krenek	*Concerto 'l'Olmeneta'* Concerto	2 vc 2 pf	orchestra orchestra
1952	Bloch Tailleferre Tansman	Concerto grosso No. 2 Concertino Concertino	str qt fl/pf ob/cl	orchestra orchestra orchestra
1953				
1954	Malipiero Tansman	*Fantasie concertanti* Concerto	pf trio --	orchestra orchestra

Not all the concertante works of the 1920s are relevant to this suggestion: composers well beyond Martinů's personal network (Ghedini) or stylistic propensity (Berg) serve to indicate the breadth of the field. Significantly, Martinů's String Quartet Concerto followed recent works from within his Parisian circle—concertante pieces by Alexander Tcherepnin, Alexandre Tansman, and Conrad Beck, and by Marcel Mihalovici's teacher, Vincent d'Indy.[9] Martinů would certainly have known Beck's String Quartet Concerto from 1929, given their close friendship (Schulhoff's had yet to be published or performed). Looking further, we see the proximity of Tcherepnin and Casella's Triple Concerti for piano trio and orchestra to Martinů's similar pair, H 231 and H 232; of two-piano concerti by Poulenc and Tailleferre to Martinů's Concerto Grosso; of flute/violin concerti by Martinů, Françaix, and Milhaud; as well as many possible interconnections besides. Each work negotiates a relationship with multiple layers of "pastness," be they self-conscious anachronisms invoking eighteenth-century models, unconscious inheritances from the Romantic era, or even discursive dialogues arising from last season's concerts. Seen from the vibrant chaos that was interwar Paris, all of these interchangeable points of historical reference might be equally valid to a composer of concertante music.

Modes of Imitation: Hyde's Four "Metamorphic Anachronisms"

To parse out these reference points, I turn to Hyde's four overlapping modes of anachronistic imitation. Hyde terms these modes "reverential imitation," "eclectic imitation," "heuristic imitation," and "dialectic imitation," depending on the relationship between the new work and its imagined antecedents. I consider three of these in relation to a triptych of Martinů's works from 1937–38; these are often acknowledged as the peak of Martinů's concertante pieces, forming a bridge between his Parisian and American years. (The third mode, heuristic imitation, will appear in greater detail below.)

Martinů's Concerto grosso, H 263 (1937), is a work replete with neoclassical, or, as often labeled, neo-Baroque anachronisms. Its outer movements adapt ritornello structure to the textural palette of a modern chamber orchestra; its thematic material is unified within each movement; and it features two pianos in what might, at times, be considered soloistic roles. The juxtaposition of these ingredients resonates most closely with Hyde's category of reverential imitation, where the new work "follows the classical model with a nearly religious fidelity or fastidiousness . . . perhaps implying a sacramental version of history."[10] Martinů's model in this case was likely Corelli's concerti grossi—but the model goes only so far. The two pianists are not soloists in the traditional sense of a concerto grosso: only in the first half of the third movement do they act independently of the orchestra. By and large, the presence of their duo points to an expansion of

Martinů's tendency to include a piano in his larger orchestral forces, rather than a systematic dialogue with each other and the ripieno.[11]

Solos abound in *Tre ricercari*, H 267 (1938), a work that evokes the sixteenth and seventeenth centuries in both name and contrapuntal technique, but these solo voices are each soon swallowed by the mass of textures that control the flow of the piece. The oboe takes the lead in all three movements, often in combination with other soprano instruments: violin and flute, as well as the ubiquitous piano. In the outer movements, Martinů develops the material by pitting orchestral sections against each other in a freely contrapuntal style, but not one that is necessarily imitative. Martinů's second movement, Largo, begins and ends with a flute-oboe duet that incorporates a certain rhythmic and contrapuntal variety, but its cantilena is ultimately of a melody-and-accompaniment texture. I read *Tre ricercari* as an example of what Hyde terms eclectic imitation, wherein "allusions, echoes, phrases, techniques, structures, and forms from an unspecified group of earlier composers and styles all jostle each other indifferently."[12]

Lastly, the Double Concerto for two string orchestras, piano, and timpani, H 271 (1938), exemplifies a technique utilized by Martinů and his contemporaries with lesser frequency, but to great effect. Instead of multiple soloists, this concerto has multiple ripienos, a device also employed in his first Sinfonia Concertante, H 219 (1931), though without the solo element that the single piano provides in the Double Concerto.[13] His subversion of the basic premise of eighteenth-century concertante technique presents us with an example of Hyde's dialectic imitation, which is "not merely a compositional technique; it [is] an aesthetic stance, a sometimes polemical definition and recreation of a tradition that provoked and tolerated tangled attitudes and intense ambivalences."[14] Perhaps unsurprisingly, this work is anything but neoclassical in detail or design: as an emotional reaction to the Munich crisis, it is among Martinů's darkest, most expressionist works.

This triptych has occupied a central position in almost all historiographies of Martinů's concertante repertoire, often to the exclusion of the majority of his work in the genre. In what follows, I investigate Martinů's modes of anachronism in ways that the celebrated triptych does not fully represent.

The Concerto Grosso as Style and Philosophy

In various public and private documents, Martinů contributed to the broad understanding we have of the concertante genre within his career. Thomas Svatoš has shown that the composer was conscious of stylistic changes in his music and their effect on groups of his pieces, essentially a type of periodization.[15] As concerns the eras of the concertante works, Martinů cites his Piano Trio No. 1 (*Cinq pièces brèves*, H 193) as the start of his neoclassical period, and the Double Concerto as the start of "hyper-neoclassicism." These categories, conceived in 1941, may have influenced subsequent commentators when discussing his development from the String Quartet Concerto to the Double Concerto as a sort of directionalized arc, although they naturally stop short of including the concertante works written after his arrival in the United States.

The question of placing specific pieces into discrete categories, however, runs counter to Martinů's own retrospective views of his career writ large. One famous statement, from an autobiographical article he published in 1946, deserves to be printed in full:

> To tell the truth, I am a Concerto Grosso type. You will find a superficial description of the form in almost all textbooks, perhaps nothing other than that the soli and orchestra alternate. But in reality, the matter goes deeper. The whole structure of this form points to quite a different understanding, a different attitude to the problem. Where the symphony allows and truly requires the application of emotional elements, often in their most Romantic conception and expression, where dynamic crests and catharses depend on them, where you can expand your themes to boundless dimensions, even to the detriment of organic order, there the Concerto Grosso only grants you strict order, restrictions, the balance of emotional elements, a limiting and adequate equalization of dynamics and pace, an altogether different and precise structure of thematic arrangement: in short, quite another world.[16]

Martinů's tantalizing formulation, "a Concerto Grosso type" as both a self-identifier and a characterization of his compositional practice, is at once helpful and vague, since it seems to apply well beyond the defining characteristics of genre or stylistic period. It can be read as an anti-Romanticist credo shared by his interwar generation, but it also reflects his deep engagement with the dynamic form of the concerto grosso. It resonates with many of his more philosophical statements about the somewhat antipodal roles of expression and form in his music and invites us to look beyond the nomenclature to find elements of the "Concerto Grosso type" throughout his oeuvre. Nevertheless, Martinů's original context for this broad statement was to qualify how he felt about composing one of his later concertante pieces, the Concerto for Two Pianos, H 292, in 1943, and how his return to the "ideal type" of the concerto grosso lifted him out of bleak spirits during the Christmas season.[17]

Within the year, Miloš Šafránek would publish his partial biography of Martinů, where he demonstrates a clear, teleological narrative strategy. "The Path to the Concerto Grosso" begins with the String Quartet Concerto and culminates in "Realization: Concerto Grosso—Double Concerto," subsuming a handful of other pieces (including solo concerti) along the way.[18] Importantly, he reprints Martinů's program note for the premiere of the Concerto Grosso, given by the Boston Symphony under Serge Koussevitzky's baton in 1941. In light of his musings five years later, it is somewhat ironic that Martinů eschews deeper analysis of concerto grosso form here, opting instead for what appears, at first, a "superficial description":

> The title "Concerto Grosso" was chosen because I have a penchant for this form, which occupies a position between chamber music and symphonic music. . . . It will be evident that *I have not followed the traditional form of "concerto grosso" but rather the characteristic alternation of "soli" and "tutti,"* which I have entrusted to the pianos, woodwinds, and strings. . . . I am reluctant to make an analysis of the form, which offers no real help in understanding a new work.[19]

In his discussion of the 1944 *Ridgefield Diary*, Svatoš reconciles the seeming inconsistencies between the "Concerto Grosso type" passage and the Concerto Grosso program note, particularly as regards form and emotional content. For one thing, Martinů felt strongly that "a musical work functions as a composite of organic relations," rather than as a fixed value defined in absolute terms.[20] Hence his deliberate avoidance of analysis for the public, since "we can never gain a definitive knowledge of the underpinnings that were responsible for a work's design," nor its emotional content beyond our ever-changing experience of it.[21] Rather than an outgrowth of Romantic psychology, for Martinů "emotion has more to do with the 'inner order' that is primary to a work's conception. . . . An inner order is responsible for a work's specific but ineffable emotional quality."[22] It is through experiential time and "self-forgetting" that composers and listeners gain access to inner order and its emotional quality, a process that Svatoš ascribes to contemporary phenomenology.

Thus we are faced with the task of reconstructing Martinů's ineffable experience of concerti grossi, past and present. But as we have seen, his relationship to his pre-Romantic models had much in common with his generation's neoclassical strategies for adapting historical models by processes of metamorphic anachronism.

Heuristic Anachronism in the Divertimento (Serenade No. 4), H 215

Although most commentators since Šafránek reference Martinů's predilection for Corelli's concerti grossi as the impulse for his concertante work, in the early 1930s he felt just as drawn to high classical models. As Martinů wrote to Václav Štěpán in 1935, "Mozart is and has always been in the top position of my favorite composers. With him I have engaged in the greatest struggles, in the attempt to get closer to that perfection and that natural and organic balance of content. Also a certain restraint, to not break free, in short, to master order."[23] One consequence of focusing on the grander achievements of Martinů's Parisian years is that historians tend to overlook his more modest essays, many of them written quickly for specific artists on commission or with individual performance venues in mind. Examining the Divertimento (renamed Serenade No. 4 after he composed three works in a similar Mozartian style) allows us to see the extent to which Martinů looked to Mozart as a model, and furthermore, to view the *symphonie concertante* subgenre as a key to understanding the Parisian years with greater nuance.

For one thing, the symphonie concertante was a historical genre with deep roots in Parisian public concerts, with a large variety of works written by both local and visiting composers from 1767 to roughly 1810, thanks to the Concert des Amateurs under François-Joseph Gossec and subsequently the Chevalier de Saint-Georges. The majority of Mozart's multi-soloist concerti, including the Concerto for flute and harp (K. 299), the Sinfonie Concertanti for woodwind quartet (K. 320) and for violin and viola (K. 364), and his Concerto for two pianos (K. 365), were all written for Parisian premieres in the years 1778–80. The sheer volume of symphonies concertantes identified by Barry S. Brook (some 570 over a sixty-year period, most of them for Paris) speaks to the depth of local significance this genre had. Not merely concerti grossi by another name nor a hybrid form, it was "a genre in its own right" that carried formal and expressive traits unique to Parisian concertgoers' tastes.[24]

Paris in the 1930s happened to be in the midst of a significant Mozart revival—what Boris de Schloezer acerbically termed "Le culte de Mozart"[25]—prompted by the re-inaugurated Société d'études mozartiennes. Led by its chief administrator and visionary, Mme Octave (Jeanne) Homberg, this Parisian institution was incorporated in 1930 under the aegis of the Salzburg Mozarteum.[26] Shortly thereafter, thanks to the patronage of Parisian titled aristocracy, the Société began a series of lavish, though infrequent concerts under the artistic direction of Félix Raugel, a student of Albert Roussel and d'Indy. It was to this Société that Martinů dedicated his Divertimento for violin, viola, and chamber orchestra (H 215), completing the work on 29 February 1932. Quite possibly, the appearance of a new concert series created, in Martinů's imagination at any rate, a potential venue for performances at a time when his household had little income. There is, however, no evidence in their extensive *Bulletin* that the Société's concerts ever contained music by any other composers but Mozart, or that they solicited or accepted newly written works in the period 1930–32.[27] Regardless, Martinů's manuscript retained the dedication when he sent it for publication to Melantrich in 1947, and its orchestral forces of solo violin and viola, with a ripieno of two oboes, piano, and strings strongly suggest Mozart's Sinfonia Concertante (K. 364) as a model.[28]

To posit any one compositional model, of course, runs the risk of discounting Martinů's warning that pieces of music do not have fixed identities. This is why I propose Hyde's concept of heuristic anachronism to shed light on the relationship between "Martinů's Mozart" (as it were) and his own piece as an experience that unfolds through time:

> Heuristic imitation accentuates rather than conceals the link it forges with the past. It advertises its dependence on an earlier model, but in a way that forces us to recognize the disparity, the anachronism, of the connection being made. Heuristic imitation dramatizes musical history and relies on the datedness of musical styles for aesthetic effect. It provides composers a means to position themselves within a culture and a tradition. It opens a transitive dialogue with the past by which composers can take, and take responsibility for, their places in music history.[29]

As such, we have no need to look for a copy, but rather, Martinů's musical acknowledgment of and departure from the Mozartian model.

Mozart's Sinfonia Concertante is much longer than Martinů's Divertimento, opening his first movement (Allegro maestoso) with a full orchestral exposition, rather than Martinů's 22-measure ritornello. After this point, however, both composers give the two soloists much more material than would be typical in a concerto grosso. This conforms to Brook's comment that the symphonie concertante "places the solo group at the forefront, assigning to it most of the important thematic material . . . while usually relegating the orchestra to a primarily accompanying function except during the initial statement."[30] While Martinů's orchestra does enter often with fragments of the ritornello, it never disrupts the flow maintained by the soloists—only a few moments of antiphony between soli and ripieno serve to segment the movement's form.

Among the many melodic allusions to the galant in Martinů's Divertimento, one repeating gesture stands out, albeit for different reasons than its putative counterpart in Mozart. One of the most iconic moments in K. 364 is the serene entrance of the soloists, overlapping with the codetta of the first exposition on a sustained tonic E♭ in high parallel octaves, which then descend in legato scalar fragments (Example 1a). Martinů employs a dramatic gesture of similar contour, in the first violin section just before the soloists' initial entrance, but his represents an apex of surface tension rather than serenity, sustaining a minor ninth rather than tonic (Example 1b). The motive returns several times more, thereby becoming one of the main gravitational points of Martinů's first movement. At the end of the developmental episode (mm. 86–92), it temporarily separates from its descending scalar release, seemingly past the point of no return, but the ensuing gentle arpeggio ushers in the retransition.

Example 1a. Wolfgang Amadeus Mozart, Sinfonia Concertante, K. 364, first movement (Allegro maestoso), mm. 70–75. Entrance of the soloists with sustained tonic and legato descent (Viola in concert pitch).

Only in its final iteration does it settle into a perfect octave between the soloists, as a trill on the dominant G before the movement's final cadence.

The slow movements of both Mozart and Martinů diverge from the lightness of atmosphere that Brook ascribes to the concertante genre generally: while Mozart's is a brooding elegy of considerable length, Martinů's brief fifty-eight measures present a chiaroscuro mosaic of dramatic rhetorical gestures. If Mozart's Andante takes the form of a *rondò* aria worthy of Donna Elvira or Vitellia's emotional depths, Martinů's Andante moderato is a *recitativo accompagnato*, which historically preceded the arias of exalted characters. The reference is quite clear: Martinů's accompaniment consists of a string of interrupted cadences, where an unexpected, chromatic chord in first inversion takes the place of the tonic. It is a deliberately anachronistic gesture that appears three times in the central, developmental section of the movement (Example 2a). Prompted by this abrupt harmonic drama, the soloists extend their phrases with elegiac *arioso* gestures in octaves. Martinů exploits this very same effect in his otherwise ebullient final Allegretto, wherein chromatic first-inversion chords interrupt the cadences expected at the ends of ritornellos (Example 2b); this time, however, the soloists break down completely into recitative-like fragments before regaining their momentum.

Example 1b. Martinů, Divertimento/Serenade No. 4, H 215, first movement (Allegro), mm. 17–20. Sustained minor ninth and legato descent (1st Violin).

Example 2a. Martinů, Divertimento/Serenade No. 4, H 215, second movement (Andante moderato), mm. 29–31. Interrupted cadence and soloists' arioso.

Example 2b. Martinů, Divertimento/Serenade No. 4, H 215, third movement (Allegretto), mm. 45–51. Interrupted cadence and soloists' recitative-like fragments.

These two features—the high sustained tones and the chromatic first-inversion interruptions—shape and challenge the identity of the piece as it unfolds, resonating with and against the Mozartian model. As such, it embodies Hyde's heuristic category of anachronistic imitation, wherein Martinů questions the old in attempting to solve the new. As we shall see, Martinů's manifold solutions to the problem of historical inheritance continued well after the abrupt conclusion of his Parisian years, through his years of American exile and the profound stylistic changes to his identity as a composer—of symphonies and large-scale solo concerti.

The Summation of All Anachronisms: Sinfonia Concertante No. 2, H 322

It is fitting that we approach Martinů's stylistic changes through the lens of another concertante piece connected with a late classical model. This time, we have authoritative evidence of his use of Haydn's Sinfonia Concertante in B-flat Major, Hob. I:105 (London, 1792), as the inspiration for the Sinfonia Concertante No. 2, H 322, both with the same quartet of soloists: violin, oboe, bassoon, and cello. As Martinů described it in his letter to Paul Sacher:

> To start at the beginning we have to go way back, to Paris, I think, in 1936.[31] It was there I heard for the first time . . . a work that made such an impression upon me that I could never forget. It was the Sinfonia Concertante by Haydn for the same group of soloists [as my piece]. For years I was, as they say here, "haunted" by this work. I searched in vain for the score in music stores and second-hand bookshops down by the Paris docks, and I believed an edition hadn't even been published. Everyone tried to convince me that I was mistaken, that it wasn't by Haydn, but rather the S[infonia] C[oncertante] by Mozart. When I became a professor at Princeton in 1948 and saw its wonderful library, my first thought was to seek the Haydn score and there it was. I even found the recording and it was the same ensemble that I had heard in Paris years ago, conducted by Charles Munch. I studied the score and was even more impressed by the simplicity and perfection and . . . well, you know what I mean. . . . I was truly inspired by this work, and if anyone perceives Haydn's influence in my piece, I would not be angry about it; rather, I would love that.[32]

Martinů's colorful anecdote reveals a reverential attitude toward Haydn, in whom he sees the personification of all the aesthetic principles he wishes for himself: balance, restraint, and humble joy without pretension, "the sign of a simple and great man."[33] The score bears out notions offered by Hyde in her concept of

Example 3a. Martinů, Sinfonia Concertante No. 2, H 322, first movement (Allegro non troppo), mm. 1–5. Anapestic rhythms in full orchestra.

Example 3b. Martinů, Sinfonia Concertante No. 2, H 322, first movement (Allegro non troppo), mm. 25–28. Chromatic descending thirds reminiscent of Wagner's "Ring motif."

reverential imitation, not only in Martinů's choice of concertino soloists but also in its balance with the ripieno and in its overall formal design. Its three movements follow the Haydnesque layout of double-exposition sonata (Allegro non troppo), through-composed variations (Andante moderato), and modified rondo (Poco allegro). Certain passages, particularly the opening of the Andante moderato, come so close to Haydn's sound world as to resemble an act of piety.

But is Haydn's Sinfonia Concertante the only point of anachronistic reference here? Martinů's first movement would tell us otherwise, its brash opening constructed entirely of full-orchestral anapestic rhythms that invoke not only Bach's third *Brandenburg Concerto*, but by 1949, Stravinsky's iconic *Dumbarton Oaks* Concerto as well (Example 3a). Inexplicably, the homophonic chords that close the first exposition—just before the first entrance of the concertino quartet—bear a suspicious resemblance to the chromatic descending thirds of the "Ring motif" from Wagner's tetralogy (though this is likely coincidental; Example 3b). Perhaps just as spuriously, the end of an extended solo quartet that forms the development section passes through the sound world of Mendelssohn's overture to *A Midsummer Night's Dream* (Example 3c). Lastly, the recapitulation brings us a variation in a

Example 3c. Martinů, Sinfonia Concertante No. 2, H 322, first movement (Allegro non troppo), mm. 144–48. Developmental passage for the solo quartet.

rollicking compound duple meter, roughly parallel to the finale of Beethoven's *Pastoral* Symphony No. 6 (Example 3d). Whether or not these allusions were deliberate on Martinů's part, he effectively bridged the stylistic gap between himself and Haydn using eclectic anachronisms from three generations of Romantics—and from the neoclassicist *par excellence*, Stravinsky.

Martinů's slow movement presents a more subtle interaction with Haydn's late orchestral work. As mentioned above, he matches his model in tone, pace, and texture in a way that demonstrates the depth of his studies in the Princeton Library. But this is no static replica. It problematizes its own form, a loose series of variations with coda, in the way that another late Haydn slow movement does—the Largo cantabile of Symphony No. 93 (written for London in the same year as

Example 3d. Martinů, Sinfonia Concertante No. 2, H 322, first movement (Allegro non troppo), mm. 207–12. Recapitulation, passage in compound duple meter.

the Sinfonia Concertante). Each of these movements becomes a testing ground for the much-vaunted restraint that Martinů sought and celebrated. Where Haydn has us question the genre, or even era, of the conventional pastoral mood by a series of interruptions from the Handelian past (see the austere G-minor passage in Example 4a, replete with dotted rhythms and abundant trills), Martinů gradually problematizes his model, ending up at a very similar goal. Martinů's classical pastoralism

Example 4a. Joseph Haydn, Symphony No. 93, second movement (Largo cantabile), mm. 17–22. G-minor passage with dotted rhythms and trills.

lasts considerably longer: after a "wrong note" chord on beat 4 of measure 3, it regains its poise for the remainder of the theme (to measure 16) and into the parallel first variation (mm. 16–36). In short order, Martinů develops his theme using

Example 4a. Continued

an intensified subdivision of the beat, first as running sixteenths, then overlapping syncopations for the second variation (mm. 36–56). These syncopations, however, result in a long, unbroken phrase for the soloists that departs both harmonically and gesturally from the classical model and truly enters Martinů's broader, symphonic expressive world. Finally, the shortened third variation (mm. 56–66)

Example 4b. Martinů, Sinfonia Concertante No. 2, H 322, second movement (Andante moderato), mm. 56–59. Third variation, rising arpeggio in dotted rhythms.

unleashes a wash of orchestral texture based on the rising arpeggio in dotted rhythms that has served as the kernel of the movement. Its effect is imposing, invoking the austerity of "Haydn's Handel," albeit in his own harmonic language of the American period (Example 4b). Importantly, as an example of heuristic imitation, Martinů once more bridges the temporal gap between his model and himself, but the route is an internal one, reenacting the artistic journey through his own ears.

Example 4b. Continued

Where we arrive at the opening of the Sinfonia Concertante's final movement is a truly remarkable place. In many ways, it stands for Martinů's dialectic engagement with the past—his own as well as others', a challenge to what has come before and to assumptions we make about his "lighter" concertante works. While many passages of this piece demonstrate Martinů's ability to achieve energetic momentum (the anapestic ostinato of the first movement; the magisterial power of the slow movement's third variation), nothing quite matches the relentless drive of the entire Poco allegro finale. The greater presence of the two horns adds depth to the sound, and the orchestra interacts with the soloists generally to a much higher degree than in previous movements, forming a complex, multi-layered texture reminiscent of Martinů's symphonies. To be sure, the concertino still receives episodic quartet solos, but oftentimes they blend into the orchestra in a manner reminiscent of a "concerto for orchestra." The melodic content of this movement—and indeed, the entire Sinfonia Concertante No. 2—is clearly grounded in the organic developmental technique of Martinů's later style: its basic kernels, which the composer named *buňky* (cells), have been extensively described by Michael Crump and many others.[34] The use of *buňky* throughout the Poco allegro transcends the bounds of the rondo form set out by the alternation of tutti and soli, emerging as a free-flowing fantasia.

It only remains to consider in what way such a movement, or its compositional style, might be considered "dialectic imitation." We might say that Martinů's symphonic style of the 1940s confronts the lightness of his Parisian works around 1930, or that the more modern his harmonic language became, the greater the disparity it provoked with his purported historical models. An even broader abstraction would be to conclude that in this finale, Martinů uses the very nomenclature of the symphonie concertante genre against itself, wherein concertante soloists blend inevitably back into the symphonic texture. But to do so would be to ignore the important through-lines in Martinů's artistic life, system of beliefs, and compositional outcomes. Neoclassicism was not a mere phase of his career, nor was it, as Taruskin once wrote, "a tendentious journey back to where we had never been."[35] Rather, it was a continuous journey back (and forth) to where Martinů had already been, many times before.

NOTES

1. Scott Messing, *Neoclassicism in Music: From the Genesis of the Concept Through the Schoenberg/Stravinsky Polemic* (Ann Arbor: UMI Research Press, 1988); Richard Taruskin, "Review: Back to Whom? Neoclassicism as Ideology," *19th-Century Music* 16/3 (Spring 1993): 286–302. All translations in this document are my own unless indicated.

2. Hereafter, I use the term "concertante" not in the broad sense as an adjective for all concertos, but in its narrow sense, denoting a work for multiple soloists with some type of orchestral accompaniment. See discussion in Barry S. Brook and Jean Gribenski, "Symphonie concertante," *Grove Music Online*, 2001. See also https://doi-org.wiulibraries.idm.oclc.org/10.1093/gmo/9781561592630.article.27252.

3. Martha M. Hyde, "Neoclassic and Anachronistic Impulses in Twentieth-Century Music," *Music Theory Spectrum* 18/2 (Autumn 1996): 200–235.

4. Ibid., 205. Hyde in turn bases her definition of anachronism on Thomas Greene: "The type of anachronism most relevant to a neoclassic aesthetic is one that 'confronts and uses the conflict of period styles self-consciously and creatively to dramatize the itinerary, the diachronic passage out of the remote past into the emergent present.'" Thomas Greene, "History and Anachronism," in *The Vulnerable Text: Essays on Renaissance Literature* (New York: Columbia University Press, 1986), 221.

5. Hyde, "Neoclassic and Anachronistic Impulses," 200.

6. Bohuslav Martinů to Victor and Georges Desarzens, 30 October 1937, Bohuslav Martinů Institute, Prague, shelfmark Des 1937-10-30. https://database.martinu.cz/mails/public_view/1130.

7. Emphasis in the original. Bohuslav Martinů to Victor and Georges Desarzens, 30 November 1937, Bohuslav Martinů Institute, Prague, shelfmark Des 1937-11-30. https://database.martinu.cz/mails/public_view/1133

8. Miloš Šafránek, *Bohuslav Martinů: His Life and Works*, trans. Roberta Finlayson-Samsourová (London: Allan Wingate, 1962), 133–34.

9. Together with Martinů and Tibor Harsányi, these composers formed a collegial circle of émigrés occasionally described as the "École de Paris"; recent scholarship, however, has shown the École de Paris label to be a construct by postwar musicologists. See Federico Lazzaro, *Écoles de Paris en Musique, 1920–1950: Identités, Nationalisme, Cosmopolitisme* (Paris: Librairie Philosophique J. Vrin, 2018), 31–41.

10. Hyde, "Neoclassic and Anachronistic Impulses," 206, 210.

11. Hyde allows for a certain amount of divergence within the reverential model: her example is Ravel's "Forlane" from *Le tombeau de Couperin.*

12. Hyde, "Neoclassic and Anachronistic Impulses," 211. Hyde's example is Stravinsky's *Octuor.*

13. See Michael Crump, *Martinů and the Symphony* (London: Toccata Press, 2010), 79–87, 95–97.

14. Hyde, "Neoclassic and Anachronistic Impulses," 222. Hyde's example is Schoenberg's Third String Quartet and its relationship to Schubert's *Rosamunde* Quartet.

15. Thomas D. Svatoš, *Martinů's Subliminal States: A Study of the Composer's Writings and Reception, with a Translation of His American Diaries* (Rochester, NY: University of Rochester Press, 2018), 41–43. Svatoš's "*Werkgruppe*" periodization collates Martinů's remarks from his 1941 *Autobiography* and two other sources.

16. "Abych řekl pravdu, jsem typ Concerta grossa. O této formě naleznete povrchní popis skoro ve všech učebnicích, snad [nic] kromě toho, že se zde soli a orchestr střídají. Ale ve skutečnosti jde věc hlouběji. Celá struktura této formy ukazuje na zcela rozdílné chápání, rozdílný postoj k problému. Tam, kde forma symfonie nechává, vlastně vyžaduje uplatnění emocionálních elementů, často i v jejich nejromantičtějším pochopení a vyjádření, kde dynamické vrcholy a katharse jsou podmíněny, kde můžete svá themata rozpínati do nekonečných dimensí i na újmu organického pořádku, tam vám forma Concerta grossa dovoluje striktní pořádek, omezení, vyrovnání emocionálních prvků, omezení i adequátní vyrovnání gradace i dynamiky, zcela jinou a přísnou strukturu thematického uspořádání, zkrátka zcela jiný svět." Bohuslav Martinů, "1938–1945," Tempo—Listy Hudební matice 18/2–3 (30 July 1946): 58; reprinted in Miloš Šafránek, ed., *Domov, hudba a svět* (Prague: Státní hudební vydavatelství, 1966), 340-41.

17. Ibid., 341. Martinů uses the English phrase "ideal type" in his original: "Koncert pro dva klavíry je 'ideal type' pro tuto formu."

18. Miloš Šafránek, *Bohuslav Martinů: The Man and His Music* (New York: Alfred A. Knopf, 1944).

19. Šafránek, *Domov, hudba a svět*, 276. Martinů's original French text was corrected in an unknown hand, and I have followed these amendments in the translation given of this quotation. Bohuslav Martinů to Serge Koussevitzky, n.d., Bohuslav Martinů Center in Polička, shelfmark MarBo 0000-00-00p_06m and MarBo 0000-00-00p_07m. https://database.martinu.cz/mails/public_view/3589. Emphasis mine.

20. Svatoš, *Martinů's Subliminal States*, 44.

21. Ibid., 45.

22. Ibid., 51.

23. "Z mých oblíbených autoru [*sic*] je a vždy byl na prvním místě Mozart. [S] ním jsem vlastně podnikal největší boje, ve snaze přiblížit se té dokonalosti a tomu vyvážení, přirozenému a organickému i obsahovému. Také určitá zdrženlivost, nevybuchnouti, ovládati zkrátka pořádek." Bohuslav Martinů to Václav Štěpán, 16 February 1935, Bohuslav Martinů Institute, Prague, shelfmark ŠtěVá 1935-02-16. https://database.martinu.cz/mails/public_view/3585. Emphasis in original.

24. Brook and Grabenski, "Symphonie concertante," *Grove Music Online*, 2001.

25. Boris de Schloezer, "Le culte de Mozart," *Esprit* 2/22 (1 July 1934): 648–51.

26. René Dumesnil, "Mme Octave Homberg et la Société d'études mozartiennes," *Le monde*, 2 October 1956. Mme Homberg was born Jeanne Boudreau (1884–1946); Jaroslav Mihule erroneously states that the 1930 Société was founded by Georges de Saint-Foix, who had in fact co-founded its previous incarnation, la Société Mozart (1901–1903) with Théodore de Wyzewa and Adolphe Boschot. See Jaroslav Mihule, *Martinů: Osud skladatele* (Prague: Karolinum, 2017), 192.

27. A. Lahure, ed., *Bulletin No. 1, 1930–1932* (Paris: Société d'études mozartiennes, 1932).

28. The dedication does not appear in the 1949 Melantrich publication. Nevertheless, we can presume that Martinů knew this work in the 1930s, based on his anecdote concerning the origin of H 322 and his ability to distinguish between Mozart's and Haydn's Sinfonie concertanti.

29. Hyde, "Neoclassic and Anachronistic Impulses," 214.

30. Brook and Grabenski, "Symphonie concertante," *Grove Music Online*, 2001.

31. Based on the reference to the Munch recording later in the quotation, Šafránek concludes that the performance Martinů attended was much earlier—in 1930 at the Société des Concerts du Conservatoire. He further states that "I recall the name of Haydn coming up in our talks about *Symphonic Fantasias* (the *Sixth Symphony*)." Šafránek, *Bohuslav Martinů: His Life and Works*, 262.

32. Martinů freely mixed English and French in this letter. Bohuslav Martinů to Paul Sacher, 14 September 1950, Bohuslav Martinů Institute, Prague, shelfmark Sac 1950-09-14. https://database.martinu.cz/mails/public_view/2998. Emphasis in original.

33. Ibid.: "la joie et cette humble attitude sans prétention, la preuve du simple et great man."

34. Crump, *Martinů and the Symphony*, 101–26.

35. Taruskin, "Back to Whom," 287.

"I changed practically nothing": Bohuslav Martinů's Collaboration on *La Revue de cuisine*

ALEŠ BŘEZINA
TRANSLATED BY ADAM PRENTIS

There is no musical trend of the 1920s to 1940s in which Bohuslav Martinů did not participate in some significant manner. His oeuvre spans one-movement symphonic works with themes of technological modernism, elements of jazz, new music integrating early musical instruments (specifically the harpsichord), experiments with electronic instruments (Thereminvox), pre-Classical forms and means of thematic development, highly abstracted folklore, anti-illusionist operas, Surrealist echoes, 1940s symphonism, and so on. In most cases Martinů was not the first to pioneer a new direction, but is rather a perceptive and inquiring observer of the music scene, always ready to expand the array of techniques and genres at his disposal. His ability to fuse experimentation with his specific musical language makes Martinů one of the most intriguing and innovative composers of the twentieth century.

As an enthusiastic supporter of dance theater, Martinů was undoubtedly aware of the ballet revolution, most notably represented in the first quarter of the twentieth century by the Ballets Russes and its ingenious manager Serge Diaghilev. Although Martinů had seen them perform while still in Prague, he was especially impressed by their rendition of *Svadebka* (*The Wedding*), by Igor Stravinsky, which he saw soon after moving to Paris in 1923. Martinů was even considered for a commission from the famous company, on the recommendation of Paul Hindemith; the plan was dropped after Diaghilev's sudden death. Martinů later composed a ballet for the troupe, *Le jugement de Paris*, H 245, a libretto by Boris Kochno. However, that work was never performed and its score was lost—it survives only as several sketches at the Paul Sacher Foundation in Basel.

Until 2011, musicologists knew of only three ballets composed by Martinů in 1927. In autumn 2011 the manager of the National Theater Archives in Prague, Matěj Dočekal, discovered in the estate of Elizaveta Nikolska the incomplete performance materials for a previously unknown fourth ballet, titled *Ruce (Hands)*.[1] Although the four stage works differ distinctively, they also share a number of commonalities. One of them is a departure, both expressively and thematically, from the pathos of late Romanticism—featuring an admiration of the modern and the mundane that Czech scholarship terms "Civilism." The first one—*La Revue de cuisine* (*The Kitchen Revue*, H 161)—is an erotic morality play in a kitchen setting, featuring cooking and cleaning utensils; *Le Raid merveilleux* (*The Amazing Flight*, H 159) describes a tragic attempt to cross the ocean by plane; a third—*On tourne* (*Lights! Camera! Action!*, H 163)—is a report about the shooting of a film. The subject matter of *Hands*, H 157bis[2] has yet to be successfully reconstructed. The first two of these four ballets share an affinity for jazz, a strong favorite of Martinů and many of his Parisian contemporaries.

Only two of the four ballets were performed in the composer's lifetime—*Hands* and *The Kitchen Revue*. The other two were given their belated world premiere by the Brno dramaturge and conductor Václav Nosek, who also conducted the first recording of *The Amazing Flight*. One possible reason for the works' lack of success was that they appeared during a time of abrupt stylistic change, as the optimism of the Roaring Twenties gave way to a devastating economic crisis.

The Kitchen Revue

The one-act jazz ballet *The Kitchen Revue* was composed during Easter 1927. The initial impetus came from the dancer and choreographer Jarmila Kröschlová (1893–1983), who came up with the concept and wrote the libretto. The circumstances surrounding the genesis of one of the composer's most popular works can be reconstructed in detail, mainly thanks to three key documents donated to the Bohuslav Martinů Institute by the daughter of Jarmila Kröschlová in 2002. The documents in question are an autograph letter from Martinů to Kröschlová from 26 April 1927, an autograph letter from Miloš Šafránek to Kröschlová from 4 August 1955, and an autograph of "intermezzos" for the libretto by Jan Löwenbach.

Before commissioning a musical setting from Martinů, Jarmila Kröschlová used her libretto for an early German version of the ballet with a choreography accompanied by music on gramophone records. Barring a few details, the libretto matches the one she later provided to Martinů. Indirect evidence places the premiere of this early version of *The Kitchen Revue* in either Hellerau near Dresden or in Vienna in 1926, as *Die Küchenrevue*; markings in the extant libretto suggest that the music was provided by one pianist and two Black percussionists ("*zwei Jazz-Neger*"), who accompanied popular contemporary hits most likely reproduced by a gramophone. Some sections have a detailed rhythmic structure, others, such as the "Charlestontanz," only contain a verbal description: "*Während des Duells Jazz-Neger, jeder an einer Seite der Bühne, feuern das Duell an*" (During the duel Black jazzmen, each on one side of the stage, cheer on the duel). The ballet included short passages with recitation—see the section "Tango du rêve" and "Und der Topf?" (Figure 1).

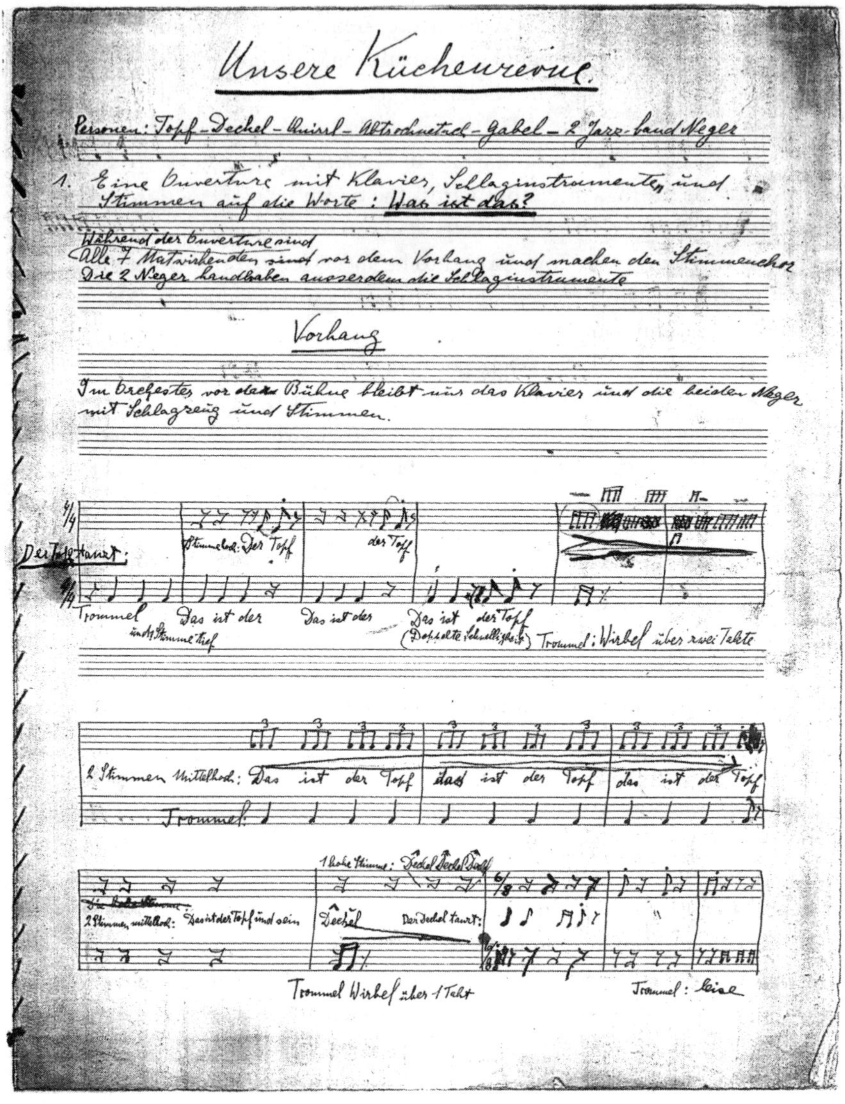

Figure 1. Sheet music of the German version of Kröschlová's ballet *Die Küchenrevue*, 1926.

The last three sections of this early version of the ballet are titled "Walentia" or "Valentia," most likely in reference to the hit song "La Valencia," a pasodoble from the zarzuela *La bien Amada* composed by José Padilla (1889–1960) in 1924.

The song was popularized in 1926 by the silent film *Valencia*, in a recording by Paul Whiteman, and went on to top the charts in America for eleven weeks beginning 30 March 1926.[3] It may be assumed that Jarmila Kröschlová's dance troupe used this very recording for their first performance. The exact instructions

Figure 2. Sheet music cover of *Valencia* by José Padilla.

provided to Martinů by Kröschlová are known thanks to a now-missing manuscript document published by the composer's biographer, Miloš Šafránek, that contains a description of the characters, a synopsis, and an outline all by Kröschlová,[4] as shown here:

Characters

Pot
Dish Towel
Broom
Lid
Twirl Whisk

Description of the Characters

Pot: Like a piece of scenery—it stands. It has openings in its belly for the actor's head and arms. The Pot is the only one to show emotion, not through motion but with words, facial expression.

Dish Towel: The nature of his movement and morality is mainly expressed by his spinelessness. He is utterly without endurance. Whenever he starts to show speed or strength or flexibility, he immediately slackens or collapses. The rhythm this creates can be either fast or slow, drawled or staccato, but mainly it changes frequently.

Broom: Shows strength without suppleness or flexibility. His spine is as if he had swallowed a ruler. All of his dance movements are in his feet and his feet only. His rhythm is mostly slow, very steady, and always the same.

Lid: Only moves in response to external impetus. The Lid is utterly passive. Her rhythm is in no way distinctive and not important to the music, nor does she have her own motive.

Twirl Whisk: She has no specific motive either. But she is very lively, mainly moving a lot from place to place, very rapidly and mostly in staccato. She is a source of provocation, constantly active.

Synopsis

The marriage of the Pot and the Lid is threatened by the change-loving Twirl Whisk. The Pot submits to her seduction. His inner being is so provoked that he knocks the Lid off himself; [she] rolls off into a corner somewhere. If it was not for the Broom, who desires order at all cost, the Dish Towel would seize the fateful moment and lure the Lid from her path of virtue, but the Broom does not allow it; he challenges the Dish Towel to a duel. The Twirl Whisk, who loves rush and commotion, is thrilled by the duel and inflames the passions of both contenders. In the blindness of battle, the Broom knocks into the Lid, who rolls off the proscenium somewhere. The fierce duel is concluded; the Broom has a broken leg and limps, the Dish Towel a broken arm that dangles helplessly. The Twirl Whisk turns back to the Pot to inflame him again, but the Pot has shaken off his infatuation and is calling for the Lid. The Lid is nowhere to be found.

The Pot is devastated, the Broom is devastated. The Broom searches all over for the Lid, but she cannot be found. They think she is lost for good; the Pot laments, when someone's enormous foot from in front of the proscenium kicks the Lid, who rolls back on to the stage. Much cheering. The Broom takes the Lid to the Pot; the Lid belongs to the Pot. The Twirl Whisk and the Dish Towel dance a merry dance together, with the Broom seconding and the Pot keeping time. Everyone is content: the Broom that he restored order, the Pot that he has his Lid, the Lid that she has her peace. The Dish Towel and the Twirl Whisk dance and dance and dance.

Outline

Curtain up.

1. *Spoken prologue*, in which the Pot-actor presents the players/ dancers to the audience. All with humor and wit. (Some 20 lines.)

2. *Musical introduction*, two-beat time signature, fast (1 minute). The dancers at their marks begin to move. They must warm up before the play begins.

3. *Dance of the Twirl Whisk Around the Pot* (2 minutes). The Twirl Whisk springs from her mark and flies to the Pot at top speed. She lures him with all of her spinning, leaping self. The Pot responds by showing his head; he follows the Twirl Whisk with his eyes and reaches out to her. The Twirl Whisk disappears.

4. *Dance of the Pot and the Lid* (1 minute). The Pot is flustered by the Twirl Whisk's disappearance. His arms and head show in swift, rhythmic gestures how he is boiling inside. The Pot becomes so impassioned that the Lid, who covers him on top, is shaken by his tremors, falls off and rolls away into a corner somewhere. In his agitation the Pot does not even notice. The Twirl Whisk reappears, takes the Lid's place with a leap, and makes herself comfortable.

5. *Love dance of two couples* (3 minutes)—the Dish Towel and the Lid, the Pot and the Twirl Whisk. A sentimental and passionate tango. The tango is written mainly for the Dish Towel, in consideration of his attributes and rhythm. The Dish Towel courts the Lid—he is passionate yet bland, bold yet ingratiating. The Lid hardly responds, but allows it all to happen. Throughout both of these dances, the Broom demonstrates his displeasure.

6. *Duel* (½ minute). A dance characterizing the Broom. The Broom can no longer endure such disorder and must vent his indignation. He challenges the Dish Towel to a duel. (Dance changes into a Charleston, 1 and ½ minutes).

The fighting is fierce, egged on by the change-loving Twirl Whisk. In the heat of the fight, the Broom knocks into the Lid, who rolls off somewhere in front of the proscenium. No one notices. When the duel is over, the Broom has a broken leg, the Dish Towel a broken arm. The fighting ends abruptly.

7. *Pause* (½ minute). In this musical intermission, the Pot rejects the Twirl Whisk and piteously calls to the Lid.

8. *Funeral march* (3 minutes). The Lid is lost, the Pot distraught. The Broom searches for the Lid everywhere. The Broom despairs as well. The Lid is gone, until someone's enormous foot hits the Lid, who rolls back onto the stage. The Pot welcomes her with a joyous shout.

9. *Boisterous dance* (1 minute). Everyone makes merry without restraint.

10. *Final dance*. Foxtrot or shimmy (3 minutes). The Broom and the Dish Towel bring the Lid to the Pot, followed by the Twirl Whisk. Everyone is in high spirits. The Pot is happy. The Broom is pleased with himself. The Twirl Whisk and the Dish Towel frolic playfully.

Curtain down, with the Dish Towel and the Twirl Whisk still dancing.

The ballet should be played and written with humor, certainly not seriously.

The Genesis of Martinů's Ballet Music

Bohuslav Martinů willingly obliged Jarmila Kröschlová's request to compose the music for *The Kitchen Revue*. One reason was that it was one of the first paid commissions he ever received. But of primary importance was that the required style of the work was a perfect match to his ongoing infatuation with jazz and technological modernism. Martinů expressed his opinions on jazz and its usage in Classical music in an article for *Dalibor* in the mid-1920s:

> The appearance of jazz in the postwar period is one of the demands of the current whim. . . . All of a sudden, elements of the jazz band are passing into symphonic music, in the manner of all previous forms. And through this creative process it constitutes a new form, like the polka back home. . . . If we take Stravinsky, who first used these forms, we see the way in which he manages the rhythmic dimension of the work, what is new in his creation, and how he stands above this rhythmic chaos. And so his music is dominated not only by the jazz band but, perhaps more so, by Slavonic rhythms.

> I often think of the amazingly evocative rhythm of our Slavonic songs, of Slovak songs, the characteristic rhythm of their instrumental accompaniment, and I feel we need not have recourse to the jazz band. Yet all the same I cannot deny its role in the general flow of life, which dictates all it needs for its expression.[5]

The composer's reply to Jarmila Kröschlová has been preserved, unlike the letter it was responding to:[6]

> I have completed the "revue" and am sending it enclosed. The performing forces are: clarinet, bassoon, trumpet, violin, cello, piano. As I wrote to you previously, I understand from your written synopsis that you have the concept of the dance fully worked out, and so I changed practically nothing and kept to the symbols you marked in the synopsis. I also sketched out a piano version of sorts into the score to make your work easier for you. But I must note that it cannot be regarded as a piano reduction, it is only a kind of outline to give you an initial idea of the music. The best would be if you heard it in the orchestra before rehearsals because much is expressed by the combination of instruments, the timbre of certain instruments, the overall sound and then the rhythm, which cannot be fitted into the piano reduction and which changes somewhat in the orchestra. Essentially therefore, and I emphasize this, the piece is written for six instruments, and no other arrangement will give you a clear idea, which you will see for yourself when you hear the sound of the orchestra. I hope you understand me. The overall flow is roughly as follows[:]
> No. 1 Overture was not detailed in the synopsis and so decide for yourself. Either the prologue starts already while the music plays or after the overture between nos. 1 and 2.
> No. 2 Musical introduction (Allegretto), abrupt crescendo, related metrically to
> No. 3 (dance of the Twirl Whisk), thus constituting a single musical number.
> No. 4 is a kind of intermission (dance of the Pot and the Lid), it opens into
> No. 5 Tango (love dance) which begins with the intermission and builds up to the duel (Charleston),
> No. 7 [is] an intermission and the Pot's lament, leading to
> No. 8 Funeral march, which leads with accelerando into
> No. 9 Scherzo and

> No. 10, which is more of a merry dance with the piano playing the rhythm and elements of the Charleston. The dance is more Czech in nature.
>
> So I think the formal structure is good and as far as the sound is concerned you need not worry, I hope you find the whole thing well suited to your dancing.
>
> Kindly confirm to me that the score arrived correctly by post. However, the score remains in my ownership because I have no copy. Let me know if you want to keep exclusive rights or if you give permission for possible performances elsewhere. Also tell me where and when you would stage the work. You will find certain remarks in places in the score. As I mentioned, I would much prefer if you heard the whole thing performed by an ensemble first, to give you an accurate idea of the music. Please respond to my question regarding the score and performances and how my conception suits you.

It is not known exactly when and how Martinů asked Jan Löwenbach to create the textual intermezzos that were already indicated by Jarmila Kröschlová in her outline. The extant autograph provides the following wording:

1. Prologue.
The Kitchen Revue begins!
What's in it, is still unclear.
It has a cast of five. More than enough.
I am Mr. Pot, master of the house.
Mrs. Lid here, my respectable wife.
This is Miss Twirl Whisk, a licentious modern seductress.
I'm a man in the best of my years: I've a hankering for a fling.
Just a glance at the Twirl Whisk's calves,
and that coquette lures me with lust.
It could have caused a marital calamity
if not for this here Broom, a proper friend of the family.
But my Lid is of a weak persuasion, for that very hour
she nearly lost herself with the Dish Towel,
if the terrible duel with the Broom
had not brought her to reason—and me in fact.
The details may be diverse,
but the morals are all unambiguous.
And now, musicians, attention! The revue begins!

4. The Pot is erotically aroused.
My heart burns!
My marriage crumbles!
Slim Twirl Whisk, you are mine!
And I a victim of your sinful appeal!

7. The Pot laments for his wife.
Where is the Lid.
My Lid, where are you, oh woe!
Come cover this gaping hole!

Alternative:
My Lid! My soul!
I've had it with that Twirl Whisk!
No never-ending twirls for me.
Warmth I want for my soul!
[My Lid! My soul!
Come cover this gaping hole!
We'll live in peace again!]

[Can be left out.]

8. The Pot rejoices in the Lid.
Praise god! What a crash!
My Lid! So polished!
Praise god on high,
I've been stoked well enough,
twirled quite perfectly.
I can sleep again now,
the Lid will hide my hole,
marriage makes me whole.

10. The Moral:
If you don't want your sinful physique
to go all flabby, you old fogey,
you mustn't want your Lid too much,
but have yourself a twirl instead
to lose the excess paunch,
then back to your Lid, you haunch.

Figure 3. Two dancers from the Jarmila Kröschlová Group put up a poster for the 1927–28 season featuring *The Kitchen Revue.*

Jarmila Kröschlová and her dance troupe premiered *The Kitchen Revue* in Prague on 17 November 1927. The first half of the program comprised Kröschlová's

Unnamed Number, a choreographed rendition of a polka by Bedřich Smetana, and *11 Childhood Scenes* by Felix Petyrek. The only male actor in the otherwise exclusively female cast of *The Kitchen Revue* was Miloš Nedbal, who played and spoke the role of the Pot. Unfortunately, no photos of the production have been preserved. The only image we have is a shot from Kröschlová's show *Scenes from the Big City* with music by Modest Musorgsky. In it, two dancers from her troupe are putting up a poster for the 1927–28 season, which shows *The Kitchen Revue* as one of the scheduled works (Figure 3).

Mirko Očadlík, a prominent conservative Czech critic and author of a number of studies on Bedřich Smetana, admitted certain qualities to Martinů's composition—"musically shape-shifting," "uses . . . the contrast in periodicity to achieve expressive value"—but described the work as a problematic experiment.[7]

A suite from *The Kitchen Revue* ballet enjoyed considerable popularity; it consisted of the Prologue, Tango (an exquisite parody of Ravel's *Bolero*), Charleston, and Finale. But in a review of the premiere of a concert performance in one of Alfred Cortot's Paris concerts in January 1930, Florent Schmitt, a prominent French composer of the older generation, dismissed the work for its supposed triviality: "As long as it's music, it's . . . politely received. But, with the Charleston, the Finale slides into triviality, vulgarity, shamelessness, obscenity, an infamy . . . that should suggest to its author the necessity of blushing."[8]

Eight years later, on the other hand, the critic Henry Prunières hailed it as a masterpiece: "*Revue de Cuisine* . . . [is] a masterpiece by a great musician who has remained too long in silence and obscurity. This time, he bursts in, covered in ornaments, wearing a bizarre mask . . . leav[ing] us stunned."[9]

The eminent Parisian publisher Leduc subsequently published not only *The Kitchen Revue* suite, but also *La bagarre*, as well as a number of Martinů's chamber, piano, and instrumental compositions.

A piano arrangement of the ballet suite, which Martinů prepared expressly for concert performances, is much less known. It is by no means a mere piano reduction of the ballet, but rather a full-fledged concert cycle. It was not recorded until 2008, when it was performed by Karel Košárek and released by Supraphon.

Martinů considered *The Kitchen Revue* one of his best works. To his closest American friend, Frank Rybka, Martinů wrote an enthusiastic description of his then thirty-seven-year-old work in a 1954 letter:

> It's already been put on records (Svoboda), but only for a small number subscribers and it would be good to record it again for the public, it will be a success. It's called Revue de cuisine and they recorded it in Paris for the company Concert – Hall. It's <u>wonderfully</u> recorded and if he [the cellist Diran Alexanian] asks he could get the same artists, all of them are in Paris (apart from the pianist

> Balsam) and all of them are first class, I would be happy if he could get them all together again, they play it with enormous gusto. . . . They gave me quite a talking to in Paris for it (it has a tango – charleston) and it's always being played somewhere, give that record a listen and you'll see that it's fine music, a joy from start to finish.[10]

And yet another four years later, he mentioned in a letter to his biographer Miloš Šafránek how "the infallible technical aspect of constructing the score of The Kitchen Revue, despite effectively having no specific technique as yet. . . . That is exactly how the work, when it is clearly formed in the mind or expresses the composer's character, itself creates the technique."[11]

Although *The Kitchen Revue* is one of the composer's most successful compositions, it was never performed in full except for the premiere; rather it was performed only as a suite. The score of the complete ballet lay unnoticed in the archives of the Paul Sacher Stiftung in Basel for decades. Finally in the early 1990s I brought attention to it in my *Catalogue of Manuscripts of B. Martinů Deposited at the Paul Sacher Foundation.*[12] The original score was reconstructed and prepared for a revised edition by Christopher Hogwood in cooperation with myself and the Bohuslav Martinů Institute. The 2004 edition—and corresponding Supraphon recording with Christopher Hogwood and members of the Czech Philharmonic—included both interludes and the funeral march (which together extended the duration of the previously known music by roughly one-quarter) and thus returned Jarmila Kröschlová and Bohuslav Martinů's work to its original form from 1927.

NOTES

This text was written within the project GA21-21228S Bohuslav Martinů's Music Theatre 1913–1937. Processing and publication of a monograph with critical edition by the Grant Agency of the Czech Republic (GAČR), Bohuslav Martinů Institute Prague.

1. See Aleš Březina, "'I Have Never Written Anything to Březina's Hands': A Newly Discovered Bohuslav Martinů Ballet," *Martinů Revue* 12/3 (2011): 8–9. See also Kateřina Lahodová, "Brněnský balet 30. let 20. století" (MA thesis, Masaryk University, 2011), http://is.muni.cz/th/217442/ff_m/Brnensky_balet_-_30._leta.txt. Translated from Czech: "Expressive dance basically became the requirement of the time. Classically trained dancers rejected it at first, speaking of it as a dilettante form that needs no technique. However, this antipathy toward new aesthetic perceptions gradually weakened, and many classically educated choreographers opened up to the influence of modern styles and even expanded the repertoire of ballet movements with new elements of their own design. Notable choreographers of this cohort in Czechoslovakia include Joe Jenčík, Saša Machov, Zora Šemberová, Nina Jirsíková, Eva Vrchlická Jr, Zdena Podhajská, Růžena Gottliebová, or Elizaveta Nikolska, who staged a ballet adaptation of Otakar Březina's poem "Ruce" (Hands), set to music by Bohuslav Martinů, at the National Theater in Prague in 1933. It was a fusion of dance and poetry, a blend of classical and expressive dance, which the critics designated as Wigmanesque. Despite the

production's mixed reception, Nikolska's experiment testifies to the presence of new influences in the art of ballet." See also Ivana Kloubková, *Výrazový tanec v ČSR: Praha, Brno (1918–1945)* (Prague: SPN, 1989), 33.

2. The designation *bis* denotes compositions that were found after the publication of Harry Halbreich's catalogue of the works of of Bohuslav Martinů in 1968. As the catalogue is arranged chronologically, it was not possible to give these compositions completely new numbers. They have therefore been placed after the closest previous composition in time and distinguished from it by the suffix *bis* (and in the case of more findings of a similar nature by the suffix *ter*).

3. For the song "La Valencia," see http://en.wikipedia.org/wiki/Valencia.

4. The text here is reprinted from Miloš Šafránek, ed., *Divadlo Bohuslava Martinů* (Prague: Editio Supraphon, 1979), 159–62.

5. Miloš Šafránek, ed., *Domov, hudba a svět* (Prague: Státní hudební vydavatelství, 1966), 46–49. Original in Czech.

6. Martinů to Jarmila Kröschlová, Paris, 26 April 1927. The letter is now housed at the Bohuslav Martinů Center in Polička. Original in Czech. A digitized copy of the letter can be found in Bohuslav Martinů Institute, Prague, shelfmark Krö 1927-04-26, https://database.martinu.cz/mails/public_view/1670.

7. "Martinů využívá svého silně vyvinutého visuálního smyslu k hodnotám hudebně tvárným.... Smysl pro symetrii výtvarné linie přechází u něho v symetrii hudební, v přesnou, předem určenou formu, která využívá jen kontrastu v periodicitě, aby dosáhla výrazové hodnoty. . . . Dílko tohoto druhu, jako je 'Kuchyňská revue,' mělo by však problém, který je nadhozen daným experimentem, vyřešiti i po všech ostatních stránkách." Mirko Očadlík, *Tempo* 7/3–4 (1927–28): 134.

8. Original French: "Et jusqu'alors, tant que c'est de la musique, ce n'est que poliment accueilli. Mais, avec le *Charleston*, le *Finale*, qui, d'échelon en échelon, glissent à une trivialité, une vulgarité, une bassesse, une obscénité, une infamie dont il faut bien suggérer à l'auteur l'idée de rougir[,] le succès devient de la sauvagerie." Florent Schmitt, *Le Temps* 70/25007 (8 February 1930): 3.

9. Original French: "*Revue de Cuisine* de Martinu . . . [c'est] un chef-d'œuvre d'un grand musicien qui reste trop longtemps dans le silence et l'obscurité. Cette fois, il fait irruption, couvert d'oripeaux, avec un masque bizarre . . . il nous laisse stupéfaits." Henry Prunières, "Concert de la Revue musicale (11 mars 1938)," *La revue musicale* 19/182 (11 March 1938): 219–20.

10. Martinů to Frank Rybka, [Nice] 9 March 1954. A digitized copy of the letter can be found in the Martinů Institute, Prague, shelfmark Ryb 1954-03-09, https://database.martinu.cz/mails/public_view/1455. Quoted after Jana Honzíková and Vít Zouhar, eds., *Dear Frank (I.): Bohuslav Martinů's Letters to Frank Rybka from 1941 to 1954* (Olomouc: Univerzita Palackého v Olomouci, 2023), 1:364ff. Translation by Thomas Prentis.

11. In Czech: "Jsem myslel hlavne na skoro neomylnou technickou stranku polozeni partitury ackoliv jsem effektivně zvlastni techniku dosud neměl. To je prave to jak dilo kdyz uz je jasne v mozku a nebo vyjadrujici charakter skladatele si tu techniku vytvori samo." Martinů to Miloš Šafránek, [Schönenberg – Pratteln], 24 April 1958. A digitized copy of the letter can be found in the Bohuslav Martinů Institute, Prague, shelfmark ŠafM 1958-04-25, https://database.martinu.cz/mails/public_view/2750.

12. Aleš Březina, "Die Martinů-Manuskripte in der Paul Sacher Stiftung Basel," in *Schweizer Jahrbuch für Musikwissenschaft*, new series, Nos. 13–14, ed. Joseph Willimann (Bern, Stuttgart, Vienna: Paul Haupt, 1994), 157–274.

Part III. Escapes and Arrivals

Martinů, Benjamin, and the Changing Experience of Historical Time

AXEL KÖRNER

On 10 June 1940 the Moravian-born pianist Rudolf Firkušný informed Bohuslav Martinů that he was about to flee Paris to escape the advancing German army.[1] Firkušný strongly recommended Martinů to do the same: the composer's connection to the Czech resistance in Paris left no other choice; and for months the Martinůs had experienced the increasingly frequent air raids terrorizing Paris.[2] Together with his wife, the composer left the following day, 11 June 1940, taking nothing but a small suitcase, leaving most of his musical manuscripts behind. After spending hours at the overcrowded Gare d'Orsay, it was by pure chance that they caught a train to Limoges, and from there the French conductor Charles Munch arranged shelter in Rancon, in the Haute Vienne.

As Martinů later remembered, "This was a moment of provisional calm, but not for long. The Germans were soon in Bordeaux and almost next to us."[3] So the couple headed for Cauterets, south of Lourdes in the Pyrenees, then east to Aix-en-Provence, to be closer to Marseille. Again, for a short moment Martinů felt a little freer: "How much time I spent at the splendid University library, as if I wanted to gain back all the lost hours and days! . . . Here I started work again, despite considerable shortages of nutrition and a crude cold, forcing me to work with gloves and a winter coat."[4] This moment of peace did not last. They returned west to Montpellier, waiting for an opportunity to cross the Spanish border and to make their way to Lisbon. From there they were hoping to leave for the United States. As Martinů's wife, Charlotte, later remembered, between leaving Paris and their arrival in New York they "slept in at least forty different beds, frequently on the barren benches of a waiting room or in a railway coach."[5] Time seemed to have stopped—"hours dragging on without end"—despite the constant movement.[6]

During those weeks, the main reason for their odyssey was bureaucracy: to emigrate they first had to follow an endless trail paved with paperwork, leaving them with a feeling of despair and impotence. Neither of them knew whether they would make their journey across the Iberian Peninsula. The misery with which the Martinůs lived this experience is well known from autobiographical

Figure 1. Martinů and Rudolf Firkušný at the piano, Marseille 1940.

sources; and most biographies of Martinů, starting with Miloš Šafránek's, report the composer's distress, his feeling of living in a vacuum where time had stopped, where agency no longer seemed to have an effect on their present or future. Hundreds and thousands of refugees shared the Martinůs' fate of waiting for a visa to cross the border into Spain to escape the Germans, Vichy France, and Nazi dictatorship. As Martinů later recalled, "Among these thousands and thousands of refugees I found nothing but cluelessness and desperation, which left a heavy impact on me."[7] Making similar observations, Alban Berg's biographer Soma Morgenstern reports that the Cannebière, the famous street in the old quarter of Marseille, was perhaps "the noisiest street of the world, where at the time one could hear so much German being spoken that one could still think to be in the camps."[8] Similar to most German speakers in southern France at the time, Morgenstern had just escaped an internment camp in the Finistère, in Bretagne.

On the Cannebière, Morgenstern could have easily met Madame Martinů, who was then trying to arrange the paperwork for her husband (it seems that as a foreigner, the composer was initially not allowed to travel to Marseille from nearby Aix, only later using the electric tram to Marseille on a regular basis). Instead of meeting the Martinůs, however, Morgenstern ran into another refugee, his old friend Walter Benjamin. Among the better-known Germans forced into French exile after 1933, Benjamin faced insurmountable administrative hurdles when trying to escape the Nazis. He knew that the collaboration settlement reached between Nazi Germany and Vichy France included a clause that obliged France to hand over any opponents of the Nazi regime to the German authorities. Disappointment over France ran deep among the victims. As Victor Klemperer recorded in a diary entry of 9 July 1941: "My idea of Germany was lost long ago, and now France! As if it were Czechoslovakia or a small state in the Balkans. First giving up militarily: Two million surrender, Metz is captured by a handful, Belfort does not defend itself at all, whole stretches of the Maginot Line, the same. And now they are convening a general assembly, in order to make their constitution 'totalitarian,' are fighting against England, which they had already harmed by accepting the conditions of the armistice, threaten death for anyone who as a Frenchmen goes on fighting in the English army, turn themselves into a German protectorate. What is left of my idea of France?"[9]

Together with his sister, Benjamin had left Paris on 13 June, just two days after Martinů, and a day before the German Wehrmacht entered the capital with orders to arrest him at his flat. First staying in Lourdes, not far from Martinů, Benjamin then moved on to Marseille, where he eventually obtained a travel visa to the United States that Max Horkheimer had negotiated for him; but he still lacked papers that would allow him to leave France. Like Martinů, Benjamin planned to reach the States from neutral Portugal, which he hoped to reach via Spain, and not via Africa, as numerous other refugees did.

In addition to having to find the financial means for his extended stay, Benjamin was in desperate need of a valid passport. In order to renew his German passport he had to hide his status as a registered refugee in France, but he also needed the approval of the Gestapo in Berlin. When the passport eventually arrived, he was afraid of collecting it from the consulate out of fear of being reported, while also worrying that a foreign document might prevent him from obtaining French citizenship. Being officially registered as a foreign refugee, he was also hoping to obtain French citizenship, although under the Vichy government this had become increasingly unlikely.[10] At some point Benjamin even considered applying for a Czech passport, though he then feared the Spanish or Portuguese authorities might discover the fraud.[11] Even after the creation of the protectorate, the former Czechoslovakian institutions in Marseille, and especially consul Vladimír Vochoč, continued to help foreign refugees, including Alma Mahler and Franz Werfel, Heinrich and Nelly Mann, and Walter Mehring.[12] Lisa Fittko, who eventually would help Benjamin cross the border into Spain, was another refugee who received a Czech passport through Vochoč. Martinů, however, left a far more critical account of the Czech consulate's activities: "We soon came to know that our consulate had no special interest in saving cultural workers (I don't speak about myself) and this bitter realization did not improve our spirits."[13]

As for Benjamin, he desperately needed that French exit visa.[14] As Morgenstern reports: "What was the recurrent theme in Marseille? Visa. Spanish visa. Portuguese visa. Exit visa. Each of us had one or the other, or several. But one outlived the other, while waiting for the French exit visa, which never came."[15] Charlotte Martinů describes the situation in almost the same words: "We got our American visa. Paul Sacher paid our ticket for an American steamer. This seemed to be in order, but the chain of permits, approvals, and stamps was never-ending. The two of us faced different difficulties, had different forms to fill in, different stamps to obtain and different obstacles to solve. One had to have a permit to leave France. Bohuš went to ask for this at an office that worked only for foreigners, I for my part had to go to an office just for the French. . . . Our steamer was supposed to leave Lisbon on 25 December. But a zealous bureaucrat of the Vichy government probably saw our departure unfavorably and so we did not receive the exit visa, and the steamer *Excambion* left Lisbon without us."[16] Martinů's own words add a note of anxiety to the description, "The postal service and the trains were not working, and I couldn't leave anyway, because everywhere you needed permission to leave or enter, permission to stay and so forth. This I obviously didn't have. In the meantime the German army was just a few kilometers away."[17]

For similar reasons, countless other writers, artists, and thinkers got stranded in southern France: Hannah Arendt, Lion Feuchtwanger, Albert Hirschman(n), Siegfried Kracauer, Heinrich Mann, Anna Seghers, Franz Werfel, and many more. Many of them, including Morgenstern, were repeatedly arrested when trying to cross the border without papers, and sent back into Vichy France.[18] "It was said that for a certain number it was possible to cross the border without a visa," Martinů later remembered; but the majority of refugees had exhausted those means many months ago.[19] As a consequence, seeking a solution in suicide was a recurrent theme among these desperate refugees.[20] Thanks to his French wife, and the considerable efforts of his friends and colleagues, Martinů eventually managed to get his paperwork in order.

Benjamin, however, crossed the border without regular papers. Led by Fittko, he decided to join a nine-hour food march via the mountains, with little to eat and drink, but a heavy case containing his last, later lost manuscript.[21] Arriving at Portbou, the group reported to the Spanish police, only to be confronted with the apparent irregularities in their paperwork.[22] Just days before, the Franco government had decided to cancel the transit visas of any refugees who did not carry a regular passport. Seeing no alternative but being sent back to France or being incarcerated in Francoist Spain, on 25 September 1940 Benjamin decided to take an overdose of morphine, which he had previously received from friends. He died the following day, just before the other members of his group learned that they would be free to continue their journey.

Throughout the 1930s, and until the late summer of 1940, Benjamin and Martinů frequently sojourned in the same place, but it is not known if they ever met, not during the years they spent in Paris, nor later in southern France, while waiting to escape to Lisbon and New York. This is despite the fact that Martinů had always been a keen reader, including of philosophical and scientific literature, and later even developed an interest in the thinkers of the Frankfurt School.[23] This lost opportunity notwithstanding, the parallels between the ways both men experienced their situation are striking. To the considerable distress of both, they had to leave many of their most precious possessions behind, in different locations and with various friends. In the case of Benjamin this meant several key manuscripts he was working on, including a copy of the *Arcades Project* which his friend, the philosopher Georges Bataille, hid in various places at the Bibliothèque nationale, as well as a copy of *Über den Begriff der Geschichte* (*On the Concept of History*), which Bataille passed on to Hannah Arendt.[24] Benjamin articulated to Gretel Adorno his worries over the fate of his papers: "What saddens me the most is the fate of my manuscripts";[25] and in a letter to Theodor W. Adorno, written from Lourdes in August 1940, Benjamin speaks "of my total uncertainty regarding the whereabouts of my works."[26] Lisa Fittko, as well as other members of her group, commented on the severely sick Benjamin carrying a heavy black case across the mountains, despite the suspected heart attack he might have suffered during the hike. His case contained a manuscript about which he reportedly cared more about than his health. Lost after his suicide, it was never clearly identified.[27]

As for Martinů, he had to leave behind the majority of his musical manuscripts, as well as printed versions of his works, in different apartments and with various friends and acquaintances in Paris. "Our only luggage was a small hand suitcase," Martinů reported.[28] He shared with Miloš Šafránek his worries about the whereabouts of his scores, and what do with his music during his flight across the mountains.[29] Shortly before leaving France, Martinů was finally able to report that "one of our friends brought from Paris my big trunk. . . . Like that I could take to America at least the score of the Double Concerto" (H 271), which would become his most frequently performed work—but paradoxically, only after the war.[30]

These examples show how artistic and philosophical production is closely intertwined with its own materiality, how the emergence of texts and music is determined by external factors, by physical and environmental conditions, but also by societal and political circumstances. These conditions and circumstances impacted the ideas behind their works, which in the case of Benjamin and Martinů often remained incomplete or were completed later on. These conditions also determine, directly or indirectly, future artistic and intellectual production that builds in complex ways on previous works and thoughts, even if in Benjamin's case the philosopher's life was cut short before his experiences and related material conditions could be fully reflected upon in subsequent works. As a consequence, meaning remains open to speculation, for which the controversies surrounding Benjamin's *Über den Begriff der Geschichte* provide a striking example.

Beyond the impact of material and circumstantial conditions on their respective intellectual and artistic development, what marked both Benjamin's and

Martinů's flight and exile was the experience of a dramatic change in the semantics of historical time, clearly evidenced in egodocuments relating to both men. Changing semantics of time determined a radically new philosophical orientation in Benjamin's thinking, and for Martinů they caused a deep consolidation of aesthetic and musical concepts that had first come to fruition during his last years in Paris and would characterize his compositional style for most of his remaining years in the United States. Due to the close interdependencies between time and sound, on which Hegel commented in his phenomenological studies on music,[31] I see both of these phenomena as closely connected: Benjamin's new philosophical orientation regarding the relationship between idealism and historical materialism, and Martinů's consolidation of stylistic parameters. In both cases these novel concepts were determined by a shared experience of time as crisis. Thus this essay, rather than comparing Benjamin's and Martinů's lives in exile, explores their experience of changing temporalities as a way to shed light on their resulting philosophical and aesthetic choices.

Experiencing Time

Remembering his experience, Martinů wrote: "It was as if time had stopped. Everything was melting under the touch of a hand, thoughts found neither response, nor support. They escaped into void, as if some kind of emptiness had opened into which humankind was sucked. Any last spark of hope seemed to be absorbed into this abyss. The purposelessness and futility of our doing crept into all consciousness. Everything I pursued, did, wrote, thought for my entire life seemed to have become meaningless. It was as if one wiped the chalk off a blackboard and what remained was just the black surface, with nothing on it and nothing that would be worth writing."[32]

In these powerful images Martinů eternalized the vacuum he felt after leaving Paris and having to wait months in the south of France for a passage to New York. A specific and novel notion of temporality characterized his consciousness during those months, clearly reflected in letters and autobiographical writings that record the self-perception of his experiences. Aware of the approaching German front, Martinů lived with a constant fear that time to cross the Atlantic might run out: "I cannot describe the strange psychological situation under which we all lived here. We did not perceive our feelings immediately, but just after a certain time. We took things as they came, without thinking, and without any mental awareness."[33]

Martinů later recorded his impressions of the years 1938 to 1945 in an article for the periodical *Malá knihovna Tempa*, published in 1947. While he emphasized the abstract psychological dimensions of his experience, his wife recorded the composer's suffering with more immediacy: "Dark clouds were gathering over Europe. . . . My husband's inner calm was shaken. He did not know what to do and felt as torn as his unhappy homeland."[34] He lost weight and suffered from a general

Figure 2. Martinů's ID, issued by the Czechoslovak Consulate in Marseille, autumn 1940.

sense of exhaustion.[35] The result was a complete lack of orientation: "We did not know what would become of us, where we would find a future."[36] The day after the outbreak of war Charlotte remembered as "full of tension, marked by fear of the future. . . . Martinů's Double Concerto for two string orchestras reflects . . . the oppressive atmosphere of that time, which lasted heavily over the whole of Europe. Paul Sacher then conducted the work in Basel in 1940. During the interval Arthur Honegger came to Martinů with tears in his eyes, embraced him, and asserted while hitting his own chest: 'This is tremendous, really tremendous.'"[37] Composing became increasingly difficult due to the couple's constant movement: "Every day that Martinů did not have a piano at his disposal, and was unable to compose, was wasted for him, sacrificed time."[38] When the Martinůs finally left France, after the composer had spent eighteen years in the country, he had lost the capacity of conceptualizing future time: "I don't think that I had any plans for the future."[39]

The parallels between Martinů's and Benjamin's description of the temporal vacuum that took hold of them seems most remarkable. "The complete uncertainty about what the next day, the next hour brings has been determining my existence for many weeks," Benjamin reported to Adorno in August 1940.[40] While on the one hand time seemed to stand still, on the other it seemed to run out. "My fear is that the time we have left could be much shorter than we thought," he wrote.[41] While Benjamin still wanted to talk about literature, his friend Morgenstern feared that we "might no longer be able to escape Marseille; with France all Europe will fall."[42] Had Benjamin given up the hope to survive, making exchanges on literature the only useful purpose of his remaining days? Benjamin took the prospect of leaving Europe with a great sense of unease, "to save oneself in New York in order to start a new life from the 20th or 30th floor of a skyscraper."[43] In the end, Benjamin never made it to New York. But Martinů's accounts frequently speak about how difficult the composer found life in the big cities of the United States, reporting his restless, nightly walks through the streets of the big city, the inappropriateness of American cafés for writing, reading, and thinking, all the things Benjamin and Martinů used to do in Paris.[44]

As with Martinů, Benjamin often struggled to retain his mental strength under the conditions of a fundamental fear for his life: "I hope that until now I gave you the impression that I remain composed also during difficult moments. Do not believe that this has changed, even if I cannot deny the dangerous character of this situation. I fear that one day those who will have been able to have saved themselves from this situation will not be many."[45] This feeling of despair had accumulated in Benjamin since the very first weeks of 1933: "The little composition with which people in my circles responded to the new regime evaporated quickly and one takes account of the fact that there is hardly any air left to breathe; a circumstance that now hardly matters, considering that we are strangled anyway."[46] In these words Benjamin described the situation to his friend Gershom Scholem as early as February 1933. Social isolation contributed to mental suffering, as he remarked to his son Stefan in August 1939: "I am saddened to hear that you are quite isolated among your contemporaries. This isolation belongs to the scourges, which Hitler and his socialist and Communist midwives have given the world."[47]

Descriptions of his declining health seemed to closely mirror Benjamin's feeling of breathlessness: "I notice only too well the extent to which my heart's capacity has become insufficient," he confessed to Gretel Adorno from Lourdes in July 1940, at a time when he had realized that his only option to escape would be crossing the Pyrenees by foot.[48] With time, it became impossible to transmit a sense of hope: "I am not in a position to lift your morale. Try not to lose hope," he wrote to Hilde Schröder in August.[49] In the end desperation won: "In a situation that can't be resolved, I have no choice other than putting an end to it. It is in a small village in the Pyrenees, where nobody knows me, that my life comes to an end," Benjamin explained to Henny Gurland on 25 September 1940.[50] It was his last letter, written after he had taken a deadly dose of morphine.

Theorizing Time

The personal accounts quoted above show how flight, exile, and existential fear caused both men to experience a profound change in the relationship between past, present, and future. In Koselleckian terms, the experience of the past no longer allowed them to designate a future.[51] In a situation of existential crisis, spaces of experience had become disconnected from horizons of expectation. This shift in the semantics of time left a decisive impact on Martinů's and Benjamin's respective creative processes, as well as on the theoretical, philosophical, and aesthetic foundations of their thought. They experienced time as crisis, a perception shared by many during those months.

Shortly before his suicide in 1942, Stefan Zweig described his experience of the present as the end of *The World of Yesterday* (to quote the title of his famous memoir).[52] One of the world's most successful writers, but also a refugee in Brazil, Zweig had lost hope for humankind. The present seemed disconnected from the past, leaving no future to hope for.[53] Others shared his perception. Around the same time, in an article titled "Denken und Leben" (Thinking and Living), Thomas Mann foretold the result of Hitler's victory on the battlefield in terms of a "Gestapo-world of general enslavement," without philosophy and democracy, without religion and morals, in short, "a moral catastrophe for humanity."[54] *Catastrophe* was also the word Charlotte Martinů associated with the couple's feelings regarding the political situation around Christmas 1939.[55] With his *Memorial to Lidice* (*Památník Lidicím*), H 296, Martinů would give the world an aesthetic response to the horrors of this world.[56]

We can find a more abstract description of time as crisis in Benedetto Croce's influential *Storia d'Europa*, written a decade earlier, in 1931, and dedicated to Thomas Mann.[57] In the book's epilogue, Croce warned against the unhistorical manipulation of time that he had witnessed for the past decade under Italy's fascist regime, which directed all human action toward the construction of a future that consciously broke with any notion of the past, where the present was no longer allowed to be nourished by what had come before. Benjamin, in his last manuscript of 1940, *Über den Begriff der Geschichte*, picked up Croce's thread of conceptual thinking about the future-oriented manipulation of historical time. Both thinkers had always been keen to identify the past in their own present, as documented in Benjamin's *Passagenwerk* or Croce's writings on Naples and its theaters. For Martinů, this idea of recognizing the past in the present informed his engagement with historical musical forms. After his 1923 move to Paris, when he had left Impressionism behind, and increasingly since the late 1930s, a creative engagement with the musical past came to form the material and philosophical basis of Martinů's compositions.

Benjamin's *Über den Begriff der Geschichte* describes historical materialism as a positivist illusion.[58] The historical materialist constructs his past and his future out of their contemporary present (including the promise of salvation). Within this manipulated process, past, present, and future lose their organic connection. To explain this dilemma, Benjamin refers to Paul Klee's colored monoprint *Angelus Novus*, which had been in his possession since 1921.[59] According to Benjamin, Klee's "angel of history" moves backwards, while staring at humanity's catastrophic past. In materialist conviction, humanity has assembled its past into a predetermined future. The storm of time, which we perceive as progress, blows the angel's wings open and pushes him into eternity, but in full view of humanity's catastrophe. According to Benjamin, the materialists' stubborn belief in time as progress is responsible for the current crisis. He denounces their conviction that the development of the productive forces will inevitably lead to socialism, an illusion that allowed the dominant classes to extend their power. Benjamin rejects the deterministic conviction of the inevitability of the revolution as a manipulation of historical time. This constellation paralyzes the working class and prevents it from acting in the present, giving the revolutionary future an aura of positive reality. According to Benjamin, this constructed reality is nothing but an illusion. Blinded by this illusion, and helplessly awaiting the realization of its manipulated future, humankind runs into its own catastrophe. This is the situation in which Benjamin found himself in the summer of 1940.

Benjamin's friend Gershom Scholem described *Über den Begriff der Geschichte* as Benjamin's "awakening from the shock of the Hitler-Stalin Pact"—a key political event that had triggered his new conceptualization of historical time.[60] After the German attack on Poland, the Hitler-Stalin Pact of August 1939 destroyed what was left of his hope in a socialist alternative for humankind, with dramatic consequences for his idea of the relationship between idealism and historical materialism.[61] As a Marxist, he had never been uncritical of Soviet Communism and of the strategies of the Communist parties in Europe. Now, however, he saw how the Hitler-Stalin Pact enabled fascism to expand across Europe, revealing the evil power behind both totalitarian ideologies. In both cases their power was based on the forced manipulation of historical time.

Aleš Březina has outlined how Martinů got in between the ideological front lines of the Age of Extremes, to employ British historian Eric Hobsbawm's phrase.[62] "Two ideologies," Březina argues, "attempted to exclude Martinů and many of his colleagues from musical life."[63] This pattern seems particularly striking when one looks at the performances of Martinů's music in Czechoslovakia, where during the German occupation from 1938 onward, and again after the Communist coup of 1948, his works almost disappeared from concert and theater programs, with just a short interval immediately following the close of World War II.[64] An example of the difficult communication across the Iron Curtain during the 1950s is Martinů's correspondence with Miloslav Bureš regarding their collaboration on the four cantatas *Opening of the Springs*, H 354, *The Legend of the Smoke from Potato Tops*, H 360, *A Dandelion Romance*, H 364, and *Mikesh from the Mountains*, H 375. The composer felt obliged in his letters to hide references to the events in Hungary in 1956 in order to circumvent censorship and not cause the poet problems.[65] Unlike Benjamin, however, Martinů was able to continue his work in the United States. In his case, the existential experience of time as crisis led him to aesthetic choices that would deeply mark his compositional output in exile.

For Martinů, the mental constraints associated with the weeks and months of suffering in southern France also made him realize the value of freedom, ultimately encouraging him to look for new avenues in his aesthetic work: "But a different value presented itself with ever more clarity, which previously we didn't consider, which we took for granted and as a given, and whose value we started to comprehend only now, when we were losing it: a sense of freedom [*pocit svobody*]. *Liberté*. Now we understood that it is not a given value, but that it had to be conquered. Personally, I had always paid for my freedom. But this was my small, private liberty. Now it was about freedom of spirit, freedom of humanity. And also another value, one of the basic human values, seemed to be falling under the pressure of events, and this was the value of conviction that determines all of our actions and the goal we set ourselves, or for which we were chosen: the human and artistic conviction, which probably is the same. There was no time for these. There was no time for anything, only the attempt to save bare life. But save—why? When we lose these two [values] what can we expect of life?"[66]

Despite the suffering of a life in exile, once Martinů arrived in the United States, he regained the mental capacity to compose, but also the liberty to do so without external obstacles.[67] His observations offer an important key to explain his stylistic development during those years, even if it had never been his intention to explain his works through words.[68]

Musical Past in the Present Tense

Central to Martinů's compositional output during his American years was his engagement with musical forms of the past. Sometimes misleadingly labeled neoclassicism, his engagement with the musical past understands the history of music as a continuum. This shows surprising parallels to Benjamin's and Croce's understanding of historical time, as well as to their rejection of the totalitarian manipulation of time and of any form of ideologically driven *antistoricismo*.[69] To Martinů the history of music offered a repertoire of aesthetic means, a past that lived on in the present, which he used as the material foundation of his poly-stylistic response to historical time. This aesthetic decision was consciously directed against an avant-garde that sought to produce a musical future without reference to its own past. The result was a historically informed plurality of styles that understood itself as modern, without falling victim to an ideology of progress.

During the mid-1920s and into the 1930s, Martinů's occasional engagement with neoclassicism stood alongside other novel forms of musical expression: new rhythmical approaches (*Half-time*, H 142), experiments with jazz (*Le jazz*, H 168, and *Jazz-Suite*, H 172), or trying out the limits of tonality (*La fantaisie*, H 180). During those years, the Impressionism of the early 1920s mostly disappeared from his work. These experiments resulted in a wide range of different genres: opera, ballet, chamber music, symphonic works. From 1938, however, his engagement with historical forms became the defining element of his style, reflected in his *Concerto grosso*, H 263, the *Tre ricercari*, H 267, the Concertino for Piano, H 269, and especially the above-mentioned Double Concerto for two orchestras, piano, and timpani, H 271, all composed in 1938. Corelli and Bach became central reference points.[70] These works formed the foundation of the composer's "classical style," which Harry Halbreich associates with Martinů's early years in the United States, characterized by "broad melodic bows" and a "newly found epical and lyrical calm."[71]

As Martinů later explained, his move across the Atlantic had accelerated his return to classical reference points,[72] and his interest in concerto forms and chamber music based on transparent harmonies and full strings. An obvious early example of this period is his Concerto da Camera for violin, strings, piano, and percussions, H 285, written in 1941. Concerto grosso elements are also present in his short Second Symphony, H 295, of 1943, exemplified by the dialogue between different groups of instruments. Although it has also been compared to Brahms's Second Symphony,[73] it was intended as a return to smaller dimensions, moving away from what the symphony had become since the closing decades of the nineteenth century.[74] In the same year, *Memorial to Lidice* was conceived even more explicitly as a concerto grosso. Its subject, the annihilation of an entire village by the Nazis, was directly related to Martinů's experience of time as crisis.[75]

Aleš Březina describes all Martinů symphonies as "a synthesis of his experiments of the concerto-grosso-trilogy," intended to revive an old form, while also overcoming the metaphysical ideas that had informed musical Romanticism.[76] All of them were written in the United States. Although Martinů's first interest in neoclassicism predates the composer's flight from Paris, it was in the United States that it became a conscious expression of experiencing time as crisis.

Beyond Czechness and Folklore

Martinů's idea of historical linearity, his universalist ambition and (as a consequence) his engagement with classical forms, make it difficult to reduce the composer's contribution to twentieth-century music to a vague notion of Czechness that found its expression in a return to local folklore.[77] The composer's opening toward the wider world, and his search for new forms of musical expression, was often viewed with suspicion in Czechoslovakia, even during the years of the First Republic,[78] when Martinů used the periodical press to voice his criticism of a too narrow understanding of nationalism in music.[79] As early as 1924, in an article for the Czech journal *Tribuna*, Martinů opined against "a return to Smetana" of contemporary Czech music.[80] The article might seem to contradict his passionate attempt, four years later, to interest French audiences in Smetana's *Prodaná nevěsta* (*The Bartered Bride*),[81] but the composer obviously followed a different agenda when introducing the French to Czech music.

As appealing as the image of the young Martinů growing up in his church tower in Polička might be, it does not equate with a composer who throughout his life experimented with different musical forms. While space as experienced from the church tower certainly marked Martinů's aesthetic concepts, the composer himself opined that viewed from the top, the streets in the little town seemed a space without potential bearers of a regional or national culture.[82] Moreover, populated not just by Czechs, but also by colonists from Silesia, Bavaria, and even Thuringia, Polička was a town with developing industrial activity, a long history of markets—in short, a sociocultural reality quite far removed from the idyllic place constructed in some of the conventional accounts of Martinů's life. When he moved to Prague, still an adolescent, he entered a modern, cosmopolitan metropolis. As for his musical experiences in the capital, the repertoire during those years was definitively international, mirrored in the composer's ballets of those years that played on models of Strauss and Debussy rather than on Czech folklore.

Works like the *Česká rapsodie* (*Czech Rhapsody*, H 118) of 1918 had an obvious patriotic connotation, even if the baritone Eugen Fuchs, who sang the solo part at the premiere, would later become known for his close involvement with the Nazi regime. But during subsequent years, when Martinů played in the Czech Philharmonic under Václav Talich, he mostly engaged with modern French composers, including Debussy, Ravel, Dukas, Roussel, alongside the Czech repertoire and Suk in particular. His ballet *Istar*, H 130, written during those years, was based on a Czech text by Julius Zeyer, but with a Sumerian plot, whereas his ballet *Kdo je na světě nejmocnější?* (*Who Is the Most Powerful in the World?*, H 133), was based on an English fairy tale, using modern dances like the Boston and foxtrot. Around the same time, he discovered the forms of the English madrigal, Palestrina, and Orlando di Lasso, works to which he would frequently return. Other influences that point beyond his love for the Czech-Moravian borderlands were his travels to Italy, the discovery of Italian city culture, then his move to Paris. According to Šafránek, rather than French Impressionism, what Martinů sought in France were "the real roots of Western culture, which he understood as closely related to Czech national character."[83] Martinů was keen to overcome any artificially constructed Czech Romanticism, which was to be replaced by an abstract, universalist musical idiom.[84]

Linked to this critical evaluation of the place of folklore and Czechness in Martinů's work is the recognition of the role of German culture in his development as a composer. The scholarly tradition of reading Czech and German music history as in essence antagonistic has made it difficult to recognize the German role.[85] In a letter to his mother from June 1929, Martinů describes his success in Berlin and the welcome he received in the German capital: an event usually ignored by research on the composer.[86] At the time, he stayed in Berlin for several weeks and also visited the seaside: "They were waiting for me to make my appearance. They were very kind to me and I have a lot of acquaintances there, they all assure me that things will be good for me in Germany, only I have to show myself there from time to time."[87] He maintained contacts in Leipzig, Baden-Baden, and Frankfurt am Main and returned to Berlin in mid-June 1930.

In letters of the years 1930–33 from Paris, Martinů regularly tells his family about his close connections to the German publisher Schott.[88] He wrote enthusiastically how the publisher promoted his work, despite difficult political and economic circumstances: "They are not paying too badly but they promise me more later on, and a permanent contract for a monthly salary."[89] At times his letters give the impression that being published in Germany, and by Schott, is one of his main objectives in seeking success.[90] His early enthusiasm for the First Republic does not stand in the way of keeping friendly relations with the German population in Prague. More importantly, he criticized the anti-German riots when the first sound films in German were screened in Prague: "It is really foolish to cause such commotion because of a film . . . it damaged us a lot, and artists especially."[91] The event was particularly noteworthy in the context of Prague's German press being favorably disposed toward Martinů. In 1931, he quoted, in German, an interview with Fritz Busch from the *Prager Presse*, where the German conductor praises Martinů, makes much of his apparent reputation in the United States, and describes his intention to have his work performed in Germany.[92]

Throughout these years, Martinů closely followed political and societal events in Germany.[93] A teleological reading of Martinů's support for the First Republic, and his concern over the German occupation of Czechoslovakia, should not stand in the way of recognizing the composer's close interests beyond the Czech lands, which forms an inherent part of his musical identity. Part of this was his interest in Bach and in particular Beethoven, which left an important mark on his first four symphonies.[94] During the 1930s, and on more than one occasion, the composer even quotes Wagner as an important influence on his aesthetic development.[95]

Reading Martinů beyond Czechness and local folklore or highlighting the role of his French and German connections is directly relevant to an assessment of the aesthetic decisions he took as a composer from the summer of 1940 onward. His creative exploration of historical musical forms reflected his universalist ambition, but also his critical engagement with the changing semantics of historical time. Accepting the musical past as an inspiration for his path into the musical future required a close engagement with Italian, English, French, and German musical traditions. Like Benjamin or Croce, Martinů relied on the continuous presence of the past as a way of approaching his musical future. In doing so, he rejected the manipulation of historical time that characterized the twentieth century's totalitarian ideologies. Although his earliest interest in historical musical forms dates back to the 1920s, it was the existential experience of time as crisis, during the difficult months of 1940 in southern France, that turned his historical curiosity into an aesthetic conviction.

NOTES

For advice and help with this chapter I am grateful to Aleš Březina and Michael Beckerman, as well as Lenka Körner Nahodilová, Quirin Lübke, and Eva Weissweiler. I owe a debt of gratitude to the late Mikael af Malmborg for the time we spent playing Martinů together.

1. For a chronology of the events, see Miloš Šafránek, *Bohuslav Martinů: Život a dílo* (Prague: Artia, 1961), 217–18. Aleš Březina has explained why Šafránek's biographical approach is not unproblematic in "Bohuslav Martinů: Der heutige Forschungsstand," *Österreichische Musikzeitschrift* 64 (November 2009): 5–13, at 7. For a personal account see Bohuslav Martinů, "1938–1945," in *Domov, hudba a svět*, ed. Miloš Šafránek (Prague: Státní hudební vydavatelství, 1966), 330–343. Also see Charlotte Martinů, *Ma vie avec Bohuslav Martinů* (typescript, Bohuslav Martinů Institute, Prague), 56. The original French version remained in typescript and in Charlotte Martinů's lifetime was published in three unauthorized translations in Czech, German, and English, languages she knew only partially, if at all. It was not until 2003 that a critical edition of the book was published in Czech, based on a thorough study of the French original: Charlotte Martinů, *Můj život s Bohuslavem Martinů*, from the French *Ma vie avec Bohuslav Martinů,* trans. Catherine Ébert-Zeminová, ed. Ludmila Sadílková and Aleš Březina (Prague: Editio Bärenreiter, 2003).

2. Aleš Březina, "Martinůs musikhistorischer Ort: Prolegomena zu einer problemorientierten Darstellung des Komponisten," in *Bohuslav Martinů*, ed. Ulrich Tadday, Musik-Konzepte NF (edition text+kritik), special issue (Munich: Richard Boorgerg, 2009), 5–23, 18; F. James Rybka, *Bohuslav Martinů: The Compulsion to Compose* (Lanham, MD: Scarecrow Press, 2011), 85–92.

3. "Byla to chvíle provizorního klidu, ale ne nadlouho. Němci byli brzy v Bordeaux a téměř okolo nás." Martinů, "1938–1945," 333–34. All English translations are by the author.

4. "Kolik času jsem strávil ve skvělé universitní knihovně, jako bych chtěl dohoniti všechny ty ztracené hodiny a dny! . . . Zde jsem začal zase pracovati přes značné obtíže výživy a přes krutou zimu, která mne donutila pracovati v rukavicích a zimníku." Ibid., 335.

5. "Nous avons couché dans au moins 40 lits différents. Quelque nuits, nous avons passé sur des durs bancs dans les gares." Martinů, *Ma vie avec Bohuslav Martinů*, 57.

6. "Les heures trainaient." Ibid.

7. "Našel jsem mezi tisíci a tisíci uprchlíky bezradnost a zoufalství, které na mne těžce působilo." Martinů, "1938–1945," 335.

8. "Vielleicht der lärmendsten Straße der Welt, wo man damals so viel deutsch hören konnte, als wäre man noch in einem Lager." Soma Morgenstern, "Aus Briefen an Gershom Scholem," in *Begegnungen mit Walter Benjamin,* ed. Erdmut Wizisla (Leipzig: Lehmstedt, 2015), 273–321, at 277. Soma Morgenstern's letters to Scholem, written decades later, have to be read with caution, as he reports on many issues following his own personal or intellectual agenda, especially regarding former communists and the later members of the Frankfurt School.

9. Viktor Klemperer, *I Will Bear Witness: The Nazi Years, 1933–1941*, trans. Martin Chalmers (New York: Modern Library, 1999), 347; originally published as *Ich will Zeugnis ablegen bis zum letzten: Tagebücher 1933–1941*, ed. Walter Nowojski (Berlin: Aufbau, 1995).

10. See Eva Weissweiler, *Villa Verde oder das Hotel in Sanremo: Das italienische Exil der Familie Benjamin* (Munich: btb, 2022), 146–47. On Benjamin's difficulties in obtaining his paperwork, see also Hannah Arendt, "Brief an Gershom Scholem, 1941," in *Begegnungen mit Walter Benjamin*, ed. Erdmut Wizisla (Leipzig: Lehmstedt, 2015), 322–27, at 326.

11. Morgenstern, "Aus Briefen an Gershom Scholem," 293.

12. Eva Weissweiler, *Lisa Fittko: Biographie einer Fluchthelferin* (Hamburg: Hoffmann und Campe, 2024), 211. See also Martinů, *Ma vie avec Bohuslav Martinů*, 69.

13. "Brzy jsme poznali, že náš konsulát nemá zvláštního zájmu na záchraně kulturních pracovníků (nemluvím jen o sobě) a toto trpké poznání samozřejmě nezlepšilo náladu." Martinů, "1938–1945," 336.

14. For a detailed report, see Walter Benjamin to Theodor W. Adorno, Lourdes, 2 August 1940 (No. 1372), in Walter Benjamin, *Gesammelte Briefe, 1938–1940*, ed. Christoph Gödde and Henri Lonitz (Frankfurt: Suhrkamp, 2000), 6:474–77, at 475. See also Benjamin to Hilde Schröder, Marseille, 22 August 1940 (No. 1375), in ibid., 480–81.

15. "Was war das ständige Thema in Marseille?: Visa. Spanisches Visum. Portugiesisches Visum. Ausreisevisum. Jeder von uns hatte schon das und jenes, und zwar mehrmals, gehabt. Aber eins überlebte das andere, alles in Erwartung eines französischen Ausreisevisums, das nicht kam." Morgenstern, "Aus Briefen an Gershom Scholem," 282. On the difficulty for foreign refugees to obtain an exit visa, see Weissweiler, *Lisa Fittko*, 207.

16. "On nous a accordé le visa américain. Paul Sacher nous a payé la place sur un bateau américain. Cela, alors, était en ordre, mais la chaine des permis, d'authorisations et d'estampilles ne prenait pas fin. Chacun de nous deux avait des difficultés différentes, de différents papiers à remplir, de différentes estampilles à obtenir et de différents obstacles à surmonter. On avait besoin d'un permis de sortie de France. Bohuš allait le chercher à un office fonctionnant seulement pour les étrangers, moi, au contraire, je devais me rendre à un office destiné pour les Français. . . . Notre bateau devait partir de Lisbonne le 25 décembre. Mais un buroviste zélé du gouvernement de Vichy regardait probablement notre départ d'un œil défavorable et nous n'avons pas reçu le visa de sortie et le bateau *Excambion* est parti de Lisbonne sans nous." Martinů, *Ma vie avec Bohuslav Martinů*, 62.

17. "Pošta ani vlaky nefungovaly a odejíti jsem stejně nemohl, protože všude bylo třeba propustky, dovolení vstupu, dovolení pobytu atd. To jsem ovšem neměl. Německá armáda zatím byla od nás jen pár kilometrů." Martinů, "1938–1945," 334.

18. Morgenstern, "Aus Briefen an Gershom Scholem," 275.

19. "Říkalo se, že je možno přejít hranice bez víza, samozřejmě za určitou částku." Martinů, "1938–1945," 334.

20. Arendt, "Brief an Gershom Scholem, 1941," 325. See also Morgenstern, "Aus Briefen an Gershom Scholem," 282, 285.

21. For a detailed description of the march, see Lisa Fittko, "Der alte Benjamin," in Wizisla, *Begegnungen mit Walter Benjamin*, 328–43. Descriptions, whether it rained or not, and how long it took, vary. See, for instance, Anon., "Bericht über einen Grenzübertritt von Frankreich nach Spanien," in ibid., 344–47. Also see the other eyewitness accounts in the same collection. For a recent account in English, see Howard Eiland and Michael W. Jennings, *Walter Benjamin: A Critical Life* (Cambridge, MA and London: Harvard University Press, 2014), 668–76.

22. There is a strong, Kafkaesque element to the unpredictability of bureaucratic hurdles the refugees faced before crossing the border into Spain, which both Martinů's and Benjamin's biographers describe as a key element of their desperation. Benjamin's ex-wife Dora, who continued to play a central role in helping him with administrative issues, was convinced that she could have prevented Benjamin from seeing suicide as the only solution to this nightmare. See Eva Weissweiler, *Das Echo deiner Frage: Dora and Walter Benjamin, Biographie einer Beziehung* (Hamburg: Hoffmann und Campe, 2020), 14.

23. On the impact of reading on his work as a composer, see Aleš Březina, "Von Experimenten, Synthesen, und definitiven Werken," in *Continuity of Change: Bohuslav Martinů in Twentieth-Century Music History*, ed. Aleš Březina and Ivana Rentsch (Bern: Peter Lang, 2010), 13–38. Martinů, in a letter to Šafránek, reported on his reading of Marcuse, alongside Marx and Hegel. Bohuslav Martinů to Miloš Šafránek, South Orleans, 30 July 1945 (No. 85). Vít Zouhar and Gabriela Coufalová, eds., *Dear Miloš: Bohuslav Martinů's Letters to Miloš Šafránek* (Olomouc: Univerzita Palackého v Olomouci, 2019), 275–77.

24. On the history of the text and the different manuscripts, see Gérard Raulet, "Entstehungs- und Publikationsgeschichte," in Walter Benjamin, *Über den Begriff der Geschichte*, in *Werke und Nachlaß: Kritische Gesamtausgabe* (Berlin: Suhrkamp, 2010), 19:161–208.

25. Benjamin to Gretel Adorno, Lourdes, 19 July 1940 (No. 180), in *Walter Benjamin–Gretel Adorno: Briefwechsel 1930–1940*, ed. Christoph Gödde and Henri Lonitz (Frankfurt: Suhrkamp, 2005), 413–14, at 413.

26. Benjamin to Theodor W. Adorno, Lourdes, 2 August 1940 (No. 1372), *Gesammelte Briefe, 1938–1940*, 6:474–77, at 475.

27. Fittko, "Der alte Benjamin," 332.

28. "Naše jediné zavazadlo byl malý ruční kufřík." Martinů, "1938–1945," 333.

29. Bohuslav Martinů to Miloš Šafránek, Aix en Provence, 13 September 1940 (No. 45); 20 September 1940 (No. 46); 1 December 1940 (No. 49). Zouhar and Coufalová, *Dear Miloš*, 167–69, 174–76, 189–90.

30. "Jedna z našich přítelkyň mi přivezla z Paříže moje velké zavazadlo. . . . Tak jsem mohl vzíti sebou do Ameriky alespoň jedinou partituru Double-concertu, které—úplně paradoxně—zde pak nikdy provedeno nebylo." Martinů, "1938–1945," 336.

31. While drawing a connection between Martinů and Hegel might seem farfetched, the composer himself wrote to Šafránek about his interest in the philosopher. Bohuslav Martinů to Miloš Šafránek, South Orleans, 30 July 1945 (No. 85). Zouhar and Coufalová, *Dear Miloš*, 275–77. Hegel's references to music are scattered across different works and include the correspondence with his wife. See in particular Georg Wilhelm Friedrich Hegel, *Ästhetik*, ed. Friedrich Bassenge (Berlin: Aufbau-Verlag, 1955), 72, 123, 806–7, 866. Also Hegel, "Aus Abend-Zeitung, 22.5.1829," in *Exzerpte und Notizen (1809–1831)*, in *Gesammelte Werke*, ed. Klaus Grotsch (Hamburg: Felix Meiner, 2013), 22:162. For a general discussion, see Wolfgang Welsch, "Warum hat Hegel Rossini so hoch geschätzt—während er Beethoven nicht einmal erwähnt?," in *Hegel und Italien—Italien und Hegel: Geistige Synergien von gestern und heute*, ed. Francesca Iannelli, Federico Vercellone, and Klaus Vieweg (Sesto San Giovanni: Mimesis, 2019), 247–68.

32. "Bylo to jako kdyby se čas zastavil. Vše mizelo pod dotekem ruky, myšlenky nenašly nikde ohlasu ani podpory. Unikaly někam do prázdna, jako by se otevřela nějaká prázdnota, do níž lidstvo bylo přitahováno. Poslední záblesky jakékoli naděje se zdály býti pohlceny touto propastí. Bezúčelnost a marnost všeho konání se vtírala do vědomí. Všechno, co jsem po celý život sledoval, dělal, psal, myslil, se zdálo býti bezpředmětné. Jako když na černé tabuli smažete křídu a zůstane jen ta černá plocha a nic na ní a nic, co by stálo za napsání." Martinů, "1938–1945," 334.

33. "Nemohu zde nepopsat zvláštní psychologický stav, ve kterém jsme asi všichni v té době žili. Své pocity jsme si neuvědomovali okamžitě, nýbrž až po určité době. Jinak jsme věci brali tak, jak přišly, bez přemýšlení, bez zvláštního stavu duševního." Martinů, "1938–1945," 335–36.

34. Martinů, *Ma vie avec Bohuslav Martinů*, 53.

35. Bohuslav Martinů to Miloš Šafránek, Aix en Provence, 1 December 1940 (No. 49). Zouhar and Coufalová, *Dear Miloš*, 189–90.

36. Martinů, *Ma vie avec Bohuslav Martinů*, 63.

37. Ibid., 53. The reference to the "oppressive atmosphere" relating to the Double Concerto appears in the book's German version, *Mein Leben mit Bohuslav Martinů* (Prague: Orbis, 1978), 60, but not in any of the preserved original sources on which the edition is based. It is therefore impossible to confirm Charlotte Martinů as the statement's definite author.

38. Martinů, *Ma vie avec Bohuslav Martinů*, 59.

39. "Nemyslete, že jsem měl nějaké plány pro budoucnost." Martinů, "1938–1945," 336.

40. Benjamin to Theodor W. Adorno, Lourdes, 2 August 1940 (No. 1372), in *Gesammelte Briefe, 1938–1940*, 6:474–77, at 475.

41. Ibid., 476.

42. Morgenstern, "Aus Briefen an Gershom Scholem," 283.

43. Ibid., 280. See also Arendt, "Brief an Gershom Scholem, 1941," 322–27, at 324.

44. Šafránek, *Bohuslav Martinů: Život a dílo*, 249.

45. Benjamin to Theodor W. Adorno, Lourdes, 2 August 1940 (No. 1372), in *Gesammelte Briefe, 1938–1940*, 6:474–477, 476.

46. Benjamin to Gershom Scholem, Berlin, 28 February 1933 (No. 768), in *Gesammelte Briefe, 1931–1934*, ed. Christoph Gödde and Henri Lonitz (Frankfurt: Suhrkamp, 1998), 4:162–65, at 162.

47. Benjamin to Stefan Benjamin, Paris, 6 August 1939 (No. 1310), in *Gesammelte Briefe, 1938–1940*, 6:319–21, at 319.

48. Benjamin to Gretel Adorno, Lourdes, 19 July 1940 (No. 180), in *Walter Benjamin–Gretel Adorno: Briefwechsel 1930–1940*, 413–14, at 414.

49. Benjamin to Hilde Schröder, Marseille, 22 August 1940 (No. 1375), in *Gesammelte Briefe, 1938–1940*, 6:480–81, at 481.

50. Benjamin to Henny Gurland, Port Bou, 25 September 1940 (No. 1378), in *Gesammelte Briefe, 1938–1940*, 6:483.

51. Reinhart Koselleck, *Futures Past: On the Semantics of Historical Time*, transl. Keith Tribe (1979; New York: Columbia University Press, 2004). For an introduction to Koselleck's temporal concepts, see Stefan Ludwig Hoffmann, *Der Riss in der Zeit: Kosellecks ungeschriebene Historik* (Berlin: Suhrkamp, 2023).

52. Stefan Zweig, *The World of Yesterday: Memoirs of a European* (*Die Welt von Gestern: Erinnerungen eines Europäers*, 1942) (New York: Viking Press, 1943).

53. For a rich documentation of Zweig's last two years, see *Stefan and Lotte Zweig's South American Letters: New York, Argentina and Brazil, 1940–1942*, ed. Darién J. Davis and Oliver Marshall (New York: Continuum, 2010).

54. Thomas Mann, "Denken und Leben" (1941), in *Gesammelte Werke, Altes und Neues: Kleine Prosa aus fünf Jahrzehnten* (Berlin: Aufbau, 1955), 11:244–49, at 248.

55. Martinů, *Ma vie avec Bohuslav Martinů*, 55.

56. For a reading of *Lidice* that takes account of the composer's own experiences, see Klaus Döge, "Das entsetzliche Grauen zum Ausdruck gebracht: Anmerkungen zu Martinůs *Memorial to Lidice*," in Tadday, *Bohuslav Martinů*, 78–91. Also Michael Crump, *Martinů and the Symphony* (London: Toccata Press, 2010), 353–56; Rybka, *Bohuslav Martinů: The Compulsion to Compose*, 128–29.

57. Benedetto Croce, *History of Europe in the Nineteenth Century*, trans. Henry Furst (London: Allen & Unwin, 1934).

58. See in particular sections 1 and 6 of the so-called Handexemplar version of the manuscript: Benjamin, *Über den Begriff der Geschichte*, in *Werke und Nachlaß*, 19:30, 33.

59. Ibid, 35. For a recent analysis of Klee's work, see Annie Bourneuf, *Behind the Angel of History: The "Angelus Novus" and Its Interleaf* (Chicago: University of Chicago Press, 2022).

60. Gershom Scholem, "Erwachen aus dem Schock des Hitler-Stalin-Paktes," in Scholem, *Walter Benjamin und sein Engel: Vierzehn Aufsätze und kleine Beiträge*, ed. Rolf Tiedemann (Frankfurt: Suhrkamp, 1967), 64.

61. For the pact's impact on Benjamin, see Morgenstern, "Aus Briefen an Gershom Scholem," 277–79, 287. See also Stéphane Hessel, "Ein verzweifelter Blick auf die Epoche," in Wizisla, *Begegnungen*, 272. For an analysis, see Lorenz Jäger, *Walter Benjamin: Das Leben eines Unvollendeten* (Berlin: Rowohlt, 2017), 316. For the theoretical and philosophical consequences, see Axel Körner, "The Experience of Time as Crisis: On Croce's and Benjamin's Concepts of History," *Intellectual History Review* 21/2 (2011): 151–69.

62. Eric Hobsbawm, *Age of Extremes: The Short Twentieth Century, 1914–1991* (London: Penguin, 1997).

63. Aleš Březina, "Bohuslav Martinů," 5–13, 55, at 8. For the Communist regime's changing attitude toward Martinů and attempts to distort his intentions, see Březina, "Preface," in *Martinů's Letters Home: Five Decades of Correspondence with Family and Friends*, ed. Iša Popelka (London: Toccata Press, 2012), 7–10. Also Březina, "Martinůs musikhistorischer Ort."

64. Jarmila Gabrielová, "Zur Martinů Rezeption in Böhmen," in Tadday, *Bohuslav Martinů*, 140–43. See also Tomáš D. Svatoš, "Über die Probleme der Martinů: Rezeption in der Anglo-Amerikanischen Musikwissenschaft," *Österreichische Musikzeitschrift* 64 (11–12): 22–26, at 25. For the campaign against Martinů after 1938, see Aleš Březina, "Martinůs musikhistorischer Ort," 18. On the wider political context, see Jiří Fukač, "Bohuslav Martinůs Tschechentum," in *Bohuslav Martinů: His Pupils, Friends and Contemporaries*, ed. Petr Macek, Colloquium, Brno 1990 (Brno: Ústav hudební vědy filozofické fakulty MU Brno, 1993), 5–12, at 7.

65. See for instance Martinů to Bureš, Rome, 10 March 1957 (No. 14) and Rome, 26 August 1957 (No. 16). Vít Zouhar and Gabriela Coufalová, eds., *Dear Friend Bureš: Bohuslav Martinů's Letters to Miloslav Bureš* (Olomouc: Univerzita Palackého v Olomouci, 2017), 111–15 and 121–25.

66. "Ale jiná hodnota se nyní jasněji představila, o níž jsme dříve málo přemýšleli, již jsme považovali za samozřejmou, za danou, ale jejíž cenu jsme počínali chápati nyní, když jsme ji ztráceli: pocit svobody. Liberté. Teď' jsme mohli poznat, že to není daná hodnota, nýbrž že musí býti dobyta. Osobně jsem za svou volnost vždy platil. Ale to byla moje malá, soukromá svoboda. Oč nyní šlo, byl svobodný duch, svobodné lidství. I jiná hodnota, jedna z lidsky základních, se zdála hroutiti pod tlakem událostí, totiž hodnota přesvědčení, jež řídí celé naše jednání i náš cíl, jejž jsme si vytkli, nebo k němuž jsme zvoleni, přesvědčení lidské i umělecké, což je asi totéž. Nebyl na ně čas. Nebyl čas na nic, jen snaha zachránit holý život. Ale zachránit – proč? Ztratíme-li obě tyto složky, co můžeme od života čekat?" Martinů, "1938–1945," 334–35.

67. Martinů published his essay in 1947 and did not know the philosophical debate of the following decades on the two concepts of liberty, in which Benedetto Croce, Norberto Bobbio, Robin George Collingwood, and Isaiah Berlin played a crucial role; but his reference to the term "liberty" seems to go in a similar direction. For the distinction between freedom and liberty, see Ian Carter, "Positive and Negative Liberty," in *Stanford Encyclopedia of Philosophy* (Spring 2022), ed. Edward N. Zalta, https://plato.stanford.edu/archives/spr2022/entries/liberty-positive-negative/.

68. Although reflecting his own experiences, Martinů saw his works as musical facts in themselves. See Šafránek, *Bohuslav Martinů*, 15. Also Březina, "Martinůs musikhistorischer Ort," 8.

69. Croce coined the term *antistoricismo* in a paper he read in September 1930 at the Seventh International Congress of Philosophy in Oxford, where he criticized the current "decadence of historical sentiment" and the "extreme anti-historical attitude" of the new political ideologies. See Benedetto Croce, *Antistoricismo* (Bari: Laterza, 1931).

70. Šafránek, *Bohuslav Martinů*, 135ff.

71. Harry Halbreich, *Bohuslav Martinů: Werkverzeichnis und Biografie* (Mainz: Schott, 2007), 88.

72. Šafránek, *Bohuslav Martinů*, 228.

73. Crump, *Martinů and the Symphony*, 209.

74. Šafránek, *Bohuslav Martinů*, 245.

75. Ibid., 247; Halbreich, *Bohuslav Martinů: Werkverzeichnis und Biografie*, 260.

76. Březina, "Martinůs musikhistorischer Ort," 19.

77. There are elements of such a line of argument in Šafránek, *Bohuslav Martinů*, 80, 83. Also, in works like the Second Symphony Šafránek recognizes "Czech spirit" (244). See Brian Large, *Martinů* (London: Duckworth, 1975), 88, 116. For a similar line of argument, see the contributions in *Bohuslav Martinů anno 1981*, ed. Jitka Brabcová, Papers from the International Musicological Conference, Prague, 26–28 May 1981 (Prague: Česká hudební společnost, 1990).

78. In this context, see the introduction to Jaromír Synek and Gabriela Všetičková, eds., *Dear All (II.): Bohuslav Martinů's Letters to His Family in Polička in 1932 and 1933* (Olomouc: Univerzita Palackého v Olomouci, 2020), 11–13.

79. Bohuslav Martinů, "O současné hudbě," in Šafránek, *Domov, hudba a svět*, 73–78.

80. "Vraťte se k Smetanovi." Bohuslav Martinů, "Cestou k Stravinskému," in Šafránek, *Domov, hudba a svět,* 24–26; and Martinů, "Ke kritice o současné hudbě," in Ibid., 99–102; Martinů, "O hudbě a tradici," in Ibid., 41–43.

81. Bohuslav Martinů, "Bedrik Smetana et la musique nationale tchècque," Comoedia, 11 October 1928, 1–2, in Šafránek, *Domov, hudba a svět,* 107–109. See.https://www.martinu.cz/en/martinu/texts-by-bm/bohuslav-martinu-bedrik-smetana-et-la-fiancee-vendue-comoedia-11101928/.

82. Šafránek, *Bohuslav Martinů,* 18ff.

83. "To, co jsem já šel hledat do Francie, to nebyl Debussy ani impresionismus ani hudební projev, ale opravdové základy, na nichž leží západní kultura a které podle mého názoru odpovídají mnohem více našemu vlastnímu národnímu charakteru než bludiště záhad a problémů." Šafránek, *Bohuslav Martinů,* 100.

84. On this argument, see in particular Fukač, "Bohuslav Martinůs Tschechentum," 5–12.

85. For a critical discussion, see Vladimír Karbusický, *Geschichte des böhmischen Musiktheaters* (Hamburg: Bockel, 2005).

86. Not even recent overviews mention these stays. See for instance Robert C. Simon, *Bohuslav Martinů: A Research and Information Guide* (New York and London: Routledge, 2014), 17. Brian Large, *Martinů,* briefly mentions negotiations with the Charlottenburg Opera in Berlin and the composer's interest in Ernst Krenek. Large, *Martinů,* 47.

87. "Oni na to čekali abych se tam objevil. Byli ke mně moc laskaví a mám tam spoustu známostí všichni mě ujišťují že to bude v Německu pro mne dobré, jen se tam musím občas objevit." Martinů to his mother, Paris, June 1929 (No. 17). Jaromír Synek and Gabriela Všetičková, eds., *Dear All (I.): Bohuslav Martinů's letters to his family in Polička until 1931* (Olomouc: Univerzita Palackého v Olomouci, 2019), 72–75.

88. See for instance Martinů to his family, Paris, 16 November 1930 (No. 25), ibid., 111–15. The German publisher's apparent interest partly contradicts the claim that Germany had always ignored Martinů. See Ulrich Tadday, "Vorwort," in Tadday, *Bohuslav Martinů,* 3–4.

89. "Prozatím neplatí špatně ale slibují mi pro později více a stálý kontrakt na měsíční gáži." Martinů to his family, Paris, 20 May 1931 (No. 41). Synek and Všetičková, *Dear All (I.),* 219–21.

90. Martinů to his family, Paris, 7 March 1931 (No. 32). Ibid., 163–67.

91. "Je to opravdu hloupost k vůli filmu dělat takové rozbroje . . . moc nám to uškodilo, zvláště umělcům." Martinů to his family, Paris, 2 October 1930 (No. 21). Ibid., 83–89, at 85.

92. Martinů to his family, Paris, 12 March 1931 (No. 33). Ibid., 169–73.

93. Martinů to his family, Paris, 28 December 1930 (No. 27). Ibid., 129–35.

94. Šafránek, *Bohuslav Martinů,* 244, 252–53, 270, 276. See also Martinů's letter to Šafránek of 19 November 1946, in which he shares his impressions of a concert of the Budapest Quartet performing Beethoven, Op. 135 (290).

95. Bohuslav Martinů, "Tvůrce Tristana," in Šafránek, *Domov, hudba a svět,* 92–93. Also see Bohuslav Martinů, "*Hry o Marii*: K brněnské premiéře," in *Divadlo Bohuslava Martinů*, ed. Miloš Šafránek (Prague: Editio Supraphon, 1979), 215–24.

"To My Countrymen—Workers of Cleveland": The World Premiere of Bohuslav Martinů's Symphony No. 2

MARKÉTA KRATOCHVÍLOVÁ AND MAREK PECHAČ
TRANSLATED BY ADAM PRENTIS

On 28 October 1943, the premiere of Symphony No. 2, H 295, by Bohuslav Martinů, was held in Cleveland, Ohio, to commemorate the twenty-fifth anniversary of the day on which the Czechoslovak Republic was founded. Despite taking place at the height of the Second World War and far from the Nazi-occupied country it celebrated, the premiere was intended for a Czechoslovak audience and was attended by the composer himself. Martinů wished to dedicate the symphony to his "countrymen and workers in Cleveland, who have accomplished so much in the war industry," contributing with his art to the liberation of Czechoslovakia.[1] He even expressed this desire in writing, in an essay published by the New York–based expatriate daily *New-Yorské Listy* on the day of the premiere: "There is one thing we must not forget: that the fact we remain free and able to work is paid for by those who stayed; and that they will have the right to ask, and ask they will, what we did and how we used our freedom and our options and how we acquitted ourselves while they were suffering."[2]

This study presents the results of our search for primary sources in Cleveland archives in spring 2022, especially The Cleveland Orchestra (CO) Archives. Among these sources is a set of letters from 1943 that shed new light on the circumstances of the Cleveland premiere of Symphony No. 2. This extraordinary event was shaped by existing structures in the expatriate community of American Czechs and by influential yet sometimes obscure figures who fled to the United States to avoid Nazi persecution.

The opening two sections of this essay map the context of the performance of Symphony No. 2 in relation to Bohuslav Martinů's American period. The first describes the course of the Cleveland premiere based on previous knowledge, the second expands on this by adding details gleaned from the newly discovered correspondence. The third section, "Cleveland Czechs," centers on the city's expatriate community, its history and structure, and endeavors to answer the question of who exactly among the Cleveland Czechs were responsible for commissioning the symphony.

Premiere "Attack" upon the American Public

Martinů lived in the United States from spring 1941, when he and his wife fled Europe to escape the Nazis. Although surrounded by a number of people who supported and helped him, in competition with other composers forced to emigrate from the Old Continent, Martinů had to assert himself—primarily through new works. His American works differ significantly from those of the preceding period, and at the age of fifty-one he finally began to compose symphonies, one each year. The first was commissioned in 1942 by Serge Koussevitzky's music foundation in Boston, the second was requested by Czechs living in Cleveland for The Cleveland Orchestra. The third was again composed for Koussevitzky's Boston Symphony Orchestra, the fourth for the Philadelphia Orchestra, and the fifth for the Czech Philharmonic. All of the symphonies were performed soon after their completion. It may be that the specific situation Martinů found himself in favored the creation of grand-scale works aiming to reach the audiences of orchestral concerts and radio broadcasts. Chamber music could hardly have had such an impact, whereas the premiere of a symphony was always a major event—both in the United States and in Europe. Besides, Martinů continued to compose concertos, other symphonic works, and chamber music. His new works were generally very well received, and the eminent Martinů researcher Jaroslav Mihule rightly summarizes the period 1943–44 by declaring that Martinů "had secured his place as an esteemed composer universally respected by the critics thanks to a series of superb premieres in the past two years."[3]

Symphony No. 2 was composed during Martinů's summer stay in Darien, Connecticut, from 29 May to 24 July 1943.[4] The composer's memoir informs us that he had conceived of the work's substance while working on his first symphony the year before. Martinů wrote one other symphonic work that summer in Darien, *Memorial to Lidice*, H 296, which was also premiered on 28 October 1943, by Artur Rodziński and the New York Philharmonic in Carnegie Hall. Thus Martinů had a double hit with two major premieres on a single night, one in New York, the other in Cleveland. He decided to attend the Cleveland performance, despite living in New York.

Martinů arrived in Cleveland with his wife on 25 October to attend the orchestra's rehearsals and participate in events organized in his honor. He traveled there by plane, the first time he ever flew. After landing safely he sent a postcard of an airplane to his friend Frank Rybka in New York, with whom he had shared his apprehension over the new experience.[5]

On 26 October, the local Czechoslovak consul Emanuel Jan Hajný hosted a luncheon attended by some thirty-odd figures from the cultural scene in Cleveland and beyond.[6] Guests included Cleveland music teacher of Czech origin Charles Václav Rychlík; music critic Elmore Bacon; curator of the Cleveland Museum of Art Walter Blodgett; sociologist Henry Miller Busch; musicologist Albert Riemenschneider; and representatives of The Cleveland Orchestra, the press, and radio stations. The guest list also names the music critic and composer Herbert Elwell, who like Martinů had lived in Paris in the 1920s. The following day, 27 October, Hajný held another banquet for Martinů, this time with "some 40 representatives of all segments of expatriate life in Cleveland."[7] Invitees are not listed in any available sources.

Symphony No. 2 was premiered on 28 October with the orchestra conducted by its new principal conductor Erich Leinsdorf in their home venue of Severance Hall. Besides Martinů's new symphony, the program included Schubert's Symphony in C Major and Leinsdorf's transcription of Bach's chorale "O Haupt voll Blut und Wunden," and concluded with Smetana's *Vltava*, the second part of his cycle of symphonic poems *Má vlast* (*My Country*). Severance Hall was sold out both for the premiere and for the repeat performance on 30 October. Martinů was in attendance and enjoyed an enthusiastic reception. He was called up several times, presented with flowers in the Czech national colors from Cleveland expatriates, consul Hajný, and Czechoslovak foreign minister Jan Masaryk, who was unable to attend but sent a telegraphic salutation to Leinsdorf.[8] The premiere was followed by a reception for the composer and his wife in the Grand Foyer of Severance Hall, attended by eminent members of the Cleveland music scene.[9]

The Cleveland performances started off the symphony's conquest of American audiences. On 7 December, The Cleveland Orchestra brought the work to the nearby city of Oberlin,[10] followed by Columbus, Ohio, on 10 December,[11] and a live radio broadcast from Severance Hall on 19 December.[12] On 30 and 31 December 1943 and 1 January 1944, Symphony No. 2 was performed by the New York Philharmonic under Artur Rodziński.

This did not conclude Martinů's ties to The Cleveland Orchestra. The composer would maintain a long friendship with George Szell, who headed the orchestra from 1946 to 1970, during which time the ensemble gave the world premieres of his *Rhapsody-Concerto*, H 337, for viola and orchestra in 1953, and his symphonic prelude *The Rock*, H 363, in 1958.

The double premiere of Symphony No. 2 and *Memorial to Lidice* opened a new period in Martinů's life marked by great success as well as great stress and exertion. After the war he remembered how "I launched my great premiere 'attack' upon the American public. . . . We were in Cleveland when friends from New York phoned up at 3 in the morning to inform of the profound impact made by the *Memorial*. Several days later, the concerto for two pianos was premiered in Philadelphia and reprised in New York. Followed by the premiere of the violin concerto in Boston and another performance of the second symphony by Rodzinski in New York. . . . Soon there was a premiere of the violin concerto in New York. Seeing that all these concerts are repeated two or three times each, I hardly ever escaped from the stage, or from the nervous tension, rehearsals, and performances, which were mostly first-class, the way American orchestras are."[13]

THE CLEVELAND ORCHESTRA

ERICH LEINSDORF, CONDUCTOR

FOURTH PROGRAM

Thursday Evening, October 28, at Eight-thirty
Saturday Evening, October 30, at Eight-thirty

Symphony in C major, No. 7 — Schubert

Andante; Allegro ma non troppo
Andante con moto
Scherzo
Finale

INTERMISSION

Symphony No. 2 — Martinu

Allegro moderato
Andante moderato
Poco allegro
Allegro

"The Moldau," Symphonic Poem No. 2 from the Cycle "My Country" — Smetana

RUDOLPH RINGWALL will discuss the music to be heard at these concerts on Thursday, October 28, at 2:15 o'clock over STATION WGAR.

Holders of Series Tickets "A" please note that the Fourth Program is in Series "A"

Tickets on Sale at Severance Hall (55c Seats Saturday Evening at 7:30 only)

70

Figure 1. Program of the premiere performance, 28 and 30 October 1943, Cleveland Orchestra conducted by Erich Leinsdorf.

The Premiere in Light of Newly Discovered Correspondence

The correspondence in the archives of The Cleveland Orchestra supplements our understanding of the circumstances of the premiere of Symphony No. 2. The set of twenty-two letters from August to December 1943 comprises both original letters received, including seven handwritten letters by Bohuslav Martinů, and the copies of letters sent by the CO management, which makes the correspondence practically complete. Transcriptions appear at the end of this essay.

The key writers and addressees are Martinů, the Czechoslovak consul in Cleveland Emanuel Jan Hajný, Martinů's friend and biographer Miloš Šafránek (also an American exile), and members of the CO management: manager Carl J. Vosburgh, press secretary George Henry Lowett Smith, president of the board of trustees and lawyer of Czech descent Thomas L. Sidlo, and the new music director Erich Leinsdorf. The letters contain numerous organizational details and document negotiations about performance and broadcast rights as well as the preparation of program texts. They shed light on the functioning of American institutions and Czechoslovak diplomatic missions and testify to Consul Hajný's active participation as well as Martinů's own role in arranging the practicalities of the matter.

The first letter is dated 9 August 1943, two weeks after the completion of Symphony No. 2. In it, Thomas L. Sidlo informed Leinsdorf that Consul Hajný had brought the score of the new symphony to his office that morning. He was sending the score to Leinsdorf separately, in an insured parcel. The letter touches on most of the topics that appear in the subsequent correspondence: deadlines, performance rights, radio broadcasts, marketing. It mentions a debate about the wording of the symphony's dedication, which Hajný wanted "to put in better form before it is released." As for performance rights, Sidlo suggested that Martinů and the CO were under pressure to schedule the symphony early due to Artur Rodziński's interest in presenting the work in the New York Philharmonic's upcoming season.[14] Hajný had asked Martinů "to hold off doing anything whatever about [New York] until he hears from [the CO]" (letter no. 1).

If negotiations up to that point had been conducted by Martinů, Hajný, Sidlo, and Leinsdorf, it was time for the CO management to step in. The second letter, from 13 August, is from the orchestra's manager Carl J. Vosburgh: "Dear Mr. Martinu: I have just heard from Mr. Leinsdorf by telephone that he wants to do your Symphony No. 2 at our pair of concerts Thursday and Saturday, October 28th and 30th" (letter no. 2). On 13 and 18 August, Vosburgh asked the composer for exclusive performance rights for the 1943–44 season and priority permission to record the work. The CO also wanted to have the first radio broadcast of the symphony, realized through their freshly signed contract with the Mutual Broadcasting System.[15] Vosburgh justified his demand for first-season exclusivity with a plan to perform the composition on the orchestra's tour of various cities in February and March 1944 (letter nos. 2 and 4).

Martinů responded with two letters, from 19 and 21 August. He was very happy to have Symphony No. 2 premiered in Cleveland, and he also gave the CO the rights to the first radio broadcast (letter no. 5). He could not, however, give them exclusivity because he was soon to have a performance in New York and had also sent the score to London and promised it to Boston and Mexico. He offered to keep the score at their "disposition for every performance you wish." Martinů then described the rights situation: the symphony had been commissioned by friends of his who hoped for a premiere in Cleveland, but "this is very friendly and private side" unrelated to actual performance rights or royalties for the rent of orchestral materials (letter no. 6). Vosburgh replied on 24 August. He accepted the performances in Mexico, London, and Boston on condition that they would not take place until 1 January 1944. He noted that "our Mutual broadcast will go direct to Mexico and be short-waved to Europe" (letter no. 7). Pleased by news of the premiere and the radio broadcast, Martinů agreed on 27 August to maintain The Cleveland Orchestra's exclusivity until 1 January 1944. He also offered to keep the score and parts at their disposal if they planned to present the symphony at other concerts in February (letter no. 8).

Martinů was less accommodating in his 10 October letter accompanying the orchestral materials and second score: he asked for the radio performance to take place before 15 December, as Artur Rodziński was to conduct the work in New York in the last week of December and would need to be sent the parts (letter no. 13). Carl J. Vosburgh replied on 15 October that he and Erich Leinsdorf had scheduled the radio broadcast for 12 December, after which they would immediately return the orchestral materials to Martinů unless otherwise instructed (letter no. 15). The broadcast ended up taking place on 19 December, a week later than planned. There is no mention as to whether the materials were delivered to Rodziński on time, but the New York Philharmonic did in fact perform Symphony No. 2 by the end of the year.

The supply of the necessary sheet music also caused trouble before the Cleveland premiere. Starting on 8 September, Martinů was repeatedly urged to provide the orchestra with a second score ("We need two scores—one for our conductor and one for the associate conductor") and the parts (letters nos. 9 and 11). And on 11 October, Smith reminded the composer that Erich Leinsdorf was "anxious to receive the parts" (letter no. 14). When the parts did arrive, their low quality ended up costing the composer potential income from royalties, as explained in the following paragraph.

On 1 December, Martinů notified Vosburgh that he had not requested the usual rental fee for performance materials because of the special significance of the premiere chosen by The Cleveland Orchestra: "Since you made the nice gesture of giving my Second Symphony in honor of the 25th anniversary of the Republic of Czechoslovakia, I have not asked for the customary fee for lending the orchestra

December 1-1943

Dear Mr Vosburgh,

Since you made the nice gesture of giving my Second Symphony in honor of the 25th anniversary of the Republic of Czechoslovakia, I have not asked the customary fee for lending the orchestra material.

Mr Leinsdorf informed me, that there will be further performances of the Second Symphony. I would be very much obliged to you, if you would pay to me fee of $ = 60. for each performance, including the Broadcast 12. December.

Very truly yours

B. Martinu

Figure 2. Martinů's letter to Carl J. Vosburgh, 1 December 1943.

materiel." (See Figure 2.) But as he had heard from Leinsdorf that the work was to be performed several more times, he asked for a fee of $60 per performance, including the radio broadcast (letter no. 17). Vosburgh responded on 4 December, reminding Martinů that much time had been lost during the rehearsal week for the premiere of Symphony No. 2 due to the need for corrections: "Not only were bars missing, but in many cases whole lines of the music were missing." The orchestra was forced to compensate its members with one hour overtime, which cost $246. Therefore, Vosburgh reckoned the composer should waive the fee for the scheduled concerts: "At the rate you suggest of $60.00 per performance, I feel that since we spent $246.00 to correct the parts that these four performances should be given to us without payment." He emphasized that this was on top of other work needed to make changes to the music that Martinů had requested from Leinsdorf after the premiere. Vosburgh concluded by arguing that this time and money would benefit both the composer and "the New York Philharmonic and other organizations who perform your work later on" (letter no. 18).

Preparations for producing the program brochure and promoting the event in the press were also considerable. On 17 August, the head of press relations and marketing for The Cleveland Orchestra, George H. L. Smith, asked Martinů to send him his photograph (letter no. 3); on 5 October, he inquired after the composer's expected date of arrival: "The Cleveland papers are very anxious to know exactly when you plan to arrive in Cleveland" (letter no. 11). When Martinů finally arrived on 25 October, the local press covered the event extensively. Smith also asked Martinů for information he could use in his program notes, and to ensure his characterization of the symphony was as complete as possible, he added: "I should be glad to quote your own description of the symphony" (letter no. 3). Martinů obliged Smith with a theoretical treatise on his symphonic oeuvre that discussed both of his symphonies to date and showed how seriously he took his recent embrace of the genre. Smith translated the composer's French text into English, and this translation came to be quoted in various publications, the first of which was Miloš Šafránek's 1944 monograph *Bohuslav Martinů: The Man and His Music* (letter nos. 21 and 22).[16]

Although the next three letters are not directly related to the preparations for the premiere of Martinů's Symphony No. 2, they document how Hajný's activities as a diplomat included efforts to procure sheet music and deal with wartime copyright issues, as well as intimating the CO's interest in presenting other Czech compositions following this initial collaboration. The letter from 15 October shows that Hajný sent Leinsdorf the scores of four works by Josef Suk and Vítězslav Novák and informed him that further scores by Leoš Janáček, Otakar Ostrčil, and Novák were located in Montreal: "Should you be interested in the last mentioned scores I will get them from Canada in a day or two" (letter no. 16). This topic is continued in the letter from 10 December, in which George H. L. Smith explained to Hajný that Associated Music Publishers could not

SYMPHONY NO. 2

By Bohuslav Martinu

Born December 8, 1890, at Policka, Czechoslovakia

Martinu's Second Symphony was written in the summer of 1943 at Darien, Connecticut. According to notations in the score, the first movement was completed on June 28, the second on July 3, the third on July 16, and the finale on July 24. The symphony, commissioned by a group of Czechoslovaks in Cleveland, is dedicated "To my Fellow Countrymen in Cleveland."

The scoring is for two flutes and piccolo, three oboes, three clarinets, two bassoons, four horns, three trumpets, three trombones and tuba, kettledrums, side drum, bass drum, cymbals, triangle, tam-tam, harp, piano, and strings.

The symphony is receiving its first performances anywhere at these concerts.*

Martinu arrived in the United States on March 31, 1941. A year later, having composed over one hundred works and reached his forty-second year, he produced a First Symphony. When it was first performed,† he contributed, by way of introduction, a discussion of his ideas on the symphonic form to the Concert Bulletin of the Boston Symphony Orchestra. It will be of interest to quote the composer's preface to his First Symphony before turning to the supplementary remarks he has kindly written for these programs on the occasion of the première of his Second Symphony:

"The form of the symphony is one of the great problems of contemporary composers. The century past has left us a form well established not only in structure but in its content of elevated expression and grandeur. The Ninth Symphony of Beethoven has been an example. The Romantic and post-Romantic epochs have added a further and a very earnest ideology—a sentiment tragic, pathetic, even grandiloquent—have placed the symphony at the highest level of musical composition. It is certainly not my intention to dispute this natural and logical position. I wish only to clarify a certain conviction which has resulted from the development of the form in our time. In spite of several attempts of contemporary composers to change the structure, to find another solution in writing a symphony in a single movement, in five parts, etc., its essential nature remains unchanged, with rare exceptions. There enter here the problems which disturb the composer when he begins a work and when he assembles his musical, ideological and technical material.

*Subsequent performances are in preparation in New York, London, and Mexico City.

†Martinu's First Symphony, completed on September 1, 1942, was commissioned by the Koussevitzky Music Foundation, and dedicated to the memory of Mme. Natalie Koussevitzky. The first performance was at a concert of the Boston Symphony Orchestra, Serge Koussevitzky, Conductor, on November 13, 1942

Severance Hall
WAR MEMORIAL CONCERT
St. James' Festival Choir and members of The Cleveland Orchestra
Directed by Walter Blodgett
All Souls Day, November 2, 1943, at 8:30 p.m.
Brahms' 'Requiem'....Vaughan Williams' 'Dona nobis pacem'
Soloists: Mary Marting, Bruce Foote
Main Floor, $1.38 Dress Circle, $1.10 Balcony, 83 Cents
Mail orders to St. James Church, 5607 Whittier Avenue

Figure 3. Introductory text of the program for the premiere performance of Symphony No. 2, 28 and 30 October 1943.

produce the parts to Suk's *Legenda o mrtvých vítězích (Legend of the Dead Victors)* because the copyright was held by the Prague music publisher Hudební matice Umělecké besedy. He appealed to Hajný: "You, as a representative of the Czech government, should be willing to authorize the copying" (letter no. 19). Hajný handed the issue of Suk's composition to the Czechoslovak consulate in New York and told Smith he reckoned that Associated Music Publishers' stance was not entirely correct, "as similar matters pertaining to countries occupied by the enemy are administered by the Custodian of Enemy Property" (letter no. 20).

Cleveland Czechs

The Cleveland Orchestra's guest artist autograph book in the CO Archives contains Martinů's signed autograph sketch of the incipit of Symphony No. 2 together with the notation "Commissioned for the Cleveland Orchestra by Cleveland Czechs." This seemingly unambiguous and unproblematic formulation conceals a rather tangled history and begs the question: Just who were these Cleveland Czechs?

The Czech community in Cleveland has roots that reach back to the second half of the nineteenth century, when migration was motivated both by the unfavorable political climate in the Habsburg monarchy and by the rapid industrialization of cities around the Great Lakes. The region was inundated with migrants from all over Europe, who brought their own cultures with them to be infused with new, American elements. In 1910, Cleveland boasted the fourth-largest population of Czechs in the world, after Prague, Vienna, and Chicago.[17] The sheer number of Czech immigrants in Cleveland influenced the city's culture. Music was often used as a way of improving social status among nationality groups in American society, as exemplified by the silent film composer John Stepan Zamecnik, or by the Hruby family, which started out playing in circus bands and worked its way up in Cleveland society to the establishment of its own conservatory, with part of the family among the founding members of The Cleveland Orchestra.[18] By the mid-twentieth century, numerous Czech music societies of diverse types were scattered throughout Cleveland, and the Czech community also built up a number of venues for cultural events and theater. Foremost among them was Bohemian National Hall, constructed in 1889 from individual donations and still actively in use today.

The Czechs in Cleveland did not form a homogenous community but were generally centered around several loosely connected organizations, such as the Czech gymnastics movement Sokol, religious congregations, or various societies and labor associations. Starting in the nineteenth century, Cleveland Czechs could boast a high percentage of qualified craftsmen, such as carpenters, dressmakers, blacksmiths, or machinists. A second group were unskilled laborers employed in local factories, such as the Standard Oil refinery. Craftsmen tended toward Sokol or various church communities, while factory workers joined labor unions. However, this stratification was not impermeable, and contact was maintained between different groups.[19]

Although a number of greater or lesser expatriate societies were active in Cleveland, available sources suggest that none of them were responsible for commissioning Symphony No. 2. Nor was there ever any officially recognized organization named Cleveland Czechs. The role of Czech associations in Cleveland in preparations for the performance of Symphony No. 2 was limited to that of secondary assistants, who ensured the presence of women in national costumes at the premiere or the attendance of community representatives at the official reception. None of their archival materials or estates provide any information whatsoever about the premiere of Symphony No. 2. Despite documenting numerous traditional or regular activities organized by these societies, be they religious, sport-oriented, or artistic, this event is not mentioned. Nor is there a word about the premiere in the eponymously titled *Cleveland Czechs*, a book detailing these societies' history.[20] Stephen J. Sebesta's detailed history of the Czech community takes a more holistic approach to the functioning of this expatriate group, free of its institutional framework, presenting the premiere of Symphony No. 2 as one of the most important music events ever in the life of Cleveland Czechs.[21] Thus any investigation of the circumstances of the symphony's commission must search beyond established expatriate structures.

A major role in the preparations for the premiere was played by Emanuel Jan Hajný (1891–1972), the Czechoslovak consul. Existing literature on the premiere of Symphony No. 2 generally depicts Hajný as the main organizer, and new sources confirm this assessment. Hajný had been posted in the United States as a diplomat since 1928, following a colorful career serving in the Australian Army during the First World War and in the Czechoslovak Legion in Serbia and France. He moved to Cleveland in 1938 in the employ of the Czechoslovak Ministry of Foreign Affairs and Czechoslovak resistance efforts. He was made consul in 1942.[22] He had met Martinů a year earlier—when the composer and his wife disembarked in New Jersey on 31 March 1941, they were greeted by Miloš Šafránek and his wife, the pianist Rudolf Firkušný, and Hajný.[23] The nickname "Captain," which Martinů used in his recollections of Hajný—"the captain shone with joy"[24]— may have referred to Hajný's experience as a traveler or to his military past, though his official rank was that of first lieutenant.

Another influential figure was Thomas L. Sidlo (1888–1955), who lived and worked in Cleveland as a lawyer, served as Board President of the CO at the time and was also active in a similar role in the Northern Ohio Opera Association, local sponsor of New York's Metropolitan Opera tour. It was probably how Sidlo met Erich Leinsdorf and then engaged him as a conductor in Cleveland.[25] In his book *Cadenza: A Musical Career*, Leinsdorf describes Sidlo's role in the city's music scene, depicting him as a successful lawyer who built up a fortune through real estate at a relatively young age and then devoted himself to civic philanthropy, including the support of music.[26] Leinsdorf mentions that unlike New York, where patronage of the arts remained in the hands of "old money," that is, families with long-standing

American roots, the culture scene in Cleveland was largely funded by immigrants who earned their wealth relatively quickly and wanted to share the fruits of their success with society. Thomas L. Sidlo was one such successful entrepreneur, and he was able to persuade others to join him as benefactors.[27]

Correspondence in the CO Archives shows that Hajný, Sidlo, and Leinsdorf were in close contact while organizing the premiere of Symphony No. 2. Hajný delivered Martinů's score to Sidlo in person (see letter no. 1). The warmer relations between Hajný and Sidlo are corroborated by their informal mutual mode of address, "Tom" and "Jan"; Hajný did not sign himself that way to any other of the correspondents (letter no. 12). It is evident that Martinů and Hajný's primary contacts in the CO were Sidlo and Leinsdorf.

A more obscure yet key role was played by František Sigmund (1901–1989). His name has not appeared in the literature to date in connection with Martinů's Symphony No. 2, nor with Cleveland or the composer's American period. Sigmund has previously only been mentioned in connection with Martinů's Paris period and the safekeeping of the composer's autographs in Sigmund's factory in Nevers during the Nazi occupation of France. We still do not have any direct evidence of František Sigmund's part in the preparations for Symphony No. 2, and even the newly found letters make no mention of him.[28] The only clue to Sigmund's participation is one newspaper clipping in a scrapbook in the CO Archives, in which the journalist Milton Widder interviewed several key actors in the Cleveland premiere: Bohuslav Martinů, Erich Leinsdorf, and František Sigmund, here named "Frank" Sigmund, a chemical engineer and friend of the composer.[29] This single clue meshes with other facts to support the hypothesis that Sigmund was one of the main instigators behind the commissioning of Symphony No. 2 for Cleveland and that he secured the necessary finances.

František Sigmund was a prominent member of the Sigmund family, Czech industrialists from Lutín near Olomouc.[30] The Sigmunds established a factory that manufactured pumps in Lutín, which gained renown throughout Czechoslovakia, Europe, and beyond. In 1937, František was sent to Nevers to build a factory for military-issue chemical protective clothing, called Siamec. Besides this industrial function, the facility also became a center of resistance against Nazi Germany. From Nevers and from his office in Paris, he organized support for Czechoslovak resistance in exile and maintained contact with members of the Czechoslovak National Committee, headed by President Edvard Beneš. Sigmund was also friends with Czech artists living in Paris, whom he supported financially. He hid Martinů's manuscript scores from the Gestapo in his Nevers factory, and Nevers was a transition point for artists fleeing the country, such as Rudolf Firkušný. Sigmund's patronage and social life in Paris, including events attended by Martinů or Vítězslava Kaprálová, are briefly touched on by Jiří Mucha in *Podivné lásky*.[31]

France's capitulation forced Sigmund to leave the country. He departed for the States in March 1940 (a year before Martinů) and remained there for the duration of the war. Relatively few sources exist to document the life and work of František Sigmund, especially for his time in the States.[32] Ladislav Smička notes that Sigmund lived and worked in Cleveland in the early 1940s and that he was employed by Lake Erie Chemical Co., which produced weapons. The Sigmunds had established ties with the firm and its owner, F. C. Goss, in the mid-1930s.[33]

Sigmund's resistance activities may have been the reason why neither Martinů nor Šafránek, among others, ever referenced his name in connection with Cleveland. There was definitely cause for caution in this respect. One of the Sigmund brothers, Jan, who directed the Czech plant in Lutín, was executed by the Nazis in summer 1942 for the family's resistance activities and their massive military production for the Allies. František's wife, Věra, was also hunted by the Gestapo and ended up in prison, where she attempted suicide.[34] The collective attribution to "Cleveland Czechs" was thus both a symbolic gesture and, possibly, a security measure to hide the identities of the work's instigators. Either way, the dedication "to my countrymen and workers in Cleveland, who accomplished so much in the war industry" would definitely fit František Sigmund on both accounts.

Martinů dedicated Symphony No. 2 to his Cleveland compatriots, but the wording of the dedication was repeatedly adjusted and exists in several variants.[35] Halbreich's catalogue lists the dedication thus: "To my Countrymen-Workers of Cleveland."[36] However, it is unclear what source Halbreich based this on, and no such source is available to us. The autograph musical sources currently do not bear a dedication. Even so, this formulation can be regarded as the original one because it best complies with Martinů's intention to dedicate the symphony "to my countrymen and workers in Cleveland."[37]

The letter from 9 August 1943 states that Hajný intended "to put [the dedication] in better form before it is released."[38] However, the original wording of the dedication is not given in the letter and has not been preserved. It was probably on the score of Martinů's symphony that Hajný brought to the CO office. Contemporary documents, especially the program for the Cleveland premiere, give the composer's dedication as "To my Fellow Countrymen in Cleveland."[39] This dedication, printed in the program, is presumably (based on letter no. 1 and Martinů's recollection cited below) the version edited by Hajný, and was probably accepted by the composer. A third option is provided by the 1966 edition of Symphony No. 2, which states: "Martinů dedicated this work to 'My Countrymen of Cleveland.'"[40] This appears to be a reduction or combination of the first two dedications.

These edits stripped the dedication of part of its initial meaning, and so it seems prudent to quote Martinů's memory, which clearly shows the symbolic importance of the local expatriate community to which he felt he belonged: "I wanted to dedicate the symphony to my countrymen and workers in Cleveland, who accomplished so much in the war industry. The idea succeeded thanks to our consul Hajný. I think that Captain Hajný had quite a hard time with it, and the dedication changed in the details, but the premiere on 28 October 1943 had the character of a national manifestation and assuaged all mistrust. The captain shone with joy, and it was wonderful to be in Cleveland with so many friends."[41]

Conclusion

The previously unknown correspondence related to the genesis and premiere of Symphony No. 2 by Bohuslav Martinů offers a closer look at the functioning of American musical institutions during the war and the ways in which the Czech composer built his reputation as a newcomer to America. However, it also hints at a more momentous aspect of history. The activities of František Sigmund and several others show how some influential individuals act on behalf of larger communities while opting to maintain a low profile themselves. There is no doubt that many Czech workers in Cleveland factories contributed to the growth of the American war industry and thus to the Allied victory over Nazism. Yet few of them would have had the financial or organizational means to commission a symphony. Specific individuals who had previously helped in similar endeavors must have initiated the project and decided to ascribe it to the expatriate community as a whole. The event clearly became a major manifestation of national cohesion for the community of Cleveland Czechs. This is corroborated by the two sold-out performances. The *Cleveland Plain Dealer*, the city's leading newspaper, published an article headlined "Czechoslovakia Still Sings." Its author writes: "Any people who can sing under adversity as they sang last night in the stirring melodies of the Martinu Symphony are freedom's destined children."[42]

The unique confluence of circumstances—the state of war and the anniversary of Czechoslovak independence—brought together the most recognized living composer of that country, his friend and patron of the arts active in the resistance, an enlightened diplomat serving as Czechoslovak consul in Cleveland, a strong local expatriate community, and superbly functioning American institutions. This gave rise to an event of extraordinary artistic and political symbolic power. It was Cleveland, with its history of Central European immigration, thriving heavy industry, and exceptional music scene, that served as the stage for this historic conjunction.

Correspondence from the CO Archives

The correspondence that follows relating to the Symphony premiere was discovered in The Cleveland Orchestra Archives in spring 2022. The set of letters, dated from 9 August to 29 December 1943, comprises original letters received, including seven handwritten by Bohuslav Martinů, and copies of letters sent by the CO management, making the correspondence practically complete. Correspondents include Martinů (7), Czechoslovak consul Hajný (3), and fellow American exile Miloš Šafránek (1); and, from the CO management, press secretary George Henry Lowett Smith (6), manager Carl J. Vosburgh (5), and president of the CO board of trustees and lawyer of Czech descent Thomas L. Sidlo (1). The addressees are all of the above and in two cases the freshly appointed music director of the CO, Erich Leinsdorf.[43]

The letters are ordered chronologically and are provided in a diplomatic transcription. Errors in the spelling of proper nouns are marked [*sic*]; other errors are left unmarked as they do not hinder comprehension or clarity. Unfinished words are completed in square brackets; inscriptions are transcribed in italics. The letters have also been processed in the online Database of Sources of the Bohuslav Martinů Institute (https://database.martinu.cz/).

1. Thomas L. Sidlo to Erich Leinsdorf; typewritten carbon copy.

August 9, 1943.
Mr. Erich Leinsdorf,
Washington, Virginia.

Dear Erich:
Under separate cover I am sending you by parcel post, insured, the score of the new symphony by Martinu which Capt. Hajný, the local Czechoslovak consul, brought to my office this morning.

I presume you will wish to look it over at your early convenience and then let me hear from you. Capt. Hajny tells me that Rodzinski has been after Martinu about it and wants to play it in the New York season, but Hajny asked Martinu to hold off doing anything whatever about it until he hears from us. I would judge that that probably means that Martinu would prefer to have it played earlier in our season rather than later, although that is of course pure supposition.

You will note that he has written a short dedication line in long-hand which Capt. Hajny says he wishes to put in better form before it is released. I will try to work out something with him, and if you have any suggestions will be glad to have them.

Carl [J. Vosburgh] and I are having luncheon with Miller McClintock, president of Mutual, on Wednesday, and at the request of WHK have invited some nine or ten men from our Board, including Messrs. Kulas, Ernst and Williams. McClintock wants to start the ball rolling in the direction of a commercial sponsor.

Hoping you are having a pleasant time and that the news you have from Ann is all good, I am, with kindest regards from us both,

Sincerely,
Thomas L. Sidlo

3-5
cc CJV

2. Carl J. Vosburgh to Bohuslav Martinů; typewritten carbon copy.

August 13, 1943
Mr. Bohuslav Martinu
Darien
Connecticut

Dear Mr. Martinu:
I have just heard from Mr. Leinsdorf by telephone that he wants to do your Symphony No. 2 at our pair of concerts Thursday and Saturday, October 28th and 30th. Since we are giving the premiere performance at these concerts, we also want to have the right to have the premiere performance on the air. I have just signed a contract with The Mutual Broadcasting System for a series of coast-to-coast broadcasts Sunday evenings, 9:00 to 10:00 P.M., Eastern War Time, beginning October 10. We would like to have you give us the right of the premiere radio performance on one of our Sunday evening broadcasts, this broadcast to take place not later than January 1, 1944.

We, of course, are hoping that it will be possible for you to be present at the first performance, Thursday evening, October 28.

May I hear from you at an early date?

Cordially yours,
Manager

P.S. I trust you will keep the performance of your composition confidential at present, as we would like to get a good newspaper release out on it about the first of September. We would prefer doing it then rather than now, as we feel it will be a more appropriate time, coming closer to the concert season and people will be thinking more about concerts than they are in this present hot weather.

CJV:H

3. George Henry Lowett Smith to Bohuslav Martinů; typewritten carbon copy.

August 17, 1943
Mr. Bohuslav Martinu
Darien
Connecticut

Dear Mr. Martinu:
I am glad to hear that Mr. Leinsdorf has scheduled your new symphony for performance at our concerts on October 28th and 30th.

I would like to make my program notes on the new symphony as complete as possible, and hope you will send me whatever material you have about the new work and your recent activities. I should be glad to quote your own description of the symphony.

Could you also send me some pictures of yourself that we might use for newspaper publicity in Cleveland?

Sincerely yours,
GHLS:H

4. Carl J. Vosburgh to Bohuslav Martinů; typewritten carbon copy.

August 18, 1943
Mr. Bohuslav Martinu
Darien
Connecticut

Dear Mr. Martinu:
I have been given to understand that money was raised here locally to commission you to write your Second Symphony, which we are to program at our concert performances of October 28th and 30th. Therefore, I am writing to ask you to give us the sole performing rights for the 1943–1944 season, as well as the first opportunity to record this composition if we should desire. As stated before, we will, of course, want to have the first performance of the composition on the air.

The reason I am writing and asking for the sole performing right is that we may want to perform this work in various cities while we are on our tours in February and March of 1944.

Trusting that I may hear from you at your earliest convenience, I am

Very cordially yours,
Manager
CJV:H

5. Bohuslav Martinů to Carl J. Vosburgh; manuscript, sent from Darien, Connecticut.

August 19 - 1943.

Dear Mr. Vosburgh,
Thank you for your lettre, I am very glad to have first performence of my Symphony N. 2 in Cleveland. I give you also the right to the premiere radio performence on on[e] of your Sunday broadcast (not later than January 1. 1944.)

I hope it will be possible for me to be present at Cleveland to first performence.

Sincerely
yours.
B. Martinů

6. Bohuslav Martinů to Carl J. Vosburgh; manuscript, sent from Darien, Connecticut.

Augustè 21, 1943.

Dear Mr. Vosburgh,
In this moment, I can't give you the sole performence rights, you asked me for, but I can to keep the score to your disposition for every performances, you wish. I have already writen to Mr. Hajný and Mr. Leinsdorf, that I send the score to London, and promised a performence to Mexico, after the first in Cleveland, and it is very possible Dr. Koussevitzky would have a performence à Boston, and I would surely have performence in New York. If you play the Symphony in New York, it will be much easier for me to give you the rights. I think London or Mexico doesn't matter.

To avoid any misunderstanding, I would tell you that it is exacte, Symphony was commis[s]ioned by my friends, for possible first performence in Cleveland, but this is very friendly and private side and doesn't concern my jusual rights for performence and the royalty for location of orchestra materiel, which every orchestra automaticaly pays for.

The money I got from my friends, doesn't cover even the copys of orchestra-materiel, and, unfortunately I can't give myself the pleasure to writte only music. May be, all that is not necessary to writte to you.

Will you be so kind and writte me if you have intention [to] play my Symphony in N. York. In this case I will be able much easier to give you the rights for all season.

Very sincerely
yours
B. Martinů.

P.S. Please, tell to Mr. G. Smith, I will send the notes and photos in earliest convenience. Thanks.

7. Carl J. Vosburgh to Bohuslav Martinů; typewritten carbon copy.

August 24, 1943.
Mr. Bohulslave [*sic*] Martinu,
Darien, Connecticut.

Dear Mr. Martinu:
I have your letter of August 21st and have just talked long distance to Mr. Leinsdorf. We would like very much to have you give us the exclusive right of concert and radio performance of your Symphony No. 2 up to January 1, 1944. As you know, we are planning to do the first performance of this work at our pair of concerts, October 28 and 30, and will then do a radio performance of the composition sometime between October 30 and January 1, 1944.

It is agreeable to us for you to give performances to Mexico, London, and Boston with the understanding that these performances will not take place until after January 1, 1944. We ask that the performances in Mexico and London do not take place until after January 1, 1944 as our Mutual broadcast will go direct to Mexico and be short-waved to Europe.

In addition we ask to have the first opportunity to say whether or not we desire to record this work with the Columbia Recording Corporation.

I trust this is satisfactory to you and will appreciate your confirming our understanding by letter.

Sincerely yours,
Manager
CJV:lmg

8. Bohuslav Martinů to Carl J. Vosburgh; manuscript, sent from Darien, Connecticut.

August 27. -1943.

Dear Mr. Vosburgh:
I am very glad to give you my 2nd Symphony for yours concerts October 28 and 30. and for the radio-performance, and I will keep the exclusivity right for you until January 1 -1944. If you would have the rights for another concerts in the country, in February, let me know, please, the approximative dates and I will keep the score and materiel at your disposition. If you have opportunity to record this work with the Columbia Recording Company, I will be glad to give you the rights to do it.

Very sincerely
yours.
B. Martinů

9. George Henry Lowett Smith to Bohuslav Martinů; typewritten carbon copy.

September 8, 1943
Mr. Bohuslav Martinu
Darien, Connecticut

Dear Mr. Martinu,
Many thanks for your letter and the material so kindly forwarded by the Office of Information. I have also received word that the photographs are on the way.

I have one more request. Would you send us a score as soon as possible? We need two scores—one for our conductor and one for the associate conductor. If we could have one of these in the next week or two we should be very grateful. May I ask at this time about the parts? Our string requirements are 8-7-5-5-4.[44]

Thanking you again for your help, I am,

Cordially yours,
GHLS:amb

10. Bohuslav Martinů to George Henry Lowett Smith [October 1943]; presumably typewritten transcript of Martinů's original letter.

Bohuslav Martinů,
24 West 58 Street,
New York, N.Y.

Mr. A. [*sic*] Smith,
The Cleveland Orchestra,
11001 Euclid Avenue,
Cleveland, Ohio.

Dear Mr. Smith:
This is just to let you know that the score of the II. Symphony is being sent to you by First Class Mail – Registered.

Kindly note my new address.

Sincerely yours,
B. Martinů
by Božka Linhart

11. George Henry Lowett Smith to Bohuslav Martinů; typewritten carbon copy.

October 5, 1943
Mr. Bohuslav Martinu,
Darien, Connecticut.[45]

Dear Mr. Martinu:
Thank you for your letter in which you so kindly offered to send me an extra score of your Second Symphony. The score has not yet arrived, and I am a little worried that it may have gone astray. May I ask also when we may expect the orchestral parts?

The Cleveland papers are very anxious to know exactly when you plan to arrive in Cleveland. I wonder if you would be so good as to let me know about your arrival as soon as your plans become definite.

Cordially yours,
GHLS:amb

12. Emanuel Jan Hajný to Thomas L. Sidlo; typescript on letterhead paper of the Czechoslovak Consulate in Cleveland, hand-signed.

CZECHOSLOVAK CONSULATE
CLEVELAND, OHIO
October 6, 1943.

Dear Tom,
I have just received from New York a photograph of Martinů, which you will find in the enclosure.

I understand that Martinů sent few photographs already to Mr. Vosburgh of the Cleveland Orchestra.

With kind regards,
Sincerely,
Jan

Carl, You may find use for this one too. TLS[46]
Mr. Thos. L. Sidlo,
Union Commerce Building,
Cleveland, O.

13. Bohuslav Martinů to Carl J. Vosburgh; manuscript; sent from New York City.

October 10. 1943.

Dear Mr. Vosburgh,
I send the orchestra materiel and a second score. I hope you shall get it. Mr. Hajny ask me to confirm your rights. You have the rights for first performance in Cleveland and for Radio, I would ask you only to give Radio-performance before 15. Decembre. I have first performence with A. Rodzinski in New York last week in December and I shall need the materiel. I hope it will be possible for you. I will comme in Cleveland about 26–27. Octobre.

Very sincerely
yours
B. Martinů
PLAZA: 5-7937. 24 West 58th Street New York. N.Y.

14. George Henry Lowett Smith to Bohuslav Martinů; typewritten carbon copy.

October 11, 1943
Mr. Bohuslav Martinu,
24 West 58th Street,
New York, New York.

Dear Mr. Martinu:
Many thanks for the score which arrived last Saturday. Mr. Leinsdorf is anxious to receive the parts, at your earliest convenience. Can you let us know approximately when they will arrive? We are also anxious to know when you plan to arrive in Cleveland.

With sincere thanks for all your trouble, I am,

Cordially yours,
GHLS:amb

15. Carl J. Vosburgh to Bohuslav Martinů; typewritten carbon copy.

October 15, 1943.

Mr. Bohuslav Martinu,
24 West 58th Street,
New York, New York.

Dear Mr. Martinu:
I wish to acknowledge receipt of your letter of October the 10th stating that you have shipped us the orchestration and score of your Symphony.

I have discussed the matter of the broadcast with Mr. Leinsdorf and we are scheduling it for December 12th. Immediately following this broadcast, the material will be returned direct to you unless we receive instructions to the contrary.

Looking forward to seeing you in Cleveland about the 26th or 27th, I am

Sincerely yours,
Manager
CJV:lmg

16. Emanuel Jan Hajný to Erich Leinsdorf; typescript on letterhead paper of the Czechoslovak Consulate in Cleveland, hand-signed.

CZECHOSLOVAK CONSULATE
CLEVELAND, OHIO
October 15, 1943.

Mr. Erich Leinsdorf,
Cleveland Orchestra,
Cleveland, O.

Dear Mr. Leinsdorf,
I am sending to you the following scores:
Josef Suk – Legend of Dead Heroes, Op. 35 b,
Josef Suk – Ripening, Op. 34,
V. Novák – Slovak Suite, Op. 32,
Jos. Suk – St. Wenceslaus, Op. 35.
In Montreal we have the folowing scores:
V. Novák – In the Tatra Mountains, Op. 26,
Otakar Odstrčil [*sic*] – Symfonietta, Op. 20,
Leoš Janáček – Taras Bulba, Rapsody,
Leoš Janáček – Lach dances in 3 parts.

Should you be interested in the last mentioned scores I will get them from Canada in a day or two.

With kind regards,
Sincerely,
[signature]
E. J. Hajný,
Consul.

17. Bohuslav Martinů to Carl J. Vosburgh; manuscript.

December 1-1943

Dear Mr. Vosburgh,
Since you made the nice gesture of giving my Second Symphony in honor of the 25th anniversary of the Republic of Czechoslovakia, I have not asked for the customary fee for lending the orchestra materiel.

Mr. Leinsdorf informed me, that there will be further performances of the Second Symphony. I would be very much obliged to you, if you would pay to me fee of $60, for each performance, including the Broadcast 12. December.

Very truly
yours
B. Martinů

18. Carl J. Vosburgh to Bohuslav Martinů; typewritten carbon copy.

December 4, 1943

Mr. Bohuslav Martinu,
24 West 58th Street,
New York, New York.

Dear Mr. Martinu:
I have your letter of December 1st regarding royalty payments to you for our use of the material for your "Second Symphony".

You will recall that during the week that this work was in rehearsal for the premiere performance that a great amount of orchestra time was wasted in correcting the orchestra parts. Not only were bars missing, but in many cases whole lines of the music were missing. This slowed up the orchestra rehearsals to the extent that we were compelled to put in one hour overtime, for which we had to pay the orchestra members $246.00.

With the premiere performances October 28 and 30, and two scheduled performances next week, Tuesday, December 7th in Oberlin, Ohio, and Friday, December 10th in Columbus, Ohio, we will have done a total of four performances. At the rate you suggest of $60.00 per performance, I feel that since we spent $246.00 to correct the parts that these four performances should be given to us without payment. This does not include, of course, the additional work which was necessary to include the cuts and additions you sent to Mr. Leinsdorf in a letter following the premiere performances.

As to the broadcast of this work, scheduled now for Sunday, December 19th, all royalty fees are paid by the Mutual Broadcasting System, so I suggest that you write immediately to Mr. C. M. Hunter, c/o Station WHK, Terminal Tower, Cleveland, Ohio, stating that the royalty fee for the performance of this composition, Sunday evening, December 19th, will be $60.00. For any subsequent performances, we will agree to pay you the fee of $60.00 per performance.

You will realize, I am sure, that the time and money we expended will be to your benefit and the benefit of the New York Philharmonic and other organizations who perform your work later on.

With kindest regards, I am
Sincerely yours,
Manager
CJV:LGS

19. George Henry Lowett Smith to Emanuel Jan Hajný; typewritten carbon copy.

December 10, 1943
Captain E. J. Hajny,
Czechoslovak Consulate,
1900 Euclid Avenue,
Cleveland, Ohio.

Dear Captain Hajny:
I asked the Associated Music Publishers in New York if they would be able to make a set of Suk's "Legend of Dead Heroes." They reply that they would not be able to undertake the responsibility of copying the parts since the copyright is held by Hudebni [matice] in Prague.

It is very difficult and expensive to have parts of large orchestra works made at present even though you, as a representative of the Czech government, should be willing to authorize the copying, so I would suggest that we wait a few months. It is possible that the parts may come through from Prague within the next year.

We are giving the radio première of the Martinu Symphony on December 19th, and I hope it will be possible for you to be present in Severance Hall that evening. I am enclosing a ticket that will admit two, and I shall be glad to send more tickets if you need them.

Cordially,
GHLS/amb
Encl.

20. Emanuel Jan Hajný to George Henry Lowett Smith; typescript on letterhead paper of the Czechoslovak Consulate in Cleveland, hand-signed.

CZECHOSLOVAK CONSULATE
CLEVELAND, OHIO
15[47]

December 17, 1943

Mr. George H. L. Smith
The Cleveland Orchestra
Severance Hall
11001 Euclid Avenue
Cleveland 6, Ohio

Dear Mr. Smith:
I have referred the copying of the parts of Suk's "Legend of Dead Heroes" to our New York office for further attention. In my opinion the opinion of Associated Music Publishers in New York is not entirely correct as similar matters pertaining to countries occupied by the enemy are administered by the Custodian of Enemy Property.

I noted with pleasure that the Radio Premiere of the Martinu Symphony will be given in Severance Hall on December 19th at 8:00 P.M. On Sunday I will be out of town but I shall do my best to be back in time to attend.

With kind regards, I am
Sincerely yours,
[signature]
E. J. Hajný
Consul
EJH: TJ

21. Miloš Šafránek to Cleveland Orchestra; typescript, hand-signed.

891 Park Avenue
New York City
December 29, 1943.

Cleveland Orchestra,
Cleveland, Ohio.

Gentlemen:
I just finished the manuscript of my book "Bohuslav Martinů, his life and work", which will be published in 1944 by Alfred A. Knopf Inc. New York.

With your permission, I would like to quote the Cleveland Orchestra program on:

Mr. Martinů's statement on his Second Symphony.

I would be glad to have a letter from you, giving me permission to use the above mentioned quotation. Thanking you in advance, I remain,

Yours truly,
[signature]
Milos Safranek.

22. George Henry Lowett Smith to Miloš Šafránek; typewritten carbon copy.

December 31, 1943

Mr. Milos Safranek,
891 Park Avenue,
New York, New York.

Dear Mr. Safranek:
It is a pleasure to hear that your book on Martinu is complete. I am happy to give you permission to quote from my program notes on the Second Symphony.

As you probably know, Mr. Martinu wrote his statement in French, the translation is mine.

Looking forward to seeing your book, I am
Cordially yours,
GHLS/amb

NOTES

We would like to thank Andria Hoy, the head of The Cleveland Orchestra Archives for her kind cooperation during Markéta Kratochvílová's study visit in Cleveland and for her invaluable help with the Bohuslav Martinů Institute's research of primary sources in previous years.

1. Bohuslav Martinů, "1938–1945," in *Domov, hudba a svět*, ed. Miloš Šafránek (Prague: Státní hudební vydavatelství, 1966), 330–43.

2. Bohuslav Martinů, "Pařížské nábřeží," in Šafránek, *Domov, hudba a svět*, 115–17.

3. Jaroslav Mihule, *Martinů: Osud skladatele* (Prague: Karolinum, 2017), 345.

4. Harry Halbreich, *Bohuslav Martinů: Werkverzeichnis und Biografie*, 2nd rev. ed. (Mainz: Schott, 2007), 233. The first movement was completed on 28 June, the second on 3 July, the third on 16 July. See also Gabriele Jonté, *Bohuslav Martinů in den USA* (Neumünster: Bockel Verlag, 2013), 109–22.

5. Gregory Terian, "The Cleveland Connection—60 Years on," *Martinů Newsletter* 3/2 (2003): 14.

6. The list is appended to the letter in which Hajný informed the Czechoslovak Legation in Washington of the circumstances surrounding the premiere. Letter from Hajný to the Czechoslovak Legation in Washington, 12 November 1943, Archives of the Czech Ministry of Foreign Affairs, Collection: ZÚ Washington, Box 9.

7. Ibid.

8. Telegram from Jan Masaryk to Erich Leinsdorf, New York, 27 October 1943: "I am very sorry not to be able to be in Cleveland for Martinus premiere. . . . My colleagues and I are very grateful to you sir and to your great orchestra for remembering our anniversary." Telegram from Erich Leinsdorf to Jan Masaryk, New York, 28 October 1943: "It is for us to be grateful and happy to have such a great composer as Martinu in our midst today and to have the opportunity to give the first performance of his new symphony. We feel it is a privilege to commemorate Czech anniversary as a sincere tribute to the freedom on mankind for which the Czech people have always fought. Hope that your country will be freed and liberated soon."

9. Letter from Hajný to the Czechoslovak Legation in Washington, 12 November 1943, Archives of the Czech Ministry of Foreign Affairs, Collection: ZÚ Washington, Box 9. For reports in the press, see for example Elmore Bacon, "New Martinu Symphony Scores at Severance," *Cleveland News*, 29 October 1943: "Czech Consul E. Jan Hajny and other officials attended. And girls in Czech peasant costume carried baskets of flowers to the stage as a tribute to the composer. He was present and shared the ovation."

10. Letter no. 18; see also "Orchestra will play at Oberlin," *Evening Independent* (Massillon, Ohio), 3 December 1943, 10.

11. See letter no. 18.

12. Although the radio performance was not released as a commercial recording at the time, it was preserved on transcription discs (5-7900C), see Patrick Lambert, *Martinů in His Time: The Recorded Legacy* (Prague: Bohuslav Martinů Institute, 2015), 11. These were later digitalized and released on CD (St-Laurent Studio, YSL 0172 78) together with Dvořák's Sixth Symphony, which was recorded in 1946 also by the CO and Erich Leinsdorf.

13. Martinů, "1938–1945," 342.

14. Artur Rodziński served as the music director of the CO from 1933 to 1943, but in 1943 he switched to the New York Philharmonic.

15. The question of the radio broadcast of Symphony No. 2 was broached swiftly because the CO management happened to be holding a meeting about their new contract with Mutual at the time of their correspondence with Martinů. The meeting was to be attended by Miller McClintock (1894–1960), from 1943 to 1944 president of the American radio network Mutual Broadcasting System, and nine or ten members of the orchestra's board of trustees, including E. J. Kulas, A. C. Ernst, and Lewis B. Williams (letter no. 1).

16. Miloš Šafránek, *Bohuslav Martinů: The Man and His Music* (New York: Alfred A. Knopf, 1944), 96–97.

17. Nicholas J. Zentos and Wendy Marley, "Czechs," in *Encyclopedia of Cleveland History*, https://case.edu/ech/articles/c/czechs; Gregory M. Stone, "Czech Migration Patterns to Cleveland, 1865–1940," *Ročenka* 2 (Winter 1995–96): 5–10.

18. For more, see Matěj Kratochvíl, "Music as an Adaptation Strategy: The Hruby Family's Voyage from Cehnice to Cleveland," *Journal of Austrian-American History* 6/1 (2022): 1–13.

19. Stone, "Czech Migration Patterns," 2.

20. See John T. Sabol and Lisa A. Alzo, *Cleveland Czechs: Images of America* (Charleston, SC: Arcadia Publishing, 2009).

21. Stephen J. Sebesta, *The Settlement, Growth and Movement of the Czechs and Their Institutions in Cleveland, Ohio* (Bloomington, IN: Xlibris, 2020), 122–23.

22. Hajný took over the consulate from the previous consul Jaroslav Gardavský on 31 August 1942. See the record about the handover of consulate responsibilities, Archives of the Czech Ministry of Foreign Affairs, London Archives 1939–1945, ZÚ čsl., Cleveland, Box 116.

23. Martinů, "1938–1945," 337.

24. Ibid., 341.

25. Michael Charry, *George Szell: A Life of Music* (Urbana, Chicago, and Springfield: University of Illinois Press, 2011), 78–79.

26. Erich Leinsdorf, *Cadenza: A Musical Career* (Boston: Houghton Mifflin, 1976).

27. Ibid., 117–19.

28. Martinů mentions the source of the funding for his new composition and its performance in Cleveland only in one letter, stating it was "from my friends" (letter no. 6).

29. Milton Widder, "Czech Composer Confesses Heart Is in Native Land," *Cleveland Press*, 27 October 1943: "About 10 new compositions by Mr. Martinu were lost when a friend of his flew out of Paris when the Germans were approaching. This friend, Frank Sigmund, an industrial and chemical engineer now on the staff of the Lake Erie Chemical Co., said that the large case containing Martinu's music was inspected by French customs officials and, as they were all in musical notes, they were held up because they were suspected of being a 'secret code.' Where they are now no one knows."

30. Information about the Sigmund family was taken from Antonín Přichystal, *Sigmundové: Ze života a práce tří pumpařských generací* (Lutín: Sigma, 2001); and Ladislav Smička, "František Sigmund, jeden z třetí generace podnikatelského rodu Sigmundů," *Střední Morava: Vlastivědná revue* 15/28 (2009): 122–25. See also Pavel Lerch, ed., *Nejen na pumpy jsou Sigmundi: Výbor vzpomínek na významné podnikatele* (Olomouc: Burian a Tichák, 2019).

31. Jiří Mucha, *Podivné lásky* (Prague: Mladá fronta, 1988), 316–17, 343.

32. World War II was a time of extraordinary measures in Cleveland as well, and a number of Czechs found temporary refuge in the city; František Sigmund was just one of many. This would explain why there is barely any mention of him in Cleveland archives. After the war Sigmund returned to France, where he resumed his business activities and where he died in 1989.

33. Smička, "František Sigmund," 123; also confirmed by Widder, "Czech Composer Confesses."

34. Smička, "František Sigmund," 124.

35. The existence of different variants is also noted by Gregory Terian, "Martinů in Cleveland," *Czech Music: The Journal of the Dvořák Society* 20 (1997–98): 95, but without interpretation or speculation.

36. Halbreich, *Martinů: Werkverzeichnis und Biografie*, 233.

37. Martinů, "1938–1945," 341.

38. See letter no. 1, Thomas L. Sidlo to Erich Leinsdorf, Cleveland, Ohio, 9 August 1943.

39. Ibid.: "You will note that he has written a short dedication line in long-hand which Capt. Hajny says he wishes to put in better form before it is released."

40. Bohuslav Martinů, *Symphony No. 2* (London: Boosey & Hawkes, 1966).

41. Martinů, "1938–1945," 341.

42. "Czechoslovakia Still Sings," *Cleveland Plain Dealer*, 29 October 1943, 12.

43. Letters courtesy of The Cleveland Orchestra Archives. Three other items of correspondence from the Archives are related to this set in both subject matter and dating, but these had been published before and are not part of the discovered set. The first two are telegrams sent on 27 and 28 October 1943, from the Czechoslovak Foreign Minister Jan Masaryk, son of the first Czechoslovak President Tomáš Garrigue Masaryk, to the CO music director Erich Leinsdorf, and vice versa. The telegrams were published by the CO Archives on its web page in Sophie Benn's article "Bohuslav Martinů: Czech Composer, Citizen of the World, and Cleveland Favorite," https://www.clevelandorchestra.com/discover/archives/stories/bohuslav-martinu/. The third was a letter from Bohuslav Martinů to Erich Leinsdorf from 2 November 1943, in which the composer expressed his joy over the successful collaboration, sent his thanks to the orchestra, and hoped that Leinsdorf would remain as their conductor despite becoming a soldier.

44. 8 first violin desks, 7 second violin desks, 5 viola desks, 5 cello desks and 4 double bass desks.

45. "Recipient's location: Darien, Connecticut. Note on Recipient's location: BM was already back in New York at this time." Database of Sources, Bohuslav Martinů Institute, Prague, https://database.martinu.cz/mails/public_view/9028.

46. Inscription by Thomas L. Sidlo (or TLS). "Carl" is Carl J. Vosburgh (or CJV).

47. Postal zone; such city zones were in common use long before ZIP codes replaced them.

Challenging Modernism: Bohuslav Martinů's Works at the Venice International Festival of Contemporary Music

VINCENZINA C. OTTOMANO
TRANSLATED BY COURTNEY QUAINTANCE

The Venice International Festival of Contemporary Music was founded in 1930, during the height of the Fascist regime. Its primary objective, until 1942, was to promote a positive image of Mussolini's government as the regime sought to stabilize its power. The intent was to demonstrate to the rest of the world a form of enlightened dictatorship that was both open to modernity and able to foster a highly prestigious artistic environment.[1] At the same time, establishing an international music festival strengthened initiatives previously begun by the Venice Art Biennale and, two years later, by the International Film Festival in 1932. These efforts aimed to revive Venice as a political, economic, and cultural hub representing a fusion of tradition and advancement, in line with Fascism's goals of modernity. From a purely musical standpoint, appointing the conservative and ultranationalist Adriano Lualdi as the director ensured control over the music showcased during the event, balancing modernity and tradition while avoiding the more avant-garde European trends.

This tension between the past and the desire to look to the future persisted even in the years after World War II when the entire nation was compelled to question its cultural identity and negotiate its moral and intellectual redemption following the dark years of the regime. The presence of Bohuslav Martinů's music at the Venice International Festival of Contemporary Music from 1934 to 1965 provides a unique vantage point for understanding the history of the reception of his works in the international arena.[2] It also offers a transnational and transcultural perspective for a broader discourse on the tensions, crises, upheavals, and networks that swept through Italy and the entire world during the twentieth century.

Between Light and Darkness: The Years Under Fascism

The first indication of Martinů's involvement in the Venice Festival date back to 26 June 1933. During the afternoon session of the Executive Committee in Rome, Giuseppe Mulè, Alfredo Casella, Gian Francesco Malipiero, and Adriano Lualdi discussed which foreign composers should be invited to the festival's third edition. Martinů's name emerged alongside Ravel, Lambert, Kadosa, and Krenek, accompanied by a note expressing the intent to feature one of his orchestral works in the program.[3] Lualdi relayed this news to the composer shortly afterward, likely at the beginning of July. Martinů replied on 1 August, informing Lualdi that he had already scheduled premieres of his works for the upcoming season and suggesting that either his Trio for violin, cello, and piano, H 232, or his Sextet, H 224, still unknown in Italy, be performed at the festival. He added, "If this arrangement does not satisfy you, I will be happy to reserve a premiere performance of my works for next year."[4] Lualdi eagerly embraced the idea of an original work, requesting to be briefed promptly on the genre of the composition and suggesting a symphonic piece.[5] Thus began Martinů's new project, which eventually led to the creation of *Inventions*, H 234. However, the months following this initial exchange with Lualdi were critical in shaping the new composition.

When the Maggio Musicale Fiorentino changed from a triennial to a biennial format planned for odd-numbered years, with the Venice Festival occurring in even-numbered years, the potential for competition or scheduling conflicts between Italy's two major music festivals was eliminated. In the fall of 1933, Mussolini intervened personally by meeting with the Biennale leaders at Palazzo Venezia in Rome. This led to the lifting of restrictions on orchestra size, making it possible to feature large orchestras in the Biennale program.[6] Once again, Lualdi wrote to Martinů to share the important news. The composer, thrilled at the opportunity to write for a large orchestra, immediately began working on *Inventions*.[7] He completed it in early 1934, as noted in a letter of 12 February updating Lualdi on the ensemble, movements, and length of the piece:

> Dear Sir,
> I take the liberty of announcing that I have just completed the orchestral score written especially for the Venice Festival, in which I have the honor of participating at your kind invitation. The work is called "Inventions" (*Invenzione*), in 3 parts. The orchestra consists of 2 flutes, 2 oboes, 2 clarinets. 2 bassoons, 4 horns, 2 trumpets, 2 trombones, piano, drums (two musicians), strings. . . . The duration is 11 ½ minutes. The movements are I allegro moderato II andante moderato III poco allegro. I will send the manuscript to Edition Schott's Söhne in Mainz, my publisher. I don't know whether he can cope with the publishing at this difficult time. In any case, I'd like to ask when you will need the score so I can make arrangements in a timely manner.[8]

After several postal mishaps, the envelope containing the orchestral score, sent from Prague on 10 June 1934, finally arrived on Lualdi's desk on 10 July and was officially incorporated into the program for the Third International Festival of Contemporary Music.[9]

As one might expect, with the restrictions on ensemble size lifted, the 1934 Music Biennale showcased a highly prestigious, if not rigorously modern, program. From 8 to 16 September, there were four events dedicated solely to new music: a symphonic concert featuring young composers and conductors, which included Martinů's *Inventions* and Pál Kadosa's *Divertimento*, Op. 20a, for orchestra (dedicated to Mussolini) alongside works by Italian composers; a concert of Nordic music featuring Wladimir Vogel's *Tripartita*; a concert of symphonic music by Pizzetti, Lambert, Milhaud, Stravinsky, and Berg (the only composer who did not conduct his own work); and finally, a performance of three chamber works by Vittorio Rieti, Antonio Veretti, and Ernst Krenek under the baton of Hermann Scherchen.[10]

In contrast to the above were three other events: an impressive performance of Giuseppe Verdi's *Messa da Requiem* in St. Mark's Square, conducted by Tullio Serafin with an outstanding cast; a performance by the Vienna Philharmonic under Felix Weingartner of works by Vivaldi, Dukas, Wagner, and Beethoven; and lastly, the highly anticipated closing event, which for the first time allowed the Biennale to incorporate the grand repertoire of Western music theater. This event also marked the debut invitation to the entire company of the Vienna Staatsoper, conducted by Clemens Krauss in the Italian premieres of Richard Strauss's *Die Frau ohne Schatten* and Mozart's *Così fan tutte* at the Teatro La Fenice.[11] The political significance of this concluding performance was clear, highlighted by Mussolini's prominent presence in the audience.

Not surprisingly, after the assassination of his steadfast supporter Chancellor Engelbert Dollfuss by the Nazis on 25 July 1934, Mussolini deployed troops to the Brenner Pass to intimidate any potential German aggression. As a result, his visit to Venice to pay tribute to the Vienna Staatsoper was perceived by both national and international press as a clear demonstration of political and moral support for Austria. This occurred just months after the somewhat frosty meeting between Hitler and Mussolini in Venice on 14 June 1934, during which they discussed the issue of Austrian sovereignty.[12] From this perspective, the inclusion of the works of Czech composer Martinů and Hungarian composer Kadosa, alongside leading young Italian composers, should also be viewed through the lens of the foreign policy pursued by the Fascist regime, which aimed to establish Italian dominance in Eastern Europe. This is evident in the so-called Rome Protocols of 1934, established between Austria, Italy, and Hungary, as well as in the efforts to contain German political influence.[13]

Inventions featured prominently in the Festival's inaugural concert at the Teatro La Fenice on 8 September 1934. Given the exceptional nature of the event, Martinů secured funding from the Czech Ministry of Foreign Affairs to cover his travel and living expenses in Venice so he and his wife, Charlotte, could attend the world premiere of his work.[14] (See Figure 1.) His impressions of the lagoon city and the vibrancy of its musical and cultural scene are well documented in a letter to his family written in mid-September:

> I did not get round to writing sooner; there was no time in Venice, what with the rehearsals and all the people I needed to talk to there. The concert was nice, it went down well with the critics mainly, especially the Swiss and the German ones, the audience is probably not too accustomed to new music, but it was well liked even so. The conductor [Oreste Piccardi] was excellent, Stravinsky was there as well, and the whole assortment from Paris. Cassadó, who played my cello concerto, Princess Polignac, we were very nicely received in Venice; I think it did me a lot of good.[15]

Martinů's words reflect, at least in part, his critical reception. The Italian reviews were generally quite positive. Bruno Barilli granted Martinů *il posto d'onore* (the place of honor) among the composers featured in the inaugural concert, deeming his performance the "most solid, the most complex, and, in short, the most fully musical of all, possessing power and bravura to a remarkable degree."[16] Finally, the *Corriere della sera* review praised the potency and grace of the second movement for strings and piano.[17]

In contrast, the German press was much more mixed in its assessment of Martinů. In the *Allgemeine Musikzeitung*, Max Unger noted in general terms that Martinů "mixes national and supranational elements in his sometimes very energetic orchestral inventions."[18] However, Herbert Gerigk, the prominent advocate of Nazi ideology and future co-editor of the *Lexicon of Jews in Music* (1940–43), did not mince words:

> In his *Inventions* for Orchestra, the Czech composer Bohuslav Martinů developed a playful style of music that was appealing for this feature alone. But even then, there was little behind it; it remained a "moving sound form." If the first movement is sometimes problematic, the next two refute the genuineness of the problem. This is musical mediocrity (and the question remains open as to how much mediocrity in art is justified).[19]

However, these criticisms should also be viewed in light of the political and ideological climate of the 1934 Venice Festival, which emphasized the gap between Italy and Germany, underscored by the complete exclusion of works by contemporary German composers. It was no coincidence that Gerigk's review began with a clear condemnation of Italian intellectual and cultural development, guilty of ignoring

Figure 1. Martinů in Venice, 1934.

"the most primordial of all ties, that of blood and soil" in favor of more progressive tendencies and concluded with the assertion that the Festival would be "a horrible dance of the death of the past . . . of the destroyers of art and decomposers of culture who have lost their primary field, that of the German system."[20]

Gerigk's criticisms encapsulate one of the central themes that emerged during the first meeting of the Permanent Council for International Cooperation Among Composers, established by Richard Strauss in June 1934 in Wiesbaden and held in Venice during the festival from 11 to 13 September. The German delegates, unhappy with the Biennale's program featuring "Bolshevik" music, jazz influences, modernist composer Berg, and Jewish composer Milhaud representing France, had their proposal for a comprehensive redefinition of music festivals ratified. The new definition stated that at least half of the works performed at any festival claiming to be international must be by composers from outside the host country. Most important, delegates from each nation would submit lists of musical compositions they considered representative. According to Benjamin G. Martin, the Permanent Council aimed to promote a Nazi-inspired model of cultural organization, which quickly evolved into the advancement of German cultural hegemony. In this context, the programming for upcoming editions of the Venice Festival started to change, especially with the emergence of new political circumstances and an increasing rapprochement between Italy and Germany.[21]

In November 1935, in an effort to curb Mussolini's expansionist campaign in Ethiopia, the League of Nations imposed economic sanctions on Italy that included a ban on arms trade and the import of products shipped from Italian territory, as well as prohibiting the granting of loans or bank credits to the Fascist government. While this measure had little effect on the conflict in the Horn of Africa, and the sanctions were removed in July 1936, the repercussions for Italy's economic framework were far more complex. Foreign trade could not be resumed quickly, as it was necessary to renegotiate trade treaties previously made with formerly sanctioned countries, all while the international market was shaken by monetary crises that forced Italy to devalue the lira.[22] However, the most significant consequence of the sanctions episode was the Fascist government's estrangement from the League of Nations and its increasing alignment with the Nazi regime, culminating in the declaration of the Rome-Berlin Axis in November 1936 and the signing of the Pact of Steel in May 1939.

At least initially, these historical and political upheavals partially affected the Venice Music Festival. In 1936, its fourth edition took place amid economic constraints, featuring just five performances: two symphonic concerts, two chamber concerts, and one choral and instrumental performance of early Venetian music, with no music theater included. In 1937, after becoming an annual event, the Festival came under the leadership of Alfredo Casella—one of the few Italian representatives of international musical trends—and gained recognition for its modernist and cosmopolitan approach. This was thanks to the performance of two world premieres, Darius Milhaud's *Suite provençale* and Igor Stravinsky's *Jeu de cartes*, along with four Italian premieres: Bartók's *Music for Strings, Percussion, and Celesta*, the suite from Prokofiev's *Lieutenant Kijé*, de Falla's *Fantasía bética*, and Schoenberg's *Suite* Op. 29 for Septet.[23]

The political climate began to infiltrate cultural spaces when, in the fall of 1937, the National Fascist Union publicly endorsed Hitler's "Speech on Modern Art."[24] This speech condemned the perceived decline caused by Bolshevik and Jewish influences and sought to uphold the pure values of the Germanic race. Casella's internationalism (and that of others like him) was openly criticized by the press, a situation exacerbated by his second marriage, to a French Jewish woman. Consequently, he was accused of promoting modernism merely to "win the market for the Jewish cause." Despite the absurdity of the charges and Casella's fervent self-defense, he was removed from his position as director of the Venice Biennale.[25] The 1938 edition was thus entrusted to the composer Goffredo Petrassi, then superintendent of the Teatro La Fenice. For the last time in the 1930s, the Biennale program would attempt to maintain at least the appearance of aesthetic and national pluralism. This was evident in the premieres of Paul Hindemith's ballet suite *Nobilissima visione* (banned in Germany), Arthur Honegger's *Nocturne*, and William Walton's Viola Concerto. Nonetheless, the program excluded works by Jewish composers, thus adhering to the cultural requirements of the Reich.[26]

Against this ambiguous and complex backdrop, the world premiere of Martinů's *Tre ricercari*, H 267, commissioned by the Biennale,[27] took place during a chamber music concert conducted by Nino Sanzogno on 6 September 1938 at Palazzo Giustiniani. The concert featured four composers connected by their Parisian training and aesthetic experiences—Josip Slavenski, Jacques Ibert, Martinů, and Conrad Beck—alongside Italian Giorgio Federico Ghedini. This remarkable event showcased no less than five world premieres, along with the first performance in Italy of Beck's composition.

This time, Martinů did not travel to Venice. However, the very next day, Petrassi and Mario Corti, the commissioner representing the Art Biennale, sent a telegram informing him of the great success of his work.[28] Indeed, a glance at the reviews reveals the favorable reception of *Tre ricercari*, even reaching the pages of the *New York Times*. An enthusiastic article by Raymond Hall, the Venice correspondent, stated unequivocally that the composition "stood many cubits above the others and proved to be one of the few revelations of the year," adding that "the work received an ovation at the close *despite* the composer's Czech nationality."[29]

Hall's words hold particular significance given the Venetian Festival's new musical directions. What excited Italian critics amid the debate between national and international perspectives, between avant-gardism and conservatism, was the clarity and brightness of the rhythmic and melodic structures in Martinů's polyphony, his ability to transcend traditional forms yet achieve "concrete and substantial" (*concreti e sostanziosi*) results, and especially his talent for "grafting a healthy, well-conceived modernism onto classical, sometimes nearly primitive elements."[30] In this sense, the *Tre ricercari*, which drew on the principle of the concerto grosso while emphasizing freedom of form and a renewed exploration of imitative contrapuntal technique and orchestral sonorities, was regarded as a prime example of the avant-garde in harmony with tradition.[31] It embodied both a reverence for the past and a desire for a stylistic and musical synthesis that responded as much to the needs of the Festival as to the trends pursued in those years by Italian composers striving to recover the glorious music of the Baroque.[32] Moreover, the explicit homage to Venice in the title made the composition all the more appealing.

Gerigk reversed his judgment of Martinů in his lengthy article on the Festival program in *Die Musik*, where he expressed satisfaction that Italy was aligning with Germany's positions both on musical style and on the Jewish question and offered words of praise for the composer born in Czechoslovakia (a nation that was at that moment clearly in the crosshairs of the Reich):

> [Sanzogno] achieved remarkable success with Czech composer Bohuslav Martinů's *Tre ricercari* for chamber orchestra. Martinů called each of the three movements of the work—which was composed for Venice—*ricercare* because Venice is where the musical form of *ricercare* was born. Here, an original musical nature speaks that overturns all considerations and simply sweeps you away. Although one recognizes occasional jazz elements in his music, they are transformed into art impeccably. Martinů works freely with tonality, but without indulging in a lack of regularity.[33]

After the Festival was paused in 1939 and 1940, the two editions held during the early years of World War II reflected the cultural and political leanings of the alliance between Italy and Germany. This was marked by the enforcement of racial laws that had already been implemented in November 1938 and a ban on performances of music from enemy nations in theaters and symphonic institutions. Banned works included those by Russian composers (excluding those before the Bolshevik era), Anglo-Saxon composers (except for Classical works), and most French composers.[34] In 1941, the program for the seventh International Festival of Contemporary Music featured just two concerts dedicated to contemporary Italian music, an all-Wagner concert, and revivals of Rossini's *La Cenerentola*, Cimarosa's *Il matrimonio segreto*, and Mozart's singspiel *Die Entführung aus dem Serail*. Similarly, the subsequent Festival featured large numbers of German musicians and works by Japanese composers in tribute to the Rome-Berlin-Tokyo Tripartite Pact.

Political Issues: The Postwar Years

The escalation of warfare, the shift in favor of the Anglo-American allies, and the collapse of Fascism silenced Venetian events until 1946, when the Festival resumed with the explicit goal of renewal. Venice, spared from the bombing, emerged from the ashes of the turbulent first two decades of the twentieth century as a symbol of political, social, and cultural rebirth.[35] The need to rebuild the nation, despite the economic challenges of the immediate postwar period, coincided with the necessity to regain credibility on the international stage, both politically and artistically, and to address the self-segregation that had excluded Italian culture from European circulation. This was especially pressing for an institution like the Biennale, which originated and evolved during the Mussolini regime and mirrored its total decline into cultural subservience to the Reich. On the other hand, from a musical perspective, the idea of reconstruction carried additional significance: it aimed to create a bridge between the modernity experienced during Fascism—despite everything—and the isolated position of the Italian scene on the fringes of the most avant-garde artistic movements. In other words, efforts were undertaken to address the discontinuities and gaps in the 1930s musical programming through cultural updating. This included a retrospective approach, exemplified by the many performances of music from the Second Viennese School and the rediscovery of the twelve-tone technique, alongside the more complex task of creating a space for the avant-garde following World War II.[36] Alongside the vision of renewal in the music performed, a certain continuity remained in the choice to revive works from the more distant past—specifically, the greats of Italian music history. This coincided with a broader movement to reclaim the musical and cultural heritage that had been misrepresented by Fascist propaganda.

Viewed from this perspective, the program put together by the Biennale's new chief commissioner, Giovanni Ponti, closely linked to the Christian Democratic Party at the time in government, is not surprising. The Ninth Festival, the first after the referendum of June 1946 that sanctioned the birth of the Italian Republic, reflected the new modernist direction of the Biennale in both the fields of art and music. On 17 September, at the Teatro La Fenice, Ettore Gracis conducted Anton Webern's Symphony, Op. 21. During the same evening, cellist Henri Honegger performed Martinů's Sonata for Cello and Chamber Orchestra, H 283; this was followed by Luigi Dallapiccola's *Canti di prigionia* for choir and instruments. Two days later, Hermann Scherchen conducted Milhaud's *La mort d'un tyran*, Schoenberg's Second Chamber Symphony, and Shostakovich's Symphony No. 9. The Festival also showcased the debut of Bruno Maderna, then twenty-six, who led the instrumental group Benedetto Marcello in a concert dedicated to the Giovane Scuola (young Italian school) of composers. The program featured music by Valentino Bucchi, Riccardo Malipiero, Camillo Togni, and Guido Turchi, along with Maderna's own Serenata for eleven instruments (which remains lost). As Mario Labroca recalled, "It was a miraculous festival because of the music he managed to put together and the performers to whom it was entrusted. . . . It was our first encounter with the music that the war had kept from us for so many years; the barrier that had nearly blinded us had fallen."[37]

The following years were pivotal in the political and social life of the newly formed Republic. They were marked by a transition from a predominantly rural economy to one increasingly centered on industrialization, primarily due to American subsidies from the European Recovery Program. During this period, the Christian Democratic Party consolidated its power and played a significant role on the international stage. The strategic location of the Italian peninsula, positioned at the forefront of the divide between the Soviet Union and the United States, grew increasingly important.

In many ways, the Fourteenth Festival of 1951 can be seen as a laboratory for the transformations occurring in Italy. It also serves as a sounding board for the tensions between openness to contemporary ideas, the need to merge Italian culture with European culture, and the development of a new memory of Italian identity in the aftermath of Fascism and its ideological dominance over the national past. Musician and music critic Ferdinando Ballo, who organized the Music Biennale from 1947 to 1951, achieved a notable first in the postwar era by successfully featuring the world premiere of Stravinsky's *The Rake's Progress* in the program. This occasion drew international attention to Venice, not only because it marked the composer's return to Europe after he emigrated to America at the start of the war but also, more significantly, because it featured his long-awaited work for the stage, composed nearly twenty years after the composition of *Perséphone*.[38]

In contrast, a glance at the list of proposed works reveals very few world premieres. Most of the program was dedicated to honoring the fiftieth anniversary of the death of Italy's national composer Giuseppe Verdi. Verdi's *Messa da Requiem* was performed on 8 September, at the opening of the Festival, followed significantly by *Attila*, Verdi's second opera composed in 1846 for the Teatro La Fenice, presented in concert form at the same theater on 12 September.[39] Still in the spirit of commemorations, a symphonic-choral concert was scheduled to honor Schoenberg, who had died in July 1951.

While the Festival appeared "to have fulfilled its delicate task of navigating and balancing between tradition and contemporaneity"[40] with the world premiere of *The Rake's Progress* and the commemoration of Verdi, the critical reaction was much more complex. Stravinsky's opera emerged as a radical reinterpretation of the neoclassical experience, seemingly pulling the music theater genre back into history rather than propelling it toward renewal in the avant-garde sense.[41] On the other hand, critics had broader concerns regarding the Festival's true purpose, vocation, and mission as an international showcase for musical modernity. Against this contentious backdrop, Martinů's *Veselohra na mostě* (*Comedy on the Bridge*), H 247—his sole stage work featured in the Music Biennale—was performed at the Teatro La Fenice on 19 and 20 September 1951.

Born as a radio opera in 1935—commissioned by Czech Radio, which broadcast it on 18 March 1937—*Comedy on the Bridge* was already familiar in Italian circles.

The work received a special mention at the inaugural edition of the Prix Italia, the prestigious international competition dedicated to the best radio productions, held in Venice in 1949.[42] However, the staged version of the opera was new to Europe. It had premiered just a few months earlier in New York City in a production by the Mannes College Opera Studio of the New School for Music on 28 May 1951, and then at the summer music festival at Tanglewood on 17 July of the same year. In fact, the decision to feature *Comedy on the Bridge* in the 1951 Biennale was a backup plan after complications arose with Nino Rota, who was to have adapted his radio opera *I due timidi*, composed in 1950, for the stage. Ballo quickly proposed Martinů's work as a substitute in a letter to director Rodolfo Pallucchini: "It is unprofessional to change the titles of works that have already been announced. On the other hand, I cannot do anything if the author [Rota], instead of completing his score, departs for London after disagreeing with the director. The substitution has these advantages: . . . Martinů's name carries far greater international significance than Rota's, and his work requires a smaller, yet more musically interesting ensemble."[43] Thus, *Comedy on the Bridge* was included in the program for two evening performances featuring three chamber operas alongside a revival of Boccherini's *La Clementina* and Roberto Lupi's choreographic cantata *Orfeo.*

The Kafkaesque plot of the libretto, written by Martinů himself and based on the play of the same name by Václav Kliment Klicpera, shocked its audience. Set in an unspecified place and time, five characters isolated on a bridge find themselves trapped between two warring armies (Figure 2). Although the reviews were mostly positive, they all expressed discomfort with the opera's sharp satire on war and especially its themes, which resonated deeply with contemporary issues.[44] During a time when the world was indeed divided into two blocs, living in constant tension between two armies, the image of an impenetrable bridge emerged as a clear symbol of the historical circumstances of the Cold War, representing the Iron Curtain that delineated the ideological, political, and territorial division between the allies of the United States and the Soviet Union. The disquiet and bewilderment at such an enigmatic work was such that it even shocked the sensibilities of American viewers. According to a journalist for *The Guardian*: "Martinů's *Comedy on the Bridge* is more voluble, though its meaning is hardly clearer. From the decorative curtain one assumes that it is a satire on the futility of armament, and it was no doubt the realization of this subversive interpretation that drove the Americans out of the next row halfway through."[45] Martinů's polemical and actualizing intent was reinforced by the staging of the opera, entrusted to the irreverent Mino Maccari. Paratroopers dressed as Harlequins descended from the ceiling, while muzzled dogs and pigs acted as sentries guarding the bridge (see Figure 3). In the finale, the absurdity of the impossibility of escape was transformed into pure provocation with a parade of placards prominently displaying the heads of war victims.[46]

Figure 2. A performance of *Comedy on the Bridge* at the Teatro La Fenice.

Even Ballo's report on the Festival program emphasized the opera's impact: "The production was entrusted to the painter Mino Maccari, who created a brilliant and surprising representation of a distinctly polemical character. . . . The show's novelty surprised and perhaps somewhat disoriented the audience, but in the end was a great success, if primarily due to the lively discussions it ignited."[47]

This created a profound discrepancy between the flashy media circus surrounding Stravinsky and the impact of Martinů's one-act opera. In just over thirty minutes, *Comedy on the Bridge* jolted both the audience and critics from their shared amnesia during a period of economic and political recovery, forcing them to contemplate their recent past, which many might have preferred to forget.[48] In this regard, even the sharpest critics recognized the modernity of Martinů's piece, which introduced a form of musical action largely absent from Biennale programming. Indeed, it offered a critical perspective on contemporary society and history that would return with even greater intensity in the politically engaged works performed in the 1960s and 1970s.

Five years later, after a recommendation from Luigi Ferrarino, at the time director of the Italian Institute of Culture in Paris, and with the support of the violinist Blaise Calame,[49] Martinů's Suite Concertante for violin and orchestra, H 276 II, premiered in Europe on 11 September 1956. This was the inaugural

Figure 3. Mino Maccari, design drawing for *Comedy on the Bridge*'s sentinels.

concert of the Nineteenth Festival, featuring Calame as the soloist and Fabien Sevitzky conducting the Teatro La Fenice orchestra and broadcast live on Italian Radio's *Terzo programma.* In October of the same year, while in Rome for his appointment as composer-in-residence at the American Academy, Martinů heard and was pleased with a repeat performance.[50]

By 1958, the context and political implications of the Twenty-First Festival were significantly different. This time, the program featured a concert devoted entirely to Czech composers, with performances by the Prague Symphony Orchestra (Symfonický orchestr hlavního města Prahy), a Bohemian choir (Český pěvecký sbor), and the Prague Conservatory's ensemble of professors.

In June 1958, Virgilio Mortari, the Festival's artistic consultant and superintendent of Teatro La Fenice, began negotiations with Ladislav Vachulka, who at the time was actively facilitating exchanges between Italy and Czechoslovakia. Mortari also collaborated with Jaromír Fučík, the cultural attaché at the Czech embassy in Rome, to help the musicians attain entry visas for Italy.[51] The concert was to take place on 22 September in the Cini Foundation's Sala del Noviziato on the Island of San Giorgio, with performances of Emil Hlobil's Octet, Otakar Jeremiáš's Doric Serenade, Leoš Janáček's Sextet for Wind Instruments (*Mládí*), and Martinů's *The Opening of the Springs*, H 354. All appeared to be proceeding smoothly until 13 September, when Mortari wrote in strictest confidence to Giovanni Ponti, who had become a senator, that a Foreign Ministry official had informed him of "serious political difficulties with granting entry permits for Czechoslovak citizens."[52] Despite a telegram sent to Prague by Mortari on 17 September confirming that the visas had been granted, Biennale management announced in a terse statement that "due to force majeure" the concert had been canceled.[53]

The Foreign Ministry's official reasons for opposing such an event were that Czechoslovakia was guilty of hosting Radio Oggi in Italia. This clandestine station, operated by the Italian Communist Party, utilized repeaters from Radio Prague that the Czech Communist Party provided for its broadcasts.[54] The station emerged as a voice of dissent, playing a strategic role from 1950 onward in criticizing government policy and the Christian Democrats, led by the Italian Communist Party. It also played a role in ideological education and propaganda aimed at broad segments of public opinion during a time when the Communist Party was largely shut out of Italian public radio channels.[55] This significant episode, which outraged much of the press, underscored the frailties and risks of the radical positions taken by the Christian Democratic government toward Eastern Bloc countries. Simultaneously, it exposed the cultural ramifications of insufficient dialogue and interaction with Soviet-influenced nations, a concern that intellectuals and the protests of the 1960s began to recognize as an urgent priority.

A year later, at the close of the turbulent 1950s, the Twenty-Second Festival featured another work by Martinů: the *Fantasia concertante* for piano and orchestra, H 366, which he completed in 1958. This piece was part of the symphonic concert on 22 September 1959 conducted by Ferruccio Scaglia with the Italian Radio and Television Orchestra, and Margrit Weber, the dedicatee of the composition, as the piano soloist.[56] Martinů's final letters convey his enthusiasm and eagerness for this event, which he planned to attend in person after having escorted Mr. and Mrs. Weber to Venice. However, he passed away in Liestal, Switzerland, on 28 August, barely a month before the concert. The performance of the *Fantasia concertante* thus served as a tribute to the composer's recent passing, as noted in most newspapers.

Aside from Nonet, H 374, which the Czech Nonet performed on 9 September 1965 at the Twenty-Eighth Festival, no other works by Martinů have been featured at the Biennale to date. The reasons for this are complex and can, in part, be linked to the chronological and aesthetic gap between Martinů's music and the shifting focus of the Venetian institution, which increasingly leaned toward showcasing contemporary avant-garde works and the new opportunities presented by electronic and, later, digital music. On the other hand, Martinů's disappearance from the concert and music theater repertoires of the Venice Festival, which continued to feature other twentieth-century composers, reveals a broader (and unjust) neglect of the Czech composer after his death. In this regard, the production and reception of Martinů's works in the context of the Contemporary Music Festival hold unique significance in the broader narrative of his life and compositional activity. They reflect all aspects of the reception of a cosmopolitan composer positioned on the borderline between tradition and innovation, and between originality and individuality. After all, throughout the long twentieth century, the Biennale Music Festival served as an essential platform for negotiating and performing the concept of modernism from diverse and often controversial viewpoints.

NOTES

1. For a general discussion, see Marla Susan Stone, *The Patron State: Culture and Politics in Fascist Italy* (Princeton: Princeton University Press, 1998).

2. For an overview, see Robert Simon, "Martinů at the Venice Biennale," *Martinů Revue* 15/3 (2015): 8–9.

3. Archivio Storico della Biennale di Venezia (ASAC) Fondo storico, serie Musica, b. 1, Relazione del comitato esecutivo del III Festival internazionale di musica di Venezia (26 June 1933).

4. "Si cet arrangement ne vous convient pas je serai content de vous réserver une première exécution de mes œuvres pour l'année prochaine." Letter from Martinů to Lualdi, Paris, 1 August 1933, ASAC, Fondo storico, serie Scatole nere 86.

5. Lualdi to Martinů, Milan, 22 September 1933, ASAC, Fondo storico, serie Scatole nere 86.

6. See A. [Adriano] L. [Lualdi], "Mussolini e i Festival veneziani," *Musica d'Oggi* 16/8–9 (September 1934): 295–96.

7. Martinů to Lualdi, Paris, 14 January 1934, ASAC, Fondo storico, serie Scatole nere 86.

8. "Cher Monsieur, je me permets de vous annoncer, que je viens [de] terminer la partition d'orchestre écrite spécialement pour [le] Festival de Venice dont j'ai l'honneur de participer pour votre aimable invitation. L'œuvre s'appelle: «Inventions» (Invenzione), en 3 parties. L'orchestre est: 2 flauti, 2 oboi, 2 clarin[etti] 2 fagotti, 4 corni, 2 trompetti [*sic*] 2 tromboni, piano, batterie (deux joueurs), les cordes. . . . La durée est de 11 ½ minutes. Les mouvements sont: I allegro moderato

II andante moderato III poco allegro. J'envoie le manuscrit à Edition Schott's Söhne, à Mainz, qui est mon éditeur. Je ne sais pas si lui-même en ces moments difficiles va s'occuper avec la édition. En tout cas, je vous demanderais en quelle moment vous aurez besoin la partition, pour que je puisse prendre les dispositions à temps." Martinů to Lualdi, Paris, 12 February 1934, ASAC, Fondo storico, serie Scatole nere 86.

9. See the documentation in ASAC, Fondo storico, serie Musica, b. 1, III Festival internazionale di musica 1934.

10. Full details on Biennale concerts and events can be found at https://asac.labiennale.org. See also Fiamma Nicolodi, "Su alcuni aspetti dei festivals tra le due guerre," in *Musica italiana del primo Novecento: La generazione dell'80, Atti del convegno Firenze, 9–10–11 maggio 1980*, ed. Fiamma Nicolodi (Florence: Olschki, 1981), 141–204, at 169–70. On the question of Alban Berg's participation, first with the *Lyrische Suite*, then replaced with the concert aria for soprano and orchestra *Der Wein*, see Mosco Carner, "The Berg Affair, Venice 1934," *The Musical Times* 110 (November 1969): 1129–31.

11. Nicolodi, "Su alcuni aspetti dei festivals," 30.

12. See Benjamin G. Martin, *The Nazi-Fascist New Order for European Culture* (Cambridge, MA: Harvard University Press, 2016), 34–35; and Erik Levi, "The Rome-Berlin Axis: Musical Interactions between Fascist Italy and Nazi Germany in Redrawing a 'New Order for European Culture,'" in *The Routledge Handbook to Music Under German Occupation, 1938–1945*, ed. Erik Levi and David Fanning (London: Routledge, 2020), 103–21, at 107.

13. On the musical consequences of the rapprochement between Italy and Czechoslovakia, see Vincenzina C. Ottomano, "'Outdated' or 'Too Current'? *Prodaná nevěsta* (The Bartered Bride) in Milan 1905, 1934, and 1935," in *Bedřich Smetana and European Opera*, ed. Aleš Březina and Ivana Rentsch (Würzburg: Königshausen & Neumann, 2024), 233–53. On the historical context, see Stefano Santoro, *L'Italia e l'Europa orientale: Diplomazia culturale e propaganda 1918–1943* (Milan: Franco Angeli, 2005); and Luciano Monzali, *Il sogno dell'egemonia: L'Italia, la questione jugoslava e l'Europa centrale (1818–1941)* (Florence: Le Lettere, 2010).

14. See Martinů's letter to his family, Paris, 3 September 1934, in *Dear All (III.): Dopisy Bohuslava Martinů rodině v Poličce z let 1934 a 1935 / Bohuslav Martinů's Letters to his Family in Polička in 1934 and 1935*, Jaromír Synek and Gabriela Všetičková (eds.) (Olomouc: Palacký University, 2021), 195–97.

15. "[...] nedostal jsem se dříve k dopisu, v Benátkách nebyl čas, byly zkoušky a bylo tam mnoho lidí s kterými jsem musel mluvit. Koncert byl hezký, úspěch jsem měl hlavně u kritiků, zvláště švýcarských a německých, obecenstvo není asi dost zvyklé na novou hudbu ale i tak se to líbilo. Dirigent byl výborný, byl tam také Stravinský a celá společnost z Paříže. Cassado co hrál můj čelový koncert, princezna Polignace [*sic*], přijali nás v Benátkách moc hezky, myslím že mi to hodně prospělo." Letter from Martinů to his family, Menaggio (Lago di Como), mid-September 1934, in ibid., 198–201, at 136–37. https://database.martinu.cz/mails/public_view/693

16. Bruno Barilli, "Giovani compositori italiani e stranieri al Festival musicale di Venezia," *Il Giornale d'Italia* (11 September 1934); "Il più solido, il più complesso e insomma il più pienamente musicale di tutti e possiede potenza e bravura in misura molto notevole."

17. Vice (pseud.), "Corriere teatrale," *Il corriere della sera*, 9 September 1934.

18. "Nationale Bestandteile mischt der Tschechoslowake Bohuslaw [*sic*] Martinu in seinen teilweise sehr energisch gesetzten Orchesterinventionen mit übernationalen." Max Unger, "Internationales Musikfest in Venedig," *Allgemeine Musikzeitung* 61/40 (5 October 1934): 542–43, at 543.

19. "Der Tscheche Bohuslav Martinu entwickelte in den 'Invenzionen' für Orchester eine spielerische Musik, die allein dieses Zuges wegen schon sympathisch berührte. Aber auch hier steckte wenig dahinter, es blieb 'tonend bewegte Form.' Gibt sich der erste Satz teilweise problematisch, so widerlegen die beiden folgenden die Echtheit der Problematik. Es ist musikalisches Mittelmaß (wobei die Frage offen bleibt, wie weit Mittelmaß der Kunst überhaupt eine Berechtigung hat)." Herbert Gerigk, "Musikfestdämmerung," *Die Musik* 27/1 (October 1934): 45–51, at 47–48.

20. "So wurde der Hauptteil des Musikfestes ein grausiger Totentanz der Gestrigen, der Geister, die stets verneinen, der Kunstzerstörer und Kulturersetzer, die ihres Hauptfeldes, des Systemdeutschlands, verlustig gegangen sind." Ibid., 45. See also Martin, *The Nazi-Fascist New Order*, 35–36.

21. Ibid., 36–43.

22. For a general discussion of Fascist foreign policy, see in particular Renzo De Felice, *Mussolini il duce*, vol. 1: *Gli anni del consenso 1929–1936* (Turin: Einaudi, 1974); Enzo Collotti, *Fascismo e politica di potenza: Politica estera, 1922–1939* (Florence: La Nuova Italia, 2000).

23. See Fiamma Nicolodi, *Musica e musicisti nel ventennio fascista* (Florence: Discanto, 1984), 261.

24. See Alberto Ghislanzoni, "Il discorso del Cancelliere Hitler sull'arte moderna," *Il musicista* 4/1 (August 1837): 125–29, cited in Nicolodi, *Musica e musicisti*, 261–62.

25. Ibid., 261–65.

26. See Martin, *The Nazi-Fascist New Order*, 130. For a more general discussion, see Jens Petersen, "Vorspiel zu 'Stahlpakt' und Kriegsallianz: Das Deutsch-Italienische Kulturabkommen vom 23. November 1938," *Vierteljahrshefte für Zeitgeschichte* 36/1 (1988): 41–45.

27. See Martinů's letter to his family, Paris, 19 January 1938, https://database.martinu.cz/mails/public_view/782#_ftn27.

28. Telegram from Goffredo Petrassi and Mario Corti to Martinů, 7 September 1938, Bohuslav Martinů Center in Polička, https://database.martinu.cz/mails/public_view/5787.

29. Raymond Hall, "Novelties from Many Lands at Venice Festival," *New York Times*, 23 October 1938, 167. Emphasis mine.

30. "Innestare un sano, bene inteso modernismo su elementi classicheggianti, talora quasi primitivi." Michelangelo Abbado, "Il VI Festival Internazionale di Musica Contemporanea a Venezia," *Rassegna della istruzione artistica* 9–12 (1938): 429–43, at 434.

31. See Michael Crump, *Martinů and the Symphony* (Woodbridge: Boydell, 2010), 77, 95.

32. See in particular Fiamma Nicolodi, "Fonti critiche e storiografiche della riscoperta italiana di Vivaldi," *Chigiana: Rassegna annuale di studi musicologici* 41/21 (1989): 19–39.

33. "Den 'Drei Ricercaren für Kammerorchester' des Tschechen Bohuslav Martinu erspielte er [Sanzogno] einen lauten Erfolg. Ricercare hat Martinu die drei Sätze des ebenfalls für Venedig komponierten Werkes deshalb genannt, weil das Ricercar als musikalische Formbezeichnung ehemals von Venedig ausging. Hier spricht eine ursprüngliche Musikantennatur, die alle Überlegungen über Haufen wirft und einfach mitreißt. Man erkennt zwar gelegentlich Jazzelemente in seiner Musik, aber sie sind auf einer einwandfreien Ebene ins künstlerische gewendet. Martinu waltet frei mit der Tonalität, ohne jedoch der Regellosigkeit zu verfallen." Herbert Gerigk, "Das internationale Musikfest in Venedig," *Die Musik* 31/1 (October 1938): 53–57, at 55.

34. Fiamma Nicolodi, "La musica sotto il fascismo," in *Il contributo italiano alla storia del pensiero: Musica*, ed. Sandro Cappelletto (Rome: Treccani, 2018), 569–80, at 576.

35. See Christopher Duggan, "Italy in the Cold War Years and the Legacy of Fascism," in *Italy in the Cold War: Politics, Culture, and Society 1948–58*, ed. Christopher Duggan and Jonathan Wagstaff (Oxford: Berg, 1995), 1–24.

36. See in particular Guido Salvetti, "Politica, cultura, musica," in *Italia millenovecentocinquanta*, ed. Guido Salvetti and Bianca Maria Antolini (Milan: Guerini & Associati, 1999), 13–28; and Peter Roderick, "Rebuilding a Culture: Studies in Italian Music after Fascism, 1943–1953" (PhD diss., University of York, 2000). For a discussion of the Festival programming during the 1950s, see David Giovanni Leonardi, "Il Festival internazionale di musica contemporanea di Venezia (1946–54)," in *Italia millenovecentocinquanta*, 137–58; and Clementina Casula and Paolo Dal Molin, "Innovazione artistica e turismo culturale: La programmazione del Festival Internazionale di Musica Contemporanea nella rinascita post-bellica della Biennale di Venezia (1946–1951)," in *Turismo musicale: Storia, geografia, didattica*, ed. Rosa Cafiero and Guido Lucarno (Bologna: Pàtron, 2020), 121–28.

37. "Fu un festival miracoloso per le musiche che riuscì a mettere insieme e per gli esecutori a cui furono affidate . . . fu il nostro primo incontro con le musiche che la guerra aveva diviso da noi per tanti anni; era caduta la barriera che ci aveva quasi accecati." Mario Labroca, "Il festival internazionale di musica contemporanea," in *Teatri nel mondo: La Fenice* (Milan: Nuove Edizioni, 1971), 259–75. See also Michele Girardi, "La Fenice nel mondo: Repertorio, avanguardie, retroguardie, fiamme," in Anna Laura Bellina and Michele Girardi, *La Fenice 1792–1996: Il teatro, la musica, il pubblico, l'impresa* (Venice: Marsilio, 2003), 157–58.

38. See Harriet Boyd-Bennett, *Opera in Postwar Venice: Cultural Politics and the Avant-garde* (Cambridge: Cambridge University Press, 2018), 32–60.

39. Ibid., 61–90.

40. "Aver assolto il suo delicato compito di orientamento e di equilibrio tra tradizione e contemporaneità." Alessandro Piovesan, "Il XIV Festival di musica contemporanea: *Notte trasfigurata* di Schoenberg," *La fiera letteraria* 6/39 (14 October 1951): 5.

41. See "Il Festival veneziano tra eventi mondiali e routine," in Roberto Zanetti, *La musica italiana nel Novecento* III (Busto Arsizio: Bramante, 1985), 1297–307.

42. Sergio Magnani, "Commedia sul ponte," *Radiocorriere* 27/39 (24–30 September 1950): 9–10. The radio version of Martinů's opera was broadcast on 24 and 26 September 1950.

43. "Non è serio cambiare i titoli delle opere già annunciate. D'altra parte, non posso far nulla se l'autore [Rota] invece di completare il suo spartito se ne parte per Londra dopo essersi messo in disaccordo anche con il regista. La sostituzione presenta questi vantaggi: . . . Martinů è un nome d'importanza ben più alta e internazionale di quello di Rota, richiede una compagnia più piccola e musicalmente più interessante." Letter from Ferdinando Ballo to the directors of the Biennale, 5 August 1951, ASAC, Fondo storico, b. 4.

44. See N., "Composizioni italiane al Festival di Venezia," *Giornale di Trieste*, 7 October 1951: "Un pubblico, dapprima sorpreso e sconcertato, e un po' inquieto, ha compreso ben presto che si trattava più che altro d'una caricatura"; see also M. N., "Il Festival di Venezia," *La Scala*, 15 October 1951: "[*Comedy on the Bridge*] è la satira di quella che doveva essere l'Europa d'oggi, spezzettata e divisa da tanti assurdi confini"; and Giuseppe M. Pilo, "Tre brevi opere al XIV Festival musicale," *Il popolo veneto*, 21 September 1951: "È possibile scorgere certa intenzione polemica e satirica contro taluni aspetti della realtà contemporanea."

45. C. M., "The Venice Music Festival," *The Guardian*, 25 September 1951.

46. See the description of the staging in Pilo, "Tre brevi opere al XIV Festival musicale," and "Tre opere alla Fenice," *Milano sera*, 20 September 1951.

47. "L'impostazione dello spettacolo fu affidata al pittore Mino Maccari che ne trasse una brillante e sorprendente rappresentazione di carattere decisamente polemico. . . . La novità dello spettacolo sorprese e forse in parte disorientò il pubblico ma non fece mancare il successo pur attraverso le discussioni più vive." See "Relazione sul XIV Festival internazionale di musica contemporanea," ASAC, Fondo storico, b. 4.

48. On the concept of amnesia, see Rosario Forlenza, "Sacrificial Memory and Political Legitimacy in Postwar Italy: Reliving and Remembering World War II," *History and Memory* 24/2 (2012): 73–116.

49. See the correspondence between Alessandro Piovesan, Luigi Ferrarino, and Blaise Calame, ASAC, Fondo storico, b. 21.

50. See Martinů's letter to his family, Rome, 21 October 1957, Bohuslav Martinů Center in Polička. See https://database.martinu.cz/mails/public_view/1362/.

51. See the correspondence between Virgilio Mortari, Ladislav Vachulka, and Jaromír Fučík, ASAC, Fondo storico, b. 29.

52. "Serie difficoltà, per ragioni politiche, alla concessione dei permessi di entrata di cittadini cecoslovacchi." Confidential letter from Mortari to Giovanni Ponti, 13 September 1958, ASAC, Fondo storico, b. 29.

53. "Per cause di forza maggiore." Rubens Tedeschi, "Inaudito sopruso clericale che offende la democrazia e la cultura," *L'Unità*, 21 September 1958, 8.

54. Ibid.

55. On Radio Prague, see Enrico Miletto, "Onde rosse da Praga: Radio oggi in Italia, la voce cecoslovacca del PCI," in *Voci dall'Est: Radio e propaganda del blocco sovietico durante la guerra fredda*, ed. Enrico Miletto and Marco Novarino (Acireale: Bonanno Editore, 2024), 193–221; and Andrea Sangiovanni, *Specchi infiniti: Storia dei media in Italia dal dopoguerra a oggi* (Rome: Donzelli, 2021), 84–85.

56. See Martinů's letter to Marie Martinů, Schönenberg, 20 March 1959, Bohuslav Martinů Center in Polička, https://database.martinu.cz/mails/public_view/1073; and a letter to Miloš Šafránek, Nice, 14 May 1959, Bohuslav Martinů Center in Polička, https://database.martinu.cz/mails/public_view/2770.

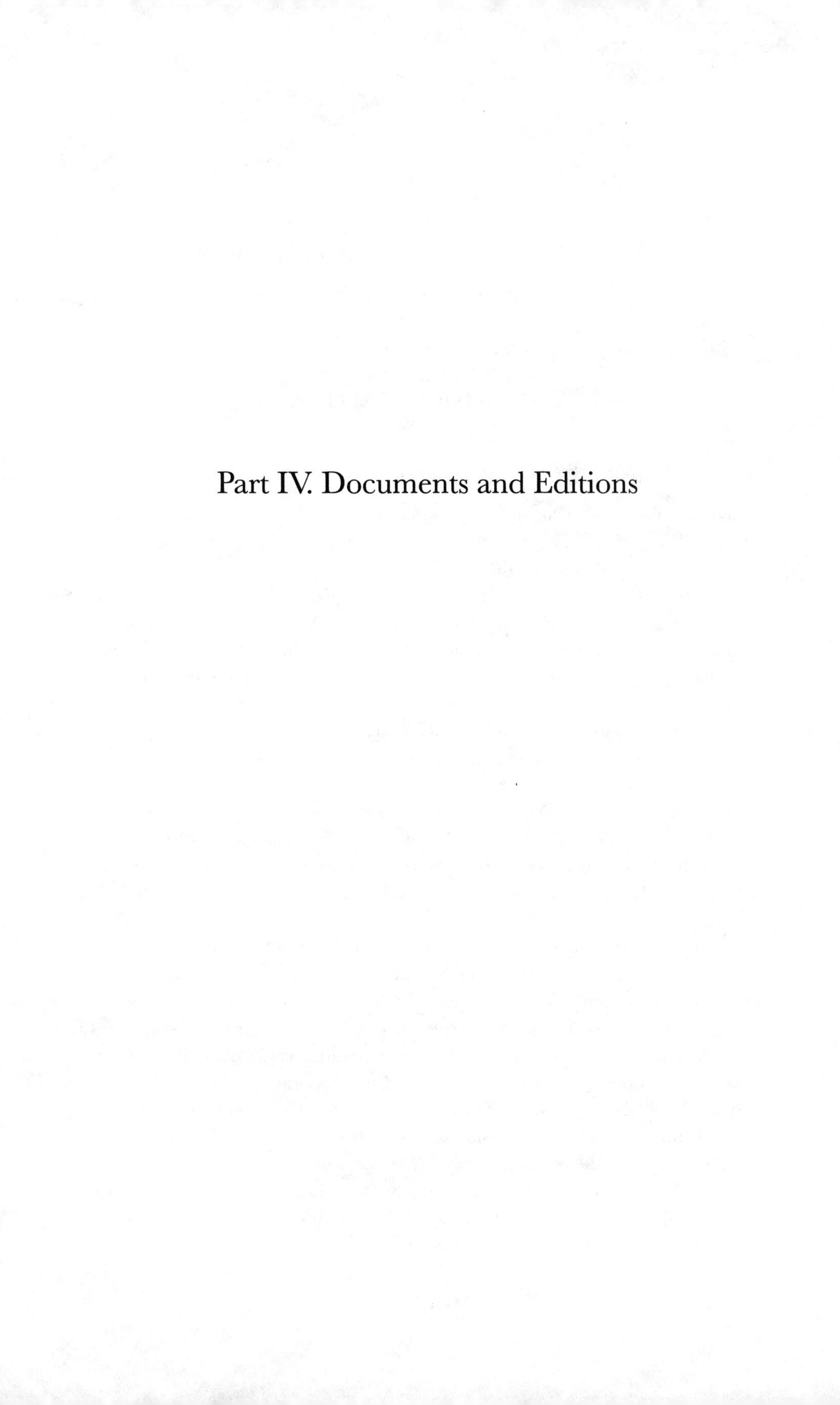

Part IV. Documents and Editions

More Than Just Corrected Notation: The Bohuslav Martinů Complete Edition

ALEŠ BŘEZINA
TRANSLATED BY ADAM PRENTIS

When the Bohuslav Martinů Foundation established the Bohuslav Martinů Institute (BMI) in 1995, it had a clear long-term goal in mind—a complete critical edition of the oeuvre of this classic composer of twentieth-century music. At the time there was not a single library in the world that housed all of the period editions of Martinů's compositions. Many of them—licensed variously to Czech, German, Austrian, French, English, and American publishers—were only available in unsatisfactory first editions, fifty or more years old and marred by unauthorized edits. Many of the older editions had been sold out for decades, causing the works to be inaccessible to the public. Some of the scores were never engraved and were (or still are, unfortunately) distributed by publishers only as reproductions of the composer's poorly legible autographs.

In 1993 the Bohuslav Martinů Foundation initiated the formation of an editorial board that included the editors of the complete editions of Dvořák and Janáček. In 1995 the BMI was tasked first with heuristic research and then with the editing of the Bohuslav Martinů Complete Edition (BMCE). The editorial board[1] was officially appointed in 2003, and in May 2004 definitive editorial guidelines were formulated.[2] Building on the years of work by leading Martinů experts of previous decades, the BMCE editors launched a systematic search of primary sources in both public and private archives. It was necessary to establish ties with the composer's still-living friends, contemporaries, and the first performers of his works in Europe and the United States, as well as with all of the publishers of Bohuslav Martinů's works, and to persuade them to provide sublicenses. Until then, this work had been undertaken by individuals who were loosely connected and thus the results were largely haphazard, with the exception of the work done at the Bohuslav Martinů Memorial (now Center) in Polička. The first major task of the BMI was to thoroughly revise the almost three decades-old catalogue of Martinů's compositions, which the institute completed in collaboration with its original author, the Belgian musicologist Harry Halbreich.[3]

Since 1994 archivists at BMI have assembled and processed the complete scholarly literature on Martinů, as well as more than 8,000 letters (received, sent, and third-party correspondence about Martinů or his compositions), rare historical recordings from private archives and radio stations, program texts from performances of Martinů's works during his lifetime, thousands of clippings from newspapers and magazine worldwide (announcements of performances, reviews, interviews with the composer, etc.), diverse pictorial matter, and so on. Notable sources, especially the composer's autographs and period copies of his works, would all be gradually digitized.[4]

Besides these heuristic activities, the preparation of the critical edition also required the formulation of a methodology that would address all of the quirks and features of the scores Martinů produced, from his autodidactic beginnings as a composer to the late works written with a shaking hand and preserved in several divergent mechanical technologies. A study of the sources showed without a doubt that for the most part the editions could not feasibly be based on just a single source. Works published in the composer's lifetime often beg the question of whether or to what degree these first prints can be considered to be authorized. The significance of extant sources has to be determined for each work individually.

The BMCE is a scholarly historical-critical series of editions of the works of Bohuslav Martinů—that is, it includes all finished and unfinished compositions in all the versions created or authorized by the composer—based on all extant autograph and other manuscript and print sources, as well as audiovisual, visual, and audio documents. It is a scholarly edition guided by the newest methods of textual criticism and philology, and is designed to meet the needs of performance practice. One of the main goals of the BMCE is to create a reliable foundation for the study of the whole of the composer's legacy and to enable a detailed understanding of its macroscopic compositional developments.

Composing was central to Bohuslav Martinů's life and, barring a few years when he taught at American music schools and universities, his only means of livelihood. This circumstance helps explain the sheer volume of his compositional legacy—with over four hundred works covering all forms and genres of music, from operas and oratorios through cantatas and ballets, to symphonies, chamber works, and concertos. Bohuslav Martinů's oeuvre holds a prominent place in twentieth-century music. Many of his best compositions came about in periods of frenetic compositional activity, which brings into question the simplistic dichotomy of quantity versus quality. The unavailability of many of Martinů's works has given rise to a largely fragmentary understanding of his multifaceted oeuvre and hinders objective evaluation of his music by both performers and musicologists. The broader public has no touchstone by which to assess his actual contributions to music, nor criteria to gauge the significance of specific works within his overall output and its broad scope of styles, compositional techniques, and genres. His tireless experimentation in the early and middle phases of his development as a composer helped him ascend to a level of creative virtuosity that he further refined in his later works. The character of compositions written as commissions is influenced by the artistic profile of their initiator, as Martinů took a bespoke approach in such cases (this can be seen, for example, in a comparison of Suite Concertante, H 276, and Concerto for Violin and Orchestra No. 2, H 293). This circumstance gives extraordinary significance to the recordings of Martinů's works performed by musicians connected to their genesis.

The fact that Bohuslav Martinů's compositions were created in various European countries as well as the United States is reflected in the complexities of their linguistic, autographic, and editorial contexts. Czech, French, English, Italian, German, and Latin texts are used in these compositions, each with a textual depth that echoes the composer's diverging levels of proficiency in the given language. The manuscripts are scattered throughout private archives and institutions across the globe. Many editions are characterized by heavy-handed editing unsupported by the composer's autograph. Martinů rarely read the proofs, and if so, his corrections were usually limited to a concise list of amendments, which suggest only a cursory comparison with the original autograph. Even some of his major works are still distributed by the publisher in the form of xerographic copies of the composer's manuscript (for example, *Rhapsody* for large orchestra, H 171, Concerto for Two Pianos and Orchestra, H 292). Numerous editions have been sold out for years and are only available as hire materials. Some compositions have yet to be published at all—besides major works (mainly those recently discovered), this is primarily true of his early works, of which there is an uncommon abundance, amounting to more than a third of all his works.

The preparation of a critical edition is a highly demanding, long-term project. Due to the extraordinary scope of the composer's work, the BMCE is divided into 106 volumes and will therefore be a project that will last for many decades. The first volume was published in 2014, after two decades of preparation. Since then, Bärenreiter Praha has been publishing at least one new volume every year. Bärenreiter presents the composer's intentions in their full breadth, providing access to unknown versions and allowing for detailed insight into Martinů's meticulous and sophisticated compositional process. The edition draws on cutting-edge scientific knowledge in the field of editing and is intended for researchers, musicians, and all fans of twentieth-century classical music. It is based on an assessment of all available sources, both musical and non-musical, that is, autographs and printed scores, sketches, short scores, manuscript copies, and the composer's extensive correspondence, as well as pictorial, audio, audiovisual, and other documents.

The 106 volumes of sheet music are divided into seven series:

I. Stage Works and Film Music

II. Orchestral Music

III. Concertos and Concertante Works

IV. Chamber Music

V. Keyboard Works

VI. Choral Works, Cantatas, Oratorios, and Songs

VII. Supplements and Varia

The first ten volumes of the BMCE aim to present Martinů's oeuvre in its breadth of scope. Few twentieth-century composers explored such a vast array of genres, and it was our intention to highlight this distinctive attribute to subscribers of the edition from the outset. Our initial subscription brochure thus covered the contents of the first ten volumes, which ranged from chamber and orchestral music to concertos and cantatas, an oratorio, and an opera. However, even ten volumes could not encompass Martinů's full scope of genres—it fails to accommodate any of his numerous songs and choral works, or his wealth of keyboard music. The reasons for relegating these categories to later volumes are mostly practical—they comprise a multitude of short compositions, which not only complicate the research and assessment of sources, but also necessitate the negotiation of sub-licenses from various publishers. Another significant factor in this decision was that many of Martinů's piano works come from his early period, when the self-taught composer was still mastering the basics of notation, creating a number of specific pitfalls for editors of his music.

To date, the Bohuslav Martinů Institute and collaborating editors have prepared thirteen volumes for publication. Volumes 1 and 2 of the BMCE, published by Bärenreiter in 2014, included two essential twentieth-century classics: *The Epic of Gilgamesh*, H 351 (ed. Aleš Březina) and Symphony No. 4, H 305 (ed. Sharon A. Choa). The editor discovered Martinů's previously wholly unknown plan to stage *Gilgamesh* as a semi-theatrical production, the consequential extrapolation of decades of experimental ruminations on vocal-instrumental theater, in continuity with his thinking from as early as the 1930s and referencing, among others, his cycle of four miracle plays *Hry o Marii* (*The Plays of Mary*), H 236. In April 1957 Martinů proposed to Sacher an original and profoundly elaborated theatrical production: "It must not be [staged] as an oratorio . . . as a static concert, but as something halfway between a concert and an opera. . . . Where necessary, the singers should turn more toward each other than to the audience, and the choir must also participate in the action, it should not remain static. What I want to say is that the Epic needs motion."[5] Sacher dismissed the composer's suggestion outright, as did the publisher, Universal Edition Wien, which did not even include Martinů's notes on the staging of *Gilgamesh* in the printed edition of the work, causing them to be completely forgotten.

Symphony No. 4 was written in the last months of World War II and premiered on 30 November 1945 by the Philadelphia Orchestra conducted by Eugene Ormandy. The composition enjoyed an excellent reception by audiences and critics alike and was soon taken up by other conductors, especially Rafael Kubelík, who gave the European premiere with the Czech Philharmonic in Prague on 10 October 1946, followed by twenty-three other performances in Europe and Australia before Kubelík emigrated from Czechoslovakia in July 1948.[6]

Instrumental music for small ensembles is represented by two volumes so far, namely Chamber Music for 6–9 Instruments (Volume 3, ed. Jitka Zichová) and String Quartets Nos. 4–7 (Volume 5, ed. Aleš Březina et al.). The stylistically diverse compositions in Volume 3 range from the years 1932 to 1959, namely, Serenade No. 1, H 217, Serenade No. 3, H 218, the septet *Les rondes*, H 200 (recte 199), the nonet *Stowe Pastorals*, H 335, and Nonet No. 2, H 374.[7] The best-known composition in the volume is Nonet No. 2, a 1959 commission for the Czech Nonet and its leader Emil Leichner, Sr. Martinů composed his cycle of four serenades in Paris in 1932, while *Les rondes* for oboe, clarinet, bassoon, trumpet, two violins, and piano was also written in Paris, in 1930. In her foreword, the editor Jitka Zichová documents that Martinů named the composition "Moravian Dances," but the title failed to catch on. The composer proudly boasted of the "great success" of "Dances" at the premiere conducted by Alfred Cortot at L'Ecole normale de la musique in Paris on 18 March 1932, in letters to his family in Polička and to Jan Kunc, "even though they are a bit brutal for the French."[8] The work was not published until 1950, by Orbis in Prague, under the somewhat inaccurate and misleading title of *Ronda* (*Rondos*), despite the composer's request for the publisher to come up with a Czech title for the composition, which was based on circle dances, and not the rondo as a musical form. *Stowe Pastorals* for five recorders, two violins, clarinet, and violoncello was composed by Martinů in November 1951. The composition was dedicated to the Trapp Family but written for a festival of recorder music in Basel, Switzerland, where it was premiered on 7 May 1952.[9]

With a total of eight string quartets (the first of these without a number), Bohuslav Martinů is one of the leading representatives of this genre in twentieth-century music. A number of string quartets were premiered by eminent European and American ensembles. In autumn 1946 Martinů received a request from Yale University to write about his music in the form of a letter for an unspecified future book. Martinů conceived the letter as a general essay on composition, the analysis of music, and musical form. In it, he highlights the importance of form as the very essence of a work. By referencing Beethoven's Opus 135 in connection with his own String Quartet No. 6, which he was composing at the time, Martinů explicitly includes himself in the evolution of this genre.

The fourth volume of the complete edition consists of Martinů's four chamber cantatas on the texts of Miloslav Bureš, edited by the composer and musicologist

Vít Zouhar, whose father, the composer and conductor Zdeněk Zouhar, was personally involved in the cantatas' history. Probably the most famous of the four is *Otvírání studánek* (*The Opening of the Springs*), H 354 (1955); the other three are *Legenda z dýmu bramborové nati* (*The Legend of the Smoke from Potato Tops*), H 360 (1956); *Romance z pampelišek* (*A Dandelion Romance*), H 364 (1957); and *Mikeš z hor* (*Mikesh from the Mountains*), H 375 (1959).

Volume 7, edited by Paul Wingfield, comprises works from the second half of the composer's Paris period (1923–1940): the cantatas *Svatební košile* (*The Spectre's Bride*), H 214A (1932), and *Polní mše* (*Field Mass*), H 279 (1939). *Field Mass* was impacted by Martinů's July 1940 flight from Paris to escape Nazi persecution. Shortly before his departure, the composer sent the scores of both *The Spectre's Bride* and *Field Mass*, along with many others, to a safe hiding place. This meant he was unable to fully participate in the preparation of the first edition of *Field Mass*, which was published in Prague in 1947. The edition was marred by various flaws and criticized by Martinů himself. The extant complete autograph score is dated "4 November 1939" in Czech. The date relates to the completion of the work's initial ending, which was discovered among unprocessed documents in the collections of the Paul Sacher Stiftung in Basel. The final page of the modified ending bears Martinů's dating in French, "Decembre 1939." Whereas the first version ends with a quotation of the fourteenth-century Czech hymn "Jezu Kriste, štědrý kněže" ("Jesus Christ, O Bountiful Lord"), the newer ending replaces it with settings of excerpts from Psalms 54, 56, and 57. The choice of an old Czech hymn imbued the work with an element of national awareness, presumably also referencing Martinů's uncertain situation as an exile in a foreign country facing invasion. The psalm settings give *Field Mass* a more universal significance.[10]

The premiere of *The Spectre's Bride*, originally part of Martinů's ballet *Špalíček* (*The Chap-Book*), composed from 30 January to 11 February 1932, took place on 19 September 1933 in Prague, and at the National Theatre in Brno on 25 November 1933. In both cases, the composer was present for the rehearsals and the opening performance. The discovery of the performance materials from both premieres and the composer's autograph markings in Balatka's score provided a wealth of input for the critical edition.

In early 1940, while in the last months of his stay in Paris, Martinů apparently decided to revise *The Chap-Book* for a prospective staging of the work in the United States. The two most momentous changes were his abbreviation of *Legend of Saint Dorothy* and the complete removal of *The Spectre's Bride*. Earlier, Martinů had been considering the possibility of separating *Legend of Saint Dorothy* and *The Spectre's Bride*, with an eye to having them performed by Ballet Russe de Monte Carlo. Yet as late as 12 July 1958, the composer remarked that he had previously proposed an independent performance of *The Spectre's Bride* to his friend Karel Šebánek but had received no reply as to the whereabouts of the score.

Volumes 6, 8, and 9 of the BMCE consist of concertante works. Volume 6, Quadruple Concertos (ed. Christopher Hogwood et al.),[11] presents both of Martinů's concerto compositions for four solo instruments and orchestra: String Quartet with Orchestra, H 207 (1931), and Sinfonia Concertante No. 2, H 322 (1949), for violin, oboe, bassoon, violoncello, and small orchestra. The form of concerto grosso, which saw a revival in the 1920s in connection with neoclassicism, links the two compositions, though they each draw from different sources of stylistic inspiration: Handel and Haydn, Baroque and Classicism. The considerable span of almost two decades between the two works is also easily discernible in Martinů's compositional techniques, which were fundamentally transformed through the decades.

The two concertos of Volume 8 (ed. Sandra Bergmannová, Paul Silverthorne) represent two stylistic periods of Martinů's oeuvre. *Concerto da Camera*, H 285 (1941), was the conclusion of his exploration of the Baroque concerto grosso. *Rhapsody-Concerto*, H 337 (1952), from eleven years later, ushered in the composer's "fantastic period," marked by looser forms and expanded tonality. This edition of Concerto da Camera was the first to present the major transformations that the work went through since its initial composition and publication, especially with regard to the solo violin part.

Volume 9 (ed. Ivana Tabak) contains two late piano concertos. Concerto for Piano and Orchestra No. 4, *Incantation*, H 358 (1956), features an atypical two-movement structure. It was written for the composer's friend Rudolf Firkušný, who played it using a copy of the autograph until 1970, when it was finally published. Concerto for Piano and Orchestra No. 5, H 366 (1957–1958), or *Fantasia concertante*, Martinů's very last concertante work differs markedly from the previous work in its compositional methods.

Volume 11, Orchestral Works, includes both *Les fresques de Piero della Francesca* (*The Frescoes of Piero della Francesca*), H 352, and *The Parables*, H 367, the culmination of Martinů's Neo-Impressionist orchestral output, marked by a fantastic, kaleidoscopic style. The composer adapted his extra-musical sources of inspiration (from fine art and literature) to the principles of musical forms, creating a space for associations that reach out from mood moments to philosophical ruminations on the fundaments of human existence. Martinů conceived *The Frescoes* after the cycle of Renaissance frescoes of Piero della Francesca in the Basilica of St. Francis of Assisi in Arezzo, Italy, in spring 1955.[12]

The first two movements of *The Parables* date from July 1957, while the third and final movement was composed half a year later (completed on 8 February 1958). Charles Munch conducted the Boston Symphony Orchestra to premiere the work in Boston on 13 February 1959. The titles of the first two movements reference Antoine de Saint-Exupéry's philosophical essay *The Wisdom of the Sands*, whereas the motto of the third movement was assembled by Martinů as a loose montage of quotes from Georges Neveux's play *Le voyage de Thésée*, which later served as the source text for Martinů's opera *Ariane*, H 370 (1958). Although the connection between the mottos and the music of *The Parables* is merely associative—even haphazard in the case of the third movement—the texts, according to the editor Arne Stollberg, form an integral part of the work.

Volumes 10, 12, and 13 are devoted to stage works—and present several challenges with regard to musical philology. A number of translations were made in the composer's lifetime, and even if they are not used in the critical edition, it is necessary for heuristic reasons to assess the extent of their authorization by Martinů, while accounting for his proficiency in the target language and the texts' natural tendency to age. Besides his native Czech, Martinů had a varying degree of knowledge of other languages, which he spoke and for which he composed; specifically, French, English, and German (as well as Italian in the 1950s). However, a study of the sources clearly show that he was the master of none of them. The sources also document just how much Martinů lost touch with native, everyday Czech during his years of life abroad. All of this explains why the librettos of his stage works, his texts discussing the compositions, and especially his correspondence are replete with non-idiomatic phrases that present a challenge to editors and translators alike. The fundamental question is how much should Martinů's very specific voice be amended, if at all. Born at the end of the nineteenth century, Martinů used various expressions that are now considered archaic, but were part of his natural language as a child and young adult. At the same time, the distinctive originality of his speech must be acknowledged and preserved. Another important factor for editors to consider is that in the last years of his life, Martinů worked on typewriters without diacritics, causing his Czech and French texts to be permeated with errors.

The specific problems of setting foreign texts to music are elucidated by his operas to the French librettos of the Dadaist poet Georges Ribemont-Dessaignes, such as *Les trois souhaits ou Les vicissitudes de la vie*, H 175 (*Three Wishes or Life's Vicissitudes*, 1929), to which there is no extant complete autograph textual source. The editor thus faces the intricate task of assessing specific grammatical expressions, the origin of which may be either the librettist's deliberate play on words or an accidental transcription error by the composer (a problem exacerbated by the Dadaist flair).

The one-act opera *Ariadne* (ed. Robert Simon) was composed by Martinů over the course of a single month in June 1958. He wrote the libretto himself, basing it, as mentioned above, on his friend Georges Neveux's 1943 play *Le voyage de Thésée*. The libretto drew mainly on scenes from the second and third acts and included Ariadne's lament, which Martinů rendered as a grand coloratura aria in the opera's finale. Immediately after completing the opera in summer 1958, Martinů presented it to Ricordi at a composer competition honoring the Italian publishing house's 150th anniversary. A hoped-for world premiere at Milan's La Scala, however, failed to materialize. The first performance took place in Gelsenkirchen in 1961.

Volumes 12 and 13, published in 2023 and 2024, contain two interwar one-act operas by Bohuslav Martinů. *Mariken de Nimègue*, H 236/2 I (part 2 of the opera, *The Plays of Mary*, 1st version), is based on the motives of a medieval Marian miracle play from the Netherlands; Martinů composed it in Paris in 1933, using a French text by Henri Ghéon. The edition by Pavel Žůrek presents the previously unpublished and unperformed first version of the opera. The second, definitive version, born out of the need to adapt the music to Vilém Závada's Czech translation of the libretto, came about in 1934 and was included by Martinů in his Czech operatic cycle *Hry o Marii* (*The Plays of Mary*), H 236. The original opera differs from the Czech reworking mainly in its orchestration, its amendments to the French text, and its extensive passages of original music that Martinů left out of the second version. The foreword details the complex genesis and fate of the first version, including the composer's difficulties in finding a suitable librettist. Martinů initially intended for the libretto to be written by the Czech Surrealist poet Vítězslav Nezval.

Bohuslav Martinů composed his last prewar stage work, the opera *Alexandre Bis*, H 255 (ed. Jitka Zichová), with the intention of staging it during the 1937 Paris World Expo. The libretto of this small opera buffa, with a cast of only five characters, was written by the French author and journalist André Wurmser. It is a lighthearted parodical text brimming with puns and hyperbole, set circa 1900. The opera was not premiered until 18 February 1964, nearly five years after the composer's death, in Mannheim, Germany, followed by a Czechoslovak premiere at the National Theatre in Brno on 5 June that same year.

NOTES

1. The board comprised Dietrich Berke, Sandra Bergmannová, Aleš Březina (chairman), Klaus Döge, Jarmila Gabrielová, Christopher Hogwood, Kateřina Maýrová, Daniela Philippi, Giselher Schubert, Eva Velická, Paul Wingfield, and Vít Zouhar.

2. The editorial guidelines draw on the work of the Bohuslav Martinů Institute (BMI) in Prague, the Bohuslav Martinů Center in Polička, and other specialized researchers of Martinů's legacy.

3. Harry Halbreich, *Bohuslav Martinů: Werkverzeichnis und Biografie* (Mainz: Schott Music, 2007).

4. Information about the archives is available to the public in the online catalogue at www.martinu.cz.

5. A digitized copy of the letter can be found in the Bohuslav Martinů Institute, Prague, shelfmark Sac 1957-04-02. https://database.martinu.cz/mails/public_view/3057. Original in French.

6. Before it was published by Boosey & Hawkes in 1950, Martinů decided to change some passages in the composition, mainly pertaining to the piano. Besides correcting several dozen errors from the printed edition of the symphony, the editor of the critical edition also directed attention to the original version of the work and included in the appendix three measures that had been later deleted by the composer.

7. Volume 3 only includes the first and third because the other two do not fit the designated number of instruments. Serenade No. 1 is for clarinet, French horn, three violins, and viola; Serenade No. 3 calls for oboe, clarinet, four violins, and violoncello. Besides their Czech titles, the

author also named them in German ("Kleine Serenaden") and French ("L'aubade"), except for the fourth, which he called "Divertimento."

8. Klára Řiháková, "Korespondence Bohuslava Martinů s Janem Kuncem" (BA thesis, Palacký University Olomouc, 2021), 47, https://theses.cz/id/mm5cam/.

9. Its first edition from 1960 was titled "Pastorely" (Pastorals); the full title was finally brought back in the critical edition.

10. The critical edition corrects the errors in the first printing of *Field Mass* and includes an appendix with the original conclusion of the work together with newly discovered contemporary English translations of the libretto by Sylva Symon (1939), Geraldine Thomsen (1945, working translation), and two of Martinů's students at Princeton, Charles Rosen and Michael Steinberg (1949).

11. Quadruple Concertos was the last work to be co-edited by the superb Martinů expert and renowned conductor Christopher Hogwood, who worked on Volume 6 during his many years of research into the Czech composer. After his death, the edition was completed at his wish by Marek Pechač and Pavel Žůrek.

12. The premiere, performed by the Vienna Philharmonic at the Salzburg Festival on 26 August 1956, was conducted by Rafael Kubelík, the composition's dedicatee.

On the Complete Edition of Bohuslav Martinů's Correspondence

VÍT ZOUHAR

The Database of Sources of the Bohuslav Martinů Institute, supported by the Bohuslav Martinů Foundation in Prague, records more than 3,000 outgoing documents of Bohuslav Martinů from 1905 to 1959 and more than 1,300 letters received between 1912 and 1959.[1] In the vast majority of cases, the received documents have not been preserved, mainly because Martinů did not live at a permanent address for a large part of his life and only sent some of the documents he received to his sister Marie Martinů in his hometown of Polička for safekeeping. These are now stored mainly in the Bohuslav Martinů Center in Polička, together with other manuscripts of the composer. Approximately 4,000 other documents in this database of the Bohuslav Martinů Institute constitute related correspondence.

Since 2005, the Martinů correspondence has been systematically processed and made accessible by a team of researchers from Palacký University Olomouc, supported by The Czech Science Foundation (GAČR). In twelve volumes of the Czech-English critical collection, more than 700 Bohuslav Martinů letters have been published. This complete edition includes correspondence to the Martinů family in Polička,[2] to his first biographer Miloš Šafránek,[3] poet and collaborator Miloslav Bureš,[4] conductor Zdeněk Zouhar,[5] publisher Karel Šebánek,[6] and musician and friend Frank Rybka.[7] The edition is based on a diplomatic transcription of the correspondence, supplemented by a detailed footnote apparatus. Parallel to this, all the edited letters are also available in the Martinů database.

These letters give us extraordinary insight into the ideas and events that inspired various compositions, such as the Double Concerto for two string orchestras, piano and timpani, H 271:

> I will send you the Double Concerto, which was written in September 38 during the events you know about,[8] and it is a sensational thing, really powerful; if accompanied with a little bit of talking, it would be a propaganda work of the highest order, just like the [Field] Mass.[9]

They also tell us something about his method of composing at the piano:

> I have my room downstairs with the piano, so I can work in utter peace, it's a Pleyel piano, small, Clara Schumann played on it, but it's still good and so I'm writing the last piano concerto on it, I've started the final movement and I think it will be good.[10]

Various letters are testimony to the astonishing speed at which he composed. He completed the first of the four cantatas he wrote to texts by Miloslav Bureš, *Otvírání studánek* (*The Opening of the Springs*), H 354, in just nine days. On 4 July 1955, Martinů assured the poet Bureš: "I will certainly write music to it, since a text as wonderful as yours does not appear every day."[11] And on 12 July, he informed his family in Polička that he had completed the twenty-minute cantata: "I have finished the Well [*Opening of the Springs*] and I will send a copy to Brno."[12]

Many letters deal with Martinů's attempts to find and secure manuscripts that got lost through the years of war, travel, and exile. To Frank Rybka he wrote:

> I've wanted to ask you for a long time, whether I stored any manuscripts with you, I can't find them, although I have almost everything from N.Y. here[13] and can't remember who I left them with. I thought it was that painter Davis,[14] but it's not there either.[15]

Like many composers, Martinů had to strive for financial arrangements that would allow him to survive, and many letters are devoted to that mundane but absolutely necessary task. For example, the composer also asked Frank Rybka to arrange a soloist for the premiere of the Concerto for Cello and Orchestra No. 2, H 304, who would pay at least 1,000 dollars for the right to play the premiere and wrote:

> I also don't have a reply from Schuster,[16] I think that he also feels it's expensive, none of them wants to hand out money, only cash it in! Which is no wonder, I'm the same![17]

Although Martinů was not politically active in a specific party or to advance a particular ideology, he often commented on the political situation in Europe and the United States, and his letters are filled with observations, sometimes ironic and other times more careful and weighty. For example, he spoke seriously about the Hungarian Uprising in November 1956, and strongly condemned its bloody suppression in letters to Rybka and other recipients in Western Europe and the United States:

> It's all messed up again and cost human lives, in short everyone has earned a medal and especially the distinguished higher-ups who

Figure 1. Martinů with Karel Šebánek, Josef Šíma, and Henriette Roget in Paris, 1949.

> brought in an army of tanks, what a lovely feeling for us and for them, who considered each other civilized nations. Dammit. I'm so mad I'd rather smash the typewriter to get back at someone, but then my common sense tells me not to, because of my sore hand.[18]

Martinů's letters are also a testimony to his clearly formulated aesthetic views. During the 1950s, when the influence and position of dodecaphony, serial music, and New Music was growing, he repeatedly criticized its authors, compositions, movements, and reviewers.

> My position will probably be pretty difficult now, because here and primarily in Germany the latest musical system for modern music is popular, it's all Schoenberg and Berg and the young folks, it's unlistenable, but they say because it's modern then all the other things with C-major chords are now out of fashion.[19]

In editing this correspondence, it was necessary to address Martinů's linguistic idiosyncracies. His accelerated style of writing heavily influenced the spelling, punctuation, and syntax of his letters. Whether written by hand or later on a typewriter, in Czech or French or from the 1940s in English, his letters and postcards functioned much like today's emails and text messages, as quick sketches. Uniform spelling was not the norm for him in any language. This does not mean that his spelling was ridden with mistakes. The punctuation, however, does bear certain common features. For example, in Czech letters, he hardly ever puts a comma before the conjunction že (if), although in Czech this comma is normal.

Martinů's inconsistent way of marking and naming compositions, people, and places often complicates their identification. Compositions underwent development and revisions in title, language, and text, and our edition seeks to make such things clear. For example, Martinů at first considered the 1956–57 cantata *Legenda z dýmu bramborové nati* (*The Legend of the Smoke from Potato Tops*), H 360, a "romance," because Miloslav Bureš originally called his poetry cycle *Romance from the Smoke from Potato Tops* and changed the title when the cantata was completed. Another example is the cantata *Romance z pampelišek* (*The Romance from the Dandelions*), H 364, which he refers to differently in different letters, its original title being *To the Old Mother's Song*. In many other cases, Martinů uses different names for the same composition, or alternates between upper- and lower-case letters. When referring to people, in some instances he used only initials or the neutral designation "friend," for fear of attracting Nazi or, later, Communist censorship.

Martinů also liked to create puns similar to the humorous drawings from his youth. For example, he addressed Frank Rybka variously as "Franconetti," "Franconnini," or "Rybi," sometimes in connection with their joint holiday trips to Italy. In a similar vein, he Italianized the surname of the cellist Gregory Piatigorsky as "Piattigrossi."[20] In some letters in Czech he produced entire humorously stylized passages, particularly in his correspondence with the diplomat Vladimír Vaněk.[21]

Martinů's correspondence also reflects the linguistic influence of the places he lived. From the 1920s, he employed French words and neologisms, as well as the circumflex accent. After arriving in the United States, his correspondence in Czech contains a large number of English expressions and neologisms, even though, or perhaps because he only learned the language once he had arrived. Similarly, in the second half of the 1950s, when he lived for a long time in Switzerland with Paul and Maja Sacher, sporadic Germanisms appeared in his writings.

Martinů approached his own and received correspondence pragmatically, spontaneously, and unsystematically. He usually did not keep incoming correspondence and did not make copies of his own documents. Nevertheless, with the help of family, colleagues, and friends, he created and accumulated an extensive collection of materials, which are an important source for understanding the composer's work, life, and time. He sent selected letters to his family in Polička, where they were kept by his sister Marie Martinů.

It is obvious that he cared about preserving the letters for the future and concentrating them in one place. However, the complicated political situation, the impediments around communications across the Iron Curtain, and the strict

Figure 2. Marie and Karolina Martinů at their house in Polička, August 1937.

censorship that not only checked but also withheld documents, required careful security measures so that the letter would not endanger the addressee. That is why Bohuslav Martinů repeatedly urged his siblings not to keep his letters and to destroy them: "I hope you are not keeping my letters, use them as kindling for the stove."[22] That this was not just a joke was confirmed by the composer's next call to destroy the documents, which he sent shortly after the first one:

> So I advise you again to make a little fire out of my letters, sometimes I write what I think and it could sometimes cause bad blood and not unnecessarily, burn them all.[23]

Fortunately, the Martinů family did not respond to these instructions and the letters have been preserved.

The composer was aware of the importance of these writings, and therefore he also commented on the binding nature of the information contained in the letters. This is also why he wrote to Miloš Šafránek:

> Now as regards the quotation from my letters and articles, that's quite important. The articles written for revues, etc. are well considered, so they can be quoted. Most of the letters are correct, at least to you or musicians, yet sometimes the more-or-less and more

private letters are not decisive, and when it comes to the articles in programs, I would give it a second thought since, as you know, articles for programs are the worst thing that a composer, I in particular, can be asked to do. They are delayed until the last possible moment and when you can put it off no longer some sort of argument is sweated out, but generally *c'est la blague*, so I would be more cautious there.[24]

A frequent reason why we read Bohuslav Martinů's correspondence is to seek information about the author's work and life. Detailed knowledge of the composer's correspondencc was the starting point for the monographs of Miloš Šafránek (1944, 1961, 1979),[25] Jaroslav Mihule (1974, 2002, 2017),[26] Zdeněk Zouhar (1957, 2001),[27] Harry Halbreich (1968, 2007),[28] and for many papers and articles. Correspondence is also a key source of information for the Bohuslav Martinů Complete Edition and is the starting point for every critical edition of Martinů's compositions. It is particularly significant in terms of musical sources.

Through a systematic study of Martinů's correspondence, we gain knowledge about the composer's time, socioeconomic conditions, political situation, aesthetic influences, social stratification, technological or the cultural parameters within which he lived and worked. Through the composer's letters, we get to know both him and his time and thus they complement the mosaic of the known.

NOTES

Please note: CBM is the Bohuslav Martinů Centre in Polička, formerly called the PBM or Památník Bohuslav Martinů Memorial. The abbreviation PBM is retained for all shelf marks signatures.

1. Database of Sources of the Bohuslav Martinů Institute (IBM), available at https://database.martinu.cz

2. Jaromír Synek and Gabriela Všetičková Žatková, eds., *Dear All (I.): Bohuslav Martinů's Letters to His Family in Polička until 1931; Dear All (II.): Bohuslav Martinů's Letters to His Family in Polička in 1932 and 1933; Dear All (III.): Bohuslav Martinů's Letters to His Family in Polička in 1934 and 1935; Dear All (IV.): Bohuslav Martinů's Letters to His Family in Polička in 1936 and 1937; Dear All (V.) Bohuslav Martinů's Letters to His Family in Polička in 1938 and 1939* (Olomouc: Univerzita Palackého v Olomouci, 2019, 2020, 2021, 2023, 2024).

3. Vít Zouhar and Gabriela Coufalová, eds., *Dear Miloš: Bohuslav Martinů's Letters to Miloš Šafránek* (Olomouc: Univerzita Palackého v Olomouci, 2019).

4. Vít Zouhar and Gabriela Coufalová, eds., *Dear Friend Bureš: Bohuslav Martinů's Letters to Miloslav Bureš* (Olomouc: Univerzita Palackého v Olomouci, 2017).

5. Zdeněk Zouhar and Vít Zouhar, eds., *Dear Friend: Bohuslav Martinů's Letters to Zdeněk Zouhar* (Olomouc: Univerzita Palackého v Olomouci, 2008).

6. Gabriela Coufalová, ed., *Dear Karel I: Bohuslav Martinů's Letters to Karel Šebánek from 1931 to 1949* (Olomouc: Univerzita Palackého v Olomouci, 2025).

7. Jana Honzíková and Vít Zouhar, eds., *Dear Frank (I): Bohuslav Martinů Letters to Frank Rybka from 1941 to 1954* (Olomouc: Olomouc Univerzita Palackého v Olomouci, 2023); Jana Honzíková and Vít Zouhar, eds., *Dear Frank (II.): Bohuslav Martinů Letters to Frank Rybka from 1955 to 1959* (Olomouc: Univerzita Palackého v Olomouci, 2025.)

8. Martinů completed the composition on 29 September 1938 in Switzerland (Harry Halbreich, *Bohuslav Martinů: Werkverzeichnis und Biografie* [Mainz: Schott Music, 2007], 275) one day before the Munich Agreement between Nazi Germany, the United Kingdom, France and Fascist Italy, which enabled the occupation of Czechoslovakia by the Nazis and was the starting point for World War II.

9. "Pošlu Vám Double concert, který byl napsán v septembru 38, při událostech o kterých víte, a je to věc senzační a opravdu silná, s trochou mluvení okolo by to musela býti propagační práce I. řádu zrovna jako [Polní] mše." Martinů to Miloš Šafránek, Paris, 3 June 1940 (CBM, PBM Kmš 748; copy at IBM, ŠafM 1940-06-03; Zouhar and Coufalová, *Dear Miloš*, 160). See https://database.martinu.cz/mails/public_view/2631.

10. "[…] ja mam svuj pokoj dole s pianem, takze mam uplny klid k praci, je to piano Pleyel, male hrala na nem Klara Schumann ale je jeste dobre a tak radim [řádím] na tom poslednim klavirnim koncerte, zacinam posledni vetu a myslim ze bude dobry." Martinů to Frank Rybka, [Schönenberg], 7 December 1957 (CBM, PBM Kfr 1303; copy at IBM, Ryb 1957-12-07; Honzíková and Zouhar, *Dear Frank (II.)*, 276, 277). See https://database.martinu.cz/mails/public_view/1823

11. "Ovšem že na ni [Píseň o studánce rubínce] napíšu hudbu tak krásný text se nenajde každý den." Martinů to Miloslav Bureš, [Nice], 4 July 1955 (CBM, PBM Kb 639; copy at IBM, BurM 1955-07-04; Zouhar and Coufalová, *Dear Friend Bureš*, 29, 30). See https://database.martinu.cz/mails/public_view/4883.

12. "Tu Studánku jsem dokončil a pošlu kopii do Brna." Martinů to his family in Polička, [Nice], 12 July 1955 (CBM, PBM Kr 497; copy at IBM, Mar 1955-07-12). See https://database.martinu.cz/mails/public_view/1320

13. Martinů sent the letter from Schönenberg, Pratteln, near Basel in Switzerland, where the Martinůs had lived in Paul and Maja Sacher's house since 1957.

14. Gerald Vivian Davis (1899–1987), American painter, author of portraits of Bohuslav and Charlotte Martinů.

15. "Chtel jsem te uz davno zeptat zdali jsem u tebe neulozil nejake rukopisy, nemohu je najit ac uz tu mam skoro vsechno z N.Y. a nemohu si vzpomenout u koho jsem to nechal. Myslel jsem u Davise toho malire ale tam to take neni, tak si vzpomen a napis." Martinů to Frank Rybka, [Schönenberg], 3 March 1959 (CBM, BM Kfr 1320; copy at IBM, Ryb 1959-03-03; Honzíková and Zouhar, *Dear Frank (II.)*, 428, 429). See https://database.martinu.cz/mails/public_view/1842

16. Joseph Schuster (1903–1969), cellist, during 1936–1944 a member of the New York Philharmonic.

17. "Od Schustera také nemám odpověď, myslím že se mu to zdá drahé také, on žádný z nich nechce peníze vydat jenom brát! Což se nedivím, ja taky!" Letter from Martinů to Frank Rybka, [South Orleans], 11 July 1945 (CBM, PBM Kfr 1228; copy at IBM, Ryb 1945-07-11; Honzíková and Zouhar, *Dear Frank (I.)*, 138, 139). See https://database.martinu.cz/mails/public_view/1781.

18. "Je to zase zvorané a stalo to lidské životy, zkratka kde kdo se vyznamenal a hlavne ti Velici Mocipani kteři na to šli s armádou tanků, moc přijemny pocit pro nas i pro ně, kteři jsme se považovali za civilisované národy. Pro kočku. Mam takový vztek, že bych nejradeji rozbil typewriter abych se na někom pomstil, ale zase rozum mi říká abych to nedělal k vuli té bolavé ruce." Martinů to Frank Rybka, [Rome], 28 November 1956 (CBM, PBM Kfr 1293; copy at IBM, Ryb 1956-11-28; Honzíková and Zouhar, *Dear Frank (II.)*, 198, 199). See https://database.martinu.cz/mails/public_view/1816.

19. "Budu miti asi dost tezkou posici ted, nebot zde a hlavne v Nemecku je ted v oblibe ten poslední hudebni system moderni hudby, je to samy Schonberg a Beck [Berg] a i ti mladi, neni to sice k poslouchani ale protoze je pry to moderni tak vsechny ostatni veci, ktere mají C dur akkord uz jsou out of Fashion." Martinů to Frank Rybka, [Schönenberg], 7 December 1957, CBM, PBM Kfr 1303; copy at IBM, Ryb 1957-07-12; Honzíková and Zouhar, *Dear Frank (II.)*, 276–79. See https://database.martinu.cz/mails/public_view/1823.

20. For example, Martinů to Frank Rybka, [South Orleans], 11 July 1945 (CBM, PBM Kfr 1228; copy at IBM, Ryb 1945-07-11; Honzíková and Zouhar, *Dear Frank (I.)*, 138–39). See https://database.martinu.cz/mails/public_view/1781.

21. For example, the letter from Bohuslav Martinů to Vladimír Vaněk, [Schönenberg], 21 October 1957, copy at IBM, VanV 1957-10-21. See https://database.martinu.cz/mails/public_view/8295.

22. "Doufám že neschováváte moje dopisy, zapalte si s nimi v kamnech." Martinů to his family in Polička, [Rome], 14 March 1957, CBM, PBM Kr 559; copy at IBM, Mar 1957-03-14; Zouhar and Coufalová, *Dear Miloš*, 8. See https://database.martinu.cz/mails/public_view/1382.

23. "Tak vam znovu radim abyste si z mych dopisu udelali Ohynek, nekdy tak pisu co si myslim a mohlo by to nekdy delat zlou krev a zbyte ne, spalte je vsechny." Martinů to his family in Polička, [Rome], 5 June 1957, CBM, PBM Kr 569; copy at IBM, Mar 1957-06-05. See https://database.martinu.cz/mails/public_view/1392.

24. "Ted co se tyce qoutation z mych dopisu a clanku, to jest dosti dulezite. totiz clanky psane do revue atd jsou premyslene, mohou byti quotovane. Dopisy jsou ve vetsine spravne alespon tobe nebo hudebnikum, dopisy vice mene a vice privatni jsou ovsem nekdy ne smerodatne a co se tyce clanku v programech, zde bych se zamyslil, nebot jak vis clanky do programu jsou ta nejhorsi vec ktera skladatele muze potkat a hlavne mne a tak jsou odkladane az na posledni chvili a kdyz uz vyhnuti neni tedy se vypoti nejaky ten argument ale v celku c'est la blague, tak tam bych byl opatrny." Martinů to Miloš Šafránek, [Schönenberg], 20 April 1958, CBM, PBM Kmš 872; copy at IBM, ŠafM 1958-20-04; Zouhar and Coufalová, *Dear Miloš*, 2019, 596. See https://databaseß.martinu.cz/mails/public_view/4687.

25. Miloš Šafránek, *Bohuslav Martinů: The Man and His Music* (New York: Knopf, 1944); Miloš Šafránek, *Bohuslav Martinů: Život a dílo* (Prague: Státní hudební vydavatelství, 1961); Miloš Šafránek, ed., *Divadlo Bohuslava Martinů* (Prague: Editio Supraphon, 1979).

26. Jaroslav Mihule, *Bohuslav Martinů: Osud skladatele* (Prague: Karolinum, 2002, 2017).

27. Zdeněk Zouhar ed., *Bohuslav Martinů. Sborník vzpomínek a studií* (Brno: Krajské nakladatelství, 1957); Zdeněk Zouhar, *Sborové dílo Bohuslava Martinů* (Prague: Academia, 2001).

28. Harry Halbreich, *Bohuslav Martinů: Werkverzeichnis, Dokumentation und Biographie* (Zürich: Atlantis, 1968); Halbreich, *Bohuslav Martinů: Werkverzeichnis und Biographie*, op. cit.

Martinů's Notebook of Dreams

INTRODUCED AND ANNOTATED BY MICHAEL BECKERMAN

On 23 August 2023, my wife and I had lunch with the distinguished Martinů scholar Jaroslav Mihule, also a former vice chancellor of Charles University and ambassador to the Netherlands. We first met in the 1980s and enjoyed a warm friendship over many years. At lunch, Mihule surprised me with a gift. Wrapped in a brown paper bag was a small spiral-bound notebook filled with Martinů's writing, given to Mihule, he said, by the composer's widow. Consisting of personal observations, descriptions, and quotations from a wide variety of sources, the book gives a picture of Martinů's thinking during a critical moment of his life.

It is an extraordinary volume in the scope and nature of the things quoted, mentioned, and discussed. Perhaps its primary value is the perspective it gives on the composer. Because he wrote so much, and so quickly, and also because he was, in the end, a fairly reticent person, it has been easy to cast Martinů as a kind of savant scribbler. This diary, along with other writings, reveals that this was far from the case. Martinů was a subtle, deep, and careful thinker, who struggled with ideas, just as he did with the materials of his compositions. In the words of his student Jan Novák, "I always thought that music just pours out of Martinů, but now that I'm with him, I see how he spends time on every motive and polishes it until he gets out of it what he wants."

The Physical Notebook

The notebook was probably purchased at Golde's Stationers at 1891 Sixth Ave. in Manhattan at some point after the composer's arrival in New York in April 1941 (Golde's opened in 1905 and was still going strong during Martinů's time in the city).

The notebook is light brown, marked "Schoolife" and is 5 x 9 inches, something easy enough to carry around. It has 36 pages, of which 28 have some kind of writing. While the majority of the writing is in English, there are substantial passages in French, and a page of definitions in Czech. The writing is in pencil, black and blue pen, and ranges from extremely readable to almost impossible to decipher.

Dating

Several things in the notebook help us to date it. On the last page there is a mention of *Gilgamesh*, as part of a list of possible works to compose, with the word "currently" next to it. Since *Gilgamesh* was completed in 1955 this year would probably be the end date for the notebook. While it is not possible to pinpoint the date Martinů began it, on page 7 there is a reference to his *Fantaisies symphoniques*, composed between 1951 and 1953. Since he writes, "Will I finish it or the atom bomb interfere any moment?" the latest possible date for the entry would be some time in 1953. While the atomic bomb was quite often in the news, Martinů could be referring to the Upshot nuclear test done on 25 May 1953. Another anchoring date may be found on page 10, a reference to the Danish seaman Captain Kurt Carlsen, who bravely remained with his sinking ship in January 1952. Somerset Maugham's *Vagrant Mood*, extensively quoted on pages 21–22, was published in the same month. Obviously, these entries could not have been written before 1952. H. V. Morton's book, *In the Steps of the Master*, was a critical source for Martinů's cantata *The Mount of Three Lights*, completed in 1954. Long passages in the notebook suggest a pre-compositional process for this work, again helping us to date it to around 1953. Other works likely written in the "orbit" of this notebook include the operas *What Men Live By* and *The Marriage*, the *Rhapsody Concerto*, the Concerto for Violin, Piano and Orchestra, and the Cello Sonata No. 3.

General Character

The notebook consists of several kinds of writing. There are many verbal snapshots that cannot be attributed at this point that are almost certainly Martinů's own thoughts on a range of subjects, from science to language, and from dignity to the nature of art. There are two stories from Martinů's own experience, about which more below, and then an invocation of a number of authors including Anatole France, Kafka, and Gogol. In particular, he also draws on the work of a collection of writers who, while considered important in their day, have faded from view: Lytton Strachey, Somerset Maugham, and H. V. Morton. In addition to these there are many passages that read like quotations, in both French and English, but are obscure, at least to us.

Main Themes

Although Martinů references a plethora of ideas, several main themes run through the notebook like a thread. Martinů continually rejects the notion that there is some system that could "reveal everything" to us (page 2). This is something of a key to his approach as a creative artist, one of pragmatism and nuance, rejecting any kind of totalizing theory or explanation. On page 7 he advances the idea that we only have our own systems, and that (unnamed) artists have a tendency to adopt systems in a false way, leading to "confusion." He continues on this page with ideas about the artist expanding to infinity, and follows with the observation on page 8 that the real charm of the unknown is that it *is* unknown. On this subject, he could be speaking of today's overreliance on a broad range of theories and theoretical systems when he says, "System[s] which overlook half the facts [are] trying to have the key to the whole in some details." And perhaps he states his fundamental artistic credo with the words, "I have the right to differ with myself. I am not a conforming to__. Simple I do not [need] to pretend dignity. I do not have to save 'face.'" The right to "differ from myself" appears as a statement of artistic courage, a refusal to be typecast, and a kind of pledge to develop in directions as yet uncertain.

This invocation of "dignity" on page 7 is another one of Martinů's primary considerations. The word appears on the very first page of the notebook and is used again in one of the longest non-quotations in the notebook, the story on page 5 of the "displaced person" on the Fifth Avenue bus. Martinů struggles with the relationship between this man, so confused and desperate, and his own state, leaving a certain ambivalence: is Martinů, himself an exile, similar to this man—or are his circumstances entirely different? Is he inside . . . or outside?

The other personal story in the notebook, on page 13, involves an anecdote that encapsulates the surreal, the disjointed, and the unpredictable, which are essential to Martinů's thoughts and aesthetic. At the very moment that the independence of Czechoslovakia was declared, the Czech Philharmonic was rehearsing, ironically, Josef Suk's *Epilog.* According to Martinů, who was a violinist in the orchestra, instead of some kind of dignified celebration, the orchestra spontaneously launched into a kind of "vulgar" pop tune, "Twenty Crowns Is Not Enough," and they all went out into the street.

Some of the most arresting moments in the notebook are short, simple questions or statements, such as on page 2: "Who is reading comics?" Of these perhaps the most intriguing is found on page 13, the query "Are we sincere at all?" This question has ramifications for confronting Martinů's compositions. One would imagine that one of his "stocks in trade" is that very sincerity, the manner in which so much of his music goes in and out of what we might term, "zones of purity," with their lush and syncopated lyricism. And yet there is always something in Martinů pulling against this "differing from himself" by problematizing the very sincerity that seems to lie at the heart of many works. While the notebook cannot provide a simple key to Martinů's works, in its questioning, struggling, and attempts to comprehend, it is a rich and worthy companion to his compositions

Editorial Approach

We offer a compromise between a completely diplomatic transcription and one that makes for greater ease in reading and comprehension. Because of the size of the notebook pages, sentences are often broken up into two or more lines. We have combined these whenever it is clear that the thought continues on the next line. If we are not absolutely sure, we retain Martinů's spacing. Martinů makes many mistakes in his use of English. We have retained these, indicating departures from acceptable grammar, spelling, and word choice. We have added notes where necessary, either to identify various quotations, provide the passages in the original language, or to elaborate or speculate on a particular passage.

I am grateful to Tomas Bazika for his help with the Czech translations and to Prof. Stamos Metzidakis for assistance with the French passages. My co-editor, Aleš Březina, provided invaluable insights into several passages and made numerous corrections in my transcription.

Finally, this chapter is most warmly dedicated to the memory of Jaroslav Mihule who passed away on 20 December 2024. While he gave me a priceless treasure with this notebook, he gave us so much more. That he traversed the path from being a humble assistant professor during normalization, despite his eminence, to distinguished positions in academe and diplomacy, was a tribute to his stamina, his intelligence, and his rather devilish wit. His departure leaves a great emptiness, filled only by the memory of his sparkling personality and the depth of his work.

Martinů's Notebook

[Page 1]

Preestablished connections
Self delusion -
Intentional - intentionally mystifying ourselves
Incompatible
Outline - outlining
Spellbound -
Incidentally
which underlay - -
make-believe[1]

Question of what is aimed at and of the chances of its working out

1. This list is understandable probably only to Martinů. Here he seems to be practicing the vocabulary necessary for his reading.

Conditioning circumstances are not the same[2]

Economy means "juste" not a little.
Artist is haunted by perfection.

Hang it. –

(The comfort[s] of unreason - R. Crawshay Williams[3]
Kegan Paul - C - London)

Every moment in life is unique, and as such, no [*sic*] what give get in for[4]

Something about dignity. I remember a man, refugee in bus.[5]

Story of Sabath[6]

---

2. This and the quotation above are taken from an article by Thorstein Veblen, "The Intellectual Pre-Eminence of Jews in Modern Europe" (*Political Science Quarterly* 34/1 [March 1919]: 33–42) dealing with the question of Jewish achievement. I have boldfaced relevant passages in the context of the longer one: "Yet much can doubtless be done by taking thought and making the most of that spirit of stubborn clannishness which has never been the least among the traits of this people. But again, to any disinterested bystander there will come the question: What is the use of it all? It is not so much a **question of what is aimed at, as of the chances of its working-out**. The logic of the Zionist project plainly runs to the effect that, whereas this people have achieved great things while living under conditions of great adversity, scattered piecemeal among the gentiles of Europe, they are due to achieve much greater things and to reach an unexampled prosperity so soon as they shall have a chance to follow their own devices untroubled within the shelter of their own frontiers. But the doubt presents itself that **the conditioning circumstances are not the same** or of the same kind in the occidental twentieth century A. D. as in the oriental twelfth century B. C.; nor need it follow that those things which scattered Jews have achieved during their dispersion among the gentiles of Europe are a safe index of what things may be expected of a nation of Jews turned in upon themselves within the insulating frontiers of the Holy Land."

3. Rupert Crawshay Williams, *The Comforts of Unreason: A Study of the Motives Behind Irrational Thought* (London: Kegan Paul, Trench, Trubner & Co., Ltd., 1946). The approach can be encapsulated from this passage on p. 6: "I propose, therefore, to try and demonstrate that during the greater part of our lives we, as human beings, tend to prefer unreason to reason and that, the more important the question, the greater is this tendency. At the same time, I hope to show, by indicating its causes, that there is no reason whatsoever for feeling either worried by or ashamed of this tendency, provided we acknowledge its existence and provided we are aware of its dangers and of its peculiar temptations."

4. Perhaps he means something like, "Every moment in life is unique and there you never know what you're in for."

5. This brief reminiscence is further elaborated in an extended passage on the top of page 5 of the notebook.

6. Not clear what this refers to. Considering later references to Berlioz's *Symphonie fantastique* in the notebook, it is most likely about the final movement, the "Witches Sabbath." It could also be a general reference to the Jewish sabbath.

[Page 2]

We are acting as though some mystery would be behind all this, one that somebody could relieve to us
There is a mystery, but nobody who could relieve it[7]
Speaking correctly we think there is some "trick" and if we know it we would know everything.
If the "job" of music disappears for some reason. (economics, practical --) there will be no music.-
Somebody has to play.- compose

We ask too many questiones.[*sic*]

Who is reading "comics"

What I mean by "craft."-

The thing is that we suddenly are thinking too much about ourselves. (Leisure?)
The problem of "man."

We still do not know much about the problem of flowers, of stone, of cat, anyway.
Because we put the label and classified them we think we know all about it.
So we make quick - ready-made solutions
"scientifier" (Psychoanalyst)
As a matter of fact we know now "man" well enough, but what we know [about him] we do not like it.[8]

[Page 3]

To write or create from necessity
" " as a reaction to somebody
Or both?

My ideal is to have plenty of time to correct.... I never ~~did~~ hade [*sic*]

7. Martinů uses the word "relieve" rather than what he probably means which is, "reveal," clearly meaning that no one can explain the mystery to us.

8. This passage is apparently not a quotation from any readings, but a record of Bohuslav Martinů's own reflections and recollections. Perhaps a handout for teaching composition at the Mannes School of Music?

When we start to be aware of something it prouves [*sic*] only that something goes wrong
(Kidneys, lungs, cold)

Do not let ourselves to be caught by words (clasification, label, tag. –

–that in the end of life we wouldn't deceive ourselves

Gogol – Overcoat[9]

Fal[l]acy of "contrast" !!![10]

Imposing a simple logical pattern upon a complex situation.—[11]

Creating when nothing is on the stake
(see Tao – p. 52. Ph[ilosophical] system[12]

Where the ~~creation~~ creative act is free!
forgetting ourselves (?)
Paradoxical conclusion of personality.[13]

[Page 4]

Very good question in any Problem.
Where have you been?

---

9. "The Overcoat" is a short story by Nikolai Gogol, published in 1842. It has had a great influence on Russian literature. Martinů was inspired by Gogol's short story "Marriage" for his television opera of the same name (1952).

10. The fallacy of contrast, also known as the fallacy of the suppressed correlative, is a logical fallacy where one person would say "Certain things are either x or not x" and the response would be, "The things you consider 'not x' are actually x." So for example, to answer, "If hunger is the capacity to eat then I am hungry" to the question "Are you hungry or not hungry?" would involve the fallacy of contrast. Or one could create the same conditions by responding to the statement, "some things are scientific and some are not," by saying, "really, everything is scientific."

11. Helmut Kuhn, *The Humanist Library Encounter With Nothingness: An Essay on Existentialism* (Washington, DC: Henry Regnery Company, 1949), 158. Though Kuhn does not specifically mention the "fallacy of contrast," it is likely that the idea emerges from his writing.

12. Martinů refers to the *Tao Te Ching*, a classical Chinese text and foundational work of Taoism, traditionally attributed to the sage Laozi. To identify the text on p. 52, it would be necessary to know the edition of the book to which he was referring. On p. 52 we find chapter 30 which deals with not trying to force issues.

13. This passage is apparently not a quotation from any readings, but a record of Bohuslav Martinů's own reflections and recollections.

Of pseudo-sensibility, emotion
faked emotions of grandeur.

Oeuvre d'art
To proofe [*sic*] something.
What does [*sic*] we proof?

"Personall [*sic*] expression could still be a bad piece - (Beethoven Triple C[oncerto])

Concept – Conceptual –

Artist doesn't communicate the emotions, he communicat[e]s the faith.[14]

Practical problem of r[h]ythm[15]

II violin. r[h]ythm connected with con[s]cious melodie [*sic*] in the mind of composer but

<u>not</u> in mind of performers.
considerind [*sic*] long way[16]

[Page 5]

Displaced person on the 5th Ave.-[bus]
I have a very high consideration of what we call dignity of human being. (very often quoted now) I felt so miserable looking at this man. What was 5th Ave. to him? He was as lost in his environment and in himself, no human dignity was there and

14. This passage is apparently not a quotation from any readings, but a record of Bohuslav Martinů's own reflections and recollections.

15. This seems to be a constant in Martinů's thinking. There is a similar but much longer passage in his Ridgefield Diary of 1944. See "Question of Rhythm" in *Domov, hudba a svět*, ed. Miloš Šafránek (Prague: Státní hudební vydavatelství, 1966) 165–69.

16. This is a reference to the musician, and he seems to mean something like, "in the broad frame" so that if you see the melody as a whole, you see the logic, but if you see one measure it's quite different.

he was like I am, like you are, a man. He could not control his reactions, they were only the reaction of an animal, he felt liberty but he couldn't believe in it.
After I get from bus and I was in N.Y.[17]

Gogol: What are you laughing for
To yourself are you laughing[18]
And the laugh stop[p]ed suddenly

Kafka questiones[*sic*]! Trial.[19]
Striving for happiness.
Is it classic, is it romantic?

Automation. That what the artist is struggling against.
But this feeling could be cal[l]ed romantic.
S[ymphony] F[antastic] was written already by B[erlioz] He describes his life - but behind ----is something.
Whole program is discontinuous – nonsense![20]

Anatol France comment on the majestic impartiality of the law which forbid [*sic*] rich and poor alike to sleep under bridge and beg their crust of bread on the street.[21]

[Page 6]

Notre generation is working on the empty space, *nous n'avons* the performers, conductors, sol[o]ist, who are connected directly with us, convictions.
They thinks [*sic*] it was better donne [*sic*] with Brahms.[22]

Story of America.

---

17. This is a continuation of the phrase, "refugee in the bus." Martinů of course identified with the man as a refugee, seemingly moved by the man's desperation, particularly surrounded by the wealth of Fifth Ave., and at the same time wondering about the differences between them. See Axel Körner's essay in this volume, noting the different fates of Martinů and Walter Benjamin. In this time Martinů composed the one-act opera on Tolstoy's *What Men Live By*. On page 1, Martinů refers to the man as a "refugee" and on page 5 as a "displaced person."

18. From Gogol's *The Inspector General*.

19. Martinů refers to Kafka's novel written in 1914–15.

20. A reference to Berlioz' *Symphonie fantastique*. It's not entirely clear what Martinů is getting at, but it probably involves his views on musical abstraction as essential. What he means here is that the symphony is Romantic, and about Berlioz's life, but also that there is so much more to the work than the written program that it amounts to what he calls, "discontinuous nonsense."

21. Anatole France, *Le lys rouche* (*The Red Lily*) (1894), chap. 7: "The *law*, in its *majestic* equality, forbids the rich as well as the poor to sleep under bridges, to beg in the streets, and to steal bread."

22. Here he seems to mean that these things were much better connected in Brahms's time.

They were looking for water and were furious to find oil.

Artist is going backwards. [The] Farther he goes, [the] more he sees the distance to reach his ideal[23]

When the psychological moment is reached to pass from the subconscious (instinct?) to the conscious plan of control[24]

State of perversion and delusions when---the call for complexity rather than simplicity in procedure.

complicated and complex
Not the same meaning.

There is a limit of musical expression. If we try to be powerful the music immediately shift[s] somewhere where it cease[s] to be music (I do not mean a genuine power, real) but <u>is</u> powerful
(elaborate)

[Page 7]

S. is not really fantastic, the meaning involved is now distant (date) Will I finish it or the atom bomb interfere any moment?[25]

Musical life in N.Y. is competition. But competition is not the goal of art-the goal is collaboration
It is *sportif* but not artistic
History *choisira* [will decide]!! not we

Some writers expres[s] my feeling better than I can do it.
Concept, Concept

---

23. Possibly related to the sentence attributed (falsely) to Winston Churchill: "The farther back you can look, the farther forward you are likely to see."

24. Possibly a reflection on his own creative process, where ideas emerge from the unconscious to a place of conscious control.

25. A reference to Martinů's *Fantasies symphoniques* (Symphony No. 6), H 343, which Martinů began composing in 1951 and completed after a two-year hiatus in 1953, places the date of these notes in 1953. He likely had time to write them after moving from the United States to Nice in the summer of 1953. This entry also illustrates a central aspect underlying the Cold War period: the genuine fear of an atomic war. It could be a specific reference to the Operation Upshot nuclear test in Nevada carried out on 25 May, the day before he finished the final revision of the symphony or the news that the Soviet Union had created an atomic bomb.

Conceptual –[26]

Is the sun doing its daily motion [so] that we can sleep?

I am used to be misunderstood.[27]
Could we experience something which has no begginning [*sic*] and no end?

Maya!

I have no system. The real "system" we do not know, we have only "our" system, i.e. *adapte* system to our ideas. If idea changes

[Page 8]

system change too, but there some of us are relucting [reluctant] to change and so adapt ideas to system in a fals[e] way and there [is] confusion.

Person[n]ell - imperson[n]el[l], when do we not act as person[n]el[l]
not only artist.
Only when we feel infinite, [does] our ego evaporate The capacity of this is artist's.
Universal is near but not infinity

Finit[e] with (in) the infinite = art piece

We all would like to know the unknow[n]. But the real charm of it is that it is unknown.

The responsibility of a[n] artist is immediately control[l]ed (performance)
(Doesn't mean that it is accepted but it <u>is</u> control[l]ed by every member of orchestra-and by _________,

Sometimes it happen[e]d that in the same moment somebody ask, (a letter for ex[ample])
I get a glimpse of idea, work, which he is asking for.-—

26. Could be either way: a gloss on the movement from the unconscious to the conscious; or the opposite, that he is commenting on the tendency of certain schools of composition, such as serialism, to be over-reliant on a concept.

27. Possibly his reaction to the new generation of composers and critics of the 1940s who often dismissed Martinů's music as being outdated and old-fashioned.

[Page 9]

System which overlook half the facts trying to have the key to the whole in some details.

We are running from ourselves. We would accept anything [other] then to be with ourselves. Is it something from the Nature?

I have the right to differ with myself. I am not a conforming to —
Simple I do not [need] to pretend dignity. I do not have to save "face."

What shall it await [avail] a man if he gain the whole world and lose his soul?[28]

<u>Absolute faith is necessary</u> RGB[29] Not because we have no more strength to fight but because [we have] hearts to fight.[30]

Never he believed in doing things by halves.[31]

What is going to happen is already happening.

[Page 10]

In order to try to explain, to speak about music we have, first to know how the mind work[s]. We [k]now it by observing ourselves and the other. (there are big hole? In this knowledge)
so we look for experts books.

Tension. Tension of Mozart
unknown order.

Somes [*sic*] of the things, events are experience, some are accomplishment.

Trial and error school of living experience

---

28. Matthew 16:26: "For what is a man profited, if he shall *gain the whole world, and lose his own soul*?" Or what shall a man give in exchange for *his soul*?

29. While this quote and the following ones can be found in Louis Fischer's *The Life of Mahatma Gandhi* (New York: Harper & Brothers, 1950), concerning Gandhi's meeting with Romain Rolland, chap. 18 "On the Way Home," 320, we can find no explanation for the initials RGB.

30. Ibid., 136.

31. Ibid., 320.

vydechnout
Opera nenechat lidem čas myslit[32]
jinak poznají co to je. Nesmysl.

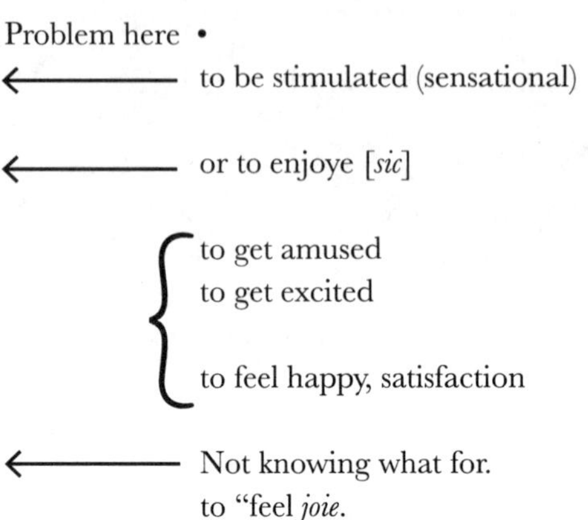

[Page 11]

I will distinguish
The real emotion
[the] false emotion
[the] conventional emotion
[the] instinct (reflex) emotion
[the] emotion which we would like
to feel, we put at ourself [*sic*]
(imagination)

Tout finit par des chansons[33]

The more things change the more remain the same.

32. "Opera doesn't give people time to think, or they'll recognize what it is. [That's] nonsense."

33. "Everthing ends in song" or "everything ends with songs" is the final sentence in Beaumarchais's play and Mozart's opera *Le mariage de Figaro*: "Messieurs la comédie, Que l'on juge en cet instant, sauf erreur, nous peint la vie du bon peuple qui l'entend. Qu'on l'opprime, il peste, il crie, Il s'agite en cent façons, tout finit par des chansons."

Capt. Carlson. [*sic*] The ethic of the sea.[34] He did it because he had to in order to be himself. He did it because it was part of his craftsmanship and calling, because it was in the nature of a good captain to do it, because he loved his ship and the sea as well.

Analysis of my students.

Mr. T. was always looking what is bad in the score, but you look what is good.—

leave a clean taste in your mouth.

To prouve [*sic*] to somebody

[Page 12][35]

Tautology - expressing the same thing (or matter) by same or similar words[36]

Teleology - the doctrine of purpose (or purposefulness)[37]

Empiricism.
a movement (or tendency) that derives all knowledge (or knowing) from experience.[38]

Agnosticism
a philosophical movement that claims the impossibility of knowing supernatural things.[39]

Gnosticism
a philosophical concept (or view) of Christianity supplementing faith by knowing (or knowledge)[40]

Gnosis = knowing
understanding of Christian teachings[41]

---

34. This is a reference to Capt. Kurt Carlsen (1914–1989) who became famous when he stayed with his sinking ship, the *Flying Enterprise*, in January 1952, allowing us to contextualize the date of the entry.

35. This page is in Czech.

36. Tautology: "vyjádření téže věci slovy týmiž nebo podobnými."

37. Teleology: "nauka o účelnosti."

38. Empiricism: "směr odvozující všechno poznání ze zkušenosti."

39. Agnosticism: "filosofický směr hlásající nemožnost poznati nadpřirozené věci."

40. Gnosticism: "filozofické pojetí křesťanství, doplňující víru poznáním."

41. Gnosis: "poznání, pochopení křesťanské nauky."

Monism

A world view presupposing a sole (only one) foundation (or basis) of phenomena.[42]

Eurythmic = relating to movement[43]

Kinetics = science of movement[44]

Eugenics = the cultivation of healthful origin and development of mankind.[45]

Genetics = the science of the origin, hereditability [and] mutability of organs.[46]

Genetic relation = developmental[47]

Metaphysics - a part of (or branch of) philosophy about that, which lies outside of nature, what cannot be perceived by the senses.[48]

Metaphor = figurative expression[49]

[Page 13]

When the independes [*sic*] of C[zechoslovakia] was declared,[50] we were rehearsing C[zech] Philharmonic. Suk- Epilog[51]-The impact of the news was that we spontaneously, wholle [*sic*] orchestra started to play the most vulgar song Dvacetikoruna ta není tak veliká!—[52] And we went on street.

To have another guess coming —

---

42. Monism: "světový názor předpokládající jediný základ jevů."
43. Eurythmic: "pohybový."
44. Kinetics: "nauka o pohybu."
45. Eugenics: "péče o zdravý základ a vývoj člověka."
46. Genetics: "nauka o vzniku, dědičnosti proměnlivosti organu."
47. "Genetický vztah = vývojový."
48. Metaphysics: "část filosofie o tom, co je mimo přírodu, co nelze postihnouti smysly."
49. Metaphor: "obrazový výraz."
50. The independence of Czechoslovakia was declared on 28 October 1918.
51. From 1915 Bohuslav Martinů was an occasional and, from 1920 to 1923, a permanent member of the violin section of the Czech Philharmonic Orchestra.
52. The opening two lines of this song are: "Dvacetikoruna, ta není tak veliká, aby rozházela žižkovskýho Pepíka." Žižkovský Pepík refers to a certain type of person from the Žižkov district of Prague who is something like a Bohemian or *flaneur*, and the words suggest that the small sum of 20 crowns is not enough to tempt Pepík. It's more nonsense than vulgar. This story probably relates to the previous passage about emotions and their various forms and consequences.

True Artist is always far ahead in spirit not in the actuel life

Are we sincere at all?

Everything has a deep significance in one moment (?)

We are not accustomed to recognizing that what is inevitable is [in fact] natural, we cannot give up gracefully that which must go away, we stand fast until everything is taken away from us. Truth comes through conquest because we have lost the art of receiving it as if invited.[53]

The stem of the ripening fruit loosens, its pulp [skin] softens but its seeds harden to furnish future life.[54]

Our external losses, due to aging[55]

[Page 14]

also have internal gains[56]

Wisdom attains fullness only through living.[57]

Subject to direct experience only not logic.
Truth, inherently limited, has no value for man.
It becomes priceless when it takes shape in a living person[ality][58]

Mencken[59]

---

53. This passage is in French. We have not yet found a source for these statements: "Nous ne sommes pas exercé à reconnaitre l'inevitable comme naturel, nous ne pouvons abandonner avec grâce ce qui doit s'en aller, nous nous crampounons jusqu'a ce que tout nous soit ravi. La verité vient en conquerant, parce que nous avons perdu l'art de la recevoir en invitee."

54. "La tige du fruit murissant devient lâche, sa pulpe s'adoucit mais ses grains durcissent pour approvisionner la vie prochaine."

55. "Nos perditions esterieuses dues á l'âge"

56. ". . . ont egalement les gains interieueses."

57. "La sagesse n'atteint sa plenitude qu'en vivant."

58. "Sujet d'experience direct et non de logique. La verité limitée en elle[-]même n'a aucun valeur pour l'homme. Elle devient sans prix quand elle prend corps dans une personnalité vivant[e]."

59. H. L. Mencken (1880–1956) was one of the most prominent public intellectuals of the time. He wrote essays, criticism, and journalism, and was a rapier-like cultural critic of contemporary American values. He was a master of the epigram and especially the first phrases below could be by Mencken, but it is not among those that could be located. And of course the first epigram under his name could actually represent Martinů's view of Mencken.

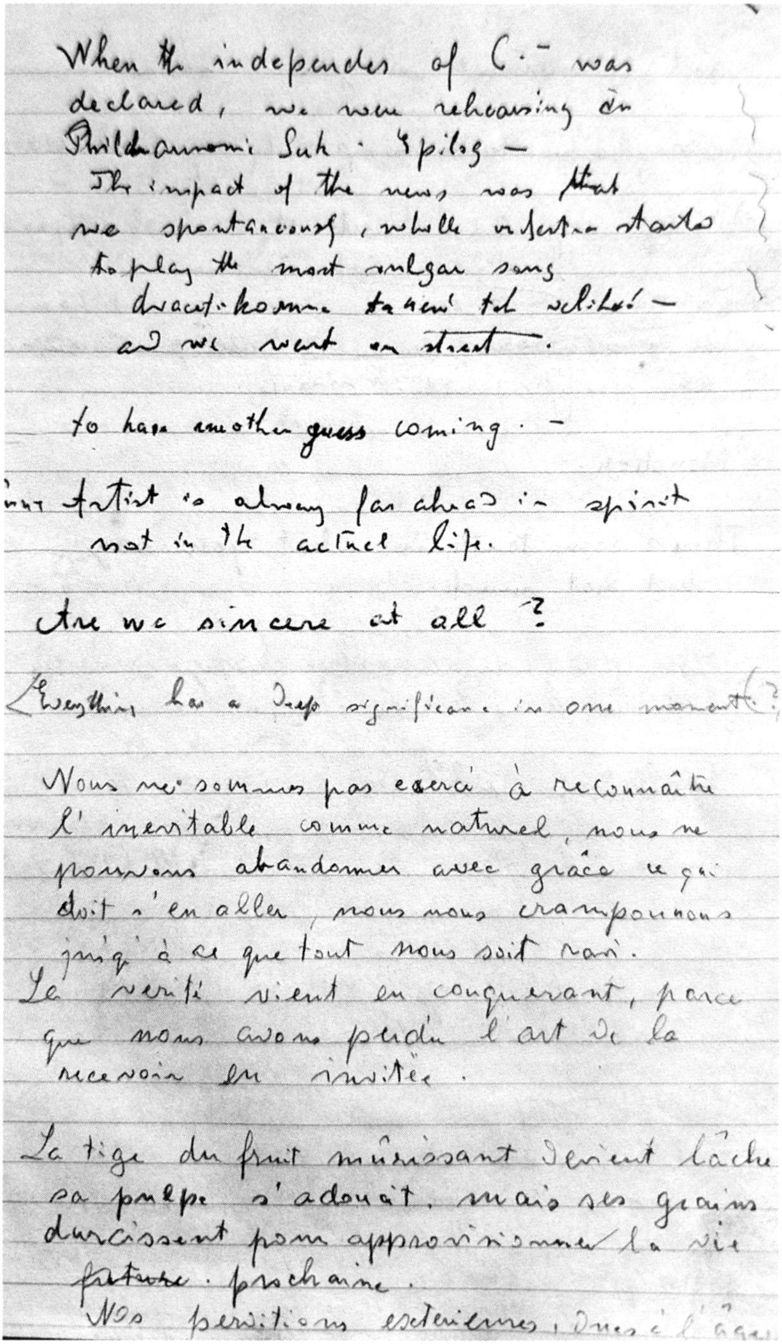

When the independence of C.– was declared, we were rehearsing in Philharmonic Suk · Epilog —
The impact of the news was that we spontaneously, while orchestra started to play the most vulgar song
dvacetikoruna ta není tak veliká! —
and we went on street.

to have another guess coming. —

our Artist is always far ahead in spirit not in the actual life.

Are we sincere at all?

<Everything has a deep significance in one moment?)

Nous ne sommes pas exercé à reconnaître l'inévitable comme naturel, nous ne pouvons abandonner avec grâce ce qui doit s'en aller, nous nous cramponnons jusq'à ce que tout nous soit ravi.
La vérité vient en conquérant, parce que nous avons perdu l'art de la recevoir en invitée.

La tige du fruit mûrissant devient lâche, sa pulpe s'adoucit, mais ses grains durcissent pour approvisionner la vie ~~future~~ prochaine.
Nos pertitions exterieures, dues à l'âge

Figure 1. Page 13 of Martinů's notebook.

There's some truth in what you say, but not much

You could do anything / everything if you know how to do it.

Intellectual ambition is terribly tempting

in order to prove himself - as that were so necessary?

To spend life in the pursuit of (that) which was not worth the finding.

sluggish	self improvement	impish
allouf [*sic*, recte aloof]	freakish	life size
lump	frighten	naughtiness
bitterness	thrilling	repelled
sheming [*sic*]	numb	
	SIGHT-SEER	

[Page 15]

When you find lies beautiful you are an idealist.

- as long as you avoid anything like *naturel* - normal solution.
The old always was normal and never had any of the horrors of abnormality.

The approach could seem to be intellectual, it is not.

When needed to drive home a point.

Something more is needed than a faith?
conventional.
For convinience [*sic*] - as efficiency

That we can wish opposite thing in the same time -.
Contradictions +

merely repeating – not accepting.
pitfalls that lurk in the written or spoken words.

There is <u>not</u> only one – stand to the subject
-"- philosophy - (China?)
-"- conception of world.

distinction +
Advantage to learn languaches [*sic*]
that you cannot talk for a certain [indecipherable]

[Page 16]

Isn't it a strange fact that the greatest ideas about humain [*sic*] aspirations come from the beggining of the human kind – Indian – mysticism!

To extend something – a meaning until it has no meaning at all

90.[60]
Luxury of Spirit[61]
If you have an abundance of music for example, you wouldn't appreciate it

[Page 17]

Do no violence to yourself, respect in yourself the oscillation of feeling. They are your life and your nature; one wiser than you ordained them. Do not abandon yourself altogether either to instinct or to will. Instinct is a siren, will a despot. Be neither slave of your impulses and sensations of the moment, nor of an abstract and general plan; be open to what life brings from within and without and welcome the unforeseen; but give to your life unity and bring the unforeseen within the lines of your plan. Let what is naturel in you raise itself to the level of the spiritual and let the spiritual become once more *naturel*. Thus will your development be harmonious and the peace of heaven will shine upon your brow—always on condition that your peace is made and that you have climbed your Calvary.

The soul too is a butterfly. [62]

learned innocence.
calculated simplicity.

[Page 18 blank]

60. Almost certainly refers to a page number in a book that we could not identify.

61. Maybe a reference to "The Dark Night of the Soul" as a phase of passive purification in the mystical development of the individual's spirit, according to the sixteenth-century Spanish mystic and Catholic poet St. John of the Cross.

62. The entire passage at the top of page 16 is taken from the *Journal intime* of the Swiss philosopher Henri Frédéric Amiel (1821–1881), originally published in 1884.

[Page 19]

Lytton Strachey.[63] Racine.
Sens of duty (to be cultured)

amplify a greatness already recognized by all.[64]

~~it is not possible~~ not the writing but the principle of (his) art.

Exclusion of visible action!
Conception of drama as the history of spiritual crisis.

intensified vision.

always the limitations of range of his interest.[65]
Relation between man & universe.[66]
the spark is important
he brings—by simplest means effects which other poet must strain every nerve to produce.

It is not the daring of adventure but of intensity.

no metaphysical speculation, no suggestions of the transcendental, no hints of the ultimate nature of reality and the constitution of the world but the mystery of man's mind.

unerring fidelity to truth[67]

---

63. All the following references, through note 71, are to the Racine chapter in Lytton Strachey's 1922 volume, *Books and Characters, French & English*. Multiple editions are available in English. Available at https://www.gutenberg.org/files/12478/12478-h/12478-h.htm#RACINE.

64. "Nothing shows more clearly Racine's supreme dominion over his countrymen than the fact that M. Lemaître never questions it for a moment, and tacitly assumes on every page of his book that his only duty is to illustrate and amplify a greatness already recognised by all."

65. "We do not find in his plays 'the whole pell-mell of human existence,' and this is true, because the particular effects which Racine wished to produce necessarily involved this limitation of the range of his interests."

66. The longer passage: "All truly great poets, he asserts, have 'a wide view of humanity,' 'a large view of life'—a profound sense, in short, of the relations between man and the universe; and, since Racine is without this quality, his claim to true poetic greatness must be denied."

67. From this passage: "On the contrary, his admirers are now tending more and more to lay stress upon the brilliance of his portraits, the combined vigor and intimacy of his painting, his amazing knowledge, and his unerring fidelity to truth."

Every art is based upon the selection[68]

[Page 20 blank]

[Page 21]

State of (society) which has already ceased to be actual and become historical.
the last phase of doomed society.

l'art de dire en un mot tout ce qu'un mot peut dire[69]
all the dottings of i's[70]

avec lui on est plus bête que l'on ne l'est tout seul[71]
what really bound her to him was the fact that they so rarely met[72]

The purposiveness = by peculiar constitution
of our cognitive faculties.[73] S. Maugham.[74]

It is a principle we make use of to provide ourselves with concepts in the vast multiplicity of nature, so that we may take our bearings in it and enable our understanding to feel itself at home in it

It may be that beauty, like happiness and originality, is more likely to be obtained when it is not deliberately attempted.

--that spiritual pleasures are obviously higher than physical pleasures.

---

68. A slight misquote or a fragment. The original: "Every art is based upon a selection, and the art of Racine selected the things of the spirit for the material of its work."

69. "The art of saying in one word all that a word can say."

70. "Madame du Deffand carries the classical ideal to its furthest point. She never strikes more than once, and she always hits the nail on the head. Such is her skill that she sometimes seems to beat the Romantics even on their own ground: her reticences make a deeper impression than all the dottings of their i's."

71. "One is more foolish with him than one would be alone."

72. A reference to the relationship between Madame du Deffand and Horace Walpole.

73. "The purposiveness which we seem to find in nature may be occasioned only by the peculiar constitution of our cognitive faculties." This and the following quotations to the end of page 22 are taken from Somerset Maugham's *Vagrant Mood*, first published on 1 January 1952, again allowing us to more or less to date this part of the diary.

74. Although not much studied today, William Somerset Maugham was an intellectual and artistic leader of his generation, whose plays, novels, and short stories were considered top drawer. A figure of Martinů-like productivity, he wrote 31 plays, 9 collections of stories, and 20 novels in addition to nonfiction works.

But who say so?
Those who prefer spiritual pleasures.[75]

[Page 22 blank]

[Page 23]

Every art has its limitations and the better the artist the more comfortably does he exercise his creative instinct within them.
The difficulties he was asked to cope with excite and inspire him.[76]

Mallarmé to Degas
But one doesn't write a sonnet with ideas,
one writes it with words.[77]

Zurbaran:[78] He was old to attempt a new manner. Such communication as an artist has to make is primarily to his contemporaries[,] he speaks to them in the idiom of his day. Another generation adopts another idiom.

There is one thing that is fairly certain, an artist can only develop on the line which nature has marked out for him, his mode of expression is of the essence of his personality and the attempt to assume a new one is futile

[Page 24]

In the step[s] of the Master
By H.V. Morton

Rich & Cowan LTD.
25 Soho Square
London (1934)
Reprinted (1935)

---

75. The original reads: "The indignant retort to Bentham's statement was that spiritual pleasures are obviously higher than physical pleasures. But who say so? Those who prefer spiritual pleasures."

76. An extended response to the statement "It is news to me that the artist who knows his business is hampered by the limitations that are imposed upon him."

77. The longer quote is "Degas arrived late at one of Mallarmé's celebrated Tuesdays and said he'd been trying all day to write a sonnet and couldn't get an idea. To this Mallarmé replied: 'But, my dear Degas, one doesn't write a sonnet with ideas, one writes it with words.'"

78. This is part of an extended meditation on the life and career of Francisco de Zurbarán (1598–1664), a Spanish painter known for powerful religious scenes.

Garden of Gethsemane

(*Mont* of three lights)[79]

[Page 25]

It was the habit in ancient time[s] to treat any stranger as if he might be a wandering Christ and this beautiful courtesy still exist[s] in out-of-the-way parts of the earth. We have lost it and with it something fine and beautiful has gone from our lives.
(on the half way to the Mount of *Tentation* - Greek monk)

Bethlehem has known the Jews, the Romans, the Arabs, the Crusaders, the Saracens the Turks. And now there is one (border sign) in English asking you "drive slowly."

One feels that these pillars are really the pillars of a temple to Jupiter.
(Church of Nativity.) in Bethlehem)

The camel - the trouble to get in the water. Once they had been persuaded to sit down in the sea; appeared to enjoy themselves. They refused to move.

For His hour had come and He stood waiting in the light. The eight disciples had seen lamps mounted on staves swinging against the darkness of the Temple mount. These lanterns descended into the valley of the Kedron and then advanced up the slight hill towards the garden. They recognized the tramp of the Roman soldiers. The approaching men came swinging their lights so that they could see into all the caves and dark places.

[Page 26 blank]

[Page 27]

In mountain country there is nothing older than a road. Cities may come and go, the most splendid buildings may live and die, but the little road that runs between the rocks lives for ever.

On the Mount of Olives, one knows that these little stony tracks that twist and turn over the rocks are the very paths that He must have taken. This is the road to the Garden of Gethsemane.

79. Martinů composed a cantata, *The Mount of Three Lights*, H 349, based in part on the book by H. V. Morton.

The walls of Jerusalem stand like a challenge, golden in the morning sun.

As I sat on the stone thinking of these things a light began to fill the sky.

It swept up the stony flanks of the opposite valley and I felt my face and my hands warm in its light.

[Page 28 blank]

[Page 29]

Know that effluences flow from all things that have come into being.
Empedocles.[80]

of those people who are encouraged because they are known as "characters"

Their antigonial behavior becomes legendary—instead of being run out of the vicinity as they deserve, they become *objets* of perverse local pride.[81]
[word in parentheses we cannot decipher]

[Page 30 blank]

[Page 31][82]

The key to everything premeditated, desired, created by trick [ruse] will finally be found [out].
Whatever is made naturally remains mysterious.[83]

80. Greek pre-Socratic philosopher Empedocles was born in Sicily, and known for his role in theories of the four classical elements. His work was preserved in various sources. This short passage was taken from chapter 5 of *Early Greek Philosophy* by John Burnet, published in London in 1920. Burnet also translated the passage.

81. Even though the ultimate intent of this passage is clear, the word "antigonial" is not an English word. Given the context it might be more like "antagonistic" or Martinů may have intended the word "antinomial" in the sense of "rejecting all laws." At the end of the passage is a word in parentheses we have not been able to decipher.

82. This entire page as well as the next two are in French.

83. "De toute chose premeditée, voulue creé par ruse, on trouvera enfin la clé. Toute chose faite naturellement demeure mysterieuse." For this and the following quotes originally written in French we have not been able to find sources yet.

Some claim that he [unnamed] is not a poet but a pure philosopher, others that he is a philosopher but not a pure poet — a Distinction.[84]

It's healthy for a young man to realize that the grass is green or that he has discovered the sun in the sky.[85]

that they cling to a desire to fix everything up by themselves?[86]

The grass will grow at night even if we don't watch it.[87]
Carlyle and Browning, whose [poem] Sordello his wife had read with great interest, [and] she wanted to know if Sordello was a man, or a city, or a book.[88]

He was not unintelligible because these ideas were vague, but because for him they were obvious.

He doesn't care to explain his discoveries because he doesn't think he's discovered anything.[89]

[Page 32]

The idea will become so fixed in his mind that he forgets that no association of the same type could form in the mind of others.[90]

---

84. "Les uns pretendent qu'il n'est pas un poète mais un par philosophe. Les autres qu'il est un philosphe e[t] non un pur poèt[e] – Distinction."

85. "Il est sain pour un jeune homme de confes[s]er que l'herbe est verte ou quil a decouvert le soleit dans le ciel."

86. "qu'il sera raccrochent à un [*sic*] désir de tout arranger eux-mêmes."

87. "L'herbe poussera la nuit même si on ne le surveille."

88. "Carlyle à Browning, que sa femme avait lu Sordello avec un grand interêt et qu'elle desirait savoir si Sordello était un humane, une ville ou un livre." For English original see https://thewholegardenwillbow.wordpress.com/2013/03/24/robert-browning-sordello/.

89. "Il ne prend pas le soin d'expliquer ses decouvertes car il ne croit pas avoir rien decouvert."

90. "L'idée deviendra si fixe dans son esprit il oublie qu'aucun associations d'idee du même genre ne se forme dans l'esprit des autres."

[Page 33]

So, it appears that Hegel-Benda[91] were directing the world. But what if I didn't know his writings? And what of another person, who does know them, does that help him somehow?[92] ---x

Concentration ------- camp. +

[pages 34–35 blank]

[page 36 (upside down)]

Gilgamesh[93]	+	currently?[94]
Komenský[95]	+	
Bible Agony[96]	+	
Kvintett avec string	+	
Concerto de Prague	+	
Cello Concerto	+	Sonata?
Opera	+	

91. A reference to the famous essay by Julien Benda, "The Treason of the Intellectuals from 1928," in which Benda argues, among other things, with Hegel.

92. "Tout se passe comme si Hegel - Benda . . . dirigais le monde. Mais si je ne connais pas les écrits? Et l'autre qui les connaît, ce que cela lui aide?"

93. Martinů composed *The Epic of Gilgamesh*, H 351, in 1955.

94. "aktuelní?" Meaning he is currently working on the piece.

95. Jan Amos Komenský (J. A. Comenius) was an internationally renowned Czech educator who lived between 1592 and 1670. For some time Martinů considered using one of his books as a textual basis for his music. In October 1954, he wrote to the director of the Haghe Sanghers choir that he had found a suitable text for his next work, J. A. Comenius's *Cantionale*, published in Amsterdam in 1659.

96. Agony, in a biblical context, refers to intense physical or emotional suffering, often associated with spiritual struggle or distress. The term is most notably connected to the experiences of Jesus Christ, particularly during His time in the Garden of Gethsemane. This is probably again a reference to the aforementioned Martinů cantata, *The Mount of Three Lights*.

Martinů in the U.S.A.: Interviews with the Composer's American Friends and Students

CONDUCTED BY ALEŠ BŘEZINA
EDITED AND INTRODUCED BY
MICHAEL BECKERMAN AND ALEŠ BŘEZINA

This section of *Martinů and His World* features six interviews with people who knew and worked with Martinů during his time in the United States. Michael Steinberg, Zaidee Parkinson, and Chou Wen-Chung studied with Martinů; Charles Rosen was an early performer of his piano and chamber music in this country; Boris Rybka was a musician whose family was close to Martinů; and the composer David Diamond was a friend and associate. Taken together they give us an intimate portrait of the composer. The interviews, except that with Chou Wen-Chung, were made for the film *Martinů and America*, produced by Czech Television in 2000 (the documentary used only short excerpts). The interviews presented here have been edited for continuity and to remove unimportant words that would only make sense if they were spoken. Except for Chou Wen-Chung's, all interviews were conducted between the 8th and 24th of April 2000. Each interview is preceded by a brief biography of the interviewee.

"You Can't Force a Theme to Become a Rondo": An Interview with Boris Rybka

Boris Igor Rybka (1926–2023) was raised in Jamaica, Queens, New York, by his musical parents Doris Campbell Summers and František "Frank" Rybka, a former student of Leoš Janáček and best American friend to Bohuslav Martinů. Boris earned bachelor's and master's degrees from the Yale University School of Music, and at age 17 volunteer-enlisted in the U.S. Navy, playing in the band on the USS Prairie, and serving in the Pacific Theatre near the Caroline Islands. A French horn player, pianist, and conductor, he performed nationally and internationally.

AB: Do you remember your first meeting with Martinů?

BR: The very first meeting with the Martinůs took place toward the end of the summer of 1941. They came out to Jamaica from midtown Manhattan on the subway, and walked up the hill, which is three city blocks to walk, and then made a turn to the right, and I saw this tall man with his wife on his arm, walking slowly, coming along the street there. And I ran inside the house, and I said, Daddy, they are here, they are here. And he said, OK, OK, don't worry. So he was fixing things inside the house, and I immediately went into the backyard, and there was a nice quince tree right in the backyard, which was in bloom at that time.

And the Martinůs came, and there was a big meeting there, and Mrs. Martinů, in a few minutes, she came into the backyard, and we all met, and we talked a little bit, and she loved the backyard and being out in the country. She said it reminded her of France.

And then . . . he used to come to the house very often, and both of them together to dinner, and they enjoyed having the children around; the kids were running up and down the stairs, and whenever there was something on the kitchen table that was supposed to be on the dining room table, one of the children was ordered to go get it from the kitchen, and Martinů enjoyed . . . the activity with the children around. And that is probably the most important time that I remember Martinů in our home and also at dinner. He was a gourmet. He loved to eat, and he loved fine food, and he loved also, after dinner, having coffee and brandy or rum . . . and just to sit around and talk, to smoke a cigarette, and to partake in conversation, and he was very good at it. Martinů felt our house was like a second home to him.

AB: Did you also see Martinů after the war?

BR: The next time I really remember seeing him was in the summer of '47 up in Keene Valley . . . and he asked about my military service and what I was doing and what I was going to do with my life. I had decided by then I wanted to go to the Yale School of Music to study there and get a broader background beyond music, more of an academic background than if I were to go to a conservatory such as Juilliard's School of Music. And he thought that was a good idea that I go for a broader background rather than specialize in my instrument, which was French horn.

When I went to school . . . and working hard on the horn . . . he would come into our home for dinner, often I would be playing the horn. And he asked me a number of questions about the instrument because he said, I don't know that much about the horn, and I would like to know more. And he would write out a little piece, and he said, does this fit very well with the horn? And I would look at it, and I would play it for him, and I said, yes, this is very easy to play. . . . And I'm sorry to this day that while he had an interest in me as a French horn player, I never asked him if he would write a composition for a French horn, because he has written very little for the horn as an individual instrument.

In 1951 . . . I received my master's degree from the Yale School of Music. And during that spring semester, I took a course with Hindemith, which was called "Exercises in Composition for Non-Composition Majors," for people who were just interested in composition. . . . and Hindemith gave us many little pieces to write. One time, he gave me a larger piece to write for string orchestra.

He would start the piece out with the theme, with the instruments, and then he would leave places blank and he would say, I expect you to develop this into a polyphonic style, and here would be a certain high point, here would be the coda, and so on. And . . . he said, I would like you to compose a rondo. And so I brought this piece home . . . on the weekend . . . and Martinů was at our house for dinner. I said, I have this piece, could you help me with it? And he and I went into the other room alone, . . . and he looked at the piece and I can still see him. He would just look at the composition, he always used to put his hand under his chin, and would not say very much, just look at things, and I looked at his eyes and I tried to discern exactly what he was thinking at that moment, but I couldn't.

He was into the composition. I could see that he was working to hear what these sounds were doing. And I remember him correcting a couple of things that I had written. For instance, the string bass line. He told me to put the string bass line an octave higher, that it would be too low where I had placed it. . . . And although I was surprised at this, I just said, oh really? And I think that he thought I was being somewhat antagonistic. I was not. I was just curious . . . and he told me why. And then we went on and I told him that I wanted to make it into a rondo. And after a little while, he was getting more and more frustrated. I could see him getting more and more upset. And he said, this is not how to write a rondo. You will not write a good rondo this way. He said, a rondo has to come out of a theme that turns itself into a rondo. You don't force the theme to become a rondo. And I didn't really understand what he was talking about too much, only a little bit.

But I, again, I was just listening. And I said, well that's interesting. Then I said to him, well, I still have to finish the piece so . . . so that it wouldn't end up with you finishing it. He said, it's all right. And you'll do okay. But this is not really good. Then he put the music aside and said, well, you know, not everything that Hindemith wrote is great music. I said, well, I'm sure that's the case. But I said, I'm not trying to write great music. I just want to write something that will be good enough so it will be a nice piece. And he let it go.

And we talked more about that and he corrected a few things. I remember, he corrected, . . . as anyone knows his handwriting, he writes in very small, quick notation. It was interesting to see him write something in there very quickly. I didn't want him to write too much because I didn't want him to compose the piece that was supposed to be my creation. But I think that he did help me and I did understand what he meant later on. Then later that same semester, which was the springtime, I had to play my recital, which was a recital for my master's degree.

And I chose to play an all-contemporary music recital. I chose three different pieces, three different sonatas. And then I looked for a piece by Martinů. I found a little serenade, I think it's maybe Serenade No. 2[1] or something like that, which is for three violins, maybe clarinet and a horn. And it's a short and it's a lovely little piece.

One other aspect, in that semester I took a course on modern composers in which I had to find some composer and I had to learn the piece, I had to be able to play it on the piano, whatever the piece was, or at least parts of it on the piano, and then talk about it to the rest of the students.

That was our assignment. I came home to Jamaica, Long Island, and again at the dinner table my first question to Mr. Martinů was, do you have a composition, a recording, a very good composition that I could present to my class? And he said, yes I do. And by the next weekend, he said, I'll give it to you next Friday. I said, that's fine.

I came back home after being up in school for that week and he had a recording there of his Concerto Grosso[2] performed by the NBC Symphony Orchestra with Ernest Ansermet. I asked him about the composition and about how he wrote it. And he said that he was . . . following a lot of the Italian madrigals of that particular period. As a matter of fact, he left me something like four different books of madrigals at that point which he had purchased in France. . . . He felt that this was a period that was very neglected in our music and understanding. And he was completely correct about it. It is only more recently that we have more interest and a broader interest in early music as it is known today. I took that and I was very, very happy that I received a very good round of applause from my fellow students after I gave that lecture on Martinů and . . . I played part of the Concerto Grosso on the piano and I used the recording for the rest of it.

AB: Do you remember something more about what he told you about the Concerto Grosso? You mentioned madrigals, did he also mention Bach?

BR: He didn't mention Bach right there. I remember him mentioning Monteverdi and he said that Monteverdi was a composer who is really underappreciated. [And he spoke about] how he could take a melody and then invert it and put it into a different place in the madrigal or the chorale and he said today you can put it in the third place, the fourth place and so on down and it still makes great musical sense. He said we have never been able to figure out how he did that.

AB: You also saw his music library. What was in Martinů's music library?

BR: I saw that he had a whole collection of things like Purcell, Morley, those compositions. I think I still have a number of them. Again, the madrigals and the works of some of the French composers, Janequin, and you know Claude

Le Jeune and many of the others of this particular period. . . . I remember how thoroughly he had learned these compositions.

AB: Once you mentioned Martinů advising you not to write the same way as Hindemith.

BR: That's exactly correct, yes. He said, do not become a little Hindemith. You must create on your own. You must find your own style and I understand that very well now and I wish I had taken that advice. I probably would have gone into composition at that point but perhaps it's better I didn't. But yes . . . he taught from the idea that one should create from one's own feelings and one's own ideas, whereas it was quite different from Hindemith. Not that they were totally opposite, but Hindemith would set you up a model and a form and would project part of it and it would be like a bit of a crossword puzzle to him, and he would give you the first clues to this part and he would give you the conclusions and he would want you to fill in the other things. Martinů didn't see it [composing] as a puzzle but he saw it as something that just flowed naturally from what your feelings toward the music were.

AB: What do you think Martinů regarded as being the most Hindemith-like aspect of your composition?

BR: Oh, I think that was the polyphonic character that we were going for, the fugal effects that we had to put in. I had to have some fugatos take place, and it was getting more and more difficult as I was going through it because the theme did not lend itself very well to that and I was having problems. He [Martinů] could see that and I think that's what he objected to more—that I was fitting my own things into a form, instead of having my things become creative and then taking the form on. It was more or less as we say the cart before the horse.

AB: One of the very first compositions Martinů wrote in America was dedicated to your mother.

BR: Yes, for her birthday on September 21st, 1942, he wrote a composition that was called *Dumka*.[3] Of course that's a well-known term that we use to mean "reverie," but it means many different things to many different people. He wrote this lovely little composition. It was only three pages long and it . . . was very sensitive and I loved the composition and it reminds me that I can see a certain French-type influence it has. I can hear chords that were similar to Debussy chords yet in the middle of it I see his own Czech nature coming out there because of the cross rhythms that he presents in the composition. Lovely.

AB: Did he write the piece in your house?

BR: No, he wrote it very quickly, I think in the morning. I'm sure he composed the *Dumka* at the Castagnola house and brought it over in the evening for a surprise party for my mother's birthday.

And at the party Firkušný was there and he brought it in, put it on the piano and Rudolf played it right away and we all just said, oh what a nice, lovely little piece, what a wonderful little birthday present it is. I will remember that my whole life as I said, I felt that it represented a certain calmness that Martinů felt, and I felt a certain tenderness that he felt toward women and my mother in particular. He could compose so rapidly and he always knew what he wanted before he wrote it down. He never had to stall over things to write them, but everyone who knows Martinů, knows that that's the case.

AB: Do you want to talk about how he walked around Jamaica at night?

BR: This was during 1942 or around 1941–1942, around the time he was out in Jamaica. It was a time when America was preparing for war, and so there were blackouts and the streets were quite dark, and we would not have very many lights on. Certain evenings were definitely like drills, air raid drills, but even without these drills the evenings were very dark, and not too many people were out after ten or eleven o'clock at night. Bohuslav Martinů loved to take walks at night, and it would be no problem for him to leave his house and start to walk maybe a mile, two miles, three miles until one or two o'clock. He would be just thinking by himself.

Very often, he would get disoriented and not know where he was, and there were calls from him that would come in at one o'clock or so in the morning. My father would get on the phone, and he would ask where he was, and he would say, okay, and more or less he'd say in Czech, of course, he said, I'll be there in ten minutes. He would go and pick up Bohuslav, and he would bring him back to his house.

AB: Do you know why his First Symphony[4] is nicknamed the "Spy Symphony"?

BR: I have heard that was because when he was up in Massachusetts he was targeted as somebody strange walking around the area. At that time, people were worried about spies. Why? Because out on Long Island, some spies were found to be out near Southampton. They had landed from a U-boat. . . . And then they came into town, and this became a big thing in the paper that, oh, the United States is being invaded by German spies. We were very worried about it. It was in the papers all the time, this talking about the spies. And there, poor Bohuslav Martinů, who was on the German blacklist, was accused of being a German spy. I think the story goes with the First Symphony. He was walking around the area near the water, probably, at night. And because it was near the water, people were very suspicious about who would be walking late at night. . . . They were suspicious. And he was brought in for questioning, I believe. Martinů was a bit terrified of something like that.

AB: Can you talk about Martinů's emotional side?

BR: I think he had an inwardly and simple quality of love in him . . . and I don't think he was a type of person who was highly complex from an emotional point of view, as far as going through, say, German psychoanalysis. I could never imagine him becoming psychoanalyzed. . . . He felt very close to his brother and his sister, and he missed them very much throughout his stay in America, and I heard him mention them once in a while there, not too often, but I think he thought of them in a, in a very, just loving, simple, brotherly type of relationship . . .

AB: How do you remember the premieres and performances of Martinů's works?

BR: I was at the premiere of the *Memorial to Lidice*,[5] and Martinů was not there, but I asked them to hold the tickets. It's a fairly short work. I was surprised at that. I was expecting to sit down for a twenty-minute work, and it was only, what, ten minutes or so, it took twelve minutes. And I applauded greatly from the top, up there in the balcony, and it received a very good review, if I remember it correctly.

AB: Would you describe Martinů in the '40s, '50s as being a famous composer in America?

BR: Really, he was very well known, very well respected. He had more premieres during his stay here, I think, than practically any other composer that I know of. The Boston Symphony, not only with Koussevitzky, with Munch, Philadelphia with Ormandy, the Cleveland Orchestra with the Second Symphony[6] that he wrote, with Erich Leinsdorf. . . . And then he wrote many other pieces of chamber music that were performed. I think that is the area of Martinů's music that is most appreciated. Performers . . . just love to play Martinů. I don't know of any violinists or string players who have played Martinů who just say, oh, I don't want to play that again. They love his music. And also wind players, people who have played the trio Madrigals,[7] that's a long piece. It's twenty some-odd minutes or twenty-five minutes long. And that, if you ask an oboe or a bassoon and clarinet player, they just love that piece.

I'll offer one anecdote. One time I interviewed Sylvia Goldstein, who was a worker for Boosey and Hawkes, and she told me how she had networked with Martinů for many years, and he kept sending them another string quartet or another chamber music, and she said, you know, we have trouble, Bohuš, to place these. Can you hold off a minute and give us more symphonies? But he just composed what he wanted.

"He Was a World Thinker": An Interview with Zaidee Parkinson

Zaidee Parkinson (b. 1937) studied with acclaimed pianists/teachers Leon Fleisher and Rosina Lhevinne and subsequently studied composition with Bohuslav Martinů and Stephan Wolpe. Throughout her career Zaidee Parkinson has been celebrated for her technical proficiency and expressive depth, contributing significantly to the Classical music landscape. She has long been a major supporter of contemporary American composers, commissioning new works from them.

AB: How did you come to know Martinů?

ZP: I was a little girl, I was fourteen years old, and I was a composer, a composition student, and they submitted my compositions to Martinů at the Mannes School, and he selected me to teach. I was waiting for him in the hall, and he came out, this tall, handsome, wonderful-looking man, came out and put his hands on my shoulders and said, so you're the one, and that started three years of just the most inspiring sessions with this great man. You could imagine what it was like for a little girl to be in the presence of such a person, learning.

AB: And what compositions did you show him during your studies?

ZP: We worked together. He had his students copy him. This was his method of teaching, at least for me, and so if he was making a cello sonata, then I was to make the same sonata in my style, but using the same measure-lengths and the same development material, and in other words, following his road, his track, and that was the way I learned composition.

AB: Was he pushing you to follow his own way of composing?

ZP: He wouldn't have done that. He wanted me to have germinal material, so that I would, you know, create the motive myself, and then I would bring it to him, and from that time on, we would extend it and work it out, and my composition became very similar to his at that time. He did a lot of improvising during sessions and nudging, feeling the way. He wasn't didactic. He didn't have theories or a counterpoint or a set way in which he taught. It was very instinctive, very intuitive. We felt our way. We groped our way.

AB: Did he try to show you what he would have done on piano?

ZP: Yes, precisely, and then I would go home and expand on the material that we had dealt with during the lesson, that we had nosed around and played with and felt, and then I would go home and extend it, and it was sonata form, of course, this cello sonata was strict sonata form. He was a classicist, as you know, in his formal, structural—

AB: Did you work on large themes with him, or on only small patterns?

ZP: On small patterns, the development of it. My view of Martinů is, that he just started at one point and tried to develop the material. It was like telling a story, you know, it would just unfold itself, and then he would either approve or disapprove of the material that I brought to him, and we would proceed again over the same ground.

AB: What role did your mother and family play in Martinů's life?

ZP: Yes, that was very important. Martinů was not happy in New York, and he was vociferous about it. He made it very clear that he would prefer to be in a café in Paris, and there were no cafés in New York, and he minded that, but he said, there couldn't be any because of the stench and smell of the automobiles.

AB: Did you ever visit Martinů when he went back to Europe?

ZP: Yes, he was living in a grotto, like a cave, on a hill overlooking the sea. It was like perhaps a monk would live, very, very stringent, and the only thing he had in this small room was a big, big art book of Piero della Francesca, and he was in the process of writing the *Frescoes*,[8] and we took him down to the town to have dinner.

AB: Would you describe Martinů as being a poor man?

ZP: Yes, there was this one occasion when my mother and I, it was in the first year that I was studying with him, so for me he was a god, and I had never met anybody like him . . . and I worshiped him. We were getting dressed to go to a wedding, my mother and I, and the doorbell rang, it was pouring rain outside, and here was Martinů with his wife, Charlotte, with his hat in his hands, I remember, and he said, Betty, we have nowhere to live, we have nowhere to go. I don't know what she did at that point, it's just a flashback, you know, it has no continuity to it. I don't remember if she immediately made a phone call, or what he did that night, but I remember I was deeply shocked, I was in a state of deep shock over it. I was humiliated, embarrassed, that here we were, dressed up for a wedding, and here was this man in poverty, and in need, and I was mortified. It made a deep impression on me.

AB: Did you have other discussions with Martinů?

ZP: What comes to mind immediately is his love of books, and how much he loved to read, and he was not a citizen of any country, he was a world thinker, and a tremendous mind. [He] . . . was very left-wing, which is interesting, because he wasn't a communist, but he certainly wasn't a capitalist. He loved Dostoevsky, and he didn't care for Tolstoy.

AB: You told me a funny story about finding a theme for an opera.

ZP: Yes, we finished the cello sonata, and he decided I should write an opera. As I say, I did everything to copy him. He must have been starting an opera at that time. And so he sent me to the library, and he said that he thought Chinese themes would be interesting. I got a book, and I brought it to him, and it was sheer pornography. And he said, I think we won't write this.

AB: Did you play his Piano Sonata?[9]

ZP: Yes, I did. That was after I was married, and I was giving concerts in New York. And my husband came home from Europe one day with this First Sonata, which was not played in this country. It had been written for Rudolf Serkin, [but] he had not premiered it. And it had not been played in New York, and I gave the first performance of it. And it's a monumental piece. I wrote the program notes for it. And it's a powerful piece, full of war, tragedy, lyricism. It's Martinů at his best.

AB: You wrote mostly instrumental music with Martinů?

ZP: I wrote a piano sonata and a cello sonata and several songs. And I don't remember doing much else than that. Although, when I look over my material, I saved everything. There are some parts, choral parts, and I'm sure that my memory lacks precision on how many pieces I worked on with him.

AB: And do you remember any circles of friends around Martinů?

ZP: Well, as I said, there was a circle around my grandparents who lived in the country, and also in New York and had many guests staying. And Jarmila Novotná[10] and her husband stayed with us many times and Rudolf Firkušný[11] and Jan Masaryk.[12] And that was the circle. We were very close. We spent Christmases together every year. And he was well known by all of them and a friend of all of theirs. But he never became part of that group. He remained very isolated in my recollection. He lived unto himself.

"He Never Complained About Lack of Performances": An Interview with David Diamond

David Leo Diamond (1915–2005) was a major American composer of Classical music. He studied at the Cleveland Institute of Music and the Eastman School of Music under Bernard Rogers, also receiving lessons from Roger Sessions in New York City and Nadia Boulanger in Paris. He was a longtime member of the Juilliard School faculty and honorary composer-in-residence of the Seattle Symphony.

AB: When Martinů composed, he sometimes had aches and pains. He suffered very badly from writer's cramp. Did taking any medications help?

DD: It . . . didn't help. What he had to do was stop writing music altogether. . . . Bohuslav stopped for I think a week, and then he would go back. But . . . with him it came and went, and he would take so much aspirin, and then he began taking other painkillers, and I said that's not very good, it'll make you feel terrible. But this Dr. Epstein, I think, told him what to do about soaking his head in cold water and then in hot water and cold water. This is a composer's disease, as you know, and if you compose a great deal, especially for orchestra, you know how many lines there are and how many notes there have to be, and this gets to be a terrible, terrible thing, that nerve which goes all the way up, it can paralyze your whole shoulder. But I remember that he suffered a great deal from it.

In Paris, I remember, when he was living in the rue Delambre, in that tiny little apartment, there was one window and not much light came in, and he had a very small little lamp. . . . You know, French electricity wasn't very strong in those years anyway. So even if you used a strong light bulb, you weren't going to get the strength that we get in a, let's say, a 60-watt bulb in the United States. If you got a bulb that was stronger, it would blow out all the lights in an entire building. He said that he had tried to get a stronger lamp, but the landlady said that you can't use it, otherwise she would charge him for the electricity bill. So he moved out of there eventually, and he moved into an apartment in the rue Jasmin, and that was a better apartment with light. But he always had troubles about places to work.

And so one night, Bohuslav and I went into the Dingo Bar, and we really, really had a wonderful time talking to some of the Black musicians. Now somebody asked me, did I think that Bohuslav was ever interested in jazz, that is, American jazz. And frankly, I never asked him directly, but from the music that I know, I would say the symphonies have no jazz influence whatsoever. None of the scherzo-like movements have. But I did find, in the First Violin Piano Sonata,[13] there is a movement that I definitely feel has a kind of jazzy feel to it. His largos are wonderful, the very slow music.

When there's a real largo, it's very impressive. But there's also a wonderful kind of feeling, like the opening of the First Symphony,[14] which creates a whole kind of almost underwater kind of feeling. Of course, I will never forget when I heard the Boston Symphony play it, you know, that great orchestra with those great musicians.

They gave the First Symphony a special kind of texture that was exactly right for Martinů's style of music. It had an enormous success, and shortly, I think the very next year or two years after, the Second Symphony[15] was performed by, I think it was Leinsdorf. His symphonies began to really move, and I think that's why he wrote one after the other, like the piano concertos for Firkušný. When you have a pianist like that, you compose.

I think he was very fortunate with conductors like Koussevitzky,[16] and then later Szell. George Szell was very, very important in performing Martinů's music. He should have played more, but in Cleveland, you know, you just do so much contemporary music. But later on, he did do more when he guest-conducted. One thing I do remember about Bohuslav is he never complained about lack of performances, whereas Bartók complained a great deal, and he was right. There were no performances until after his death, I mean, now and then.

Bohuslav once said to me, you know, I feel very, very unhappy that I'm having such a big success in America, and Bartók had died recently, and Mrs. Bartók is very unhappy that his music is completely ignored, and my music is played all the time. So when I saw Mrs. Bartók, I told her, I said you shouldn't feel that way, because it's a rare thing, because Koussevitzky really did a great deal in commissioning the Concerto for Orchestra of Bartók's, but she said that wasn't a great deal of money. It was $1,000 and the copying of the parts.

AB: Where did Martinů meet his friends?

DD: It was mainly the Dôme that Bohuslav met his friends, and there were a lot of them. They either went to the Coupole for the seafood, which was better than the seafood at the Dôme, or they liked the terrace of the Dôme, where I remember there was a *gérant* [manager] whose name was Alexander, and he would set up seven or eight tables in a long row. And all of Bohuslav's friends, and Mihalovici's[17] friends, and Harsányi's[18] friends, they would all come and sit around these tables, and just [have] coffee, you know. They weren't big drinkers, none of them were big drinkers. I think the only time I saw a bottle of champagne being opened was a birthday celebration for Mihalovici, but that was the only [time], otherwise it was coffee, very little alcoholic drinks.

As a matter of fact, come to think of it, I don't remember Bohuslav drinking very much except good wine. He liked very good wine, and he had very good taste, and I mean taste in the sense of choosing good wines from the good wine

Figure 1. Martinů with friends in a Paris café on 15 May 1940. Present, among others, Tibor Harsányi, Georges Auric, Pierre Bernac, Marcel Mihalovici, Francis Poulenc, Lee Hsien Ming Tcherepnin, Alexandre Tansman, Charlotte Martinů, Alexander Tcherepnin.

regions in France. I think he learned that from Charlotte, because she was very good about those things, too. She was also an excellent cook. I remember they invited me for supper one night, and she made a wonderful, wonderful omelette. Then we had lamb, which she made sort of Russian-style, it was very, very good.

AB: Can you describe the personalities around Martinů, around you in the late '30s? Who were the friends of Martinů, composers, artists?

DD: Harsányi and Mihalovici . . . are the two that I remember. . . . We loved Roussel's songs, especially a song called "Jazz dans la nuit." We thought that was a very unusual song for Roussel to have written. We talked a great deal about Roussel as a composer, as a teacher, and as a human being. He was as fond of Roussel as I was. And Roussel did a great deal, as you certainly are aware, for Bohuslav. I think he was the one, as he did for me, who gave us letters to Munch. I found a letter from Munch saying that Bohuslav was coming with a new score and would I like to come over to hear it.

I would always tell American students, you must come to Paris to study. If you don't want to study with Boulanger, then you should take a course at the Conservatoire or the Ecole Normale, but you should be there just to go to concerts, you will hear so much different music, old music, new music, everything, you know, and within a period of one year and you will know the whole history of music. And at that time, the Schola Cantorum was still very active, even though d'Indy had died, I believe it was around 1935, it was still very active, the concert was still Sunday afternoons. Bohuslav was always amused when I told him that Erik Satie had been a student, had taken the counterpoint class of Roussel's at the Schola Cantorum. He said, "Vraiment?" Yes. He said, "How do you account that there's so little counterpoint in Satie's music?" I said, but Bohuslav, there is a lot of counterpoint.

So I went to Durand and I bought up all the published music that there was of Satie, and I went through it and I marked, in a work called *Choses vues à droite et à gauche (sans lunettes)*, and one of the movements is called "Fugue à tâtons."

I said, take a look at this fugue subject, Bohuslav, it's a wonderful fugue. And he looked at it and he said, Oui, vraiment, c'est bon ça. And he began to hum, da, da, di, da, di, da, da, da, dum, da, da, dum, da, da, dum, di, da, da, da, da, da, dum. He said, Very good, but he said, There's one bar too many, too many—da, da, da, dum, da, da, dum. That's not good for a fugue to repeat the same three bars over again. He was absolutely right about this.

See, those were the things about Bohuslav where you could see his face change expression, because he was half amused and half surprised that there was so much in Satie's music.

AB: What did Martinů think of the United States more broadly?

DD: I told him that you must never think of America as being New York City, because it is anything but America. It's sort of all the different parts of Europe put together. That's what New York is. But if you want to see America, you must go out west or you must go into New England. And I think that shortly after I sublet his apartment, the summer of '45, he and Charlotte took a small little house in Edgartown, Massachusetts. And that's when Koussevitzky invited him to Tanglewood to teach, I think it was two different summers, and that's where he had the bad accident, where he fell and hurt his head badly.

And other than that, he didn't know New England very well. But then he got a couple of the students at the school in Tanglewood to drive him around Vermont and New Hampshire, and he was amazed by how beautiful the country was. And he was especially impressed with Mount Monadnock. Every time I manage to get up there, I'm still amazed by how extraordinary that whole region of Mount Monadnock is near Peterborough, New Hampshire.

But I think Bohuslav had a very unusual eye. He had the kind of eye which was the kind of ear, really. He would seek color in terms of lyrical quality, and that's a little bit like Klee's looking at Bach's polyphony and seeing it as design for his own work. I think painters and composers have a great deal in common.

AB: Who were the people who helped Martinů when he came to America? Who were the most important orchestras, persons, critics?

DD: I would say Koussevitzky, because they had known each other in Paris, so it was natural that when he arrived in New York Koussevitzky should have immediately commissioned him to write a symphony. I remember years later Koussevitzky would say to me, can you imagine that he wrote a sinfonietta, he wrote a this, he wrote a that, but he never had written a big symphony. He said, Why do you think that? I said, I don't know, you must ask him, but I'm glad that you asked him to write a symphony because he will probably write you an extraordinary symphony and I hope it will be for the full Boston Symphony.

He said, Yes, I told him I want it to be for the full orchestra, and that's how the First Symphony came to be written. But I think that New York, as a city for Bohuslav, was a kind of place where he was stimulated by the energy level.

AB: How did you see the role of Rudolf Firkušný in helping Martinů?

DD: I think Rudy was one of the great blessings, because not only do we have great piano works, solo piano works and works for piano and orchestra, but they are completed, fulfilled works. They are the best of Martinů in terms of imagination and writing for the piano. I asked Rudy once, did you make any suggestions, did you ask him to change certain things in the writing for the piano, or did you feel that Bohuslav handled the piano well, because he was a violinist after all. And he said, no, no. He said he wrote extremely well. Sometimes I would say an octave here would be very good for contrast, or the left hand maybe could anticipate this, but other than that, I didn't. He did that all very, very well himself.

He conceived of the piano as basically a good solo instrument as well as an instrument for piano with orchestra. So in many ways, I think Bohuslav was a phenomenon. He is one of the few composers I know outside of maybe Mozart, Haydn, who could write for any ensemble and absolutely give as much variety to every ensemble, an invention as well.

And this is, I think, true, because if you take chamber music, if you take a string quartet by Martinů, it is a complete string quartet written for the instruments, and you could tell that this is a violinist who knows his string instruments. Then you take a quintet with piano, a piano quartet, I realized that he had written for so many different ensembles, piano quartet, piano quintet. There isn't an ensemble that Bohuslav at some time did not complete.

I think had he stayed in America longer and traveled more, he would have been even more surprised by the variety in the American landscape. And he used to ask me also about painters. I would tell him about de Kooning and I would tell him about Stuart Davis, some of the American painters. But he also wanted to know about American composers. I introduced him to Aaron Copland. As a matter of fact, Copland came with Harold Clurman, his friend. They came to the Saturday performance of Martinů's First Symphony. And I introduced Martinů and his wife to Copland and Harold Clurman. And Copland was very impressed with Bohuslav. He said, you know, that man has a quiet about him that is very impressive.

AB: At one time, Martinů had wonderful teaching jobs. It was at the Mannes School of Music, Tanglewood, and Princeton. Was it unusual to have that many teaching positions?

DD: [No.] . . . The American composer Roger Sessions taught at Princeton and at Berkeley. It was not unusual if you had the big reputation, if you were a big name. And Bohuslav was certainly a big name among European composers, so that made it possible. And then once he taught at Tanglewood, the students who were there would tell other students, you ought to try sometimes to take some lessons with Martinů. He's in New York a good deal, and you should try to call him and get in touch with him. As a teacher, he told me that he lacked patience. He said, "Ça me manque beaucoup, beaucoup, je ne peux pas penser aux autres, à la musique des jeunes. Je pense toujours de moi-même, et ça c'est un peu égoïste," he said, "mais quand même c'est moi."[19] And I could understand immediately what he meant by that, because a man who wrote that much music would have to think constantly. He told me that once, when he would walk down Sixth Avenue, he could already hear an entire piece that he wanted to compose.

And when he got back to the apartment, in one day, he would be able to get the whole piece written out. I think one of either the Violin and Piano Sonata or a Flute and Piano Sonata[20] was written in a very short period of time. Another thing that I found extraordinary in Bohuslav is he could hear the piano parts, and he could hear the orchestral parts without having to depend on either an orchestration book or the piano. He could absolutely write out an entire orchestral score without depending on testing the chords at the piano.

AB: Charlotte described Bohuslav Martinů as being a different person after the accident, not the same as he had been before. Did you notice a difference between Martinů before 1946 and then after 1946, after his fall?

DD: Yes. I definitely noticed a big change and the big change was not only in the way he walked, but also the way his head seemed to be a little bit more on one side than it had been before. And where before he would answer immediately if I would say something to him, this time there was a long pause, as though he were thinking before he spoke. There must have been some shock to his nervous system to make that happen to him, because he was not the same Bohuslav.

And the fact that you tell me he was in his sixties, he seemed much older, you see, after the accident.

If anything, what I find very unusual is that it's as though the accident created something that made his energy level become even more motivated, so that there's a kind of energy level that's very much stronger—it made me think of some of the early pieces like *La bagarre*,[21] you see. So it's hard to know what that particular kind of accident did in terms of harming the nervous system. But I did notice, as a person, it took him a longer time to reply when you spoke to him. And Rudy Firkušný said the same thing to me.

AB: How would you describe Martinů's success as a composer in the United States?

DD: I think he had the success he did because the music was immediately convincing in terms of melody, harmony, instrumentation, rhythm. You see, it was very difficult in the '40s particularly. The Greek conductor Dimitri Mitropoulos played a great deal of contemporary music of all composers, not only American. It always surprised me that I don't remember his ever playing a Martinů work. Maybe he did a concerto with Rudy Firkušný. But I think in general, Bohuslav's music stayed strong up until—oh, I would say somewhere around 1963.

AB: Do you see any conscious difference between Martinů's music written in France and his music written for an American audience?

DD: Oh, definitely. The music written in America is much warmer, I mean, emotionally warmer. It's much bigger in structural concepts. That's because he became interested in the large symphony, and even the large chamber music becomes more interesting. I think the music altogether becomes more interesting during his American period. Also there's a greater variety in his movements. There's a change between the fast movements, the presto movements, and the slow movements and the really largo movements. So there's a bigger variety, I think. And the instrumentation is, I think, much more interesting, too. We have, perhaps, Koussevitzky to thank for making him write more and more of these pieces. And even the piano concertos take on a bigger interest. It could be that his trip to Italy [caused this change], when he wrote *The Frescoes of Piero della Francesca*. You see, that already showed another attitude.

That's where I think the similarity between a Paul Klee's reaction to Bach's counterpoint and Bohuslav's reaction to what he saw in Italian painting. And for me, if somebody asked me, what basically do you feel isolates Martinů's music as a Czech composer from its just being very much recognizable as, let's say, one recognizes Smetana, or Dvořák, or Janáček, what is it about Martinů that makes him definitely stronger in recognizing this style? I would say it's basically because the structures begin to be larger. They go out. They go beyond themselves, so to speak. Now that could be also why he began to write more operatic music, because he needed the bigger structures for all this enormous amount of melodic and harmonic and orchestral music and vocal music that he heard within himself.

AB: Is there anything you would like to add about the technique of Martinů as a composer?

DD: Well, he was a master. I mean, a master that was like nobody else, you see. What you could say about certain composers is that so-and-so is a little bit like Debussy, so-and-so has been influenced by Boulez, so-and-so has been influenced by so-and-so. With Martinů, you can't do that, not even with the earliest pieces.

The most I heard said once about *La bagarre* was that it made them think of Stravinsky. I said, I don't hear any Stravinsky whatsoever in it, although I do know that Bohuslav was very interested in Stravinsky's neoclassic music when he began to change from the music like *Firebird* and *Petrushka*, and he went into the neoclassic period of the Octet. That's when I think Bohuslav really becomes interested in Stravinsky's music. He had a great many of the scores, and every time there was a new piece, I brought it back to him; I remember *Perséphone* of Stravinsky. He thought it was an extraordinary work, and he was right. . . . He knew everything that was happening in music.

He wanted to know a great deal more about American music, but of course there wasn't too much American music being played, you see, except for Copland, myself, especially in the '40s. Now and then, a Sessions symphony. He heard the Sessions Second Symphony, he said it was too complicated, and he was absolutely right. It was far too complicated. When I told him, actually, that I had seen Schoenberg in Hollywood—this was before I sublet his apartment—I saw Schoenberg in 1942, and then I saw him again in 1949, but the first time I saw Schoenberg, after he arrived, I saw him for, oh, just a short time in '35. But then I told Bohuslav about our talks that we had, and how important [Schoenberg thought] counterpoint was, and that a student must study counterpoint and harmony. He would accept no student writing twelve-note music until they had mastered traditional music, and Bohuslav smiled, he said, "Bon, c'est bien dit, ça."[22] He was very pleased that Schoenberg had said that.

AB: What was his approach to twelve-tone music?

DD: He didn't really like it. He said that it was very dry. He said everything he knew of Schoenberg that was a twelve-note work, it was dry. I said, have you had a chance to go through parts of *Moses and Aaron*? He said, no, he hadn't done that yet. But his feeling was that the moment you had to work out the twelve pitches in a certain way, he said, it's like a person looking in a mirror, he said, what would I think of myself if every day when I woke up I went into the bathroom and I looked at myself in the mirror, and I said to myself, well, today you're going to pull up this eyebrow, and then you're going to pull this one down, and you're going to pull your nose up here, and then you're going to pull your mouth down here, and that's the way you're going to look today. Then you're going to look another way the next day. He said, this is what twelve-note music seemed to me, that the moment you have to take those twelve pitches and arrange them in four different versions, or even two different versions, he said, it's not at all like what Bach did.

He said, Bach did it instinctively, and he heard it automatically, whereas Schoenberg does it all automatically and self-consciously, which is absolutely true.

AB: So did he think that twelve-tone music was unnatural?

DD: Calculated. He said it's always calculated so that you know every minute that the pitch is going to go here, it's going to go down there, and that the inversion is going to do this, and it's going to do that. He said, Bach can do it, but he makes it sound completely original so that you are constantly surprised. He said, I would say Schoenberg's twelve-note music doesn't surprise me, whereas Bach's chromatic music surprises me all the time. Absolutely right about that.

AB: I would like to ask about the flat you used to live in, in his flat in the summer of 1945.[23] How could you describe the flat, what was in it, what did it look like?

DD: You came up, it was an apartment, a furnished apartment, in a small building that had about three apartments, one on top of the other. And you came up the steps, Bohuslav's, I think, was on the second floor. And you came up, and you opened the door, and you were immediately in this very long room. And right there in front of you was this long, very long . . . grand piano. But then I found out that it wasn't playable. The strings were ripped. It had been badly, badly mauled for many, many years. It just stood there.

And Bohuslav used it as storage space to put his manuscripts in flat, on top of the strings inside the piano. So that was his storage, because otherwise there was no place for him to put all his music that he wrote, that he had manuscript paper of, or those transparencies where he could make several copies, you see. So he used the piano as a storage space.

Then to your left, after you came in, was a little pantry, but not much of a kitchen in the back, just this kind of gas range. It's amazing that Charlotte could do cooking, but the French are wonderful for just using a gas range. And then you came out, again, this large living room. And then to the back, you turned right, was the bedroom. And in that bedroom was a little upright piano, and that's where Bohuslav composed. So the upright piano was against the window, and the bed was over here. And there was a bath off the front room. And there was a nice bay window in the front where you could copy. So that's all there was to the apartment, just that very large room with the bedroom off one place, the pantry on that side, and a bathroom. That was all the apartment was.

AB: Would you say he was happy in America?

DD: I can't really say, because I'm not sure I really knew what happiness would mean for a man like Bohuslav. I had a feeling that Charlotte was not happy in America, and therefore I felt that he was not very happy either, because of that.

I had a feeling that they both—and Firkušný told me that I was not wrong about that—that they both felt as they were in a strange land. And I said, you don't think it's the fact that it's New York, that if they were in some other smaller city outside of New York, maybe in Connecticut or in Maryland, any place but this nightmare city of New York, it would be better for them? And I once asked Koussevitzky, I said, you know, it would be so good if you could get the Martinůs to move and live here in Boston. It would be wonderful for them, don't you think? He said, yes, it would. He said, it's a good idea, but you know, I think there is a big financial problem to be discussed. And so he has to be where he does some teaching. And at that time, I think he was offered a part-time job at Princeton University.

He had to commute, you see, back and forth. That was closer than had he been in Boston. I would think that the whole setup for Bohuslav, the sudden giving up a city like Paris, where he really was excited by what was happening, and then having to live in a jungle like New York, even though he had wonderful performances there, I think that personally he was not very happy.

But I didn't know one European composer who was happy there. Bartók was very unhappy, and I felt Bohuslav was unhappy, because that is not a city for a creative person to live in. Maybe a painter could enjoy New York, or a sculptor, but I don't think that a composer . . . I hated living in New York.

"Why?": An Interview with Chou Wen-Chung, Basel, 9 May 2006

Chou Wen-Chung (1923–2019) was a Chinese-born composer, teacher, and administrator who lived and worked in the United States from 1946. In his creative life he always thought about ways his training in Western music could be transformed through aspects of Chinese music and culture. He was a professor at Columbia University and also Vice Dean at Columbia's School of the Arts. He also became the musical executor of the estate of Edgard Varèse.

AB: Can you tell me how you came to study with Martinů?

CWC: I really did not study with him for very long. I began . . . at the beginning of 1949, immediately after I got to New York, and then he had to go back to Europe and he went back and forth, so he was away. And then I was looking for other opportunities and I went to Columbia University and I . . . met Varèse, so my contact with Martinů was over a short period. We became friendly very quickly, even though his English was not exactly up to easy-flow conversation, nor was I fluent in another European language. The comunication was, in some ways, very . . . indirect. On the other hand it was very instinctive. You know the story about the gesture he paid to my so-called fugue. He played a few measures, and turned around and said: "Why?" It sounds very philosophical. But maybe he couldn't continue with his objections. I very quickly, suddenly, realized, okay, this is not a fugue, it was an imitation of a fugue. So our communication was like that. He reacted to my music very well, but he probably felt he was not in a position to tell me how I should proceed.

AB: Why did you want to study with him in the first place?

CWC: In that way, looking back I was naive, although not without good reason. I was studying in Boston at New England Conservatory and at that time, back in '50s, it was very different from today. It was very, very old-fashioned, and I'm grateful for that because nowadays people don't teach that way anymore. That's a very solid foundation. . . . I studied with the head teacher of composition, Carl McKinley, who was a student of Boulanger, and our relationship was very good but he was too old-fashioned to really help me. I only remember that every time I showed him a piece, when we got to the wrong note, he would say, Wait, not yet. It was so funny, the moment he said, Not yet! So I was always looking out for teachers. But it took me many, many years to decide to study music, because I was brought up during the war, tough years, and it was very hard decision. And I always wondered whether, at my age, I should still consider studying composition. Also, I wondered, in China, how could you possibly study composition during the war? Mainly it's Western music. So, I hesitated. And when I finally got to this country after college, I got a big scholarship to go to Yale. Instead of going to class, though, I would stay in my room meditating, literally. I don't remember what I did during that week, but by the end of that week, I decided to try to study composition. So, I was very particular and when I began to find a teacher, I really was trying to find the teacher best for me. And I was so impressed with Martinů when he came to the conservatory to give lectures, so I went to study with him. Of course he was a noted composer, so it was valuable. In fact, he was the first one to say: You are a Chinese, what is your knowledge of Chinese music? Of course,

I was brought up with that, I knew it, but he said: No, what's your knowledge, he meant *your* knowledge, not just your way around. I said: Nothing. He said: If I were you, I would have studied that first. I took it to heart. That was really the first best lesson I ever had, and Martinů gave me also the second: Why? Ever since then when I do something new, something unique, personal, I always remember Martinů's word: Why? Well, too bad Martinů died because I wanted to tell him: I know why! My answer is that he didn't know the answer. The answer is, that only a few people practice their tradition. And you can define what polarity, the term polarity's meaning is, yin and yang. You realize yin and yang's polarity doesn't have to be opposite. But he was looking at it from the European heritage and saying: What are you going to do? You don't have the polarity but the contrast, the forces of contrast, you are not going to achieve anything in terms of you. He was right, but if you could define what the forces are, you can equally achieve something by not quite a fugue. In fact, my second string quartet is nothing but a fugue, because I was approached by the Brentano Quartet for commission to write a fugue in honor of art. And that was celebrated with Bach that year, and I wrote a fugue. I removed all the episodes, so it's very dense, and I used the episodes in the last section for recapitulation, the last moment as recap. Anyway, that's afterward. So therefore, Martinů's question of "Why?" is very important to me, as important to me as any composer. Whether I was right or wrong, he was right or wrong, the point is you have to ask yourself why, because it deviates from heritage, and you may gain or you may lose because of that knowlege. So it's not that. People would say, Oh as a composer, I should do it instinctively. No! Martinů to the last degree in my mind, is an instinctive composer compared to a lot of other composers. And yet, the word why is quite loaded. I'm sure he asked himself that question.

AB: How long did you study with Martinů?

CWC: Not really long. I think for over a year period but you know, only whenever he was available. It was very short but had a lot of impact. A lot of impact . . . nonverbal impact. And that's very interesting. I don't know whether you know his personality. Now, at that time when I read about him, being a Czech, he was very much aware of his own heritage, how to, you know, be a composer that's obviously strongly influenced by West European heritage and yet to retain the Czech part of himself.

AB: Did he discuss Eastern traditions with you? Because he was fairly interested in that.

CWC: We talked a bit about it. Not really actually, as I recall, as much as one might think. Again, I think it might be the language barrier. I think he was a rather shy and self-conscious person. I could see, he didn't want to talk or say anything that he wasn't comfortable with or knew enough about. So often, he was reserved, and I could sense the reserve was not really because he didn't care about something, or whatever, but rather, the language issue. And of course, my own English was not really that fluent. So the two us were communicating by way of this kind of bastard English. It was very funny. . . . Actually, this goes back to my decision of trying to study with him. I came to New York, I was looking for a teacher to study with, and there were a lot of composers. But people would say, Oh, don't study with this person. When I read this piece of news, I said to myself, well I'm from the East, yes. Basically, I tried to learn from the West, but I'm not going to write Western music and such. And then here is the composer, Martinů. Before my time, he already, more or less, did the same thing. . . . Martinů was trying to find something that's of Czech heritage, and yet within the overall framework of European music. In my case, it's just expanding that distance a little more. And so that was my reason for studying with him. Therefore, my intentions were not really that I wanted to study with this teacher, or that I wanted to study what this composer does, or in his or her style and so on, but rather, how did he get to the point? I thought I would be able to learn from him by digesting what he had to say, and comparing how that might affect my way of thinking. Yes, interesting. It's an experimental approach on my part. If he hadn't been going back and forth, I would have stayed with him, and what I would have studied from him would have been very interesting. From then on, I just felt very much attracted to the idea of Czechoslovakia.

AB: His piece, *The Fifth Day of the Fifth Moon*[24] is his reaction to the Communist coup de état, this Communist takeover.

CWC: I remember when I took it home and looked at it, I was surprised, because his music before was characteristic for mobility, and I thought, well, this is just contrary to that. I will say at the time, I was very shy, also, coming from China, at that time, the student-teacher relationship was not what it is today. If Martinů were to have given me his music, I wouldn't dare make a comment. I think I was starting to write a piano piece and he said, Oh, I have a piano piece, would you like to have it? So I got it and I never thought of going back and commenting on that. Because American students would go praise the piece. I didn't know what to say, I didn't dare say anything. But he too was also shy. He could never ask. But from his comments on the piece, I could understand he was trying to tell me that it made a difference to him at the time, I just did not make the connection. I find also that it shows another side of him, quiet and also empty and all that. In fact I was even thinking that someday he might develop it into an orchestra piece, because of course that would be very easy with a lot of tremolo.

At the time I studied with Martinů, I was really still groping, I had no sense of direction yet. And I was experimenting. I used Chinese motives based on Chinese material, and so on, but really, not knowing exactly what to do. So I was in a way, at that time, very primitive. And often, as I've said, I wonder what would have happened if I had continued with him and became a more mature student. Because he and Varèse were really very, very different.

AB: Did you know Martinů's music at that time?

CWC: I knew some. . . . A small biography by Šafránek on him came out in 1946 . . . and I read that. So I knew, when I read the newspapers. . . . And I think I got hold of some scores, not very deeply, but at least I knew of them and I was impressed with his Duos, after Mozart.[25] I loved the Mozart Duos. And, so I was at the premiere in fact. I think it was at Mannes School, or some small auditorium. I think those Duos are really one of his very fine works. But I don't know enough of his music to say what might be his best. But I felt it was a really fascinating piece. It's modern, and yet, it just floats on so naturally, and not at all relates to the Mozart, you know, only experience. And I remember I loved it so much. In fact, every time I write for strings, like my string quartets, that Duo comes to my mind.

AB: How do you consider Martinů's position in the '60s, '70s, and '80s?

CWC: He was less and less played. And I think that obviously, it's like today, a lot of composers are played less, including myself. That's the way it is, particularly in this country, because I have been observing the whole situation since I came here in 1946. We go through cycles, just like that. And his music became less popular because of this eruption of interest in the theory of music, and the interest in music technology, tape recordings, and that kind of stuff. Because the interest went in those new directions lots of older works were forgotten. I think it's understandable he suffered from that. I think there will be a revival of Martinů's work. I think his value, really to me, is exactly how I envision him as my teacher. Because if you just look at one piece of his, you say, okay here was a composer from East Europe, he was writing in his own style. But he was such a composer because he came from a different culture. And if the person is sincere in putting in words his own cultural heritage, it is bound to survive. And I've sensed it particularly because in my work I'm not interested in writing Chinese music that's identifiable as Chinese music. I'm interested in writing something that reveals what Chinese heritage can contribute to the music of my own time and the future. And in some ways, that's why I want to find out more about it. Martinů had his own ideas and I think that the value eventually would emerge because of that quality. I think as the question of fashion subsides. . . . You realize how well he was able to express . . . his Czech background. And that's legitimate. That's the step you have to go through. One can never go beyond one's generation. You are captured in that era. And I think we have to look at those composers that way. And then to say, abstractly, what is the value of the composition? Abstractly. Forget about the European tradition, or Czech indigenous feeling. I think that's really the question. And I think at his best, Martinů goes beyond that. For example, the Madrigals for violin and viola. When you listen to that piece, you forget about that. If you are aware of Mozart, you just say, Ah, this is inspired by that. But it goes beyond that. And it's a terrific piece. And you don't say, This is Czech, or that's German, you don't feel that way. You just say, this is a wonderful piece. And you say, this reminds me of Mozart, perhaps, but it has nothing to do with Mozart, and therefore it's a separate piece to me. . . . I think also politics has something to do with it. Right after the war, a composer from Czechoslovakia was very attractive, you see. It was easy to publicize. Today, you don't have too much to say about a foreign composer.

But Martinů to me, in fact, is really a universal system. I don't know his music that well and I shouldn't pretend that I understand it, but I don't feel that here is a composer who wants to show that he's a Czech, nor is this composer saying, Ah, my future is in French music, or German. He said, No. He was just being himself.

"Martinů's Music Goes Against the Bar Line": An Interview with Charles Rosen

Charles Welles Rosen (1927–2012) was an American pianist and writer on music. From the age of six to eleven he studied at the Juilliard School and then privately with Moriz Rosenthal, who had been a student of Franz Liszt. At Princeton University he studied French and completed a PhD in 1951. Rosen appeared in numerous recitals and orchestral engagements around the world and made a large number of recordings, including recording various twentieth-century works at the invitation of their composers (Stravinsky, Carter, Boulez, etc.) In 1971, Rosen published The Classical Style. *He won numerous awards for his books and recordings, including the National Book Award and the Otto Kinkeldey award of the American Musicological Society. In 2012, he received the National Humanities Medal, awarded by President Obama.*

AB: Do you remember when you first met Martinů?

CR: Well, he came to Princeton. At that time the Princeton Music Department was a very good one and the composition area was very distinguished. Roger Sessions had been there for a long time, and then Milton Babbitt was teaching there. Unfortunately, they had Randall Thompson who was not a very good composer, but then he left and Martinů who came was very distinguished.

It was wonderful for the department that he could come. I think he was there two years or something. And I met him because they asked me to play a welcome concert for him. I did the Second Piano Quintet. I was handed the music, which I didn't know. And I looked at the Etudes and Polkas,[26] wonderful pieces, so I learned quite a few of those and then I did the Cello Sonata as well.

He was a wonderful man. He was an extraordinary teacher. The students all loved him as he was a very original teacher. I can remember that he once gave the students a sort of opening theme and told them they should come back and see how the piece would go on. The students came back and he was very indignant at all of them, because they went on with the same theme, and he said no no, with a theme like that you have to do something immediately different right after. So it was quite funny.

His teaching was wonderful. The students all commented on his way with the piano, which I noticed too. He was a violinist, of course. He once told me that he flunked composition at the Prague Conservatory, but that he got wonderful marks in violin and he immediately went to the great orchestra in Prague, the Czech Philharmonic. I think Talich was conducting at the time when he was there. He was placed second desk, first violins, and then four weeks later Richard Strauss came, and a week after that, he found himself at one of the last desks, second violins. I don't know how true the story is and how much he was inventing a part of that.

It was interesting to me that he didn't play the piano very well. But he had one, and when he tried to demonstrate something on the piano there was one thing he could do very remarkably: very fast jumps, he was always very accurate. He couldn't play a scale very well, but he could do this much better than most pianists. It was very, very surprising.

He once told me an extremely funny story about playing in the Czech Philharmonic. He told me they always used to play the Dvořák *Humoresque* as an encore and that one day they played it and the audience went wild with enthusiasm so Talich said, let's do it again. . . . They'd taken the music away but everybody said, oh well we know this, we play it so often, we can all do it by heart. So they started all wanting that bum-pa-dum-pa-dum-pa-dee-da-dee and . . . the first phrase was all right, but at the second phrase, the second violinists began to forget their part, and they played the first violin part, and then gradually the winds forgot their part and finally it was all done in unison. It really sounded terrible and Talich nearly had a fit. They had to play to the end like that. I remember that.

Martinů was an extraordinary character . . . he had a wonderful sense of humor, and he was very, very generous. So it was a tremendous opportunity for me, because the contact with the music was wonderful, and it even led to my first recording. There was this small record company [that] they had just started up. . . . This very small record company was actually a music shop. . . . They had just invented LPs, and so it was very inexpensive to record. Lots of small companies started doing that because there was no breakage; you could ship the records because [the earlier] shellac was very much more delicate, and you got 25 minutes of music on to a side. You could get 50 minutes of music onto one plastic record, making it possible to record long works or lots of works which wouldn't have been possible before. There was this record company, small, just started, and they had half a record by Martinů with René Le Roy playing the Flute Sonata[27] and they asked me if I knew anybody who played Martinů and I said, well, I do. They called up Martinů and asked him if I was any good, and he said I was good—he was a very nice man, a very kind man. I recorded the pieces that I played for his welcome concert, Etudes and Polkas, and he also gave me a copy of *Les ritournelles*[28] which are very beautiful pieces which I learned and I learned some more Etudes and Polkas. I only did about 15 minutes of music, or 12 minutes of the solo pieces really, because there was the Cello Sonata and the Piano Quintet but then there's about 25 minutes of Martinů on that record I made. That was my first recording and it launched my career. I was very grateful to Martinů, and I was grateful to him for the privilege of playing the music which has a tremendous charm. It was very beautiful [even if] they are not his greatest pieces [such as] the Double Concerto[29] which I heard I think Ansermet conduct with the NBC Symphony once.

AB: If I may turn back to this welcome concert, can you remember who performed in that concert?

CR: Well, it wasn't a regular quartet. I think at least three of the four played in the Lehner Quartet, and the cellist in the Cello Sonata was Gabor Rejto, a wonderful Hungarian cellist. We got on extremely well, and we both enjoyed playing the Martinů so much that after this, we went on and gave a concert somewhere else, and I think on the radio we played some Brahms too. The concert would have been 1949, and the record would have been made in 1950. But it didn't come out and it was not issued until 1951, during the last months that I was in Princeton—I got my PhD in May 1951. In a way, this was the beginning of my playing in public and my recording.

AB: How would you describe Martinů's position in Princeton at that time as a musician, as a composer?

CR: He was an enormously respected figure, with a little bit less prestige than Bartók. . . . He was . . . one of the great representatives of European culture who had come to the United States. Basically speaking, a lot of American musicology and composition was a gift from Hitler. We inherited the composers and the musicologists, so basically Hitler created American music this way, quite a lot of it anyway.

Most people felt him as the end of a particular tradition, rather than a deliberate stimulus in their own work. Although those who actually followed him found him quite fascinating. I know many of the students spoke about the extraordinary quickness of his mind in relation to composition, but he was not a man given to very large theories. He didn't have a particular theory like Schoenberg, and he didn't actually found an idiosyncratic aesthetic the way Stravinsky did.

AB: How do you explain the big difference between the approach of both the public and interpreters to Martinů and Bartók in those years?

CR: Bartók's music is actually more difficult to play. . . . And slightly the more radical in chromaticism, so it was more difficult to accept. I remember the first time I heard a quartet by Bartók, I actually got physically nauseous. I mean, I thought it sounded terrible. Those pieces of Bartók from the Third Quartet on could be very radical. I mean, it was that period of Bartók's. It was not until the very last pieces he wrote in America that this style became slightly more acceptable publicly.

The second thing is that, as I said, the music was more difficult to play, but then there was this gradual influence of Hungarian conductors, above all, George Szell and Reiner. I don't know if Reiner was actually Hungarian, but I think he came from somewhere near Hungary. I mean, I'm sure Reiner was Hungarian and so was George Szell.[30]

And Reiner and Szell actually were the great promoters of Bartók in this country. So Bartók's music gradually was being pushed by very important conductors, basically the Cleveland Orchestra, which was certainly the best orchestra in America, along with the Chicago Symphony, which was Reiner. The two best orchestras in America were actually performing Bartók much more than Martinů.

AB: So Martinů was really mostly favored by European conductors.

CR: Yes. That would normally be the case. First of all, that had to be, because there weren't very many American conductors at all.

We imported all our conductors from Europe too, which made one think of Thomas Beecham's great joke. Why do we have so many third-rate foreign conductors when we have so many second-rate native ones? But some of the greatest conductors in the world were literally the great foreign conductors. Reiner, Szell, Toscanini, and so on, who created, in a way, the excellence of the American orchestras in the '40s and '50s, and it lasted a long time.

This was a problem. The other problem was the important difference between the repertoire that one has of Martinů and Bartók. The basis for Bartók's popularity or prestige were the quartets, which gradually went into the repertoire of so many quartets in this country that it was a kind of solid basis on which everything else was done. It's very odd because normally a composer is furthered by lots of performances, particularly of piano music, because there were more piano recitals, but neither for Bartók nor for Martinů was the piano that important an instrument. This is particularly curious in the case of Bartók, who was one of the greatest pianists of the twentieth century, but with the exception of the Etudes and the *Out of Doors* suite, the Bartók works for piano are much less interesting than the *Music for Strings, Percussion, Celesta with piano*, or the quartets, or the Concerto for Orchestra.

And in Martinů, the piano music was not very interesting because he was basically, in fact, not a pianist. Piano music was a side production.[31] What was important for Martinů were the operas which are very difficult to produce in this country, so they were almost never done here. I don't remember any performances of those at all. That, again, made it difficult to assess the music of Martinů as a whole.

With Bartók it was much easier to see what his production was and what was important.

AB: In an essay, Krenek wrote about America's influence on European composers.[32] He wrote that America changed almost every European composer who came to this country. Do you see this difference in the work of composers coming to America, especially Martinů?

CR: I'm not sure whether the change in Martinů at the end of his life was that radical, so it would be difficult for me to assess that. I presume what Krenek said was true about Stravinsky and Schoenberg, although I'm not even sure whether this was really true what Krenek said. The changes in Schoenberg that took place in America had already started before his arrival here in 1939. . . . There was a big change in Stravinsky toward the end, but that, . . . and Bartók, the change in Bartók, I don't think it's American culture.

I think that people have complained about Bartók that the last pieces are attempted popularizing, but I think that was deliberate. He wanted to write pieces that would have a greater chance of frequent performances with the orchestra, so that Martinů represented the last generation of a certain group which began with a strong inspiration from the regional culture they came from, Martinů Czech, Bartók Hungarian, Stravinsky Russian, and Hindemith was powerfully influenced by German folk culture, which is in the early pieces, which goes unperceived today. What happened then, is that these composers got a little bit left behind with the new generation of composers in this country who wanted a more dogmatic inspiration.

They wanted some kind of a flag . . . to follow. So extraordinary . . . very strict serialism was very popular in the late '40s and early '50s with the young composers, and of course it's just at that moment that you get the arrival of composers in other countries, like Pierre Boulez, Stockhausen, Ligeti, and it was an entire new generation. What is interesting is, I mean, Martinů was already fairly advanced in age by the time when I knew him in the '40s, and it was a period, the '30s and the '40s, that most of the music was written by composers who were already fairly elderly.

I mean, there are these periods, you know, in which great music is being written, but the young composers are not nearly as good as the old composers. I mean, it was literally the case. The more distinguished composers, Martinů, Bartók, Schoenberg, Webern, Stravinsky, I mean, these were all the important figures of the late '30s and the '40s.

The younger composers, like Copland and Krenek and so on, were much less interesting and much less significant, and it's not until the '50s that you suddenly get composers of enormous international prestige coming up and pushing their way in, obviously trying to push the older generation out, as in the famous essay of Boulez, often quoted, called "Schoenberg Is Dead."[33] Although I once spoke to Pierre about this, and I said that Schoenberg is dead, that means kill René Leibowitz, and he said, yes, yes, that's what you might understand.[34] I mean, what happens is with the attempt to get rid of an academic approach to serialism and to have a kind of strict serialism, which . . . finally engulfed Stravinsky as well. . . . Basically, the composers who didn't, Bartók, Martinů, remained slightly behind in influence, although their prestige remained enormous and performances continued, and it represents an important part of the heritage of the twentieth century.

AB: You wrote a great book on the Classical era, and Martinů was a so-called neoclassical composer.[35] Do you see any connection between earlier Classical music and Martinů's own music?

CR: He studied the classics. He was interested in Haydn. There was always a kind of influence of that Classical style upon the composers later. . . . Actually, the only composer for whom the Classical influence was not really important but used very ironically is the neoclassical Stravinsky, who once said that "I just use Classical formulas the way I used to use folk music."

And it's quite interesting, of course, for Stravinsky, Pergolesi and Mozart and so on were exotic, sort of like Russian folksongs, but more exotic even than that, whereas with Martinů, the whole Classical tradition was what he grew up with at the Prague Conservatory, and that's what he learned, and so it was a great part of his whole heritage, which he never tried to get away from. I just remember him as an enormously cultivated figure who knew a great deal about the music of the past, but then, actually most of the interesting composers knew the music of the past extraordinarily well. Milton Babbitt actually knew any piece of Classical music that I'd ever heard of and a great many pieces I didn't know. I mean, he knew, for example, *Theodora* [by] Handel extremely well.

When I wrote *The Classical Style*, I dedicated it to Elliott Carter because I discovered while I was staying in his apartment that he had a complete analysis of the thematic basis for the Mozart D-Minor Concerto. All these composers, the most radical as well as the most conservative, studied the music of the past. So I can't say that the influence of, say, Haydn on Martinů was greater than it was on Elliott Carter. They both studied it and both were fascinated by aspects of the music of the past.

AB: How do you see the differences between Stravinsky and Martinů?

CR: Well, Stravinsky was more radical in one respect [in] that for him his treatment of folk music was actually more radical because it was partially ironic. There was this kind of irony in Stravinsky's music, from the beginning. In other words, Stravinsky would deliberately write passages which were normally considered ugly because he enjoyed them. I mean, he loved them.

Martinů came out of a very rich use of Czech folk music from Dvořák and Smetana, where the folk music was no longer as exotic. Stravinsky, very oddly, coming from Rimsky-Korsakov, still found those folksongs extremely exotic and very strange. Deliberately, the word I would like to use is *alienated*. Stravinsky alienates the material constantly throughout his life. When he was writing neoclassical music, the material is equally alienated. That is, he over-harmonizes the tonic with the dominant; he does it all the time.

And Martinů actually loved the tradition more than Stravinsky. For him it was still a living tradition and he doesn't want to alienate it. I mean, he wants to continue it in this way. This makes him at once, in some ways, a stronger composer in relation to tradition, and also a weaker one because he is destroying the tradition much less than Stravinsky does. I mean, this is one of the problems with all composers, the music of the past, the extent to which they use it and the extent to which they subvert it when they use it. But I'm glad to see that performances of Martinů are becoming more frequent and it should be a great celebration.

"To Work Whether You Feel Like It or Not": An Interview with Michael Steinberg

Carl Michael Alfred Steinberg (1928–2009) was an American music critic and author. He graduated from Princeton University with a Bachelor of Arts in 1949 and received a Master's in Musicology from Princeton. He became music critic for the Boston Globe *in 1964 and was program annotator for the Boston Symphony Orchestra. From 1979 he worked as publications director and artistic advisor for the San Francisco Symphony. He published a number of books on music, both his collected program annotations and new writings.*

AB: When did you first meet Martinů?

MS: I met Martinů in the fall of 1948 when he came to teach composition at Princeton. He had been recommended for the position by Koussevitzky, who, of course, was a very old friend of his, and for whom he had taught at Tanglewood back in the '40s. And he came here and he was here for three years. Not long before that, but for some years before that, I already knew Martinů's music, which was very much performed in America at that time.

He was actually a very famous kind of public figure, and somebody whose music had engaged and stirred me very much, I think both for its musical qualities, but also I think the whole historical and personal background. I was born in a part of Germany that was very near to Czechoslovakia, so as a small boy I was always very aware of . . . the horrendous things that were being done to that country. And my notions of what was happening with Czechoslovakia were . . . the right ones, though I also knew enough not to say out loud in public what I knew, being Jewish in Germany in the '30s and therefore very vulnerable.

But there was something very moving about the whole situation of that country, and . . . given the whole context of what had happened in the nineteenth century, the struggle then for national identity. And so Martinů's music for me was very laden with a lot of strong emotional baggage. And even before I encountered the music, I'd read about him and heard about him.

I remember particularly the account in *Time* magazine of the first performance of the big Violin Concerto that he wrote for Mischa Elman.[36] And then finally hearing his music, which I did in December 1945 for the first time, the Suite concertante for violin in its first performance of its revised version. And then to finally to meet Martinů in 1948 was a tremendous thrill for me and very moving. As brief as it was, it was a very emotional kind of relationship for me.

AB: He came to Princeton later than you did, so you didn't go to study there especially for Martinů?

MS: No, and I was not a composer anyway. I was on the musicology side of the department, but all my life I've sort of had a habit of . . . going against the current. And so even though I was here as a musicologist, I was always a lot more interested in what was happening on the composition side of the department.

I was already nearly finished with my undergraduate work when he came. And I very eagerly went to such classes as he had. And what happened was a very strange situation. I think my impression was that he'd had very little teaching experience and didn't quite know what he was supposed to do teaching composition here. There were not many composition students here anyway, or at least none that interested him. And so, it became almost like a kind of private club involving two or three people. I was one of the principal characters in that. Another was Charles Rosen, who later became an important pianist and very important writer about music. A third one who was always very interested in Martinů was a man named Vernon Gotwals, who was a historian also and organist.

And even though he was not teaching a formal composition class, it was always a fascinating two or three hours. Sometimes he could be persuaded to bring down scores or recordings of his own music. Recordings meant enormous acetate or glass discs. It was very cumbersome. And I realize in retrospect it was an awful thing to ask of him to schlep those things down from New York. But I always had the feeling he didn't really like to talk about his own music.

He was fascinated studying any number of Haydn string quartets. He could never get enough of that. And then particularly Renaissance music, sixteenth-century music; I almost had the feeling he loved that more than anything. For him, that music was kind of paradise lost. He felt about that the way Tchaikovsky felt about Mozart, that it represented a kind of an ideal of calm and of beauty that seemed so much missing from his daily life, or seemed so much missing from the music his contemporaries were writing or that even he himself wrote. That was always for him like going to a wonderful spring to drink. We studied a lot of other music, and the real education I got out of that was . . . to see what fascinated a real composer in a piece by Haydn or in a piece by Berlioz or in a piece by Josquin or whoever.

AB: What fascinated him about this music?

MS: With, well, with Lassus, with the other Renaissance masters . . . what he loved most was . . . a kind of the Apollonian . . . simplicity. He was very admiring of the technical brilliance of somebody like Josquin, the incredible ingenuities in Ockeghem and people like that. But I think that was not what appealed to him most. I think it was the calmness of spirit that he sensed in that music. Though he also loved Gesualdo, which is anything other than calming of the spirit. In that case, it was the harmonic adventures, I mean, the sheer craziness of that music that got to him.

In Haydn, I remember particularly it was the lightness of touch, that so much could be said seemingly so effortlessly, and that, how shall I put it, it wasn't sweaty. And I always had the feeling he loved Haydn much more than Mozart. I mean, obviously, he knew who Mozart was, and how great he was, but Haydn corresponded more to his own spirit, the wit and a certain *sec* [dry] quality in that music, and that was a favorite word of his. That appealed to him much more than the sort of sensuous, sensual sexiness of Mozart. In Berlioz, again, it was the originality.

I don't remember him talking much about the actual structural side of composition, but again, harmonic details, color, and again, in [Berlioz's] *Les nuits d'été*, the wonder of saying so much with so much intensity, but seemingly with such . . . lightness and effortlessness, a kind of quality of elegance in that music that he treasured very much. He had strong opinions about every kind of music. I mean, he loved the earlier Stravinsky and the neoclassical Stravinsky of the '20s.

The [Stravinsky] Violin Concerto was a piece . . . he particularly loved, and I remember we spent an afternoon studying it, but he really disliked what Stravinsky was doing in the '40s, pieces like the *Mass*. . . . [It] irritated him, and he called it *sheesh*, stingy. We did a program once in the chapel, we being the chapel choir, when we performed his *Field Mass*,[37] and we did the Stravinsky *Mass* on the same program because it was for male chorus and it was an orchestra of all winds, so it fit from that point of view very well, but I think it really annoyed him.

The whole Schoenberg, Webern, Berg world: the word he used about that. . . was *exaspéré*. That got his goat. . . . He just felt no spiritual consonance, but he also realized these were remarkable composers, and I remember when Mitropoulos conducted the *Wozzeck* concert performance at the New York Philharmonic, he absolutely insisted that I go up to New York to hear it.

His great hero among his contemporaries, or slightly older contemporaries, was Bartók. We spent a lot of time looking at Bartók's music and I think the first movement of the *Music for Strings, Percussion, and Celesta* was the piece for which he had most reverence . . . and we actually went through that in great detail. . . . He loved and was very moved by the darkness of the first movement . . . .

I remember something that he enjoyed and which is I think very prominent in his own music [is] the sort of athleticism, the sheer physical energy of the music and the . . . excitement of it. But it was the dark side and the mysterious side too; the night music in Bartók that he marveled at in some of the earlier piano music for example, or in the Fourth and Fifth string quartets, the middle movement of the Third Piano Concerto. He was a very nature-loving man.

AB: Did Martinů analyze all the movements or all the pieces with you, or just special places in the music?

MS: Martinů hardly did anything that I would call analysis. Very, very rarely. The first movement of the *Music for Strings* of Bartók is one exception where I think he wanted to find out about it himself, so he just walked through it very slowly and let us watch. But mostly what he did was that he would point to things that fascinated him, and say, what a wonderful idea it was to put the flute into this register, or what a great effect it is to have a 6/4 chord right here. I remember one session of talking about 6/4 chords in Verdi and how effective those were and it was always just oh, look at that, that kind of thing. Virtually never real analysis. It was a kind of discovering in front of you. . . . Discovering and letting us, the students, watch him discover.

He knew the pieces he brought, but the longer he stayed here over those three years, the more he liked being surprised. He liked having me or Charles Rosen, we were really the two main ones, pick out something to bring to him that we thought he might not know. That's how we came to the Berlioz *Les nuits d'été*, for example.

That had interesting consequences of a strange sort [when] he got interested in other Berlioz pieces, and we spent an afternoon once with the *Symphonie fantastique*, and that sort of indirectly led to his idea to write a piece that he called "Nouvelle Symphonie Fantastique" which eventually changed . . . well, not only its name, nearly everything changed but it became the *Fantaisies symphoniques*.[38] In a remote way that was a kind of descendant of that first encounter with *Les nuits d'été*.

Another instance where something that happened here had an interesting and very . . . lovely consequence. . . . He vaguely remembered having heard in Paris Haydn's Sinfonia Concertante for violin and cello and oboe and bassoon, and he had this very vague recollection of hearing Munch conduct this piece before the war, and in fact Munch had recorded [it then]. This was still soon enough after the war that imported recordings were very hard to come by, but somehow we managed to get ahold of this recording from Paris 1938 or something like that, and one of the professors here at that time, Oliver Strunk, one of the great Haydn scholars, had a hand-copied score of the Sinfonia Concertante so we were able to find a recording and then get from Mr. Strunk, what we learned later was a very inaccurate score of the piece and we brought it to him. He loved this piece and . . . later on, not very much later, wrote a Sinfonia Concertante of his own for the same combination which we had no idea that he was doing. He just brought it in from New York one Thursday with a rather shy and somewhat sly little smile and he said, *regardez*.

AB: Did he talk with you about his own music?

MS: Very reluctantly. Martinů was very shy about talking about his own music. I was the one who really was longing to hear more about it because I just loved it madly. It moved me so very much and I used to just beg him to bring whatever he had by way of recordings and he would bring these enormous glass or acetate platters with him and he would play something for us and he never wanted to talk about it or analyze it. The one remark I recall his making is that the critic and composer Virgil Thomson[39] had written in the *New York Herald Tribune*[40] that the Second Symphony[41] was a disappointment after the First Symphony[42] and Martinů said Thomson was wrong, that he thought the Second Symphony was much better and he was very proud of the Second Symphony and at least Two, Three and Five were the ones that he brought to us and that he took great pleasure in. Three he particularly liked, and he referred to it as, I can't remember now whether it was the Dark Brother or the Dark Sister, but somehow that it was in a mood that was a bit different from the others and then by the time the *Fantaisies symphoniques* came around he was already gone from here and I was hardly in contact with him.

AB: What do you think about the idea of Martinů repeating himself as a composer?

MS: Martinů did repeat himself as a composer. He had this stern discipline that he recommended to us as something to think about no matter what we ended up doing, whether we were composers . . . or whatever, which is to work whether you feel like it or not. My recollection is that he composed every morning. You know, he just sat down and did it until lunchtime, and I think there are a lot of pieces where he's kind of freewheeling, you know with his wonderful technique, and not all of the pieces are as personal as the greatest of them are. He would hate me for this; I was going to say like Hindemith he had a very recognizable vocabulary. You can spot a Martinů piece in a few seconds when it comes on, almost no matter from what period of his life.

AB: You mentioned the *Field Mass* by Martinů. Can you recall this performance? Was Martinů there? Was Martinů in it?

MS: Martinů was here for the performance of the *Field Mass* that came about because I had read about the piece in Šafránek's biography, and Princeton at that time was an all-male college. When I was in the chapel choir I was always looking for interesting things for a male chorus to do. I'd read about this piece, and the combination of that and you know, my reverence for Martinů, led me to suggest it to the choir director. I asked Martinů about this piece and I had this very strange experience, because he absolutely denied ever having written such a piece. He had no recollection of it at all, and for the following Thursday I had to get the book out of the library and bring it to him, and show it to him and he sort of said, ah, perhaps. Then he actually found a score of it somewhere, and Charles Rosen and I made an English translation of it, with Martinů sort of telling us roughly—I think he sort of translated it into French, and then we went from the French into English—and it was performed in, I don't remember what year, I would think in maybe '49 or '50 in the University Chapel. I remember it was on a program with a brass piece by Charles Ruggles called *Angels* and the Stravinsky *Mass* and it made a very deep impression. It was a very moving piece, and I was very disappointed that not more people took it up at the time. I mean, it sort of came into its day, what, thirty years later, or something like that with, I guess, the Mackerras recording and so forth. I still love that piece, I must say I have very happy memories and also, in a sense, it was a very moving and sort of rather fulfilling thing for me to have the sense of having been able to do something for him on a level beyond bringing him, you know, a recording of a nice piece by Berlioz or Ockeghem or whatever but something directly for his music. And we had done that at Princeton before; when he first came in '48 we organized a concert of his chamber music too, and that was a great joy to be involved in that, and actually I was involved primarily in sort of helping to organize it and then as a page-turner for the pianist but still, it was a wonderful way of introducing him to this community. I think the program included the Madrigals[43] for violin and viola and the Second Cello Sonata[44] and the Second Piano Quintet.[45]

AB: Did Martinů enjoy this concert?

MS: He was always very cautious in talking about performances about his own music. I remember going to hear the Third Piano Concerto[46] once when the Boston Symphony came to New York, and I went to the Brooklyn Academy and it was with Firkušný and Munch. He always spoke well of Munch . . . and he was very fond of Firkušný personally. But I remember it was about Firkušný that he also said, about one of his performances—I forget what piece—oh, František Xaver Dušek—[that Firkušný made] too many of these kind of rubatos of George Szell playing Smetana kind of thing. One thing I recall that came up often in general about performances was about conductors sort of mooning, or soloists kind of being too moony/dreamy sometimes and especially about slow movements. He would say, Too slow, too slow. I remember he talked about Koussevitzky in connection with "too slow" and I remember he told with great relish a story that Arthur Rubinstein had told him about trying to move Koussevitzky along in a Rachmaninoff piano concerto and saying to Koussevitzky "Maestro, I am dying," and Koussevitzky saying, "Not worrying, we carry on."

AB: Did he say anything about Ansermet, who did many great analyses of the music of his symphonies?

MS: Well, I remember one of the recordings he brought down and that he liked very much was the Fifth Symphony,[47] the performance with the NBC Symphony and which I remember was a tremendous success. And he spoke about Ansermet's great intelligence and his sort of analytical acuity and that sort of thing. I don't remember that he said much about the conducting.

AB: Can you remember what a typical day was like with Martinů?

MS: He came once a week on Thursday afternoons. He usually arrived toward noon, and Charles Rosen and I usually or sometimes I by myself would go down to the railway station and we would collect him there and we would walk into town. There was this one place that had pretensions to being a good restaurant called Lahiere's and it was actually run by a real honest-to-goodness Frenchman, and we would take Martinů in there. It was almost the only place where you could get a glass of wine.

The music department had a tiny building of its own with not enough room for classes, and they used this room. There was a grand piano in there and a blackboard and some chairs and I have to say many of the most important things I know about music I learned in that room from Martinů, from Milton Babbitt, from Edward Cone, from many others. We would come there and there would be two, three, four people and we would usually have already picked out some scores and records or he would have brought something down, and we would be in there for maybe two and a half, three hours and then we would go back to my room which was in a dormitory along that way. We would go up to my room and . . . he never wanted anything to eat, but he always wanted . . . tea with either lots of bourbon or . . . rum in it . . . and we would sit there and he would talk. He would sometimes get loosened up and tell stories about his young years as a violinist in the Czech Philharmonic, or his early years in Paris, or his troubles at the Conservatory in Prague and things like that. He would stay maybe another half an hour to an hour and then we would take him back down to catch his train and he would go off and then we would see him again the next Thursday unless I saw him in between at a concert in New York.

AB: Can you recall anything of the conversations you had with him about his time at the Conservatory in Prague?

MS: Not in great detail, but I remember he was inclined to laugh it off. He said that it made him very angry that he was thrown out for, what was it, incorrigible laziness or negligence or something of that kind?[48] He always made the point that it doesn't really matter what you do in school, it's who you are.

AB: Do you recall his talking about any pieces he performed at the Czech Philharmonic? Because it was in those years, playing under Talich, that he discovered French music and he performed compositions by Debussy and Ravel for the first time.

MS: Yes, he mentioned the importance of Debussy and Roussel and to some extent Ravel also, but I don't recall his connecting that with his having learned them first in the orchestra. He said the piece he always enjoyed playing was the Dvořák *Carnival Overture*, because the horn parts were so awkward, and he loved to hear the horn just having a hard time playing those octaves, beep boop beep boop. Another thing about orchestra stuff that I remember him saying that was funny is that I asked him about using the piano in his symphonies, and he said it was because he never could figure out how to work out the transpositions for the harp. C-flat major was just too much, and he couldn't do that, and so he thought it was just easier [to use the piano]. He had a very strange, a very primitive piano style actually in his compositions, but it's very effective in the orchestral pieces.

AB: You yourself are not American-born, and Martinů also came to the United States under difficult circumstances. Do you have a sense of him as an émigré, and can you recall whether Martinů spoke about himself in that way?

MS: Martinů was very much a sort of alien plant in . . . in this country. . . . He felt the sense of foreignness and exile very keenly here, he looked very alien. I think in the middle of Cleveland, or in some other community where there are many Czech people, he might not have. He had an ethnically specific kind of face; the manner was very European. It's one of the things that we talked about in my dormitory room over there; the more personal part of the conversation was that he felt very exiled. As he got to know us better, he spoke more about his unease about life in America. In public, he had nothing but good things to say about America, and he was grateful that it was a country that had welcomed him when he had come as a refugee, and where he had tremendous professional success. . . . One thing he hated about New York was . . . the grid layout . . . you know, the endless rectangles of streets and square blocks. He lived, I have to say, in a particularly dark and dismal one. I mean it's just a block up from Carnegie Hall and a block below Central Park South, but still 58th Street is wanting in charm . . . and he found New York just terribly impersonal. You could see that somebody coming from Paris or somebody coming from Prague before that naturally would [have that response]. The other thing that he talked about very hesitantly—but he did talk about it—was that he felt this growing unease about the political situation in this country . . . after the war there was a swing to the right and the growth of anti-Russian feeling. I mean it's not that he was fond of the Soviet Union himself, to say the least, and you know that the whole Communist takeover of Czechoslovakia in 1948 was a matter of great grief to him. . . . With the kind of idealism with which a lot of European Hitler refugees viewed America, it was disappointing for him to discover, like the rest of us, that something else was happening. . . . He was a perfect example of an exile doing very well—in the sense of his career going brilliantly, but feeling totally out of place here.

I think it's characteristic unfortunately of America that people don't know any history, [but] they know that Martinů came from Czechoslovakia, and that Czechoslovakia is a Communist country. They are unable to understand that he had come over here for reasons that were as opposed to that as possible. I've met the same thing with my situation, that of having come here as a Jewish refugee from Hitler's Germany. I run into Americans who say "where were you born you come from Germany oh it's my favorite country." You run into people who just have no sense of historical context.

During the Communist years, which were the same as the Princeton years, it was very clear how strong he was longing to be back in Czechoslovakia. But at that time it seemed like there was no prospect of ever going back, and that was very painful for him. I never understood clearly the balance between the French side and the Czech side. I always had the feeling that he had become in many respects very French, and he'd lived in Paris so long, he had a French wife, he spoke French with her at home and so forth, and that somehow the whole Czech side of him had been pushed underground in certain parts of his life, though not in his music.

AB: You see this in his works, for example, his opera *Juliette*. It doesn't sound Czech, it's just Martinů's language and it owes more to French opera dramaturgy than to Czech operas.

MS: I think *Juliette* is the work I heard him talk about more than any other, and I think that he always yearned to see a production of it. I know he spoke with Charles Rosen and me about possibly making a translation of it, since we had translated the *Field Mass*. . . . The opera climate in this country is unfortunately so different now from what it was then. I mean in those days there was nearly no regional opera. There was the Metropolitan Opera, there was the New York City Opera, the San Francisco Opera that was pretty darn near it. There were opera workshops in schools and universities, but there was almost no place where work like that could have been performed at that time. Only the New York City Opera did a certain number of adventurous things, but they never got to that one.

AB: How would you describe Martinů's reputation in America during the '40s and '50s?

MS: I became aware of Martinů around '44–'45. I'd come to America myself at the end of '43 and I knew very little about music; I was just sort of beginning to find my way then, and what sticks in my mind is reading about the Violin Concerto, hearing about this piece . . . full of fervor and passion, and pain, nostalgia . . . and having this very exciting kind of premiere. I became aware . . . of Martinů everywhere. . . . There were constant performances of Martinů and his reputation at that time was really very high . . . and there was always a lot of excitement about them.

Martinů was regarded as one of the most important composers. . . . I don't know that that was a word that was ever attached to him particularly but he was very communicative and in that sense very needed, very necessary—one always got some kind of important spiritual nourishment from hearing the best of his music. He was very much admired, and I think that continued to be so until I left the country, which was in '52—I went to Europe to study for a couple of years. He had left just before that. I guess he came back once for the performances of the *Fantaisies symphoniques*, and he did a year at the Curtis Institute in Philadelphia which I seem to recall made him very unhappy. By the time of his death at the end of the '50s he had kind of vanished from the scene, and it was very frustrating to me that the music was just not to be heard anywhere. It was later that the music began to come back. . . . I think we still have a very narrow view of him here, centered on the symphonies and on a couple of the concertos. The operas are almost totally unknown, the other big choral things like *Gilgamesh*[49]—I don't recall ever encountering a performance of that piece—some of the chamber music gets played. I do constantly find, though, that when people encounter one of these pieces there's often this sense of amazement of, you know, my god where has this been all my life?

NOTES

1. Serenade No. 1, for clarinet, French horn, three violins, and viola, H 217 (1932).

2. Concerto grosso for chamber orchestra, H 263 (1937).

3. *Dumka* No. 3, H 285bis (1941).

4. Symphony No. 1, H 289 (1942).

5. *Memorial to Lidice*, H 296 (1943).

6. Symphony No. 2, H 295 (1943).

7. Four Madrigals, for oboe, clarinet, and bassoon, H 266 (1938).

8. *Frescoes of Piero della Francesca*, for large orchestra, H 352 (1955).

9. Piano Sonata No. 1, H 350 (1954).

10. The Czech soprano Jarmila Novotná (1907–1994) was one of the most outstanding singers of the twentieth century.

11. Rudolf Firkušný (1912–1994) was a Czech pianist of world renown. In 1917 he met Leoš Janáček, who recognized his extraordinary musical talent and taught him music theory. Firkušný studied in Paris with Alfred Cortot and Artur Schnabel in Berlin. From 1948 he lived in the United States. He was one of the closest personal friends of Martinů, who dedicated several of his compositions to him.

12. Jan Masaryk, son of the first Czechoslovak president Tomáš Garrigue Masaryk and a famous Czech foreign minister, was a good friend of Martinů, and as an accomplished pianist he premiered the song cycle *Nový Špalíček* (New Chap-Book), H 288 (1942), which the composer dedicated to him, with Jarmila Novotná, soloist, at the MET.

13. Sonata No. 1 for Violin and Piano, H 182 (1929).

14. Symphony No. 1, H 289 (1942).

15. Symphony No. 2, H 295 (1943).

16. Serge Koussevitzky (1874–1951), Russian and American conductor, composer, and double-bassist, music director of the Boston Symphony Orchestra from 1924 to 1949.

17. Marcel Mihalovici (1898–1985) was a Romanian-French composer and an intimate friend of Martinů.

18. Tibor Harsányi (1898–1954) was a Hungarian composer and pianist and a close friend of Martinů.

19. "I completely lack (patience), I can't think about other people, about young people's music. I always think of myself, and that's a bit selfish, but still, it's me."

20. Sonata for Flute and Piano, H 306 (1945).

21. *La bagarre*, Allegro for large orchestra, H 155 (1926).

22. "Thats well put."

23. Diamond rented Martinů's Manhattan apartment in the summer of 1945 while the composer was on holiday.

24. *The Fifth Day of the Fifth Moon*, H 318 (1948).

25. Three Madrigals (Duo No. 1), for violin and viola, H 313 (1947).

26. Etudes and Polkas, for piano, H 308 (1945).

27. Sonata for Flute and Piano, H 306 (1945).

28. *Les ritournelles*, six piano pieces, H 227 (1932).

29. Double Concerto, for two string orchestras, piano and timpani, H 271 (1938).

30. Both Fritz Reiner and George Szell were born in Hungary. Szell's family moved to Vienna, and Reiner, after studying with Bartók, moved to the United States.

31. Martinů composed five piano concertos and dozens of solo piano pieces, from the Piano Sonata up to a series of piano cycles. He also used the piano often in his orchestral works as well as in his numerous chamber music.

32. Ernst Krenek and Don Harran, "America's Influence on Its Emigré Composers," *Perspectives of New Music* 8/2 (Spring–Summer, 1970): 112–17.

33. Pierre Boulez, "Schoenberg Is Dead," *The Score* (May 1952): 18–22.

34. René Leibowitz (1913–1972) was a composer, conductor, music theorist who advocated for Schoenberg and his music. The comment implies that Boulez was not attacking Schoenberg himself as much as his followers.

35. *The Classical Style: Haydn, Mozart and Beethoven*, 1971.

36. Concerto for Violin and Orchestra No. 2, H 293 (1943).

37. *The Field Mass*, cantata for baritone, male choir, and orchestra, H 279 (1938).

38. *Fantaisies symphoniques* (Symphony No. 6), H 343 (1951–53).

39. Virgil Thomson (1896–1989) was an American critic and composer. He studied at Harvard University and with Nadia Boulanger in Paris, where he lived from 1925 to 1940. From 1940 to 1954 he worked as a music critic for the *New York Herald-Tribune*.

40. Virgil Thomson,"Repeating Pattern," *New York Herald Tribune*, 31 December, 1943. Critique of the first New York performance of Symphony No. 2, which took place on 30 December 1943 at Carnegie Hall, performed by the New York Philharmonic Orchestra under the direction of A. Rodzinski. Also printed in Virgil Thomson's *The Musical Scene* (New York: Knopf, 1945), 107–8.

41. Symphony No. 2, H 295.

42. Symphony No. 1, H 289.

43. Three Madrigals (Duo No. 1) for Violin and Viola, H 313 (1947).

44. Sonata No. 2 for Violoncello and Piano, H 286 (1941). The piece is dedicated to Frank Rybka.

45. Piano Quintet No. 2, H 298 (1944).

46. Concerto for Piano and Orchestra No. 3, H 316 (1948).

47. Symphony No. 5, H 310 (1946).

48. He was expelled "for irreparable negligence."

49. *The Epic of Gilgamesh*, oratorio for soli, mixed choir, and orchestra, H 351 (1955).

Part V. CODA

Music and Politics in the Twentieth Century: The Parallel Lives of Bohuslav Martinů and Rudolf Firkušný

LEON BOTSTEIN

Bohuslav Martinů was a strikingly original, prolific, and eclectic composer. This essay places his life and work within the turbulent politics of the twentieth century; it also addresses a twentieth-century characteristic of classical music at odds with its nineteenth-century heritage: the separation between the profession of composition from that of concert performer. In Martinů's case, the consequences of that separation were compensated for by the composer's close friendship and collaboration with his countryman, Rudolf Firkušný (1912–94), one of the great pianists of the century.

Martinů enjoyed enormous success and fame in his lifetime, particularly during the last decades of his life. But after his death, Martinů's music drifted, with unexpected rapidity, into the margins. The scale and variety of his music seemed more worthy of note than its character. Martinů's erosion in visibility and stature coincided with a gradual general decline of classical music's stature in culture and politics in the West, especially with respect to new music. The fall of Communism in the 1990s, however, challenged the dynamics between culture and politics; it inspired a reconsideration of the twentieth century and the character of modernism in music. In that context, a revival of interest in Martinů began to take shape.[1]

In the Czech lands, where Martinů was born and lived until he was in his early thirties, his music had consistently experienced a mixed reception. This ambivalence became stronger under Communism despite de-Stalinization in the Soviet Union after 1956 and Dimitri Shostakovich's admiration for his music. In the pernicious alliance between Communism and nationalism that prevailed in Eastern Europe during the second half of the twentieth century, especially in post-1948 Czechoslovakia, nationalism helped to shape the dominant aesthetic orthodoxy of Socialist Realism in music.

In 1979, the Czechoslovakian government arranged for Martinů to be reburied in Czechoslovakia, exhuming his body from its original resting place in Switzerland, where the composer had died twenty years earlier. The controversial event was designed to exploit Martinů as a nationalist symbol. It was well known that Martinů had been a "free thinker" and very critical of the Communists. It was equally transparent that his modernism and eclectic experimentalism were downplayed in favor of his loyalty to Czech folklore and his prestige as a significant Czech cultural figure.[2]

The revival of interest in Martinů that survived Communism's collapse ironically has been contained in a convenient if narrow nationalist framework. Martinů has become the heir, as predicted by Vitězslav Novák in 1945, to the great Czech musical tradition represented by Bedřich Smetana, Antonín Dvořák, and Leoš Janáček. This circumscribed appropriation of Martinů's music as distinctly national and even exotic may help to market him to audiences accustomed to nationalist rubrics, but it obscures and distorts the wide range and cosmopolitan character of Martinů's achievement. Michael Beckerman, the eminent scholar on the Czech tradition, has consistently argued that the actual connection between national elements and folk traditions in Dvořák, Smetana, and Janáček demands rethinking. Insofar as Martinů can be understood as representative of a national sensibility, it is because "no composer is a greater poet of nostalgia and loss. Surely, Martinů is the champion of musical homesickness."[3]

Martinů's music possesses a range, quality, and variety that confirm that he was a non-doctrinaire twentieth-century modernist who, in a manner reminiscent of Stravinsky, transcended the influence of the place and circumstances of his birth. His music merits a central place in the repertory of Europe, Asia, and America (where he spent arguably the most productive period of his life) on account of its idiosyncratic modernism. Martinů reached a wide audience. He explored, provocatively and persuasively, the interaction between musical thinking and the contemporary world around him. His achievement is worthy of emulation in the twenty-first century.[4]

Martinů's personality, simultaneously intense and opaque, his erratic habits, his complex relationship to his homeland, his inimitable chameleon-like flirtation with many musical styles, including the neoclassical and neo-Baroque, and his response as an artist to exile all can be illuminated by the life and career of his close, albeit younger friend, Firkušný, a great pianist with an international career, who was also a protégé of Janáček. Firkušný and Martinů crossed paths in exile, first in Paris in the 1930s and then in America in the 1940s and '50s. Martinů was a friend to whom Firkušný was devoted. Firkušný was the only major pianist of his era to play Martinů with regularity, a commitment that helped sustain the composer's reputation in the decades after his death.

Martinů and Firkušný both grew up and came of age in a world in which the practice and culture of classical music remained vital and secure, despite radical political and social upheaval. In the major cities of Central and Eastern Europe, music was a key constituent of cultural norms, social aspirations, and collective self-images around debates over national and linguistic distinctiveness. Music as both amateur activity and spectator entertainment reached even market towns such as Polička (with 5,600 inhabitants in 1890), Martinů's birthplace in a rural region near the border between Bohemia and Moravia, and Napajedla (3,700 inhabitants in 1912), Firkušný's birthplace in Moravia. Both musicians were born as Czech subjects of the multinational Habsburg Empire, in which the German language and culture were dominant.

Martinů was not born into a family of musicians, but his parents, despite the modesty of their circumstances, recognized his intense interest and striking aptitude and found local instructors. Martinů ended up studying in Prague, the largest Czech city and the third largest of the Habsburg Empire, a place where music had flourished for at least three centuries.[5] By gaining an opportunity to study there, Martinů seemed destined to become a professional violinist, or perhaps a church organist and music teacher.

In Martinů's childhood and youth, the Czech-speaking population of Bohemia and Moravia was caught up in a protracted and complex political struggle of competing visions of how Czech traditions and a Czech collective self-image ought to flourish in modernity. The language and history shared among Czechs seemed to justify greater political and cultural autonomy within the Empire, or perhaps even a separate Czech nation. Nationalist sentiments arose that contested the primacy of the German language in the affairs of the Empire and rejected the legitimacy of a multinational heritage based on a shared dynastic entity.

Language, however, was not the only instrument of politics. The gestures and rhetoric of music developed during the Romantic era after 1815 lent music, even when left on its own—that is, without the words of a song or the decorations and movements of theater and dance—the capacity to convey meanings to a rapidly growing audience in public arenas. Music, like writing and painting, became a powerful shaping force of cultural ideals. The influence exerted by Richard Wagner throughout Europe and North America secured a connection between late Romanticism in music and European nationalism. Romanticism, in Wagner's hands, expanded music's capacity to evoke feelings, ideas, and symbols in ways readily correlated with words and images that were easily grasped by a broad public. Music ceased to be an abstract formalist art, the province of aristocratic amateurs and connoisseurs. By the turn of the century, music was practiced and heard as being "about" something other than itself. It was associated with distinct languages and literatures, national landscapes, myths, and histories.

Within the vast multinational and multi-ethnic Habsburg Empire, wedged between Imperial Germany and tsarist Russia, music was written that encouraged the quest for autonomy and recognition by distinct populations. Cultural minorities throughout the Empire were following the lead of Germany, Russia, France, and Great Britain, where music had secured a place in the public sphere by fostering and defining national conceits and ambitions, especially in the celebration of imperial and national pride.

Musical Romanticism's alliance with nationalism sharpened the contrast with the eighteenth-century's aesthetic norms, specifically the ideal of classicism. The eighteenth century understood music as a transnational artform defined by criteria of aesthetic judgment that celebrated its unique nature, its patent artificiality vis-à-vis nature and therefore its autonomy from words and images. The musical Romanticism of the nineteenth century was strikingly successful in adapting the rhetoric and forms of musical classicism as allies of prose, poetry, politics, and painting. During the nineteenth century, however, anti-Romantic classicist ideals for music were never entirely vanquished. Martinů himself would be forced to confront the apparent contradiction between his attraction to neoclassicism as a style and strategy for writing modern music and his allegiance to modern nationalist sentiments early in his career, sentiments that in many instances resembled exclusionary claims of ethnic and racial superiority. Music had developed into a cosmopolitan art, one that created a universal discourse that thrived by adhering to shared international styles and norms. The alliance of the national with the Romantic threatened to make music a vehicle of divisive sectarianism.

These tensions were acutely present when Martinů turned his attention away from pursuing a career as a performer and teacher and toward one as a composer during his years in Prague. He made that decision fully aware of music's growth in popularity and prestige. Martinů and his generation of composers sought to retain if not augment music's place by making their own distinct mark at a time of political change. They challenged the premises and practices of late Romanticism and charted novel directions for new music. They were persuaded that they were witnesses to a new, unprecedented age in history, an age that demanded a new kind of music.

Older contemporaries, particularly Richard Strauss, sought, in contrast, to radically magnify musical Romanticism's allure by expanding, beyond Wagner, the musical manipulation of classicism's capacity to foster illusions of realism. Strauss, despite his underlying pessimism about modernity and a nostalgia for the eighteenth century (particularly Mozart), cultivated an anti-metaphysical hyper-realism analogous to innovations in narrative techniques in contemporary prose. But he remained indebted to nineteenth-century Romanticism's narrative power, utilizing his expansive use of tonality and sonority. Through his harmonies and orchestration, Strauss achieved notoriety as a modernist and challenged reigning norms of musical beauty. The so-called musical Impressionists, Debussy and Ravel, suppressed a functional approach to harmony and wrote music that transformed the experience of time in ways that inspired a comparison to the radical subjectivity visible in Impressionist and Expressionist painting.

But many composers—Igor Stravinsky, Anton von Webern, Leo Ornstein, and Edgard Varèse—went further and rejected more dramatically the premises and conventions of late Romanticism. They sought to develop something new, including a revival of a rigorous ascetic modernist classicism reminiscent of the eighteenth century and rooted in music's essential quality as a uniquely universal and formal autonomous art free of narratives, confessions (e.g. Mahler), and symbolic meanings.

These turn-of-the-century debates about the nature of music and its proper future did not, however, diminish the perceived need to connect music to the expression of national sympathies. How might it be possible to replace the symbiosis between the practices and forms of late nineteenth-century musical Romanticism and modern national consciousness? The radical anti-academicism and turn to premodern national folklore promoted by the Russian "Mighty Handful" of composers offered one model.

Between 1900 and 1938, young composers charted many paths of experiment and eclecticism that would define a multifaceted musical modernism. This modernism would often run afoul of both the middle-class audience and mass political movements with a strident populist and nationalist core and their conservative aesthetic principles. In Prague in the 1920s, Martinů would find himself accused of favoring a new international style at the expense of local and national traditions. During the same period, innovative modernist Czech architects and designers experienced similar accusations. They were seen as abandoning a populist nativist cultural cause.[6]

What was at stake vis-á-vis music throughout Europe was nothing less than the soul of a nation. Twentieth-century musical modernism unfolded just as the practices of music, including music education, public performance, and domestic music making, were reaching their zenith. The apex of music's place in culture and society occurred in the 1920s, after the end of the "long nineteenth century." That end was marked by the redrawing of the map of Europe in 1918, and the creation of new nation-states in Central and Eastern Europe. In Prague and Paris between 1923 and 1940, Martinů witnessed how musical culture was being captured and expanded by increasingly novel, user-friendly technologies of sound production, reproduction, and transmission. How might one reconcile the ambition to be true to modernity, make use of industrial and technological progress and still retain the traditional audience for music nurtured by the aesthetics of Romanticism?

During Martinů's lifetime, classical music would struggle with this predicament and begin an extended journey into the shadow of irrelevance in politics and culture. By the end of the interwar era, the late 1930s, the chances seemed increasingly slim that a new generation of composers of concert music would experience the level of success and prominence achieved by their predecessors—Brahms, Wagner, Verdi, Dvořák, and Tchaikovsky. By the outbreak of World War II, it had become apparent that music, by comparison with the visual arts, architecture, and literature, was failing to retain the loyalty of its inherited public. As young protagonists of the modern, Martinů and his contemporaries faced a concert-going public ever more tied to a standard repertoire rooted in the eighteenth and nineteenth centuries, and increasingly resistant to anything new, especially if it was labeled "modern."

There was a further paradox. After 1918, the success of a modern composer's music, even when it sought to define and express nationalism (as was the case with Janáček in the 1920s) became contingent on the achievement of international success. Wide recognition beyond national borders and the demand for performances of new works in the cosmopolitan, international concert world, were necessary before a composer could be appropriated as a modern nationalist symbol at home and abroad.

A few composers from the first half of the twentieth century navigated these treacherous waters, achieving and sustaining wide international public recognition and an appreciative public of listeners. They caught the attention of politicians and public opinion as representatives of both modernity and of distinct national cultures. Martinů was one of them. He was neither a doctrinaire modernist like Arnold Schoenberg or Alois Hába, nor an arch-conservative like Hans Pfitzner. His music intentionally reflected twentieth-century discontinuities with the nineteenth century.

In exile, Bohuslav Martinů became both a national figure and an international composer of repute. He can be compared to a few contemporaries, among them Igor Stravinsky, Paul Hindemith, Aaron Copland, Ralph Vaughan Williams, Dimitri Shostakovich, Karol Szymanowski, and Béla Bartók.[7]

Martinů's preeminent contemporary was Stravinsky, who, after Richard Strauss, was the most famous and influential composer of the first decades of the century. Stravinsky's career began in Russia, but after the Bolshevik Revolution of 1917 his staunch anti-Communism, religious posturing, and reactionary politics ensured that by the 1920s he was regarded as somewhat more French than Russian. Ultimately, he would play a role in post–World War II musical culture as an American.

Hindemith came to be regarded both at home and abroad as an admirable and palatable protagonist of a distinctly German tradition of composition. Like Martinů, he was prolific; unlike Martinů, he was a legendary performer as violinist and violist, and an intimidating presence as teacher and theorist. His technical skill and command of the composer's craft were reminiscent of the disciplined approach to musical structure found in Bach, Haydn, Brahms, Busoni, and with respect to Germany's pre-eminence in music, Max Reger, who died in 1916.

Hindemith's international notoriety was enhanced perversely by national politics. He first gained attention in Germany during the early 1920s as a radical Expressionist composer intent on exposing the moral and aesthetic hypocrisy of the ruling elites whom he held responsible for the carnage of World War I. When the Nazis came to power, they were divided on whether to embrace him as properly representative of the new Germany. This struggle ended in a public 1934 controversy involving Wilhelm Furtwängler, the eventual banning of Hindemith's music, and his dismissal as a teacher. Hindemith emigrated and ended up in America. He taught at Tanglewood, like Martinů, and at Yale. He subsequently returned to

West Germany. Hindemith secured his place during the Cold War as representative of a particularly German, yet cosmopolitan modernist musical traditionalism. Strauss's collaboration with the Nazi regime rendered him problematic as a symbol of German culture after 1945.

Aaron Copland, an unashamed homosexual and politically progressive Jew from Brooklyn, managed to fashion sonorities that celebrated the open landscape and progressive democracy of midcentury America. Copland, like Martinů, went to France in the early 1920s to study composition. Upon his return, he abandoned radical modernism. His 1935 *Statements* revealed his intent to perfect an accessible modernism evocative of the pluralist American democracy fostered during the New Deal under Franklin Delano Roosevelt. Unlike Martinů, Copland was lionized in his home country. Although Copland turned toward a more brutalist modernism in the 1960s, Copland and Martinů shared an overriding commitment to music as central to liberal democracy and patriotism.

Shostakovich struggled with his official status as the Soviet Union's leading composer. It was his fate to be regarded as such, particularly during World War II under Stalin and at the end of his life under Brezhnev. Vaughan Williams was an outspoken advocate of the relevance of national folk traditions to twentieth-century music and, like Martinů, turned to the symphony as a modernist genre. Vaughan Williams's commitment to nationalism in music, however, was more explicit and pronounced than that of Martinů, although both men achieved fame as important symphonists.

Szymanowski may have died early in the century, in 1937, but he assumed and retained an uncontested reputation as Poland's greatest composer after Chopin, even during the Communist era when Poland boasted two internationally significant composers, Witold Lutosławski and Krzystof Penderecki. Szymanowski, unlike Martinů, took on an official role in the musical life of the newly constituted Polish Republic after 1919. Like Vaughan Williams, he also participated in researching and foregrounding national folk traditions. Much like Martinů and Vaughan Williams, Szymanowski was influenced by Paris and French music but was also fascinated by sources from "oriental," non-European traditions.[8]

Bartók was internationally acclaimed as the musical voice of twentieth-century Hungary, first during Béla Kun's revolutionary rule, then under Admiral Miklós Horthy's regency, and posthumously throughout the Communist rule of Hungary. He did not have an extended exposure to Paris, despite French influences in his work. Like Martinů, Bartók rejected fascism and emigrated to the United States. He pioneered in the ethnographic documentation of his nation's premodern rural folk music, only to become persuaded that all folk music traditions were interrelated, thereby exploding their utility as evidence for nationalist cultural conceits.

Within this group Martinů displayed a more inconsistent, complex, and ultimately ambivalent relationship to his national origins. He left his rural town for

Prague at age seventeen in 1906. In 1923, he went to Paris, where later he met and married his French wife, Charlotte. Paris became his base before he escaped to America in 1941. Despite living as an émigré in Paris, and being a contested figure in his homeland without any official role, by 1940 he had become internationally celebrated as the greatest living Czech composer since Leoš Janáček, who had died in 1928.

In exile in wartime America, Martinů's public prominence as a specifically Czech modernist grew; being Czech in America turned out to be an advantage. He represented continental Europe's most admired pluralist democracy and therefore the nation most similar to the United States. But from 1948 on Martinů, due to his repudiation of any sort of totalitarianism, was shunned by Communist Czechoslovakia. Only after 1989 and the end of Communist rule and the subsequent breakup of Czechoslovakia did Martinů, posthumously, claim broad acceptance within the Czech Republic and the status as modernity's rightful heir to Smetana, Dvořák, and Janáček.

During the Cold War, however, it was Janáček rather than Martinů who was celebrated in the West as the most successful Czech composer of the century. The suppression of Martinů during the four decades of Communism in Czechoslovakia, particularly after his death in 1959, reinforced the decline in Martinů's posthumous standing and presence outside of the Soviet bloc. Radical modernism, especially the disavowal of tonality, enjoyed prestige and governmental support in the West, reinforcing the idea that Martinů was too conservative to properly mirror the uniqueness of the twentieth century. The same criticism was leveled at Stravinsky, most notably by Theodor W. Adorno.

The contrasts between Martinů and Stravinsky are illuminating. In biographical terms, Stravinsky remained more isolated from Russia in exile than Martinů from his homeland. During his Paris years, Martinů's works were, more often than not, premiered in Czechoslovakia, making the composer a presence in the musical life of the republic between 1924 and 1938. In Stravinsky's life, music and politics diverged. He was modern as a composer but politically and religiously an overt and severe reactionary.

Both pursued careers without much formal training within the structured framework of a conservatory curriculum. They exhibited eclecticism in style and a flair for the neoclassical, and shared an affinity for the language and literature of their homelands. Both achieved international recognition through music in multiple genres that appealed to the wider public. But Stravinsky had a brilliant meteoric start and remained far more prominent than Martinů; he outlived him long enough to embrace, like Copland, more radical facets of modernism at the end of his career. Stravinsky's influence on Martinů became the cause of the critical controversy in 1924 that surrounded Martinů's *Half-Time*, his first great success in Prague.[9]

Stark biographical contrasts amplified both the strictures and claims by Czech critics of Martinů. Martinů came of age isolated in a small market town. His forebears were of unassuming modest peasant stock, whereas Stravinsky grew up in St. Petersburg where his father was a celebrated opera singer. Stravinsky was influenced first by a teacher, Nikolai Rimsky-Korsakov, who was himself a leader in an explicitly nationalist school of composition. Martinů's approach to composition was decisively supported not by Czech nationalists, but by the eminent French composer, Albert Roussel, and relatively late in Martinů's life, in his thirties. Roussel nonetheless delighted in saying that his own place in history would be secured by the fact that he had encouraged Martinů.

The most telling biographical contrast, and the one that suggests Martinů's relevance to the twenty-first century, is that his finest music was written in the final two decades of his life, in exile, whereas Stravinsky's reputation remained anchored in his spectacular early works written before 1930. Martinů's return to international prominence in recent years has been led by the great symphonic works composed after 1942, scores that reveal his expansive musical palette and idiosyncratic connection to politics and the fate of Czech culture forged in exile. These qualities are expressed through Martinů's affection for the "fantasy" form he excelled in during the 1950s. Consider the Viola Concerto, the Fourth Piano Concerto, the *Parables*, the Sixth Symphony, and *The Frescoes of Piero della Francesca*.

Martinů was remarkably industrious, rivaling his contemporaries Hindemith, Darius Milhaud, or his Tanglewood student Alan Hovhaness. But Martinů stood out as a composer unusually adept at writing both light and serious music. For a twentieth-century composer, he had an astonishing sense of humor. Like early Hindemith, he engaged shifting popular fashions in music and the visual arts of his time, again like Stravinsky, but more so. His numerous piano pieces from the 1920s reveal humor and his sly capacity to inject commercial idioms popular in France with a touch of modernism. Many of these piano works are riffs on jazz and dance idioms of the time like the foxtrot.[10]

At the same time Martinů remained close to contemporary Czech visual artists who were fellow émigrés in Paris. He was attracted to modernist drama and stage design and identified avant-garde directors for his theater music.[11] And like Stravinsky, he drew on a wide range of literary sources; he was particularly fascinated by surrealism. However, Martinů was more committed than Stravinsky to finding ways to reconcile modernism, formal structural integrity, and a link to his homeland with comprehensibility on the part of an international audience. Stravinsky, particularly toward the end of his career, clung to a rigid distaste for the idea of music as "expressive," and cultivated an increasingly abstract and astringent surface in his music, in which an expressive power inadvertently could break through, as in his 1966 *Requiem Canticles*. Martinů's humor and talent for grace and charm, and his attention to accessibility without blatant concessions to imitative nostalgic evocations, or faux simplicities, made his late works models for an approachable, modernist classical music.

Martinů's ballet scores from the 1920s—*Istar* (1921), *Who is the Most Powerful in the World* (1921), *The Butterfly that Stamped* (1926), and *On tourne* (1927, but received its premiere only in 1979)—may reveal the influence of French rather than Czech composers, but they also display Martinů's talent for integrating disparate sources, including jazz, Czech folk materials, marionette plays, fairy tales, and film. In all its variety, Martinů's idiosyncratic modernism revealed a central objective: a formal clarity conducive to winning an audience at first hearing.

The accessibility and elegance of Martinů's diverse output, including works for large orchestra such as the charming *Inventions* (1934), *La bagarre* from 1926 (the first orchestral work performed in the United States), and *Thunderbolt P-47* (1945, a work that briefly became widely programmed during the 1940s) all account for Martinů's prominence as a composer during his American years. But as the composer David Diamond, a Martinů pupil, observed, his success would turn out to be fragile. Martinů was widely performed and written about in the United States in the 1940s, whereas Bartók, also an exile, languished in relative obscurity until his death in 1945. But by the time of Martinů's death in 1959, his work was no longer well represented on concert programs, whereas Bartók posthumously assumed a secure place in history as one of the greatest and most widely performed composers of modern times.[12]

Martinů's posthumous fate was ironic. His "rediscovery" after Communism was as a Czech composer, even though the national elements in his great later works were subtle and flourished at a considerable distance from his homeland. During the last years of his life, 1953 to 1959, Martinů retained professional and personal links to America even though he based himself in Europe. His love of country became tinged with the distortions of memory and nostalgia. As Martinů himself realized, his first emigration to Paris had been voluntary. Then, from 1938 on, and again in 1948, after the Communist coup that brought an end to democratic Czechoslovakia, exile became involuntary. [13]

Ambivalence and inconsistency accompanied Martinů's exile. Despite complex personal circumstances related to his marriage to a French woman who did not speak Czech, in 1938 he suddenly seemed determined to return to his homeland, and after the Munich Agreement, he even contemplated moving to Prague as late as early 1939. But Martinů failed to obtain a position at home, and he came to resent the provincialism of local Czech musical politics of the 1930s;[14] its persistence fueled his unease at the prospect of returning to Prague after the Allied victory in May 1945.

For all his nostalgic musings about Polička, the town of his birth, Martinů's career would have been doomed had he not left for Paris. He had been a poor student in Prague, psychologically ill-suited to the classroom, the authority of teachers, and the routine of assignments and examinations. He showed little interest in practicing and achieving a competitive standard as a violinist. He had no powerful figure's protection, as Josef Suk had found in his relationship to Dvořák, who became his father-in-law. Martinů never completed his conservatory degree. The composition of music, a solitary enterprise, became a separate and protected psychological space, carved out largely as an autodidact. It required an intensity of concentration that shielded Martinů from the intrusions of the outside world.[15] Stravinsky had by the mid-1920s become a suave, assured, and world-famous public personality, increasingly unaffected by his emigration from Russia.

The most revealing clue to Martinů's recognition of the benefits of his status as an exile can be found in how recurrent Czech materials are transformed in his work by a virtuosic command of cross-cultural and cosmopolitan strategies of modernist transformation. Martinů did not foreground the Czech as exotic in his major works. Martinů's pattern of elongating small units into larger melodic shapes in the Fourth Symphony (1945), for example, has led some scholars to speculate that the original melodic material came from a Czech source. The final musical result, however, overwhelms anything originally identifiable as Czech.[16]

Martinů's attachment to pre-Romantic forms, most evident in one of his most admired works, the *Double Concerto* (1938), provided him with the structure to transform sources using musical means of compositional development, both in rhythm and harmony. The *Double Concerto* was finished the day the Munich Agreement was signed. It was premiered in Basel and Geneva, and performed in Prague only in 1947. This three-movement piece does not assert the composer's love of country directly, but transfigures it. Martinů's longing for hope, and his recognition of national suffering becomes an engrossing musical event, a tightly structured, brilliant, and complex score characterized by a masterful command of melodic materials, counterpoint, and sonority within an imaginative reworking of a neoclassical model.

National elements were consistently subordinated to the composer's unique voice, suggesting a spiritual homesickness tinged with resentment, if not some measure of guilt. His fiercest Czech critics, notably doctrinaire right-wing nationalists but also Communists such as musicologist Zdeněk Nejedlý—who emulated Stalin in merging cultural national sentiment with Communism, thereby blunting Communism's fundamental universalism—sensed in Martinů an attachment to the Czech heritage that resisted political appropriation.[17] His internationalist aesthetic stood in opposition to the unabashed advocacy of a nationalist aesthetic agenda that elevated Smetana as the true Czech musical voice in the interwar years, when Smetana's *Bartered Bride* and *Má vlast* became idealized as musical monuments of Czech nationalism.

Martinů resolutely rejected German Romanticism; his credo placed "absolute musical values" in opposition to "Romanticism and subjectivism," both characteristics readily applied to Smetana's large-scale works, but less so to Dvořák's.[18] Martinů's belief in objective international norms brought him into conflict with a nationalism that rejected the validity of such "absolute" criteria of judgment. In the 1920s and '30s, the clash between internationalism in aesthetic modernism and provincial and exclusively national norms in art reached its apex in the Nazi condemnation of modernism as "degenerate." In the Czech context, Martinů sided with Novák and others who opposed Nejedlý's denigration of Dvořák as having betrayed the national cause by adapting German compositional practices from Brahms and Wagner, among others.

Martinů repeatedly asserted a lack of interest in narrowly sectarian politics. Although his pronouncements on political subjects were rare, no composer of his generation could shield his work from the history unfolding around him. He stood apart from factions but not political ideals, as his 1935 anti-war opera *Comedy on the Bridge* suggests.[19] The politics that surrounded Martinů early in his life had been consumed with the struggle over how Czech national aspirations for independence from the Habsburg monarchy should be realized. His virulent opposition to the use of music as an instrument of ideas and political ideology was itself a political reaction to the intensity of such debates. Martinů developed a distaste early in his career for the late nineteenth-century, post-Wagnerian medium of the tone poem, but not before he achieved his first major public success with an overtly nationalist cantata, his *Czech Rhapsody* (1918), written to celebrate the new republic of Czechoslovakia. Bartók did something similar when he emulated Strauss in his massive patriotic symphonic poem *Kossuth* (1903).

Martinů's sources shifted, while still in Prague, from the German to the French. Early orchestral compositions, such as *La mort de Tintagiles* (1910) after Maeterlinck, and the *Ballade: Villa by the Sea* (1915), inspired by Arnold Böcklin (a visual source for music shared by Max Reger and Sergei Rachmaninoff), reveal his eclectic search for models, which led him in the 1920s to his own idiosyncratic aesthetic formulation. Martinů postulated a belief in music as a unique—cognitive but still intuitive—human psychological capacity inherently independent of language and images that leads the composer to identify and unlock the immanent formal possibilities of melodies and rhythms. This permitted him to write remarkable, modernist, and original ballet and stage music based on everything from Russian to American sources.[20]

When Martinů returned to writing concise works for orchestra near the close of his career, his model remained equally distant from the extreme realist musical narrative of Strauss and from Socialist Realism. Martinů perfected his command of form in compact orchestral works by turning impressions of visual images into subjective musical fantasies developed through the coherent elaboration of the self-referential musical implications of his constituent materials. This trend can be heard in *The Frescoes of Piero della Francesca* (1955) and in *The Rock* and *The Parables*, both from 1957, all written in Europe and premiered in the United States. In their sonority they may hark back to early twentieth-century French models of orchestral use, such as Ravel and Honegger, but not to Martinů's Czech experience. Martinů remained, to the end of his life, a spiritual nomad, a wanderer who realized musical time and sound the way an abstract painter would. Michael Beckerman once suggested that Martinů might best be seen as "the brilliant, distinctive, and incisive painter of musical canvases." Beckerman's examples were, properly, not Czech artists, but the leading mid-twentieth-century abstract painters in America: Jackson Pollock and Mark Rothko.[21]

The direction Martinů pursued as a composer reflected not merely a strong anti-Wagnerian streak but a general anti-German philosophical conception of the nature of music. Music did not exist to express sentiments or ideas; it was not a surrogate for religion and could not "save the world." Even Smetana's *Bartered Bride* was an example of music as instrument of extramusical ideology by which music "was carried over to a different sphere and the limitations of judgment were overstepped considerably." Martinů became convinced that music in Czech culture before 1918 had been driven into "political opposition" because it had been "surrounded" by "calculated German propaganda" that led Czech music to be judged by how it "*fits in*."[22] Martinů concluded that the idea of having a "message" in music came from "sentimentality, self-pity and selfishness" that all worked against any professed effort "to save humanity" through art. He emigrated to Paris "looking for . . . the actual foundations upon [which] Western culture lies." Martinů, however, slipped in his own personal patriotic confession; he added the phrase, "which, in my opinion, reflect our national character."[23]

This mix of resentment of and distaste for German Romanticism partly explains the distance between Martinů and his almost exact contemporary, the Czech composer Erwin Schulhoff. Schulhoff was born in Prague in 1894 into the German-speaking Jewish community from which both Franz Kafka and Max Brod came. Like Martinů, Schulhoff was influenced by directions in French music, notably Debussy, and like Martinů, he went through a jazz-inspired phase. A fabulous pianist, he ended up returning to Prague and taught at the Conservatory, only to be caught up in the Nazi takeover and die in 1942 while incarcerated in Germany.

Schulhoff became a committed Communist in the 1930s. His overt political engagement alone would have been an impediment to closer ties with Martinů, a barrier that derived from the long-standing tension and ambivalence toward Czech nationalism within the German-speaking community of Prague. For Martinů, Schulhoff might have seemed more a German than a Czech composer. From his perspective, Schulhoff carried forward Romanticism's philosophical conceits concerning music's meaning and its capacity to convey ideas, a "German" tradition most evident in his choral-orchestral setting of *The Communist Manifesto* (1932).

Martinů's unique realization of an "objective" but expressive musical modernism—music that is at once the carrier of meaning but without a fixed ideological program or message—is best understood through the opera *Juliette* (1938), which he considered his masterpiece. Based on a 1930 French play by Georges Neveux, the Czech libretto was Martinů's own and was his translation from the French. The opera is a mix of Freudian psychological drama and surrealism. Martinů produced the Czech libretto expressly for the March 1938 Prague premiere (at which Firkušný was present) conducted by Václav Talich.

The sequence in the work's genesis, from French to Czech, helps place the Czech sources in Martinů's music in their proper place. The opera suggests no particular locale or landscape. The personal and national materials, indeed all autobiographical sources and references, serve music's inherent nature and therefore the larger cross-cultural and international practice of music. Martinů believed that Czech music had been "led astray" in the nineteenth century by its encouragement of "contrived pathos" and the "manufacturing" of emotions, among them a musical nationalism (e.g., in Smetana).[24]

An affinity exists between Martinů and Dvořák (largely unacknowledged by Martinů). It rests in the priority they both gave to "absolute" norms and forms in musical practice as validated by the history of music. As Czech composers they drew upon the distinctive sources and ethos of their homeland to generate unique works of art. Martinů was sparing in his musical references to his Czech predecessors. There are echoes of Dvořák's *Requiem*, particularly in the masterful Sixth Symphony, but Martinů claimed not to know the work, although, as observers have noted, he participated as an orchestral musician in performances of Suk's *Asrael* Symphony, in which he would have encountered Suk's own allusions to (and direct quotations from) the *Requiem*.[25]

The Prague premiere of the surrealist *Juliette* took place just three years after two great surrealist French poets, André Breton and Paul Éluard, visited Prague. Breton praised the city as uniquely seductive and magical. For Martinů, surrealism was evidence of an international spiritual movement linking Paris, contemporary Czech modernism in literature and art, and Prague. Exemplary of Martinů's engagement with surrealism as both Czech and international was his collaboration with the writer Vítězslav Nezval.[26] Intense relationships with friends and lovers notwithstanding, Martinů was understandably attracted to surrealism as a solitary and introspective personality. It was consistent with his marked abhorrence of absolutist political ideologies that brought music closer to aesthetic realism, particularly the use of music as emblematic of a defined national character.

Martinů's aversion derived from his encounter with post–World War I radical Czech nationalism and the attendant conflicts that surrounded him during his years in Prague, despite its vibrant modernist culture. When the war ended, Prague had become a city of more than 700,000 inhabitants that included Czechs, Slovaks, Germans, several Slavic nationalities, and Jews. The Czech nationalism from within the majority community posed a challenge to the city's minorities.

Within the Jewish community, allegiance to the German language had declined since the late nineteenth century, but a veneration of German culture still lingered. A significant number of adherents to the ideology of Czech nationalism were anti-Semitic and did not welcome the embrace of the Czech national cause among many Jews.[27]

Unsurprisingly, a Zionist movement flourished in Prague alongside the pursuit of a non-Zionist Jewish nationalist arrangement within the new republic. Interwar Czechoslovakia legally recognized Jews as members of a separate nation, equal in status to Germans, Hungarians, Slovaks, and Eastern Slavs (then called Ruthenians). In the years immediately following the establishment of the interwar republic, some optimism owing to its democratic nature notwithstanding, it became apparent that the ethnic conflicts inherited from the Habsburg era were on the rise, not in retreat. In the case of the Jews of Prague, despite their advocacy of contemporary Czech culture—as exemplified by the German Jewish writer Max Brod's decisive intervention on behalf of Jaroslav Hašek, Kafka, and Janáček—anti-Semitic sentiment was in the ascendancy, a prejudice Martinů did not share.[28]

Martinů's tenure as a violinist in the Czech Philharmonic under Václav Talich led him in the direction of a universalist normative aesthetic. Martinů had managed to secure a place in the second violin section, owing to his close friendship with Stanislav Novák, the Philharmonic's concertmaster.[29] This proved to be decisive. Talich exposed him to a cosmopolitan view, particularly that music, properly understood as possessing norms, could be a means to blunt xenophobia and discredit cultural chauvinism. Talich had adopted an admirably expansive version of Czech national pride.

Under Talich, the Philharmonic's repertoire was wide-ranging and open to new European trends. Talich not only widened Martinů's horizons, he fostered his career as a composer. The resolute commitment to an international repertoire mirrored a cultural agenda that sought to bolster the ideals of the new Czechoslovakia as a multi-ethnic pluralist democracy. An advocate of Janáček, Talich was independent and, like Martinů, respected the individuality of artistic creation and privileged objective criteria of judgment over political allegiances. He would be accused, ironically, of collaborating with the Germans during their occupation, only to be exonerated fully in 1946.[30]

Martinů found the competing politics of Prague unnerving, making his existence as an émigré in Paris liberating. The ability to set sectarian politics aside was conducive to his calling as a composer committed to the ideal of music—and particularly new music—as self-referential and reflective of music's inherent unique logic. Martinů expressed this by admitting that he "instinctively" feared the "diversion" of the natural "spiritual development" of "national Czech expression" by efforts both of artificial preservation and the "exaggerated" imposition of "metaphysical systems" that were residues of a historic German hegemony. A reductive chauvinist construct of what was authentically Czech was a "caricature" and "not native to our Czech expression." Martinů was determined to honor an internationalist Czech tradition in music that had "a greater bias toward concretization" and "logical thought."[31]

It is instructive to compare Martinů's reactions to the dominance of German musical traditions in Eastern Europe to those of his Polish contemporary Szymanowski. Writing after the Great War, Szymanowski welcomed the end of German influence, particularly that of Strauss. He, like Martinů, embraced the French composers of his time, especially Paul Dukas, and celebrated Stravinsky. But Szymanowski held to the belief that music, even when shedding the trappings of Romanticism, had to take "its proper place in the national consciousness." Hence, Bartók represented the compelling model. Stravinsky's "exoticism," his use of Russian materials, made him distinctive, without diminishing his centrality to modern European music. Stravinsky remained "fundamentally" Russian. Szymanowski, again like Martinů, regarded Stravinsky as "the greatest living musician" because he rejected "metaphysical banalities," and realized beauty based on craftsmanship. The result was an "objective" command of form that avoided a subordination of form to content. Like the masters of the Classical era and of the Renaissance, Stravinsky restored the "organic" implications of music to renew it as a unique "craft."[32] But Szymanowski saw his own role as using Stravinsky's principles to shape the modern culture of his nation, using Polish traditions in ways that emulated the achievement of Chopin.

By contrast, Martinů stressed a cross-national "clarity and conciseness of form and expression" that even when based on national materials, transcended them, thereby diminishing music's future role in strengthening a divisive nationalism.[33] The "Czech" elements Martinů used in works written in France and later in America—with few exceptions—signaled a national pride that foregrounded an alignment between Czech traditions and a universalist humanism. Martinů left Prague for Paris to pursue music in "the style of the West" that he first associated with Stravinsky. Martinů recalled arriving in Paris with "confused ideas." Looking for clarity, he discovered Roussel, who encouraged him to write music that had "order, transparency, balance, taste and a clear, exact expressive language."[34]

Martinů's humanist version of Czech pride blunted the divisive character of the politics of language use under Habsburg rule. Music had to be an instrument of reconciliation. Martinů knew of Brod's vigorous defense of Janáček's *Jenůfa* after its 1918 German-language premiere in Vienna against the charge by outraged critics that the opera was little more than an assertion of Czech nationalism. According to Brod, *Jenůfa* was "a human opera," not a "national one." It was a work that set a distinctly Moravian experience in a truly "universal" and "purely musical" manner, reconciling genuine "national" sentiment with the essence of the "ocean of humanity."[35] Brod's defense mirrors Martinů's musical aesthetics. The affinity between Janáček and Martinů—despite stark contrasts—rests in how the local communicates the universal in their music. Janáček crafted a new, anti-Wagnerian rhetoric of intense musical expressiveness from Czech materials that captured audiences even when sung in translation. Martinů sought to exploit his Czech material to strengthen the clarity of his musical structures and the transparency of his sonorities, even when writing instrumental music.

Martinů joined the public fray over the direction of music in the new republic in 1924, the year of an ISCM (International Society for Contemporary Music) festival in Salzburg and Prague. He wrote a defense of Stravinsky in which he openly challenged the call for a "return to Smetana," and expressed his skepticism about the elevation of Smetana by Czech nationalists. There was no need to emulate the monuments of the past. The example Czech music needed to follow was that of Stravinsky, who took into account the momentous historical changes between past and present, and who experimented, "searching and preparing the field for those who are coming." The goal was to supplant the worn-out rhetoric and sonority of German Romanticism with music that was "lucid" and "healthy" and not overly subjective and diffuse.[36] Martinů understood that the nationalist appropriation of Smetana was a distortion of the composer's musical achievement.

Martinů's rejection of undisciplined subjectivity in music rested also on his conception of the discontinuity in history that faced his generation in the post–World War I era. "Life is inconsiderate, strict and fast; it does not leave time for fumbling around in the extremities of feeling," he wrote. "It demands intensity—a forceful compact form and concentrated contents." The example of the postwar generation of French composers, and the Stravinsky of *Le sacre du printemps* and *Les noces*, revealed the bankruptcy of Romantic nationalism in music. Stravinsky may have relied on archaic Russian sources in these works, but Martinů focused on the brilliant formalist transfiguration of the musical logic contained within folk sources. An organic musical shape and form resulted that stripped the source material of its superficial political and cultural overtones. Musical laws took over; music spoke "for itself."[37]

This aesthetic fit the newly created Czech nation, Martinů argued, since it historically had not been "an overtly emotional nation," but rather one characterized by a "simple and healthy sentiment, strictness rather than abandon, sobriety rather than hysterical enthusiasm, and a natural sense for simple explanation and a simple relationship to things." This valorization of the "simple" made the Czech national character, in Martinů's view, essentially democratic and egalitarian, not dominated by an aristocratic political mythology like the Polish.[38]

Martinů rejected the predilection among postwar Czech musicians and intellectuals for metaphysics and aesthetics, a symptom of the still lingering German tradition. As late as 1947 he wrote, "So despite how badly we suffered at the hands of German culture, we still cannot get rid of it." By the mid-1920s, Prague was not the place to pursue "principles of rationality and clarity," its enviable multilingual, cosmopolitan character notwithstanding.[39] Martinů was not surprised that after the 1946 performance of his Fourth Symphony, he was condemned as a "formalist traitor" by left-wing Czech critics.

Martinů's putatively naïve but actually commonsensical appeal to the virtues of reason and clarity within the Czech nation can be heard in his music, despite its eclecticism of idiom and subject matter. His beliefs and the rhetoric that accompanied them were not entirely original. The popular Czech writer and political advocate of Czech nationalism, Jan Neruda, gave a speech in 1884 on the occasion of his fiftieth birthday in which he said, "We often lament having no friends or too few. Why this lament? It is completely gratuitous. We need no other friends than work and a love for our country. Work is an honest friend: honor her and she will never leave you. Likewise, our love of country: there can be no nation so low that such a love cannot raise it up to victory. Thus, the Czech nation, a nation of honest, tireless labor, will emerge victorious."[40] There was nothing in Neruda of the grandiose chauvinism that flourished in neighboring Hungary or Poland, rooted, respectively, in the myths of the valor of the Magyar defense of Christendom, or the past glory of the Polish-Lithuanian Commonwealth, an empire that once stretched from the Baltic to the Black Sea, a heroic and chivalric heritage enshrined in Adam Mickiewicz and Henryk Sienkiewicz, and shared both by Chopin and Szymanowski.

Neruda died in 1891. He may have been the most widely read Czech poet, prose author, and political commentator of the late nineteenth century. Although greatly influenced by German literary models, Neruda was a leader in the revival of the Czech language. An avid reader, Martinů knew of Neruda's advocacy of the Czech language and his resistance to recurrent Austrian schemes to Germanize the Czech lands.[41] The merits of things distinctly Czech were not even rooted in religious uniformity, especially given the proto-Protestantism of the reformist cleric Jan Hus and his successors, the Bohemian Brethren. Czech culture extolled the courage, resolve, and dignity of ordinary individuals. In Neruda's *Prague Tales* (1878), a character resists the enforced use of German and chides the many fellow Czechs who refrain from using their native language, proudly saying, "I speak Czech long and loudly. My colleagues avoid me like the plague."[42]

In formal terms, what is true of Neruda's short fiction can be said of Martinů's music. Both combine an accessible surface with wit, formal invention, and philosophic insight. Both are democratic and innovative, despite Neruda's conservative adherence to realism. Martinů's shifting experiments in the appropriation of competing strategies for modern music reflects a Neruda-like intent to capture his audience across barriers of class and religion, in a manner that cultivates a humanist sympathy in the listening public, a synthesis of nativist loyalty and pride consistent with tolerance. This suggests a cosmopolitan liberalism in politics that was the presumed goal of the constitutional regimes in all four of the nations for which Martinů had the greatest sympathy—interwar Czechoslovakia, France's Third Republic, wartime and postwar America, and Switzerland, his last refuge and the place of his death.

Martinů believed modern music could reinforce the core values of democracy. He was in this sense a direct analogue of his contemporary and friend Aaron Copland, who worked to forge a synthesis of formal excellence and wide accessibility that cohered with a commitment to freedom and equality. Martinů's *Brigand Songs* from 1957, ten difficult pieces for male choir a capella, are based not on Moravian or Bohemian sources but on Slovak folk texts that derive from the peasant resistance to the Turkish invasion of 1663, and later, to German and Hungarian invaders. As Martinů worked on the songs, he lamented that there were not enough people in Czechoslovakia willing to resist the tyranny of his own time, a sentiment only strengthened by the composer's disappointment at the West's failure to come to the aid of the Hungarian revolutionaries in 1956.[43] He was so livid that he fantasized about a bomb destroying the United Nations headquarters as punishment for failing to stop the Soviets from crushing a revolution against Communism he hoped the Czechs would emulate.[44] These songs were written alongside *The Rock*, Martinů's celebration of the *Mayflower* landing, a milestone in the history of the New World.

The folk ballet *Špalíček* (1932), Martinů's finest ballet score, has origins in Bohemian culture and history and its debt to Roussel and the Stravinsky of *L'histoire du soldat* reveals his effort to produce a work rooted in his homeland, a modern national work of musical theater. It can be properly compared to Copland's ballet scores from the 1930s and '40s, *Billy the Kid*, *Rodeo*, and *Appalachian Spring*, in its modernist but populist transformation of native folk materials into musical forms with a transnational appeal. The enmity shown Martinů by the advocates of Smetana notwithstanding, he would receive the Smetana Prize for Composition in 1934 for *The Miracles of Mary*.[45]

That Martinů emerged as a distinctly "Czech" voice in twentieth-century music after the 1989 "Velvet Revolution" (despite the breakup of Czechoslovakia in 1992/93) was fitting. The Czech element he sought to express was indeed a construct of music as exemplary of a shared and simple universal humanism and consistent with Václav Havel's politics. Martinů and Havel, in their separate ways, considered that "the actual foundations" of Western culture defined the Czech nation. What made Martinů's synthesis of a commitment to freedom and tolerance and a modernist reassertion of the power of music's unique logic and accessibility successful was his belief in the immanent implications of musical motifs, their thematic character, and the rhythmic structure required to realize an organic musical form.

Musical composition was ultimately motivated by an internal psychic dynamic sparked by musical ideas. Composing was psychologically detached from the conduct of ordinary life. It was propelled subconsciously by an organic dynamic that emanated from the constituent musical materials themselves. Musical thinking was an independent way of being. It permitted the composer to take a fragment and fashion what Martinů, consistent with the psychological fashion of his era, termed a *gestalt*.[46] The melody, or motivic fragment, may have had a national or ethnic character, but what happens in the compositional process is less the work of "intellectual effort" than something "dictated spontaneously by an organism that became crystallized in the composer's mind beforehand." The shape of a work emerges from a dynamic between the "variable" and "invariable" objective consequences of a musical phrase. Martinů argued this idiosyncratic claim in his analysis of Beethoven's *Pastoral* Symphony, a work endlessly cited as a defense of music with literary or visual programs, music understood (following Beethoven's example) as concerned with a primary purpose of expressing emotions, narrating stories, and promoting ideas, both philosophical and political.[47]

Martinů's provocative musings on how music takes shape and gets written explains in part the scale of his output and its varied character. It also accounts for the consistent formal musical coherence of his works, and, despite shifts in outward style, their highly personal and idiosyncratic sound. Martinů lived, so to speak, isolated in a world of his own, even though he was responsive to the musical movements that surrounded him. French Impressionism, Stravinsky, neoclassicism, and surrealism left their mark, as did events and phenomena from the contemporary environment, including sports and technology. But the personal in Martinů prevailed. Translated into musical terms, the personal resulted in a self-contained use of harmony that utilized the complex array of tonal strategies in an unpredictable and novel way, generating clear, simple, and eloquent melodic shapes that were developed with rhythmic virtuosity, using idiomatic instrumental textures that confront the listener with a unique approach to musical time.

This explains why, even in his most explicitly neoclassical works, Martinů exhibits an acute sense of musical duration and its limits. A comparison to Bartók is illuminating. Bartók had an uncanny sense of elapsed time and a quasi-mathematical instinct about structure that prevented him from overstaying his welcome. Martinů's internal clock was as acute, but it was guided by the implications of specific melodies and timbres and a fascination with shifts in music that seemed to run parallel with subjective shifts in mood, comparable to shades of light in a landscape. Martinů's music, for all its variety, is consistently concise. He rarely miscalculates the duration his musical materials will tolerate. His music engages the listener through the economy of time calculated to enhance comprehensibility at first hearing. Despite the formal demands of neoclassicist models, Martinů avoids monotony and excessive repetition. He manipulates rhythm in a manner that surprises without breaking continuity. The intensity of the later orchestral works retains this quality of economy but suggests a wide expressive range without an explicit narrative (as in Alban Berg's *Kammerkonzert* from 1925) or hidden confessional program (as in Berg's 1926 *Lyric Suite*).

Martinů's mature thoughts on the character of music were perhaps best expressed in the English-language note he wrote and sent to the dedicatee of the Fourth Piano Concerto, Rudolf Firkušný, in 1956. He gave the title "Incantation" to the two-movement work "in the form of Symphony or Fantasy." He wanted to "break out" of the traditional concerto form that seemed too "geometrical and static." The title implied some sort of "magic." Martinů conceded that "there is always some sort of program in music," but that program does not need to be "verbal"; "magic" pointed to Martinů's conviction that music's nature cannot be contained within the framework of language. Rather, it stems from "the inner life of the composer, his framework and logic of language of the world, his struggle to express himself, and it could mean even a refuge or a protest." Music is always "searching for a meaning of life," not only in a personal sense but for "mankind." Music is a path toward "searching for truth." The specific context for the search Martinů cites is the contemporary world, which he characterizes as beset by "contradictory forces" and a "system of uncertainty" in "our daily life." But most important, Martinů describes daily life in modernity as under the "pressure of mechanization and uncertainty." To "evoke" a genuine "protest" against this existential reality, music is "the one means" capable of expressing that protest.[48]

The protest then goes through many emotions for which the composer seeks to find "tangible forms." But once the composer gets "control" of a melody, gives it "substance and form" and commits it to paper, he starts "something of a quite different order." The "emotional" impulses that started the process of composition and led to melodies then "cease to be important." "Music has different laws," Martinů observed, even though drama and tragedy in the composer's life may have spurred its initial creation. Even when "a deeper conception of human destiny and faith" are at stake, the "formal building" of music takes over. Meaning contained in emotions and ideas is "displaced" by a focus on the "musical form problem." The question "what the music means" therefore becomes "rather embarrassing," since "music has to speak for itself." Martinů ends his note with a simple "Amen."[49]

The essence of Martinů's approach to composition and view of the unique agency of music can be found in his last major compositional effort, his setting, not entirely complete, of passages from *Isaiah* written at the very end of his life in 1959. The composition was inspired by Peter Gradenwitz, the German-Jewish Israeli musicologist and publisher whose 1949 book on the music of Israel was widely influential. Gradenwitz had studied with Josef Rufer and Arnold Schering and was an expert on Classical style.[50]

Gradenwitz, by working with Martinů, sought to achieve two main objectives. First was to underscore the universality of musical logic and the second the power of musical modernism. A third implicit objective was to compare the historical fate of the Czech and Jewish nations. Martinů's settings are dramatic, spare, energetic, and also lyrical. He uses his small but powerful forces—male choir, four instruments, and three soloists—to great effect and realizes the power of the prophetic text in a manner that conveys the beauty and gravity of the human condition through a disciplined use of sonority, melody, and counterpoint. There is no suggestion of any particularistic nationalism, whether Czech or Jewish, Western, or "oriental." Martinů is in complete command of the unique universalist potential of modern music as a communicative medium of reason, virtue, and profound recognition of the human predicament as all humankind searches for peace, justice, and freedom.[51]

As the *Isaiah* settings suggest, the exile Martinů may have dreamed of his Czech homeland and even hoped to return, but he resisted the possibility that he might end up being remembered only as a "Czech" composer. He believed it was "necessary for a Latin element to emerge in my work." When contemplating the post-Communist elevation of Martinů as modernism's uniquely Czech master, it is important to remember that Martinů himself observed, "Is it possible that some of my ancestors were Italian, French, or Spanish in origin and that their name might have been Martini, Martin, or Martinez? If I had a choice, I would choose Italian ancestors."[52]

The contradictions and tensions between Martinů's public profile as a representative Czech, an exile and patriot, and his ambition to be a voice that transcended national distinctions, strengthened his instinct that to return when it might have been possible, between 1945 and 1948, would put his career and international standing at risk. Martinů's referencing of his homeland in his later music must be seen as a nostalgic illusion that functions as part apology and part confession that seeks to lessen the guilt of ambivalent feelings and any suggestion of a betrayal of his homeland. And then there was the personal element. Neither of the major romantic attachments of his later life, his long marriage to Charlotte or his intense infatuation with the American Roe Barstow, were with Czech partners.

The Czech materials in Martinů's later music was sustained by their musical potential, their residual assistance in the reception of his music, and the psychological stability they provided. They confirmed the narrative of the struggling exiled artist who shielded his private thoughts and internal dialogue from view. That being said, Martinů's love of country had a specific content that justified his exile, particularly after 1948. Martinů's loyalty was to the democratic republic of Czechoslovakia that came into being after World War I. The dominant virtue of this new democratic state was its valorization of ordinary individuals and freedom. At the end of World War II, Martinů wrote derisively of the "worship of heroes" encouraged in his homeland. He asked, "I am the one who takes responsibility for my work, and not Smetana, right?" He cited the revered founder and first president of interwar Czechoslovakia, Tomáš G. Masaryk, who expressed the primacy of the individual and the ethics of responsibility that freedom and democracy permit. Martinů approvingly quoted Masaryk as saying, "if I can do something and I am capable, then I will do it myself."[53]

Martinů died a few years after Khruschev's 1956 "de-Stalinization" in Soviet Russia and the failed Hungarian Revolution of the same year. He did not experience the Prague Spring of 1968 and the harsh neo-Stalinism that followed in its wake. But his friend and colleague Rudolf Firkušný did witness all these.[54] Firkušný was the finest exponent of Martinů's music for the piano. His 1993 recording of three Martinů concertos, including *Incantation*, with Libor Pešek and the Czech Philharmonic, is astonishing. Its pianistic power, eloquence, and the incisiveness of the sound and interpretation display the integrity of Firkušný's musicianship and his unequalled pianism—Firkušný was over eighty years old when he made that recording.

Like Martinů, Firkušný was an ardent patriot but not a partisan nationalist. They shared a loyalty to a Czech tradition that found its political realization in the ideas of Masaryk and the democratic multi-ethnic republic Masaryk forged. Both men emigrated to America in 1941 after the fall of Paris in 1940, but Martinů never quite adjusted to the United States; it was as much the Europe of Paris as his Czech homeland that he missed. Firkušný, by contrast, adapted to America with great enthusiasm. Both musicians produced their finest work while based in America, and they enjoyed the support of American audiences and institutions. Firkušný and Martinů's attachment to their Czech homeland was rooted not in a sentimental construct of ethnic homogeneity, but in political principles. The experience of democracy in America made the loss of their homeland somewhat more tolerable.

Firkušný became part of a circle of Czech artists, writers, and musicians in Paris in the early 1930s. Like Martinů nearly ten years earlier, Firkušný shared the ambition of his contemporaries to escape from "German culture" and "go to France and see Paris." Like Martinů, he sensed the limitations and sectarian conflicts that dominated his homeland, despite its new lease on life as an independent nation. In Paris, Firkušný became close to Martinů and subsequently his wife, Charlotte, whom he sought to protect during tensions in the marriage stemming from Martinů's infidelity, particularly with the composer Vitězslava Kaprálová, even though her 1937 *April Preludes*, Op. 13, were dedicated to him.

It was Firkušný who alerted Martinů that he had to flee Paris in 1940, and made sure that he would be able to obtain a visa and get to America. In the United States he performed Martinů's music, became the dedicatee of several key works, particularly two concertos, the Third and Fourth (*Incantation*). Firkušný became an indispensable friend. He rushed to help Martinů after his disastrous fall in 1946 at Tanglewood; he watched over Martinů for the rest of the composer's stay in the United States.[55] The short appreciation of Martinů that Firkušný wrote in 1990, four years before his own death, written to celebrate the 100th anniversary of Martinů's birth, is a tribute to Firkušný's discretion, grace, and loyalty (see Appendix 1). They both shared the patronage, friendship, and admiration of George Szell, who, among other things, rescued the score of Martinů's 1937 Concerto Grosso.[56]

Firkušný was born in 1912, to a more prosperous family than Martinů's, in Napajedla in eastern Moravia. His father, also Rudolf, was a notary and a classmate, in secondary school, of Gustav Mahler. Firkušný had two older siblings, a brother, Leoš, a trained musicologist who died young, and an older sister, Marie. Firkušný's mother, Karla, lived a long life, and Rudolf, although he refused to perform in Communist Czechoslovakia, visited her regularly.

Firkušný's father died when Rudolf was three, in 1915. The family subsequently moved to Brno. It was there that Karla had the wisdom and determination to recognize her son's exceptional talent and seek out the best guidance she could find. That led her to Janáček, who despite misgivings about prodigies, took the five-year-old Rudolf under his wing.[57] The two remained close until Janáček's death. Janáček taught Firkušný (in his own iconoclastic manner) and exposed him to new music, particularly Debussy and Stravinsky. He went with him to concerts and operas, and even collaborated on a cadenza for a Mozart concerto. He encouraged the boy's interest in the world apart from music. Under Janáček's watchful eye, Firkušný began a public career at the piano as a child prodigy.

Firkušný observed how Janáček expressed his sympathies for the new Czechoslovak Republic with music that was modern in form and sonority. One of Janáček's celebrated late works is the *Sinfonietta* (1926), written initially for the multilingual Czechoslovak army. Janáček believed he was inspired by the ideal of the "free man" in the contemporary world. Without referencing late-Romantic musical rhetoric or conceding the rigor of compositional structure, but using familiar folk patterns in angular and arresting ways, the *Sinfonietta* managed to express patriotic enthusiasm and the courage "to do battle" for the young Czech republic."[58]

Firkušný witnessed Janáček's increasing fame late in life, in the 1920s, first in the Czech lands (after the premieres of *Jenůfa*, first in Brno and Prague) and then internationally after the Vienna premiere in 1918. But for most of his career, Janáček's life and reputation remained local to Brno. He insisted that Firkušný become more than a virtuoso and cultivate musicianship. Janáček's influence lasted for Firkušný's entire life; a decisive aspect of that legacy was Firkušný's ideal of interpretive integrity based on the structure of a composition. Beyond Janáček's works for solo piano, Firkušný maintained two Janáček works for piano and large ensemble in his repertoire: the *Concertino* (1925) and *Capriccio* (1926).[59]

Janáček treated the young Firkušný as an adult. Janáček's example inspired Firkušný to contemplate a career as a composer, an ambition that led him to continue his studies in Prague, albeit briefly, with Josef Suk. The piano, however, came first. Firkušný, as a performer, experienced the kind of early success and acclaim that eluded Martinů. At eleven years of age, he played Mozart's "Coronation"

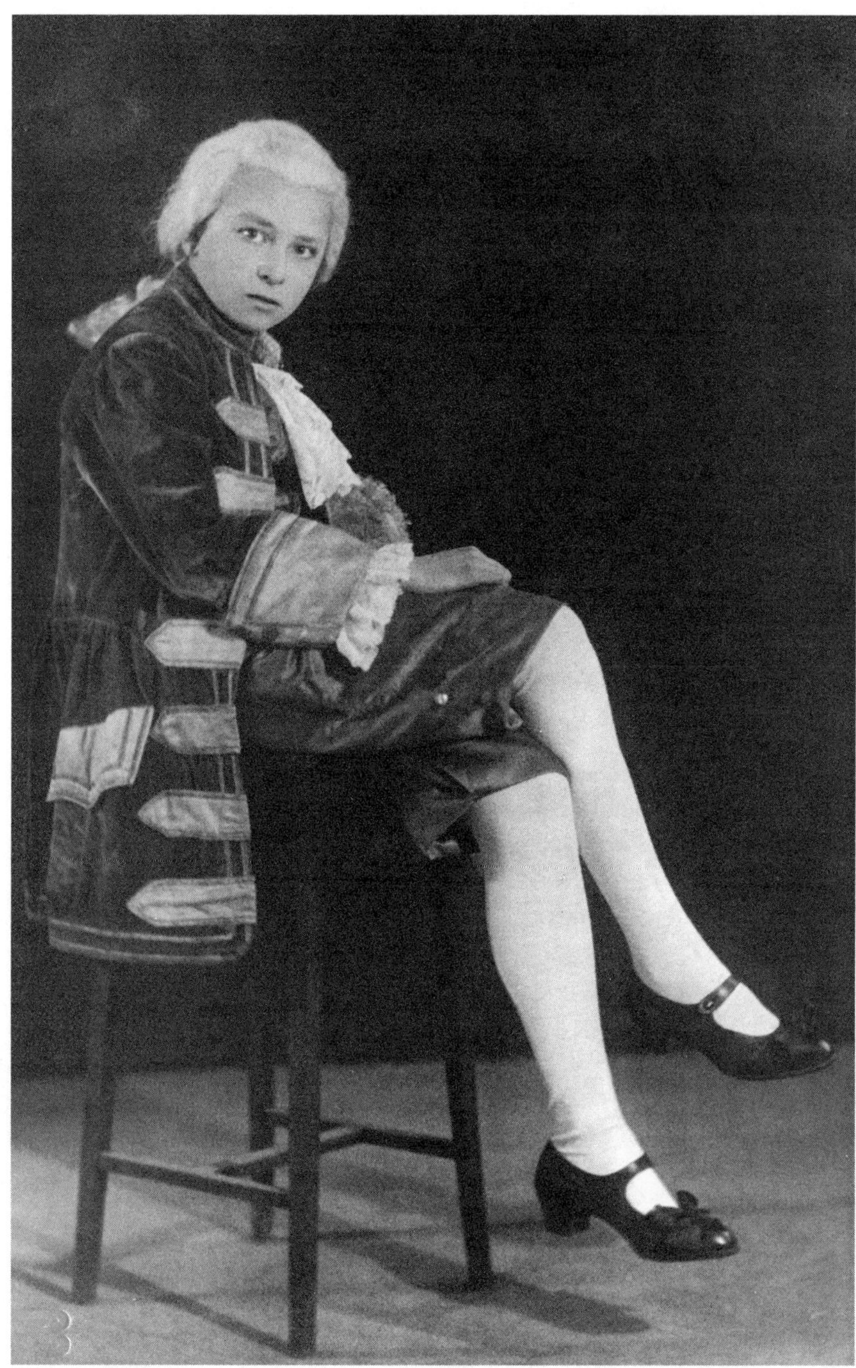

Figure 1. Rudolf Firkušný, dressed as Mozart, 1925.

Concerto, K 537, with the Czech Philharmonic. He quickly became celebrated, sufficiently so as to warrant appearing in public dressed up as Mozart (Figure 1).

Although Firkušný shied away from the sort of grand philosophical speculations Martinů indulged in, he shared with Martinů the idea that the Czech musical tradition, particularly exemplified by Dvořák, was inherently humanist and universalist. In Czech music, the local folk element was transformed into a constituent of a long-standing pan-European cultural tradition. Janáček had achieved this, and Firkušný recognized the same ambition and talent in Martinů. The Czech was not embraced as exotic but as a significant distinct contribution to the international tradition of the art of music. During the Cold War era, Firkušný, as an advocate of the Czech tradition, sought to reconcile old rivalries (e.g. Smetana with Dvořák) and bring Suk, Novák, Martinů, and of course Janáček within a unified account of the Czech contribution to European music.[60]

Firkušný became one of the most admired and successful pianists of the twentieth century; his repertoire ranged from Bach and Mozart to Beethoven, Brahms, Chopin, Schubert, Schumann, Debussy, and a wide array of contemporary composers, including Samuel Barber, Alberto Ginastera, Copland, Prokofiev, Bartók, Stravinsky, Poulenc, Messiaen, and even Schoenberg and Webern. Firkušný's playing of Stravinsky's *Trois mouvements de Petrouchka* was particularly admired. He premiered Gian Carlo Menotti's Piano Concerto, an attractive neoclassical score of which Firkušný rightly continued to think highly.[61]

He was an exponent of an aesthetic of refinement, lyricism, tonal beauty, insight, and interpretive integrity coincident with the anti-Romantic impulses of modernism. He combined a resistance to interpretive excess with a stunning and complete technical command of the piano characteristic of late Romanticism. Unlike Martinů, he harbored no particular resentment toward German culture, partly on account of the non-parochial influence of Janáček, whose thoroughly original musical mind transcended essentialist nationalisms, even though the sonorities in Wagner and Strauss appealed less to Janáček than the Italianate lyricism of Puccini. Firkušný, following Janáček and Masaryk's advice to broaden his education, pursued an intense wide-ranging interest in painting and literature from around the world throughout his life.

Firkušný soon abandoned his ambition to become a composer. However, he graduated from the Prague Conservatory with an elegant, finely written one-movement piano concerto that has recently been performed in Brno and is scheduled for an American premiere. The concerto may not be original, but neither is it merely imitative. It is an engaging foray into more than one style, held together by an impressive display of pianism. One regrets that Firkušný did not write more music.[62] He periodically mused that he regretted less that he had stopped composing and more that he had not become a conductor. His conception of conducting, like that of being a pianist, revealed the mindset of a composer. The influence of

Janáček, and Firkušný's own forays into composition, illuminate the easy affinity he developed with Martinů.

Firkušný went on to study with Vilém Kurz, the legendary Czech piano pedagogue. That relationship was not altogether easy, given Kurz's intense desire to control his protégés. Since Firkušný's aesthetic was, like Janáček's and Martinů's, shaped by a suspicion of late-Romantic practices and preferences, he avoided many of the monumental virtuosic staples of the repertoire, such as the Tchaikovsky and Rachmaninoff concertos that increasingly defined the signature works of leading piano virtuosos. He rejected the practices of interpretive freedom of Ignacy Paderewski and Vladimir de Pachmann, without cultivating an inflexible and uninflected approach. He did, however, avoid reliance on a piano repertoire whose primary virtue was the display of pianistic athleticism or the superficial sentimentalism frequently apparent in late-Romantic expressive piano literature. As Noel Straus, the highly regarded *New York Times* critic, put it in a review of an early recital in New York, Firkušný embodied a "pianism of pronounced fascination" on an "altogether exalted interpretive plane."[63] Firkušný sought to achieve this high standard in all styles. It required the disciplined cultivation of a translucent clarity from the piano that mirrored Janáček's approach to orchestration. And it demanded the command of formal structures and the functional economy characteristic of the fabric of Martinů's music.

Not surprisingly, Firkušný helped Martinů to understand how the piano could further his compositional aims. Firkušný's ability to render a musical text without distortion appealed to Martinů. The composer's *Fantasy and Toccata* (1940), written as both were fleeing the Nazi invasion of France, was dedicated to the pianist. Firkušný played a role for Martinů vis-à-vis writing for the piano comparable to Joachim's influence on Brahms's understanding of the violin. Firkušný's command of dramatic thundering *fortissimos* as in Brahms's D-minor Concerto and Martinů's Fourth was complemented by the ethereal *pianissimos* that were essential to renderings of Schubert and Janáček.

When Firkušný arrived in Paris, he was already a rising star. He was the most feted pianist to come out of Czechoslovakia. His friendship with Martinů was cemented less by their shared Czech heritage or membership in a close-knit circle of countrymen than by shared musical values. The two musicians shared an affection for recent French music. Firkušný recognized immediately that the reproach directed at Martinů in Prague—that he was an imitator and not sufficiently Czech—was mistaken. He recognized that Martinů was sensitive to shifting trends and influences, but that responsiveness lent his output an unusual, unexpected, and welcome variety. Firkušný rapidly realized that Martinů's works shared a disciplined craftsmanship, rhythmic originality, an intuition for structure, and an ear for instrumental sonority that were distinct and individual. No work demonstrated this more than *Juliette*, which some scholars suggest is a product of a Czech-French symbiosis in Martinů's work. This symbiosis shaped both composer and pianist. Firkušný was so taken by the opera at its Prague premiere that he wandered the streets of Prague all night thinking about it. He asked Martinů for permission to adapt part of the opera for piano solo, which he did, using his phenomenal memory, directly from the full score.

Firkušný's aesthetic was neither rigid nor doctrinaire, though it resembled Martinů's affinity for anti-Romantic modernist neoclassicism. But neoclassicism did not lead to antiquarianism. Firkušný showed limited interest in the period instrument movement, and Martinů rendered the harpsichord, in his 1935 concerto for the instrument and small orchestra, a protagonist of modernist neoclassicism.[64] Like Martinů, Firkušný had a sharp critical eye, but he maintained catholic tastes. He admired Horowitz's crystalline sound and electric power, even though he chose to follow the path pioneered by Artur Schnabel, with whom he studied briefly—that of a disciplined effort to realize the classical era masterpieces free of Romanticism's distortions. For Horowitz's part, he greatly admired Firkušný's Schubert.[65] Not surprisingly, Firkušný's repertoire reveals an extraordinary commitment to the intimacy and interiority of chamber music, as his recordings of the Mozart violin sonatas with Erica Morini and his admiration of Suk's chamber music with piano, particularly the Opus 8 Piano Quintet, suggest.

Firkušný was incapable, it seemed, of making an ugly sound on the piano, at any dynamic. He was never overconfident. The threat of stage fright remained with him. Firkušný was reluctant to include Rachmaninoff's Third Piano Concerto or the Chopin concertos into his repertoire, which in retrospect, is a shame. But the Dvořák Piano Concerto (in both the Kurz edition with its rewriting of the piano part, and later in its original version), which languished for decades in relative obscurity, became his specialty. Its current place in the repertoire is the consequence of Firkušný's advocacy. But with respect to Czech piano literature, Martinů's piano music took pride of place alongside Janáček.[66]

Firkušný remained partial to Janáček in part because it was from him that he developed the highly sophisticated grasp of how to think like a composer, and merge his command of the keyboard with the richness of his interpretive imagination. This led Firkušný to the informed pianism for which he became famous, an impeccable virtuosity free of antics and the cult of personality. Rudolf Serkin (to whom Martinů's 1954 Piano Sonata was dedicated) wrote to Firkušný in 1981, imploring him to join the Marlboro Festival in Vermont, arguing that the rising generation of musicians needed his guidance as an exemplar of music making. For Serkin, Firkušný exemplified the cultivation of technique on behalf of musical ideas and the logic of a musical text.[67]

A distinguishing feature of Firkušný's pianism that made an appearance early in his career was his ability to improvise, a gift connected with his early ambitions to compose. Firkušný won a prize in 1930 sponsored by the Polish and

Czech governments. It sought to promote collaboration between the Warsaw Conservatory and the Prague Conservatory. The prize therefore had two winners, one Czech and one Polish. Each winner was given a recital in the opposite country—in Warsaw for the Czech winner and in Prague for the Polish prize recipient. The Polish winner was the violinist Roman Totenberg.

Totenberg went to Firkušný's recital in Warsaw; it was a sensation. Totenberg (who played in the 1942 New York premiere of Martinů's Madrigal-Sonata for flute, violin, and piano), remembered vividly the concert's astonishing close. Firkušný turned to the audience and invited its members to give him tunes to improvise on, which he did, with mesmerizing results.[68]

The realities of the international concert circuit immediately after World War II allowed Firkušný to have a lifelong international career. Such careers and admiration did not always sit well with composers, particularly Stravinsky and Schoenberg, who viewed performers with suspicion. Martinů did not share this prejudice. Stravinsky (who appeared as a pianist and conductor with mixed success) and Schoenberg (who thought of himself as a conductor) were envious of the recognition and financial rewards earned by star performers. Interpreters—mere performers—captured the imagination of audiences more than composers. Their success rested on interpretations often arbitrary and theatrical and they concentrated on the performance of music of the premodern past, largely avoiding modernist works. Martinů did not resent a dependency on star instrumentalists. The arch-Romantic violinist Mischa Elman, for whom Martinů's Second Violin Concerto was written, put the work into circulation.

Performance of the familiar had already come to dominate concert life when Firkušný embarked on his international career in the interwar era. Firkušný benefited from this phenomenon in his post–World War II tours of South America, where he was lionized. Firkušný fan clubs sprung up, particularly in Argentina and Brazil. This took Firkušný by surprise since he never cultivated the level of fame achieved by Artur Rubinstein, Horowitz, and even Serkin, much less their larger fees. But until the end of his career, Firkušný routinely inserted new and unfamiliar Czech music into his recitals.

A career in performance defined separately from composition emerged slowly at the end of the nineteenth century and became dominant in the era of modern recording and high fidelity. Firkušný, although he had abandoned composition (in part because his facility in improvisation had undermined his compositional ambitions), remained committed through Janáček's teaching to the ideal of the performer-composer. He identified with Liszt, and, later, with Eugen d'Albert and Sergei Rachmaninoff. Firkušný was not alone among his contemporary performers, particularly conductors, who had tried their hand at composing, and even continued to pursue it. Schnabel took pride in his own compositions. The era's most famous violinist, Fritz Kreisler, composed, as did the cellist Pablo Casals, albeit more seriously. Alexander Zemlinsky (with whom Firkušný played the C-major Beethoven Concerto in the 1920s in Prague), Felix Weingartner, Wilhelm Furtwängler, Bruno Walter, Dimitri Mitropoulos, George Szell (the last three conductors delighted in performing with Firkušný), all composed. Firkušný stood out as a pianist whose approach to music had not been shaped primarily by a pianist and trainer of pianists. His fundamental and distinct musicianship explains why in 1931, at age nineteen, when Firkušný arrived in Paris, ostensibly to study with Alfred Cortot, Cortot remarked, after hearing him play, that he did not need a teacher, only a public.[69]

Both Martinů and Firkušný ended up living in the United States where their astonishingly successful careers, marked by a sustained interaction between composer and performer, reaped mutual benefits. Both turned to teaching, Martinů at Tanglewood, then at Mannes, Curtis, and Princeton, and Firkušný, a participant early in the history of the Aspen Festival, at Juilliard, where he launched a large number of distinguished pianists.

It has become convenient and commonplace to categorize composers and performers by nationality, and to assume that they represent a distinctive national musical tradition in some "authentic" manner. That strategy falsifies the complexity and variation in the way composers and performers construe themselves as musicians and citizens. In the cases of Martinů and Firkušný, they were both Czech patriots. The allegiance they shared, however, was to the newly formed independent state of Czechoslovakia that emerged from the multinational Habsburg Empire, and not to the divisive debates about the political destiny of the Czech people that dominated discussions before the collapse of that dynasty. Their careers and development as Czech artists were shaped in post-Habsburg Prague, in interwar France, and in wartime and postwar United States; in Firkušný's case, his political commitment to democracy was also shaped by international touring before the war.

Firkušný's fame and the admiration of his colleagues—he was a pianist's pianist—did not depend on his advocacy of Czech music but on his interpretations of the defining works of the repertoire for the piano. Like Firkušný's pianism, Martinů's compositions gained visibility not primarily as emblems of Czech identity. As is the case with writers of fiction, Martinů appropriated materials associated with the fabric of his life, including memories and sensibilities taken from the place of his birth, his childhood, and early adulthood. Martinů's eclectic and accessible modernism, often cast in neoclassical forms, incorporated these details and lent them a new significance.

As one leading American critic put it, writing about Martinů's Third Piano Concerto in 1950, "rhythms and melodic ideas" rather than "folksongs" "emanated" from Martinů, whom he nonetheless identified as a "Czech composer." Martinů's music represented "the classic ideal of music, form, design, for their own sake . . . the soundest craftsmanship and essential sincerity of musical thinking."[70] Martinů's compositions, especially late stage works such as the comic opera *Mirandolina* (1954), after Goldoni (with its original Italian libretto), *The Epic of Gilgamesh* (1954), and the *Greek Passion* (1957; libretto in English), are not defined by exotically Czech music, but are "cosmopolitan" in character. Even when Martinů's music is reliant on the Czech language and Czech scenarios, the music is distinguished by an allegiance to the autonomy of music's form and logic, and the transnational traditions of compositional craft required to realize music's communicative power.

The Czech patriotism of Martinů and Firkušný was not narrowly ethnic and provincial. It centered on the ideals of freedom and democracy, which is why their enthusiasm for their homeland flourished in America. Martinů and Firkušný chose to leave their homeland on account of their artistic ambitions before the external threat from Nazi Germany became actual. They understood the limitations and comparative isolation of Prague and sought fame and fortune in the wider world. Martinů, albeit with ambivalence, expected to return to Czechoslovakia. But before World War II, criticism and opposition at home troubled him. When the dismemberment of Czechoslovakia was complete and war broke out, a return became impossible and Czech identity became linked with an idealized image of interwar Czechoslovakia as a pluralist democracy. For all its limitations and periods of unrest, from 1939 to 1948, the Czechoslovak democracy created by Masaryk symbolized the promise of human freedom and dignity within a constitutional democracy largely free of sectarian nationalism.

Martinů's and Firkušný's Czech patriotism was grounded in their admiration for Tomáš G. Masaryk. They identified Masaryk with tolerance, pluralist liberal democracy, and the freedom of the individual. As a recent Czech biographer of Firkušný put it, "He never ceased to feel Czech. . . . He embodied all the glory of the Masaryk era, which was arguably the pinnacle of our nation's history."[71]

The unique prestige attached to exiles from Czechoslovakia reaped benefits for both men. Writing in 1951, Olin Downes, New York's leading music critic, reported, "Many students of Martinů's music believe that it is more truly Czech in its actual substance than it was before he came to America. He said that he substantially agreed. He said that no American could fully realize the freedom of the atmosphere in America, the absolute lack of restriction of act, of thought. This affected in him a certain release, and that release resulted in the crystallization of his utmost creative ideas."[72]

The Czech "substance" that, according to Downes, made its appearance in Martinů's late work was more a fantastic object, a glorified ideal, than a reality. Those caught up in a diaspora, particularly to America, nurture over time selective and idealized images of their homelands of origin. Consider the Irish in Boston who supported Irish resistance to British rule; the "White Russian" émigrés after 1917 who reveled in nostalgic (and unrealistic) images of a tsarist past, and the Cubans in twentieth-century America, whose allegiance is to a selective memory about a paradisiacal pre-Castro Cuba. When returning to Prague seemed plausible, between 1945 and 1948, Martinů hesitated to return and vacillated between the guilt of not wanting to return, bouts of nostalgia, and resentment about the inadequate recognition in his native country, and the recognition that his work and career would flourish better if he remained in exile.[73]

The loyalty to the Czechoslovak nation shown by Czech émigré artists and intellectuals after 1938 and through to the era of Václav Havel, was markedly different, however, as was its international reputation. In the 1940s, the ideals of freedom and democracy were Czech ideals. Czechoslovakia seemed to show that humanist values could thrive over emotional nativism and mythic histories. Czech musical and artistic traditions, particularly in the early years of modernism, took pride in their resolute Europeanism. For Firkušný, this was the consistent thread in the history of the eighteenth and nineteenth centuries, including Prague's place in Mozart's career and Dvořák's achievement, particularly after returning from America. Martinů's and Firkušný's commitment to the art of music was as an international, cosmopolitan form of life that transcended national distinctions. In America, the legacy of Czech participation in the pan-European music tradition, and its link to the Czech community in America, from New York to New Spillville, Iowa, stemmed from Dvořák's highly influential (albeit brief) presence in the United States in the 1890s.

The composer and pioneer in the music of Bali, Colin McPhee, reviewing Miloš Šafránek's first brief biography of Martinů in 1944, concluded that in Martinů's case, "it is not easy to define his warm and colorful musical style, which is neither radical nor conservative. He is at times the innovator, but never the revolutionary. Form, the problems of musical organization, a style that was personal, rather than colored by a facile nationalism—these have always been his first preoccupations." No matter the wide range of Martinů's historical models and his Czech sources, his music is "not esoteric, but aims at a wide and popular appeal" beyond the borders of a single nation.[74]

The suggestion of a special compatibility between Czech identity and the wider European musical heritage was observed by American critics and audiences with respect to Martinů and Firkušný. While praising Martinů's music as "personal and individual," Virgil Thomson compared Martinů, ironically, to Smetana, since in Martinů, "the shining sounds of it sing as well as shine." Thomson placed Martinů above Dvořák, in the "high company of Smetana, greatest of all those symphonic composers in whose work patriotism is of the essence."[75] Thomson mistook the evident individuality of Martinů's music and reduced it to a reflexive and superficial category of Czech musical "patriotism."

In a similar vein, in February 1943, after Firkušný's Town Hall recital, Downes wrote: "It is good to hear a pianist who plays like a genuine artist with something to say." Downes reserved his highest praise for the performance of Schumann's

Fantasie in C Major, Op. 17. It was "full of passion, yet conspicuous for the penetrating and cohesive treatment of the free form." Firkušný, whom Downes identified as a "Czechoslovak artist," played the finale "without mawkishness which makes the movement anti-climactic after the glowing poetry of the preceding pages." At the same time, "Firkušný proved, in performance of "a new work by Martinů" (described in the article as being "of Czechoslovakia") that "his technique is the equal to any modern demand and that he has virtuoso blood for this indispensable requisite of a concert pianist's art." Downes predicted that Firkušný will "go far" since he "has already won a high position among virtuosos of his generation."[76]

Martinů sought to view politics objectively rather than personally, professionally, or through the lens of sectarian ideology. Nevertheless, the political commitments of both Martinů and Firkušný derived from Masaryk. A world-famous figure, a philosopher, historian, teacher, and writer, Masaryk during his presidency became a direct patron of Firkušný, and indirectly, through government support, of Martinů. Martinů's first great success, the Prague premiere in 1918 of his most overtly patriotic work, *The Czech Rhapsody*, was delayed to ensure that Masaryk himself would be present.

Masaryk's son, Jan, who represented the hope of a post–World War II restoration of Czech democracy, was a close friend of Martinů and of Firkušný. His sudden death in 1948 (whose cause—suicide or murder—is still a matter of controversy) and the subsequent Communist takeover made the thought of a return to Czechoslovakia unthinkable for both.[77] Jan was a fine amateur pianist and Martinů dedicated a Moravian song cycle to him in 1942, which he performed in New York with the legendary Czech opera and movie star Jarmila Novotná. As Downes observed in 1950, the character of the final movement of Martinů's Third Piano Concerto was widely thought to have been influenced by Martinů's reaction to Jan Masaryk's death during the Communist coup d'état of February 1948.[78]

Downes noted that despite Martinů's resolute resistance to instrumental music defined by "programs," it was nevertheless hard, in the shadow of the recent end of the Second World War, not to sense some musical meaning outside of the realm of pure objectivity. Listening to Martinů's Fourth Symphony in December of 1945, Downes concluded that despite the absence of an "avowed" program, "we cannot listen to this music . . . without thinking of a resurgent Czechoslovakia, and a world of better horizons, and courage and vision for the future."[79] In this case Downes intuited Martinů's uncanny ability to convey his Czech patriotism in the form of a personal commitment to the liberal, ethical, and democratic political ideals he and Firkušný identified with Masaryk.

Firkušný's personal connection to Tomáš Masaryk was closer than Martinů's, even though Masaryk arranged for financial support for Martinů during the composer's Paris years. Masaryk became aware of Firkušný during the 1920s, gave his mother a monthly stipend, and later sponsored the pianist's travel to Italy and Paris. Firkušný had been a frequent guest in the Masaryk home and became friendly with the president's daughter. He played for Masaryk often, in the relaxed surroundings of the president's summer residences in Central Bohemia, Lány Castle and Topolčianky Castle in Slovakia.[80] Jarmila Novotná recalled meeting Firkušný there. He was still a prodigy and "quite young," and proud of the fact that he was wearing long pants "for the first time in his life."[81] Much later, Firkušný admitted that the president's understanding of music was limited—he adored Beethoven, albeit selectively—but Firkušný idolized him nonetheless. He once observed that only in the presence of three men would he be "turned to stone": Janáček, Masaryk, and Toscanini.[82]

The Czech state's constitution and objectives—its synthesis of nationalism and democracy—was created and defined in the image of America. Masaryk had married an American and took her last name, Garrigue, as his middle name. He was enamored of the American constitution and political ideals. Between the memory of Dvořák and the visible presence of Masaryk, pro-Czech sentiment in America before and during the war was high. As an early victim of Nazi aggression and viewed as a pawn in Neville Chamberlain's (and France's) shameful capitulation to Hitler, Czechoslovakia commanded broad sympathy as a democracy uniquely aligned with American values. No such sympathy was provoked by the 1938 Anschluss of Austria that supplanted an Austro-fascist regime. Edvard Beneš, Masaryk's protégé and successor as president, inherited Czechoslovakia's admirers.

Masaryk had realized that a commitment to democracy in a pluralist nation-state would necessarily involve the weakening and, if necessary, the subordination of the reflexive and often irrational love of what one believes is unique about one's country, its people, and its land. Visceral nationalism and democratic and pluralistic ideals were natural enemies, as Masaryk knew from his fame as an opponent of anti-Semitism. In his book of conversations with the great playwright Karel Čapek, Masaryk argued that the laws and practices of democracy derived from the Christian imperative to love one's neighbor as oneself. Masaryk cited Christ's admonition as the second fundamental commandment that should govern human conduct and define laws (as Jesus explained, echoing Hillel, in *Matthew* 22).[83]

Masaryk never entirely shed a residual attachment to the unrealized potential of a multinational state that existed under the Habsburgs. He excoriated the monarchy's failure to provide sufficient autonomy to the distinct national communities, particularly during the reforms of 1867 that followed Austria's 1866 military defeat by the Prussians. Only a dual monarchy emerged, as opposed to a triple or quadruple monarchy that might have made the Czech lands and Galicia, the Polish part of the Empire, equals of the Austrian and Hungarian crowns.

Masaryk briefly flirted with the multinational alternatives to independence that attracted some Czechs before World War I, including a pan-Slavic confederation and the possibility of a radical reform of the Habsburg framework. However, by 1919 the Czech lands were bordered on one side by Russian autocracy, and on the other, by an increasingly racialized and strident German nationalism (even in republican Austria), as well as extreme nationalisms to the north in Poland and in an independent Hungary to the south.

Masaryk saw no alternative but to lead the Czechs and Slovaks into a political entity that, after World War I, was pluralist, not homogeneous. Masaryk's legendary and courageous defense of the Jews, particularly his defense of a Jewish defendant in a blood libel case in 1899, was famous internationally, as was his sympathy during the 1920s for the Jewish settlement in Palestine. Masaryk's reputation as a philo-Semite enraged Czech nationalists and even triggered suspicion among wary leaders of the Czech Jewish community. But the rarity and nobility of Masaryk's behavior and reputation had no contemporary parallel. No wonder that so many towns in Israel have either a square or a street named for Masaryk; there is even one in Mexico City.

Interwar Czechoslovakia was democratic and remained so until 1938. This made the nation unique among the Eastern European states that came into being with the Treaty of Versailles. The new republic was, as Martinů and Firkušný recognized, not immune to the influence of radical nationalism, much of it inherited from discrete national aspirations cultivated under the Habsburg Empire. Precisely because it sought to be multi-ethnic, Masaryk's Czechoslovakia experienced no shortage of crises and injustices that stemmed from the political dominance of the Czechs. As the historian Tara Zahra has observed, after 1918 Czech nationalists encouraged the international impression that the Czechs were civilized and cultivated and therefore best suited among the Eastern European nations to the ideals of Western liberal democracy, while they acted explicitly to prevent full equality for minorities.[84]

The shortcomings of interwar Czechoslovakia notwithstanding, the republic was indeed unique in terms of democratic values, especially when compared to its proximate neighbors—Soviet Russia, Poland under Józef Piłsudski, the regency in Hungary under Admiral Horthy, the Austria of Dollfuss and Schuschnigg, not to speak of the unstable Weimar Republic and its evolution into Nazi Germany in 1933.[85] The philosopher Karl Popper, in his 1945 *Open Society and Its Enemies*, reminded his readers that no political figure emerged out of the dissolution of the Habsburg empire who matched the aura and prominence of Masaryk as an embodiment of a humanist tradition of learning and universalist political commitment to the tenets of classic liberalism, particularly freedom and tolerance.[86] Masaryk himself, however, was not free of doubt as to whether he would succeed. Writing after the outbreak of World War I, he recalled, "in all this thinking and deciding upon the fight against Austria, there rang through the depths of my soul the questions: Are we ripe for the struggle, are we mature for freedom, can we administer and preserve an independent State made up of the Bohemian Lands, Slovakia, and considerable non-Czech and non-Slovak minorities?"[87]

But for Martinů and Firkušný, Masaryk as the representative of Czech exceptionalism was not an illusion.[88] They transferred the aura of the elder Masaryk to his son Jan. The Czech embrace of democracy and the Czech contribution to modernism in music, art, and literature were closely connected. Firkušný and Martinů were aware of the striking achievements in the visual arts and literature that emerged during the first three decades of the twentieth century in the Czech lands, notably in Prague and Brno. The artistic soul of the new republic needed to embody the ideals Martinů associated with his parents and Neruda: "common sense, loyalty, honor and justice."[89] This form of patriotism defined both men's ambitions as artists living in exile and tempered their sense of loss and the allure of nostalgia.

As fascism and war made their way through Europe, the idealized image of a democratic Czechoslovakia achieved an unusual boost to its already widespread visibility. The idealization of the interwar Czech nation and its values found its way, curiously enough, into one of the most popular and celebrated cultural documents of the period, the film *Casablanca*. Released in 1942, shortly after Martinů and Firkušný successfully had made their way to the United States, the film's plot centers on the fate of an opponent of fascism, a fighter for freedom and the face of the resistance by all European nationalities to the Nazis.

The film's pan-European hero is the fictional Viktor Laszlo, played by Paul Henried, who, ironically, resembled Martinů physically. Laszlo is explicitly not a Jewish victim of the Nazis; neither is he a Communist. The leader who can defeat fascism is portrayed as the wise, calm, rational representative of a nation committed to the core values of Western humanism and democracy. This representative of European liberalism is explicitly identified in the film as a Czechoslovak freedom fighter working on behalf of all oppressed nationalities. In one scene he leads a defiant rendition of the French national anthem to drown out the singing of German soldiers in Rick's Café, a gathering place for victims, refugees, and resistance fighters. Rick, the American owner (Humphrey Bogart), is a veteran, on the republican side, of the Spanish Civil War. The characterization of Laszlo (despite his rather Hungarian name) bears an uncanny resemblance to the idealized personality of Masaryk (who died in 1937) as a dignified and principled proponent of European and Western freedom and justice. The choice of assigning a Czechoslovak identity to the film's ideological hero aligned with the ideals of his American counterpart, despite their shared love of a woman, was, in 1940, neither thoughtless nor arbitrary.

Firkušný lived to see Václav Havel assume the status once achieved by Masaryk as an international symbol of the cause of freedom, human dignity, and democracy. But Firkušný also witnessed the breakup of Czechoslovakia, an unexpected harbinger of a post-Communist political reaction against liberal democracy. Firkušný embraced this new promise of Czech democracy as he returned in the early 1990s alongside his contemporary, the conductor Rafael Kubelík, also an exile during

Communist rule, and the anti-totalitarian composer Karel Husa. They were honored widely as representatives of the interwar Czech tradition of a cosmopolitan commitment to freedom and justice rooted in loyalty to Czechoslovakia and not defined by nativism and exclusionary nationalism. Firkušný died in 1994. He was spared becoming witness to the growth of xenophobic populism and corruption throughout Eastern and Central Europe, the rise of autocracy, and the disintegration of the utopian dreams of the early 1990s about what politics would prevail in the post-Communist world. Firkušný never witnessed the shattering of optimism in post-Communist Eastern Europe by populist autocracy, exemplified by Viktor Orbán in Hungary and Vladimir Putin in Russia.

In retrospect, Martinů's output as a composer reveals the ambitions of a different vision of populism, a democratic one consistent with modernism in the aesthetic realm. Martinů was a populist composer who sought to retain classical music's historic internationalism; a nearly obsessive reader, he drew inspiration from the widest range of literary and philosophical sources. In his lifetime, he reached a broad public, as did Bartók, with a public art form that was a force for humanism and the freedom of the individual. Martinů's quirky originality, astonishing productivity, and his eclecticism in genre and style were realized without sacrifice to the imperative of modernism; neither revolutionary nor conservative, the work is rooted in musical logic, clarity, and economy, thereby ensuring broad accessibility.

What are we to make, then, of Martinů in the third decade of the twenty-first century, now that liberal democracy is threatened, and, perhaps, mortally wounded, in Europe and the United States? This question is particularly pertinent in the context of the ever-shrinking public significance of classical music. It is increasingly sustained by star performers, whose half-life as stars gets ever shorter. These star performers are cast not in the mold of Firkušný, but resemble the highly stylized virtuosi of the fin de siècle. In the arena of composition, there is renewed enthusiasm for young composers, particularly of opera. There is, however, little patience for the complexity, subtlety, variety, and resolute referencing of music's history that characterizes Martinů's music. Pianism in the sense of Firkušný's artistry exists, but his unique blend of intellect and composer's intuition is less likely to sustain a career.[90]

The aesthetics of both Martinů and Firkušný, given their link to the promise and practice of liberal democracy, suggest that Martinů's music ought to become a model for new music now that the public life of classical music seeks to ally itself with the struggle against materialism, prejudice, thoughtlessness, conformism, passivity, tyranny, and autocracy, and acts in defense of freedom of speech, the protection of minorities, civil and religious liberty, the rule of law, and the respect for learning. Martinů's music reminds us of the power and range of the best traditions of classical music and the specific potential of music to promote the neighborly love that Masaryk believed was the essential basis of democracy's commitment to freedom. Martinů successfully transformed the Czech into the universal without shying away from the provocative, the ironic, and the joyful. He embraced complexity, experiment, and accessible beauty.

Masaryk's Czechoslovakia may have been flawed, but its reality and promise were greater than anything that has transpired since then in Eastern Europe, just as the America of Franklin Delano Roosevelt remains the high-water mark for American democratic pluralism. Martinů's music suggests how democratic idealism and contemporary music, by reaching a wide public, can reinforce one another. Likewise, Firkušný's artistry can serve as a model for how the performing and teaching of music as a humanist endeavor can resist dictatorship and tyranny.

NOTES

I want to thank Christopher Gibbs, Michael Beckerman, Aleš Březina, Byron Adams, Irene Zedlacher, and especially Véronique Firkusny for their invaluable help and advice. Thanks go also to Jeremiah Sheehan and the archivists at The Juilliard School.

1. This essay skirts the ambiguities in usage between "Czech" and "Czechoslovak" as adjectives, given the dissolution of Czechoslovakia in 1992/93. They are used interchangeably. The disappearance of "Czechoslovak" as a modifier of something connected to a present political reality has resulted in more common general use of the word "Czech." For the lifetimes of Martinů and Firkušný, however, "Czechoslovak" signified something significant, despite the clear historical and cultural differences between the Czech, the Bohemian, the Moravian, and the Slovak.

2. See Michael Beckerman, "Introduction," in *Martinů's Mysterious Accident: Essays in Honor of Michael Henderson*, ed. Michael Beckerman (Hillsdale, NY: Pendragon Press, 2007), 4–6. A similar celebratory public reburial in Hungary in 1988 under Communist rule was organized for Béla Bartók, who like Martinů died in exile, in 1945 in America.

3. Michael Beckerman, "Letter from Michael to Michael," in *Martinů's Mysterious Accident*, 42, see also 38–39.

4. Information on Martinů in this essay leans on the work by earlier scholars on the composer: Miloš Šafránek, *Bohuslav Martinů: The Man and His Work*, ed. Scott Goodard (London: Dobson, 1946); Jaroslav Mihule, *Bohuslav Martinů* (Prague: Orbis, 1978); and Mihule, ed., *Martinů: Osud skladatele* (Prague: Karolinum, 2002); Michael Crump, *Martinů and the Symphony* (London: Toccata Press, 2010); F. James Rybka, *Bohuslav Martinů: The Compulsion to Compose* (London: Scarecrow Press, 2011); Thomas D. Svatos, *Martinů's Subliminal States: A Study of the Composer's Writings and Reception, with a Translation of His American Diaries* (Rochester: University of Rochester Press, 2018); and Brian Large, *Martinů* (New York: Holmes and Meier, 1975), to name a few.

5. Valuable sources about the history of Prague and its population and conflicts are, among others, Scott Spector, *Prague Territories: National Conflict and Cultural Innovation in Franz Kafka's Fin de Siècle* (Berkley: University of California Press, 2000); Peter Demetz, *Prague in Black and Gold: Scenes from the Life of a European City* (New York: Hill & Wang, 1997); and Peter Stephan Jungk, *Franz Werfel: A Life in Prague, Vienna, and Hollywood* (London: Grove Weidenfeld, 1987).

6. See Eve Blau and Monika Platzer, eds., *Shaping the Great City: Modern Architecture in Central Europe, 1890–1937* (Munich: Prestel, 2000), 117–24.

7. This list is selective and not exhaustive. Georges Enescu, for example, is missing and there were others in German-speaking Europe who might have been included, particularly Berg, Othmar

Schoeck, and Karl Amadeus Hartmann. The examples were chosen for their utility in framing Martinů's career.

8. See Alistair Wightman, *Karol Szymanowski: His Life and Work* (Aldershot, UK: Ashgate, 1999) and *Szymanowski on Music: Selected Writings of Karol Szymanowski*, ed. and trans. Alistair Wightman (London: Toccata Press, 1999).

9. See Svatos, *Martinů's Sublime States*, 17–19. Martinů's susceptibility in the 1920s to the influence of others extends to Arthur Honegger, whose *Pacific 231* and *Rugby* from the 1920s bear comparison to Martinů's orchestral music from the same period.

10. Striking among these is the 1929 set of Eight Preludes for Piano dedicated to Charlotte Quennehen, whom Martinů would later marry. Humorous and very short works also include the *Instructive Duet for Nervous People* (1925) and the three-handed *Avec un doigt* (1930), a foxtrot.

11. See John Allison, "The Art of Exile: Martinů and a Circle of Painters," *Opera (with Opera News)*, May 2025, 682–86.

12. See the interview with David Diamond in this volume.

13. Crump, *Martinů and the Symphony*, 359–60.

14. He applied for the post of professor of composition at the Prague Conservatory, a position occupied by J. B. Foerster, a fascinating personality no longer remembered for his music but for his autobiography and his friendship with Gustav Mahler.

15. Martinů, "*The Ridgefield Diary* (Summer 1944)," in Svatos, *Martinů's Subliminal States*, 109–10, 134–35.

16. Crump, *Martinů and the Symphony*, 105.

17. Nejedlý (1878–1962) was the biographer and a proponent of Smetana and musically conservative. He disparaged Martinů's *Juliette* after its Prague premiere in 1938. Nejedlý was an ardent supporter of the Communist Party since the 1920s and became a government official. He was responsible for the attack on Talich after World War II.

18. Svatos, *Martinů's Sublime States*, 16–17, and Martinů, "*Essays from Fall 1945*," in ibid., 139–40.

19. I would like to thank Byron Adams for bringing this work to my attention. Its radio premiere took place in Prague in 1937, and its very successful stage premiere in New York in 1951.

20. Consider, for example, Martinů's ballet for Martha Graham, *The Strangler: A Rite of Passage*. Based on a text by Robert Fitzgerald, the translator from Ancient Greek, on Oedipus and the Sphynx, it premiered in 1948 to a mixed reception. It used, among other things, Mexican percussion instruments. See Harry Halbreich, *Bohuslav Martinů: Werkverzeichnis und Biografie*, (Mainz: Schott, 2007), 222–23, and Šafránek, *Martinů: The Man and His Work*, 259.

21. Beckerman, "Letter from Michael to Michael," 40.

22. Martinů, "Something about that 'French' Influence II," in Svatos, *Martinů's Subliminal States*, 140.

23. Martinů, "Something about that 'French' Influence," in ibid., 139.

24. Bohuslav Martinů, "Igor Stravinsky," *Listy* 4/3 (1924): 57–59. English translation from Svatos, *Martinů's Subliminal States*, 17.

25. Crump, *Martinů and the Symphony*, 109–10.

26. Vítězslav Nezval (1900–58) was a writer, poet, and translator and a proponent of surrealism. He provided the text for the 1935 radio opera *The Voice of the Forest*, which had its stage premiere posthumously in 1964. He subsequently became, improbably, a Stalinist Communist apologist and functionary. See Demetz, *Prague in Black and Gold*, 349–52.

27. Ibid., 357–58.

28. See Hillel J. Kieval, *Languages of Community: The Jewish Experiment in the Czech Lands* (Berkeley: University of California Press, 2000), and his *The Making of Czech Jewry: National Conflict and Jewish Society in Bohemia 1870–1918* (New York: Oxford University Press, 1988), esp. 183–97.

29. See Svatos, *Martinů's Subliminal States*, 194n22.

30. See ibid., 14–15.

31. See ibid., 12–13, 22–29.

32. Szymanowski, "Igor Stravinsky," in *Szymanowski on Music*, 223–27.

33. Martinů, "*The Ridgefield Diary* (Summer 1944)," in Svatos, *Martinů's Subliminal States*, 103–12.

34. Ibid., 121–30, and Šafránek, *Martinů: The Man and His Work*, 86–87.

35. Brod was the translator of Janáček's operas into German. Brod, "Jenufa Übersetzung," in Max Brod, *Prager Sternenhimmel: Musik und Theatererlebnisse der zwanziger Jahre* (Vienna: Zsolnay, 1966), 22–34. See also Leon Botstein, "The Cultural Politics of Language and Music: Max Brod and Leoš Janáček," in *Janáček and His World*, ed. Michael Beckerman (Princeton, NJ: Princeton University Press, 2003), 13–54.

36. Martinů on Stravinsky. A poignant irony with respect to the legacy of the nationalist privileging of Smetana is revealed by the enthusiasm of Heinrich Schenker for his music. Schenker was a notorious German cultural chauvinist, and the influential twentieth-century defender of the superiority of the formal classical musical procedures found in Haydn, Mozart, Beethoven, and Brahms. For him, Dvořák was inferior to Smetana as a composer and Smetana comparable to Brahms. See Schenker's articles on Smetana from the 1890s: "Friedrich Smetana," "Smetana's 'Kuss' (Zur ersten Aufführung in der Hofoper)," and "Aus dem Leben Smetana's (Ein Besuch bei Fr. Smetana's Witwe)," in *Heinrich Schenker als Essayist und Kritiker*, ed. Hellmut Federhofer (Hildesheim: Olms, 1990), 48–54, 70–75, and 109–14 respectively, and Hellmut Federhofer, *Heinrich Schenker: Nach Tagebüchern und Briefen in der Oswald Jonas Memorial Collection* (Hildesheim, Olms, 1985), 252–54.

37. "Martinů's 'Parisian Criticism,'" in Svatos, *Martinů's Subliminal States*, 19–20.

38. Martinů, "Notes from 1947" (Excerpts), in ibid., 166–69.

39. Martinů, "My Latin Origins?" in ibid., 168.

40. Cited in Ivan Klíma, "Introduction," in Jan Neruda, *Prague Tales*, trans. Michael Henry Heim; introduction by Ivan Klíma (London: Chatto & Windus, 1993), xvi.

41. According to his biographer Miloš Šafránek, Martinů used a text by Neruda in 1917 as the closing recitation in his *Koleda* (*Christmas Carol*), a theater piece that combined song, dance, and recitation, all settings of old Czech Christmas celebrations. See Šafránek, *Martinů: The Man and His Work*, 62.

42. Jan Neruda, "A Week in a Quiet House," in *Prague Tales*, 57.

43. Halbreich, *Martinů: Werkverzeichnis und Biografie*, 435–36; also Šafránek, *Martinů: The Man and His Work*, 302–3.

44. Michael Henderson, "Two Letters by Michael Henderson," in *Martinů's Mysterious Accident*, 31.

45. It is interesting to read the characterization of Martinů in Rosa Newmarch's influential 1942 *The Music of Czechoslovakia* (New York: Da Capo Press, 1978) which includes a foreword by Edward Beneš, Masaryk's successor (v–vi). Newmarch asserts that Martinů has "undoubtedly assimilated the national characteristics of his Czech predecessors" (236). She foregrounds the dominant image and influence of Smetana on Czech music.

46. See Martinů, "On the Creative Process" (Summer 1943) and "Notes from 1947" (Excerpts), in Svatos, *Martinů's Subliminal States*, 98–99 and 168-69, respectively.

47. See Martinů, "The 'Pastoral' Symphony: What are Invariable and Variable Conditions?" (1945), in Svatos, *Martinů's Subliminal States*, 152–57.

48. Martinů to Firkušný, handwritten letter, Bohuslav Martinů Center in Polička.

49. Ibid.

50. See Peter Gradenwitz, *The Music of Israel: From the Biblical Era to Modern Times*, 2nd ed., rev. and exp. (Portland, OR: Amadeus Press, 1996).

51. See Halbreich, *Martinů: Werkverzeichnis und Biografie*, 446–48.

52. Martinů, "My Latin Origins?," in Svatos, *Martinů's Subliminal States*, 169.

53. Martinů, "Further Thoughts," in ibid., 144.

54. Sources consulted for the life and time of the pianist include Jiří Šafařík, *Rudolf Firkušný* (Brno and Prague: Masaryk University Foundation, 1994); Richard Pohl, "Rudolf Firkušný—pianista a pedagog" (MA thesis, Janáček Academy, Brno, 2010); and the Firkušný Papers in the Juilliard Archives, among them transcripts of interviews recorded late in Firkušný's life (August 1986) in Staatsburg, NY. The interviews were conducted by Firkušný's wife Tatiana (TF, 9 tapes), and are in the personal archive of his children.

55. The best account of this mysterious and devastating accident is Michael Henderson, "Martinů's Mysterious Accident," in *Martinů's Mysterious Accident*, 43–54.

56. See Olin Downes, "Work by Martinu in Radio Premiere," *New York Times*, 29 January 1950.

57. Janáček, deeply interested in folk materials, the power of music as narrative, and the music inherent in speech, particularly local dialects of Czech, developed the notion of "speech melodies." Although he flirted—as did many of his generation—with the potential of pan-Slavism as a solution to the realization of Czech independence—Janáček was not an intolerant nationalist. See Svatos, "Preface," in *Martinů's Subliminal States*, xiii.

58. Nigel Simeone, John Tyrrell, Alena Nemcová, eds., *Janáček's Works: A Catalogue of the Music and Writings of Leos Janáček's* (Oxford: Clarendon Press, 1997), 208–12.

59. In rehearsal for a performance of Janáček's *Capriccio* at the 1992 Bard Music Festival, Firkušný took issue with the editors of the critical edition. In his view, they tampered with Janáček's idiosyncratic approach to notation and chose variants the composer had discarded. We used the new edition of the score and the ensemble and the piano solo part found themselves one measure apart. Firkušný discovered that an extra measure had been inserted by the editors and said, "take it out . . . it does not belong there . . . the composer removed it." When asked, "how do you know," he replied: "Janáček told me himself." Firkušný was barely fourteen at that time. He had inherited his phenomenal memory from his father. I witnessed this recall in a session reviewing the nineteenth- and early twentieth-century Czech repertoire: Firkušný recalled, played, and sang excerpts of orchestral and choral music by Suk, Fibich, Novák, and Foerster, all works he had last thought of or heard more than a half-century ago. Firkušný was a strong advocate of Dvořák's *Requiem*, which he considered a masterpiece all too rarely performed. Author's recollection.

60. The Firkušný Papers in the Juilliard School Archives contain a manuscript for a lecture on the history of the "music of my native country." He noted that music became more "important" in Bohemia, since it became "the only means of national expression" under Austrian rule, and that a "distinctive musical tradition developed out of the synthesis of international practices and the local, the folk tradition."

61. See Šafařík, *Rudolf Firkušný*, 68.

62. See the many exercises in composition and sketches for new works in the Firkušný Papers at the Juilliard School Archives.

63. Noel Straus, "Firkusny Scores in Piano Program," *New York Times*, 19 January 1946.

64. At a lecture-recital in New York at which it was argued, by means of a comparative demonstration, that a modern Steinway piano was incapable of realizing the subtle soft dynamics required by Schubert's piano music, Firkušný whispered, after hearing the demonstration, that the comparison was flawed, since the protagonist "does not know how to play a real *pianissimo*" on the modern piano. Author's recollection.

65. Jed Distler, liner notes to the CD set *Rudolf Firkušný Edition*, Deutsche Grammophon, Eleoquence Classics 484 6393, 24.

66. See, among other sources, Stephen E. Rubin, "The Making of a Non-Superstar," *New York Times*, 8 April 1973.

67. Serkin to Firkušný, 1981, Firkušný Papers, Juilliard Archives, box 2, folder 31.

68. Personal communication to the author at an oral history taping for Totenberg's ninetieth birthday in 1991. The Totenberg archives are in the Library of Congress.

69. Šafařík, *Rudolf Firkušný*, 33.

70. Olin Downes, "Bostonians Offer Martinů Concerto," *New York Times*, 19 November 1950.

71. Pohl, "Rudolf Firkušný—pianista a pedagog," unpaginated translation, last page.

72. Olin Downes, "Martinu at 60," *New York Times*, 7 January 1951.

73. Henderson, "Martinů's Mysterious Accident," in *Martinů's Mysterious Accident*, 47–53.

74. Colin McPhee, "A Czech Composer," *New York Times*, 1 October 1944.

75. Byron Adams, "Martinů and the American Critics," in *Martinů's Mysterious Accident*, 85.

76. Olin Downes, "Rudolf Firkušný in Piano Recital," *New York Times*, 3 February 1943.

77. See Zbyněk Zeman, *The Masaryks: The Making of Czechoslovakia* (London: Weidenfeld & Nicholson, 1976).

78. Downes, "Bostonians Offer Martinů Concerto."

79. Olin Downes, "Ormandy Offers Martinů's Fourth," *New York Times*, 12 December 1945.

80. See Firkušný interview tapes; tape 6, Firkušný personal family archive.

81. See Jarmila Novotná, *My Life in Song*, ed. William V. Madison, foreword Brian Kellow (Lexington: University Press of Kentucky, 2018), 21.

82. Firkušný interview tapes; Firkušný personal family archive. Martinů shared Firkušný's veneration of Toscanini. He recounted a dispute between Toscanini and an English Horn player during a rehearsal of Debussy's *La mer.* The player wished to depict "the waves" implied by the work's title. Uninterested, Toscanini, to Martinů's delight, admonished the player with "exquisite authority" to follow the notes. Toscanini followed "what is written in the score": not "waves," but "notes." Martinů, "On the Aspect of Emotion," in Svatos, *Martinů's Subliminal States*, 131.

83. Karel Čapek, *Talks with T. G. Masaryk*, trans. Dora Round, ed. Michael Henry Heim (North Haven, CT: Catbird Press, 1995), 162.

84. See Tara Zahra, *Against the World: Anti-Globalism and Mass Politics Between the World War* (New York: W. W. Norton, 2024). See also her *Kidnapped Souls: National Indifference and the Battle for Children in the Bohemian Lands, 1900–1948* (Ithaca and London: Cornell University Press, 2008) 106–18.

85. It should be noted that there has been some historical revisionism about Masaryk and interwar Czechoslovakia. See for example, Peter Bugge, "Czech Democracy, 1918–1938: Paragon or Parody," *Bohemia: Zeitschrift für Kultur der böhmischen Länder* 47/1 (2007): 3–28. See also Miloš Pojar, *T. G. Masaryk and the Jewish Question* (Prague: Karolinum Press, 2019), which makes a case for a degree of revisionism on Masaryk's attitude to the Jews of Europe.

86. See Karl Popper, *The Open Society and Its Enemies* (Princeton, NJ: Princeton University Press, 1950), 652, also 246 and 661.

87. Thomas Garrigue Masaryk, *The Making of a State: Memories and Observations, 1914–1918*, trans. Henry Wickham Steed (New York: Frederick A. Stokes, 1927), 19. See also Robert B. Pynsent, *Questions of Identity: Czech and Slovak Ideas of Nationality and Personality* (Budapest: Central European University Press, 1994).

88. See Pynsent, *Questions of Identity*, esp. 180–95.

89. Martinů, "My Latin Origins?" in Svatos, *Martinů's Subliminal States*, 168.

90. There are heirs to Firkušný's tradition of artistry, particularly András Schiff.

APPENDIX 1.
RUDOLF FIRKUŠNÝ, STAATSBURG, NY, JANUARY 1990.

My Friend Bohuslav Martinů

In this 100th anniversary year of the birth of Bohuslav Martinů much has already been said and written about his music and about him as a composer. Scholars have described, documented, and annotated his life, and musicologists have scrutinized and analyzed his works. I feel, therefore, that it would be superfluous to add more words to this already vast body of commentaries. I have decided, instead, to talk simply about the wonderful human being: Bohuslav Martinů, my friend.

Although I had known and played Martinů's music during my student years in Brno and Prague, we did not meet until 1931 in Paris. By then, he was forty-one years old, and I was barely nineteen, but the age difference did not seem to matter. We became friends right away. We moved very much in the same musical and social circles, and we began meeting frequently simply because we liked each other. His wife Charlotte often invited me to come and share their simple but delicious meals she herself took pride in cooking.

Bohuslav was a withdrawn, rather shy person. At large social gatherings he would mostly stay a bit aside, detached and pensive. He talked little, never raising his voice, never making a gesture which might draw people's attention. Tall and always standing ram-rod straight, he was visually summed up in a perfect nickname given him by our mutual friend, the painter Rudolf Kundera: "Flinta," meaning rifle. Yet among close friends with whom he felt at ease, Martinů would talk, and what he had to say was always fascinating. He was an extremely intelligent man who was interested in many things besides music, and his intellectual curiosity could never be satisfied. All his life he read voraciously. He was one of those people who not only read a lot but retain new knowledge and love passing it on to others.

His mind had a strong philosophical bent, and he was always waging battles over various highly intellectual problems. The field of his interests seemed unlimited: science, philosophy, politics, religion, the visual arts, literature, languages. His favorite gift to friends was a dictionary or an encyclopedia, and the bigger the volume the better. I still have the huge Webster's Dictionary he gave me one Christmas in New York.

But Martinů was no ascetic. The other side of his personality was that of a kind, fun-loving man who enjoyed good food and good wine, and never failed to notice a pretty woman. He felt close to nature: the spell of a childhood lived in a remote corner of unspoiled countryside never lost its power over him. Although he spent most of his adult life in large cities, every summer he would impatiently head for the country, both in Europe and later in the United States, where we both found refuge after fleeing war-torn Europe.

Life in the city stimulated his mind, but it was in the countryside where he was happiest. I paid many visits to the Martinůs at their various summer homes, both in France and in the United States, and always found a different Bohuslav there—a relaxed, smiling and contented one. He did not go fishing and hunting like Hemingway, nor did he work in the garden like Karel Čapek, and he never made notations of nature's sounds the way Janáček did. He just walked or sat among the trees, listened to birds, looked at flowers whose names he perhaps did not even know, and enjoyed one of God's rarest gifts to man: the gift of feeling one with nature.

In 1946 Bohuslav was in Tanglewood and suffered a terrible fall. He was staying alone in an unfamiliar house, went out onto the dark terrace at night, did not realize there was no banister and fell off the high edge. He suffered a brain concussion, was unconscious for some time and, as a result, partially lost his hearing.

After that, he became even more introverted, but his creative powers remained undiminished despite his physical handicaps. At that time he enjoyed, almost with boyish pleasure, camping trips with our mutual Czech-American friend, the musician Frank Rybka. The two traveled in a modest trailer, and Bohuslav was happy leading the rough life of a camper. Later on, he would describe their adventures with great relish, and we spent many hours laughing at his dry humor and wit. Always with a twinkle in his eye, he was a most lovable human being, and nobody could resist his unique charm.

Although Bohuslav was always anxious about perfect interpretation of his works, he could take less happy performances with a great deal of humor. On one particular occasion, when I performed his second cello sonata, the cellist—by the way, it was not Pierre Fournier—played so badly that, after we finished, I felt embarrassed to even look at Bohuslav, but his only comment was a dry: "I didn't exactly compose what he was playing but the piece survived it anyway."

When I returned to Prague for the first time after the war in 1946, he had originally planned to come with me, but due to his commitments in Tanglewood, he had to postpone. Then came his accident and a trip to Prague was impossible that year. The second time he wanted to return with me to Prague was in 1948, when I was to play his Piano Concerto No. 3—which he wrote for and dedicated to me—at the Prague Spring Festival. Once again, though, an unforeseen event prevented his (and my own) trip: the Communist coup d'état. He never returned, and it was nearly half a century before I performed in my native country again.

Finally, in May of this year, after a self-imposed exile of forty-four years, I was able to return professionally to the Prague Spring Festival. Unfortunately, it was without Bohuslav, but I paid tribute to my friend by playing his Piano Concerto No. 2 in Smetana Hall, where I had premiered it with the Czech Philharmonic Orchestra under Václav Talich in 1935. I am sure this time he was there with me.

Index

Note: Page numbers followed by "n" indicate chapter endnotes; page numbers in italics refer to figures, tables, and musical examples; throughout the index, BM refers to Bohuslav Martinů.

Index of Works

Index of Names and Subjects

Contributors

Michael Beckerman is Carroll and Milton Petrie Professor, New York University and the incoming Dean of the Herb Alpert School of Music at UCLA.. He served as Leonard Bernstein Scholar in Residence for the New York Philharmonic from 2016–17, and on the board of directors of the Czech Center in New York (2010–15), and vice-president of the American Musicological Society (2010–12). He has received honorary degrees from Palacký and Masaryk universities in the Czech Republic. Publications include, as author, *Janáček the Theorist* (Pendragon Press, 1994) and *New Worlds of Dvořák* (Norton, 2003); and as editor, *Martinů's Mysterious Accident* (Pendragon Press, 2007) and *Classical Music: Contemporary Perspectives and Challenges* (2021), *Janáček and Czech Music* (with Glen Bauerl; Pendragon Press, 1995). Beckerman served as scholar in residence for two Bard Music Festivals, editing the volumes *Dvořák and His World* (1993) and *Janáček and His World* (2003), both published by Princeton University Press.

Leon Botstein is president and Leon Levy Professor in the Arts of Bard College and the author of several books and editor of *The Compleat Brahms* and *The Musical Quarterly*. The music director of the American Symphony Orchestra and The Orchestra Now (TŌN), and principal guest conductor of the Jerusalem Symphony Orchestra, where he served as music director. He has recorded works by, among others, Schoeck, Honegger, Szymanowski, Hartmann, Dukas, Foulds, Bruckner, Chausson, Richard Strauss, Mendelssohn, Popov, Shostakovich, and Liszt. He is founder and co-artistic director of the Bard Music Festival. His work has been acknowledged with awards from the American Academy of Arts and Letters, Harvard University, government of Austria, and Carnegie Foundation. He was elected to the American Philosophical Society in 2011.

Aleš Březina is the director of the Bohuslav Martinů Institute in Prague and chairman of the editorial board of the Bohuslav Martinů Complete Edition. In 1998 he reconstructed the first version of Martinů's opera *The Greek Passion.* In 2016 his edition of *The Epic of Gilgamesh* received the Best Edition award from the German Music Publishers Association. In 2020 The Czech Science Foundation (GAČR) awarded the Martinů Complete Edition as "one of the five best scientific projects of the year." His recent publications include *Bedřich Smetana and European Opera* (Würzburg, 2024), and *"Making Real Theatre": Bohuslav Martinů's Music Theatre, Part I: 1913-1937* (Würzburg, 2025), both edited with Ivana Rentsch, and a chapter on Czech film music in Martin Nedbal, Kelly St. Pierre, Hana Vlhová-Wörner, eds., *A History of Music in the Czech Lands* (Cambridge, 2025). Březina is a prolific composer of film, theater and concert music.

Marios Christou is a Greek Cypriot composer, conductor, psaltis, scholar, and pedagogue based in Prague. He is the founder and director of the Archaion Kallos Festival of Orthodox music, the artistic director of the Phillokallia Ensemble, the principal Byzantine singer (psaltis) of the Church of the Nativity of the Virgin Mary in Prague. Christou received his musical education in Prague, initially studying music education and choral conducting at Charles University, followed by composition and orchestral conducting at the State Conservatory. He later pursued composition at the Academy of Performing Arts (HAMU). In 2009 he completed a doctoral degree in music theory and pedagogy at Charles University.

Susan H. Gillespie has spent her life exploring the possibilities of translation—interlingual, cultural, and educational. She is a graduate of Radcliffe College of Harvard University and attended the University of Freiburg for four years on a DAAD scholarship. She has translated Theodor W. Adorno and many other authors of philosophical and musicological works, as well as fiction and poetry. Her book-length translations include *Corona: Selected Poems of Paul Celan* and *The Correspondence of Paul Celan and Ilana Shmueli*, which was a finalist for the National Translation Award. Gillespie has worked as fundraiser for the New York Zoological Society, the New York Public Library, and, finally, Bard College where she served first as Vice President for Public Affairs and Development and then as Vice President for Special Global Initiatives. In 1998, she founded the Institute for International Liberal Education.

Jiří Gruša (1938–2011) was a Czech poet, novelist, translator, diplomat, and politician. He graduated from Charles University in Prague but was banned from publishing after the 1968 Soviet occupation of Czechoslovakia. Gruša signed the human rights manifesto Charter 77 and left the country in 1981 and lived in Germany. After the fall of Communism, he served as the Czech ambassador to Germany and Austria, and also briefly as the minister of education. From 2004 to 2009 he was the president of International PEN, and between 2005 and 2009 he served as director of the Diplomatic Academy of Vienna. He was also a member of the Board of the European Network Remembrance and Solidarity. His books include *The Questionnaire* and *Franz Kafka of Prague.*

Axel Körner is professor of modern cultural and intellectual history at Leipzig University and honorary professor at University College London, where he has been teaching since 1996. He has held visiting positions at the Institute for Advanced Study, Princeton, at the École Normale Supérieure in Paris, and the Remarque Institute at New York University, among others. In addition to his work on opera and music, he has published widely on French, Italian and Habsburg history and on transatlantic cultural and intellectual exchanges. His *America in Italy: The United*

States in the Political Thought and Imagination of the Risorgimento, 1763–1865 (Princeton, 2017) won the Marraro Prize of the American Historical Association. He currently is principal investigator on a project financed by the European Research Council entitled "Opera and the Politics of Empire in Habsburg Europe, 1815-1914."

Markéta Kratochvílová studied musicology at the faculty of arts, Palacký University Olomouc. She was a curator in the Department of Musical Instruments at the Czech Museum of Music and a music editor on Czech Radio. Between 2013 and 2018, she was a researcher at the Cabinet of Music History at the Institute of Ethnology, Czech Academy of Sciences, conducting research into the work of Antonín Dvořák and Otakar Ostrčil. In 2019, she joined the Library of Musicology at the Institute of Art History, Czech Academy of Sciences, as a bibliographer. She publishes on Czech music of the nineteenth and twentieth centuries.

Brian S. Locke is professor of musicology at Western Illinois University and has previously taught at Dalhousie University (Halifax, Nova Scotia). His research interests span a wide range of topics in the Romantic and early modernist eras, with a focus on the musical communities of Prague. Publications include *Opera and Ideology in Prague: Polemics and Practice at the National Theatre, 1900–1938* (University of Rochester Press), as well as articles in major journals and essay collections. Locke has also edited the score of Otakar Zich's opera, *Vina* (Guilt; A-R Edition). Forthcoming book chapters include studies of Erwin Schulhoff's 1932 opera *Flammen* (*Plameny*) and of the Czech swing community during the Nazi-era Protectorate of Bohemia and Moravia in *Music in World War II* (Indiana University Press). He is currently working on the musical estate of Jiří Traxler (1912–2011).

Jon Kantor Meadow is an historical musicologist who earned his PhD from New York University, where his research on Martinů's stage works culminated in the dissertation, "Traveling with Mary: Explorations of Bohuslav Martinů's Opera Cycle *Hry o Marii.*" He has taught music history at the Mannes School of Music and served as a teaching assistant at New York University. He has also contributed to musicological projects for Carnegie Hall and delivered lectures at the 92nd Street Y. His current work explores the interplay of technology, cult fandom, genre, and emotion, with a particular focus on their applications in mainstream and commercial contexts.

Martin Nedbal is professor of musicology at the University of Kansas. He is the author of two monographs: *Mozart's Operas and National Politics: Canon Formation in Prague from 1791 to the Present* (Cambridge University Press, 2023), and *Viennese Opera and Morality in the Age of Mozart and Beethoven* (Routledge, 2017). He is also the translator and editor of *The Published Theoretical Works of Leoš Janáček* and a co-editor of *A History of Music in the Czech Lands* (Cambridge University Press, 2025).

Vincenzina C. Ottomano is professor at the University Ca' Foscari Venice. She studied at the University of Pavia/Cremona (Italy) and Fribourg (Switzerland) and received her PhD in musicology at the University of Bern (Switzerland). Her publications include a book on the impact of Russian opera in France and Italy, *Quando l'opera russa diventò europea* (Ricordi-LIM, 2024), the volume *Luciano Berio: Interviste e colloqui* (Einaudi, 2017), and several articles on Russian and Italian opera of the nineteenth century and on music theater of the twentieth and twenty-first centuries. She is co-editor of the journal *verdiperspektiven*, as well as of the *Swiss Journal of Musicology*. For her project on the composition process behind *Falstaff* she has been awarded the Rotary Club Parma's "Giuseppe Verdi" International Prize (2019).

Marek Pechač earned master's degrees in musicology from Palacký University Olomouc, and in culture management from Masaryk University in Brno. He currently is a PhD student at the Palacký University, where he is writing his dissertation entitled "Jan Löwenbach: A Life for Czech Music." On the staff of the Bohuslav Martinů Institute since 2010, he coordinates the source research. He is co-editor of the Martinů Complete Edition's volume *Quadruple Concertos* (Bärenreiter Prague, 2018) and editor of works for chamber orchestra, *Toccata e due canzoni* and *Sinfonietta La Jolla* (forthcoming).

Adam Prentis was born to Czech-English parents in Scotland. Growing up in the Czech Republic, he learnt the cello and sang in amateur choirs. He graduated from journalism and Czech and English literature, linguistics, and pedagogy at Charles University in Prague. As a professional translator, he focuses on music history and has collaborated with Bärenreiter and leading Czech institutions on critical editions of Bohuslav Martinů's works and correspondence, among others.

Courtney Quaintance is programs manager at the British School at Rome. Her research centers around sixteenth- and seventeenth-century Italian literature and music. She has a PhD in Italian literature from the University of Chicago and a *dottorato di ricerca* in music history from Sapienza University of Rome. Her publications include *Textual Masculinity and the Exchange of Women in Renaissance Venice* (Toronto, 2015) and, more recently, various essays on women singers in seventeenth-century Italy. Translation projects include *Music, Place, and Identity in Italian Urban Soundscapes circa 1550–1860* (Routledge, 2023), *Noble Magnificence: Culture of the Performing Arts in Rome 1644–1740* (Brepols, 2024), and *Vincenzo Bellini on Stage and Screen, 1935–2020* (Bloomsbury, 2024).

Ivana Rentsch is professor of musicology at the University of Hamburg. Her research interests include the relationship between music and nationalism, Czech music history, seventeenth to twentieth century music and music theater. She is a member of the editorial board of *Bohuslav Martinů Complete Edition* and of the advisory board of the Staatliches Institut für Musikforschung Berlin Preußischer Kulturbesitz. Book publications include *Bohuslav Martinů: Anklänge an die Avantgarde* (Steiner, 2005), and *Bedřich Smetana and European Opera*, edited with Aleš Březina (Würzburg, 2024). At the University of Hamburg, she heads or is member of several research projects initiated or managed by the German Research Council: "Understanding Written Artefacts," "Spiritual Intermediality of the Early Modern Period," and "Digital Music Editions: Open Work Form in the 17th Century."

Giselher Schubert studied musicology, philosophy, and sociology in Bonn, Zurich, and Berlin and received his doctorate in 1971 with a dissertation on early Schoenberg. Since 1971 he has been the editorial director of the *Hindemith Complete Edition*, which he also edits and of which fifty-nine volumes have been published to date. He was director of the Hindemith Institute in Frankfurt/Main from 1991–2011 and, until 2010, chairman of the Association for the Promotion of the Schoenberg Complete Edition. He was co-editor of the journal *Musiktheorie* from 1985–95 and currently is a member of the editorial boards of the Weill, Martinů, Webern, and Eisler complete editions and of the project committees of the Richard Strauss and of the Bernd Alois Zimmermann editions. He has been a permanent contributor to the journal *FonoForum* since 1985. Schubert, who taught at the University of Mainz and the music academies of Frankfurt and Hanover, is an honorary professor at the Frankfurt University of Music.

Vít Zouhar is a composer, musicologist, performer, professor of music, and vice-dean at the Faculty of Education, Palacký University Olomouc, Czech Republic. He is the author and co-author of several operas, orchestral and chamber works, sound installations and music games. His music is placed in the context of minimalism and postmodernism and has won various awards. Zouhar's research focuses on twentieth and twenty-first-century music, mostly on Bohuslav Martinů's oeuvre. He has published several books on music. Recent works include *Bohuslav Martinů & Miloslav Bureš: 1955–1959* (Palacký University Press, 2022), a critical edition of Bohuslav Martinů's chamber cantatas (Bärenreiter Prague, 2016), and six volumes of Martinů's correspondence (together with Jana Honzíková, Gabriela Coufalová, and Zdeněk Zouhar). Since 2024, he has been the chairman of the board of trustees of the Bohuslav Martinů Foundation in Prague.

VOLUMES PUBLISHED IN CONJUNCTION WITH THE BARD MUSIC FESTIVAL

Brahms and His World
edited by Walter Frisch (1990)

Mendelssohn and His World
edited by R. Larry Todd (1991)

Richard Strauss and His World
edited by Bryan Gilliam (1992)

Dvořák and His World
edited by Michael Beckerman (1993)

Schumann and His World
edited by R. Larry Todd (1994)

Bartók and His World
edited by Peter Laki (1995)

Charles Ives and His World
edited by J. Peter Burkholder (1996)

Haydn and His World
edited by Elaine R. Sisman (1997)

Tchaikovsky and His World
edited by Leslie Kearney (1998)

Schoenberg and His World
edited by Walter Frisch (1999)

Beethoven and His World
edited by Scott Burnham and Michael P. Steinberg (2000)

Debussy and His World
edited by Jane F. Fulcher (2001)

Mahler and His World
edited by Karen Painter (2002)

Janáček and His World
edited by Michael Beckerman (2003)

Shostakovich and His World
edited by Laurel E. Fay (2004)

Aaron Copland and His World
edited by Carol J. Oja and Judith Tick (2005)

Franz Liszt and His World
edited by Christopher H. Gibbs and Dana Gooley (2006)

Edward Elgar and His World
edited by Byron Adams (2007)

Sergey Prokofiev and His World
edited by Simon Morrison (2008)

Brahms and His World (revised edition)
edited by Walter Frisch and Kevin C. Karnes (2009)

Richard Wagner and His World
edited by Thomas S. Grey (2009)

Alban Berg and His World
edited by Christopher Hailey (2010)

Jean Sibelius and His World
edited by Daniel M. Grimley (2011)

Camille Saint-Saëns and His World
edited by Jann Pasler (2012)

Stravinsky and His World
edited by Tamara Levitz (2013)

Franz Schubert and His World
edited by Christopher H. Gibbs and Morten Solvik (2014)

Carlos Chávez and His World
edited by Leonora Saavedra (2015)

Giacomo Puccini and His World
edited by Arman Schwartz and Emanuele Senici (2016)

Chopin and His World
edited by Jonathan D. Bellman and Halina Goldberg (2017)

Rimsky-Korsakov and His World
edited by Marina Frolova-Walker (2018)

Korngold and His World
edited by Daniel Goldmark and Kevin C. Karnes (2019)

Nadia Boulanger and Her World
edited by Jeanice Brooks (2020)

Rachmaninoff and His World
edited by Philip Ross Bullock (2022)

Vaughan Williams And His World
edited by Byron Adams and Daniel M. Grimley (2023)

Berlioz and His World
edited by Francesca Brittan and Sarah Hibberd (2024)